BATTLE LINES

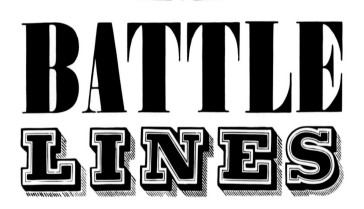

BATTLE LINES

A GRAPHIC HISTORY OF THE CIVIL WAR

JONATHAN FETTER-VORM
ARI KELMAN

A Novel Graphic from Hill and Wang

A DIVISION OF FARRAR, STRAUS AND GIROUX

NEW YORK

For Lesley, Jacob, and Ben ––AK
For Charlotte ––JFV

Hill and Wang
A division of Farrar, Straus and Giroux
18 West 18th Street, New York 10011

Library of Congress Cataloging–in–Publication Data
Kelman, Ari, 1968–
    Battle lines : a graphic history of the Civil War / Ari Kelman, Jonathan Fetter-Vorm ;
  [illustrated by] Jonathan Fetter-Vorm
     pages cm
    Includes bibliographical references.
    ISBN 978-0-8090-9474-5 (hardback)
    1. United States—History—Civil War, 1861–1865—Comic books, strips, etc. 2. United States—History—Civil
War, 1861–1865—Juvenile literature. 3. Graphic novels. I. Fetter-Vorm, Jonathan, 1983– II. Title.
  E468.K33 2014
  973.3—dc23
                                                                                                      2013033905

Designed by Jonathan Fetter-Vorm
Inks by Brendan Leach

Hill and Wang books may be purchased for educational, business, or promotional use. For information on
bulk puchases, please contact the Macmillan Corporate and Premium Sales Department at 1–800–221–7945,
extension 5442, or write to specialmarkets@macmillan.com.

www.fsgbooks.com
www.twitter.com/fsgbooks • www.facebook.com/fsgbooks

10   9   8   7   6   5   4   3   2   1

Future years will never know the seething hell and the black infernal background of countless minor scenes and interiors, (not the official surface courteousness of the Generals, not the few great battles) of the Secession war; and it is best they should not—the real war will never get in the books.

—Walt Whitman

TABLE OF CONTENTS

PREFACE

The Civil War was unspeakably bloody. Americans slaughtered each other with such abandon that even now, with a century and a half standing between us and the fighting, it is still nearly impossible to make sense of the statistics: somewhere between 620,000 and 850,000 dead, more than 1.5 million wounded.

In four years the war claimed as many lives as there are inhabitants of present-day Boston. Or Louisville. Or Las Vegas, or Detroit, or San Francisco.

At the Battle of Antietam, more Americans were shot and killed than on any other single day in the nation's history.

On Independence Day 1863, after three days of fighting, the land outside the town of Gettysburg festered under the weight of roughly 6 million pounds of flesh, the carcasses of the fallen soldiers and their horses.

One out of every four soldiers who marched off to war never came home.

Grim statistics like these go a long way toward communicating the terrible cost of the Civil War, but the numbers themselves are almost too much. Our imagination balks, and we lose sight of the anguish that nearly every American felt on a level that was—and for many still is—deeply personal. Indeed, the challenge of telling the history of the Civil War lies in bridging that gap between history on a national scale and the countless individual stories of those who fought, died, grieved, gave up, or rejoiced. Add to that the survivors' burden of confronting difficult, unanswered questions in the aftermath: How could such a thing have happened? And what hope could there be for a country so deeply divided against itself, a country so thoroughly drenched in the blood of its own people?

Those same questions endure in this book. On one level, *Battle Lines* is a study of a nation transformed. It is the history of a war that dismantled the institution of slavery and remade the social order of the South. Of a war that altered the very definition of what it meant to be an American citizen as millions of freed people joined the voting rolls and began to demand equal protection under the law. It is the history of a war that exploded the size and scope of federal authority by establishing a national currency, a precedent for military conscription, an income tax, and an expansive system of government pensions. It is also the history of a war that brought many women into the workforce, fostered innovations in medicine, photography, and military technology, and set the stage for the conquest of Native Americans in the Far West and the resettlement of the region. Much of this history is woven into the various narratives within *Battle Lines*.

But the Civil War was a vast, complicated event, so at the start of each chapter we provide context by explaining what was happening behind the scenes. These short articles—typeset to look like newspapers from the period—present the strategies and turning points of the war, from the movement of troops to the machinations of lawmakers.

On another level, *Battle Lines* is a series of portraits, of personal narratives. The Civil War drew together people from all corners of the nation—from all classes and in the name of every cause—into a crucible of shared experiences and private struggles. Each chapter of *Battle Lines* begins with an object, something specific and, on its own, unremarkable (a flag, a bullet, a brick, a photograph). In turn, each object comes to represent the history of the war from the ground up, from multiple perspectives and unexpected angles: light glints off the lens of a pair of opera glasses, reflecting the chaos and uncertainty of the Battle of Bull Run; leg shackles trip up a man as he scrambles away from a life of slavery; a mosquito, its belly full of malaria, buzzes across the battlefield, infecting soldiers and civilians alike; a jar of ink runs dry beneath the hot Georgia sun as a prisoner of war scrawls in his diary. These and others are the faces of the war. These are the stories behind the statistics.

But where do these stories come from? *Battle Lines* hews closely to the historical record, drawing from letters, diaries, speeches, and other contemporary accounts. It features the lives and words of many actual people (our notes at the end of the book catalog the various historical figures who appear throughout). Moreover, since *Battle Lines* is a work of graphic history, the obligation to fact extends beyond the words and into the images themselves. The artwork relies on a trove of visual sources, from Civil War–era photographs and sketches to advertisements, maps, engravings, and schematics. Much of the visual research also included field studies––drawings of objects and landscapes––at various museums, historic battle sites, and Civil War reenactments. In other words, although *Battle Lines* is a book about a time when violence enthralled a nation, we have taken great pains to avoid doing violence to the past.

Let us leave you with a final statistic, not nearly so grim as the others, but nevertheless illuminating: some 65,000 books have been written about the Civil War. If one had been published every day since the war ended, we'd still have ten thousand or so left over. Clearly there is something about this moment in American history that continues to fascinate and confound readers. With each generation of scholarship new voices emerge, searching for new ways to make sense of the war. We are excited to add *Battle Lines* to this tradition, excited to tell this history in a graphic form and from a new perspective.

––Ari Kelman and Jonathan Fetter–Vorm

BATTLE LINES

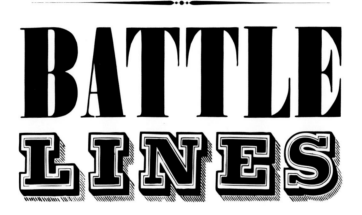

Chapter 1: The Flag

CHARLESTON COURIER

April 12, 1861

THE UNION IS DISSOLVED!

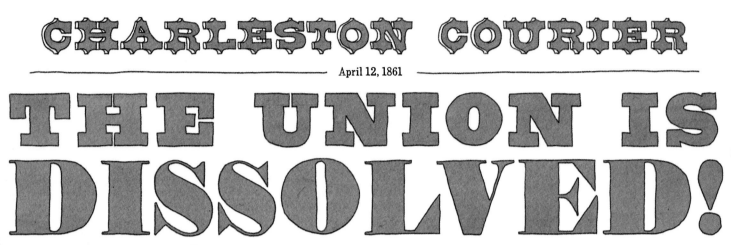

South Carolina FIRE-EATERS SUNDER UNION

Other States Follow

Although his name did not appear on ballots in the Southern states, Abraham Lincoln won a majority in the Electoral College in November 1860. Confronted with the election of a candidate they reviled, a man they believed would abolish slavery upon taking office, the states of the Deep South prepared to shred the fabric of the Union.

Secession happened on a state-by-state basis, with South Carolina assembling the first of the conventions that discussed the issue. Less than a week before Christmas, that body voted unanimously to dissolve the state's ties to the Union. Just after the new year, Mississippi followed. Next came Florida, Alabama, Georgia, Louisiana, and Texas.

President-elect Lincoln looked on, but because he had not yet taken the oath of office, he could not respond to the crisis. Meanwhile, the seated President, James Buchanan, had the authority to act but did nothing.

Would the South be allowed to go in peace? Would there be another in a line of compromises to placate slaveholders? Or would the nation find itself embroiled in a civil war?

PRESIDENT LINCOLN INAUGURAL ADDRESS "Mystic Chords of Memory"

On March 4, 1861, President Lincoln delivered his inaugural address. He reassured the Border States--Delaware, Kentucky, Maryland, Missouri, and Virginia--that they could remain loyal to the Union without fearing abolition.

Lincoln explained, as he had before, "I have no purpose, directly or indirectly, to interfere with the institution of slavery in the States where it exists. I believe I have no lawful right to do so, and I have no inclination to do so." He would, though, live up to his Republican Party's ideal that the West should remain free soil.

He next warned that secession was unconstitutional, an act of rebellion, and that the federal government would fight for the Union. In short, he reassured the nation that he did not seek armed conflict with the seceding Southern states, but should it come to it, the Union would "defend and maintain itself."

In the end, he implored all Americans, "We are not enemies, but friends. We must not be enemies. Though passion may have strained it must not break our bonds of affection." He asked both Northerners and Southerners to pay heed to their shared history, to "the mystic chords of memory, stretching from every battlefield and patriot grave to every living heart and hearthstone all over this broad land." Those chords, he promised, would "yet swell the chorus of the Union, when again touched, as surely they will be, by the better angels of our nature."

RUMORS FROM THE FRONT ☞

Rebels Poised to Attack Ft. Sumter

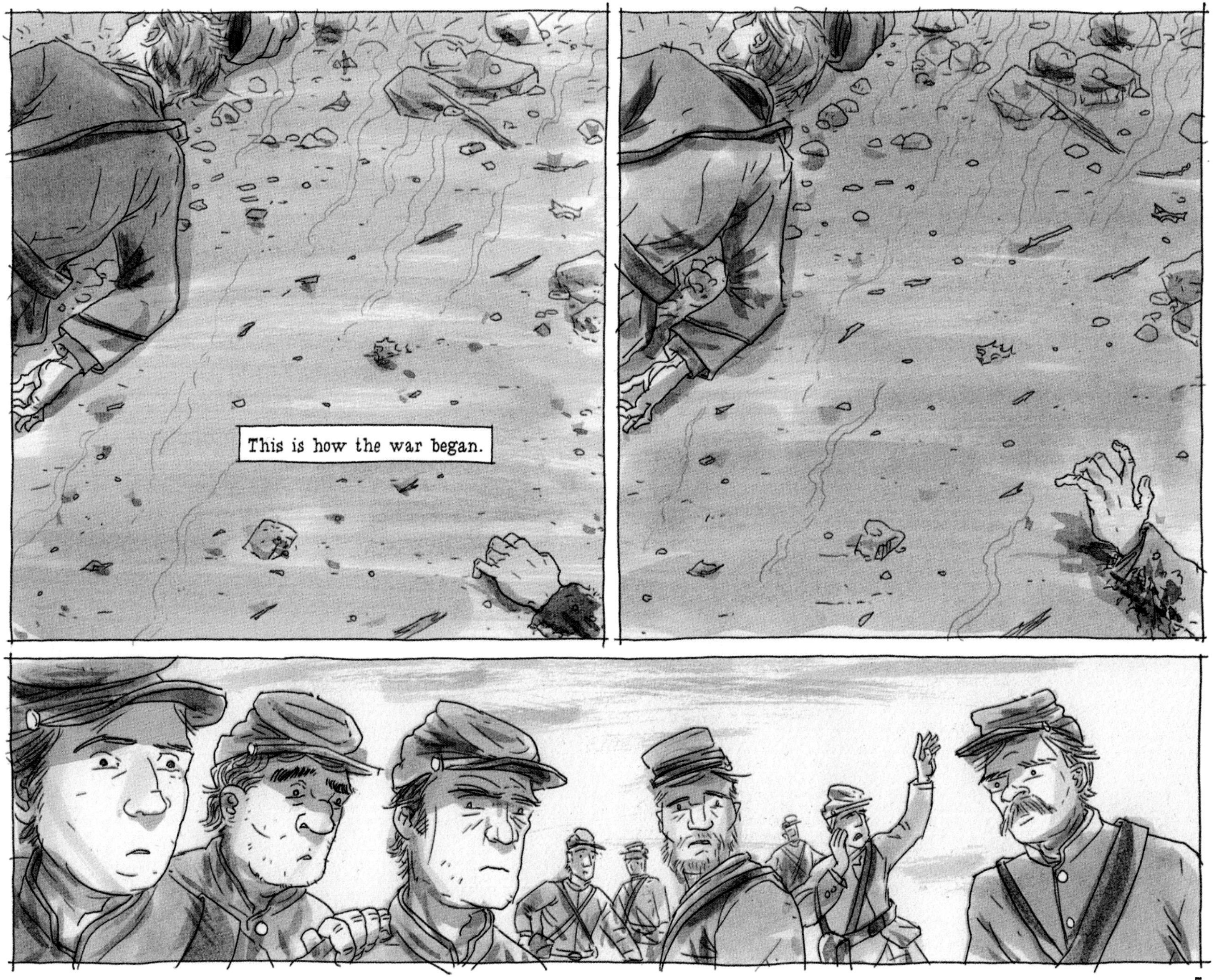
This is how the war began.

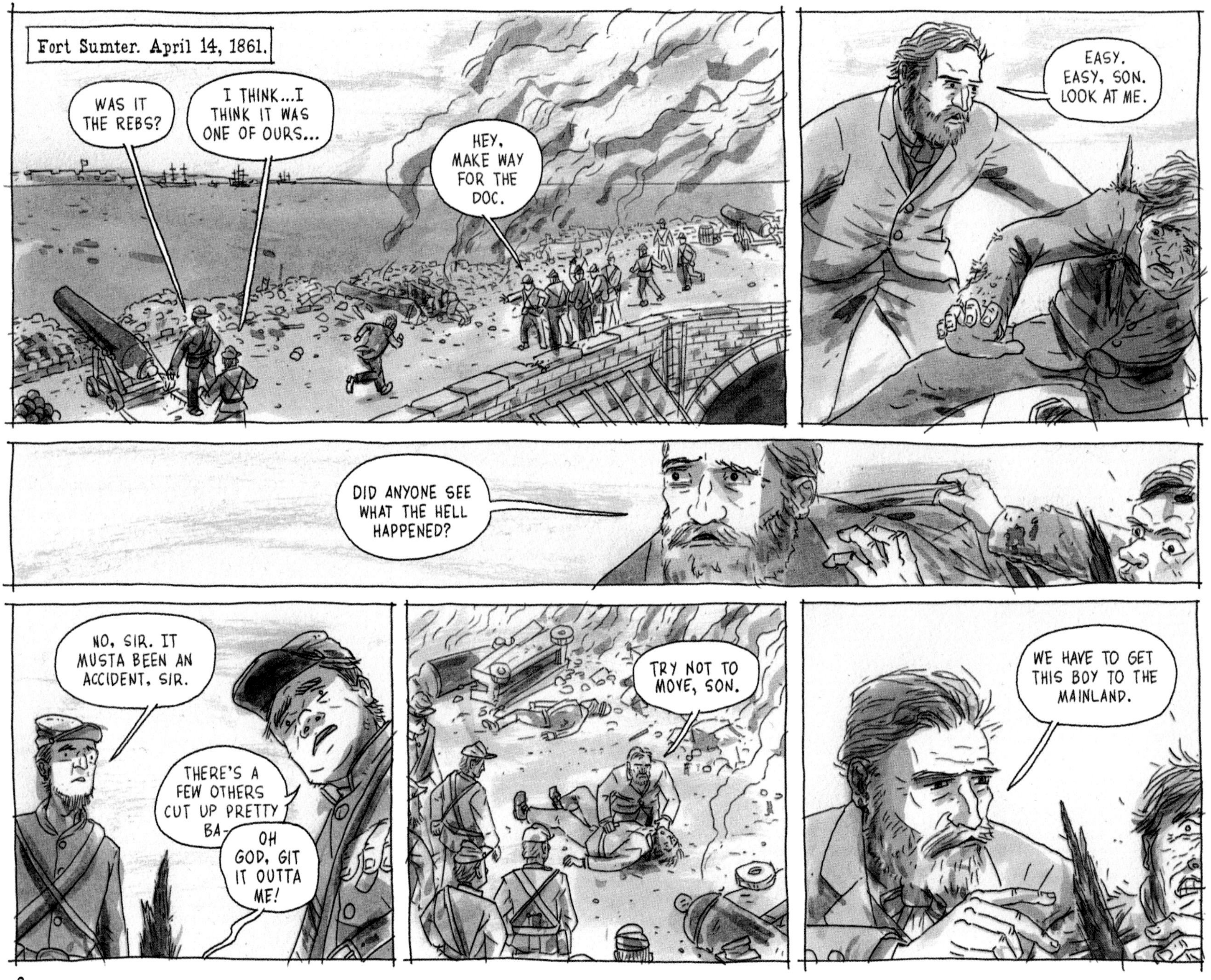
Fort Sumter. April 14, 1861.
WAS IT THE REBS?
I THINK...I THINK IT WAS ONE OF OURS...
HEY, MAKE WAY FOR THE DOC.
EASY. EASY, SON. LOOK AT ME.
DID ANYONE SEE WHAT THE HELL HAPPENED?
NO, SIR. IT MUSTA BEEN AN ACCIDENT, SIR.
THERE'S A FEW OTHERS CUT UP PRETTY BA-
OH GOD, GIT IT OUTTA ME!
TRY NOT TO MOVE, SON.
WE HAVE TO GET THIS BOY TO THE MAINLAND.

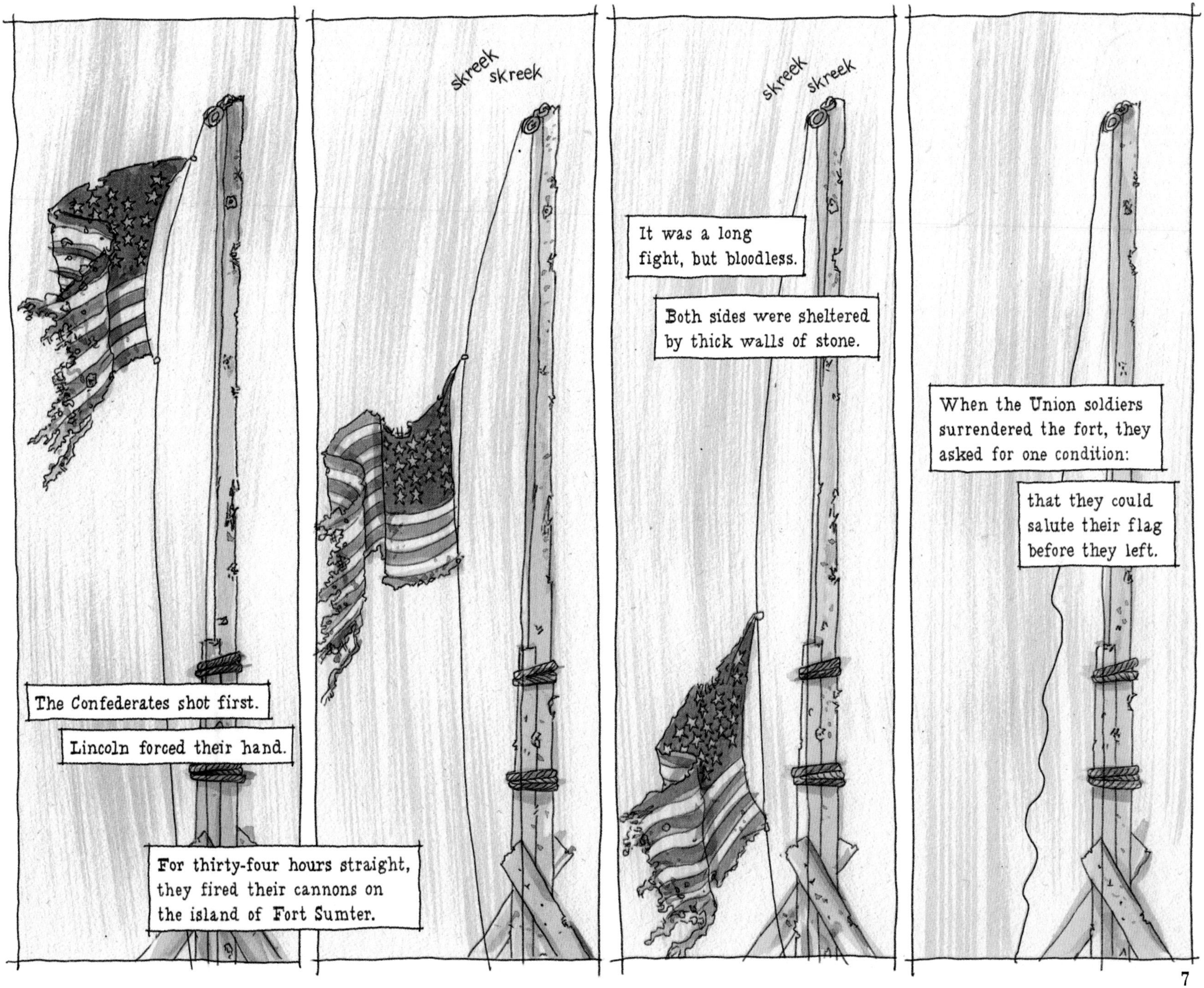
The Confederates shot first.
Lincoln forced their hand.
For thirty-four hours straight, they fired their cannons on the island of Fort Sumter.
skreek skreek
skreek skreek
It was a long fight, but bloodless.
Both sides were sheltered by thick walls of stone.
When the Union soldiers surrendered the fort, they asked for one condition:
that they could salute their flag before they left.

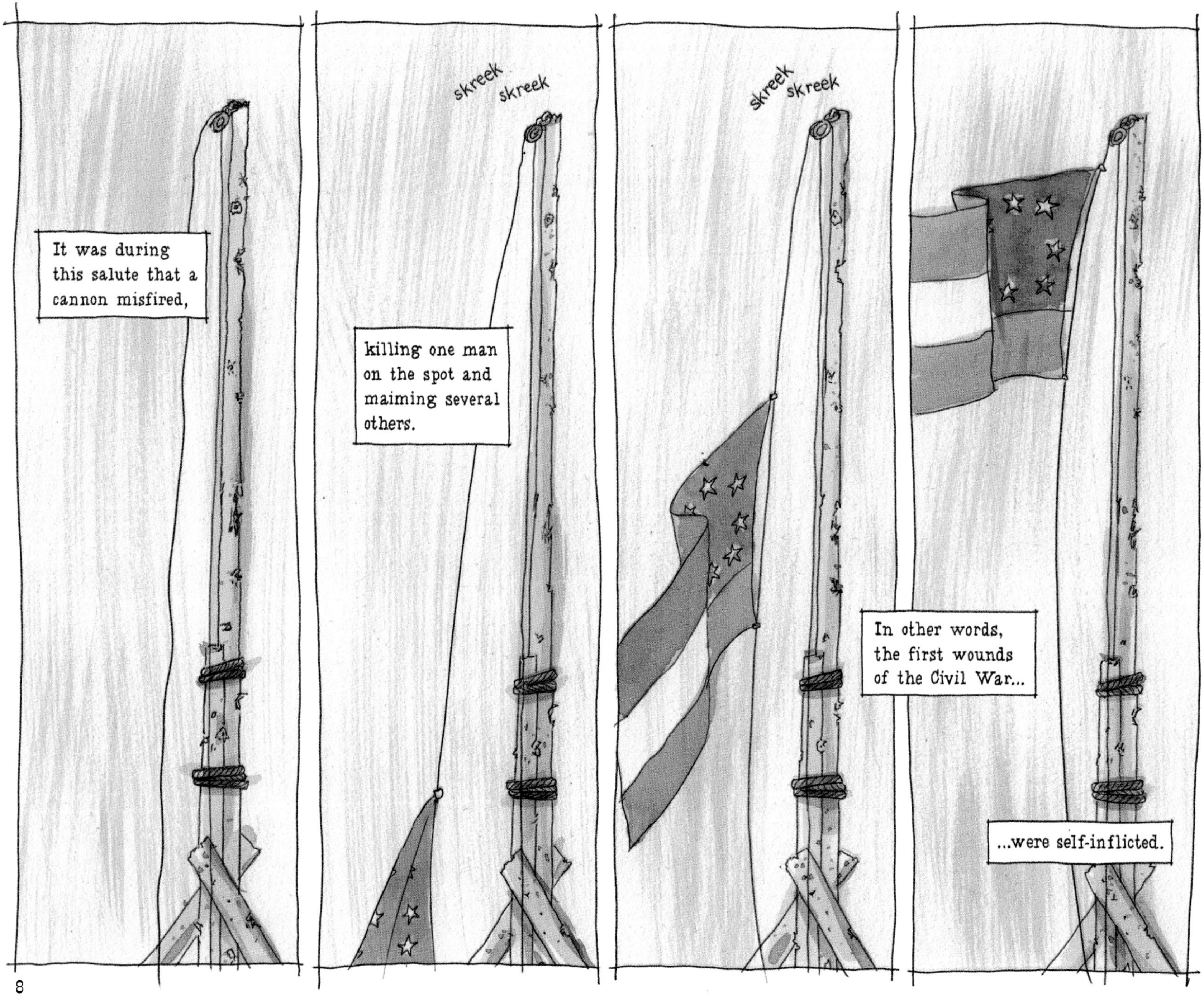
It was during this salute that a cannon misfired,
skreek
skreek
killing one man on the spot and maiming several others.
skreek
skreek
In other words, the first wounds of the Civil War...
...were self-inflicted.

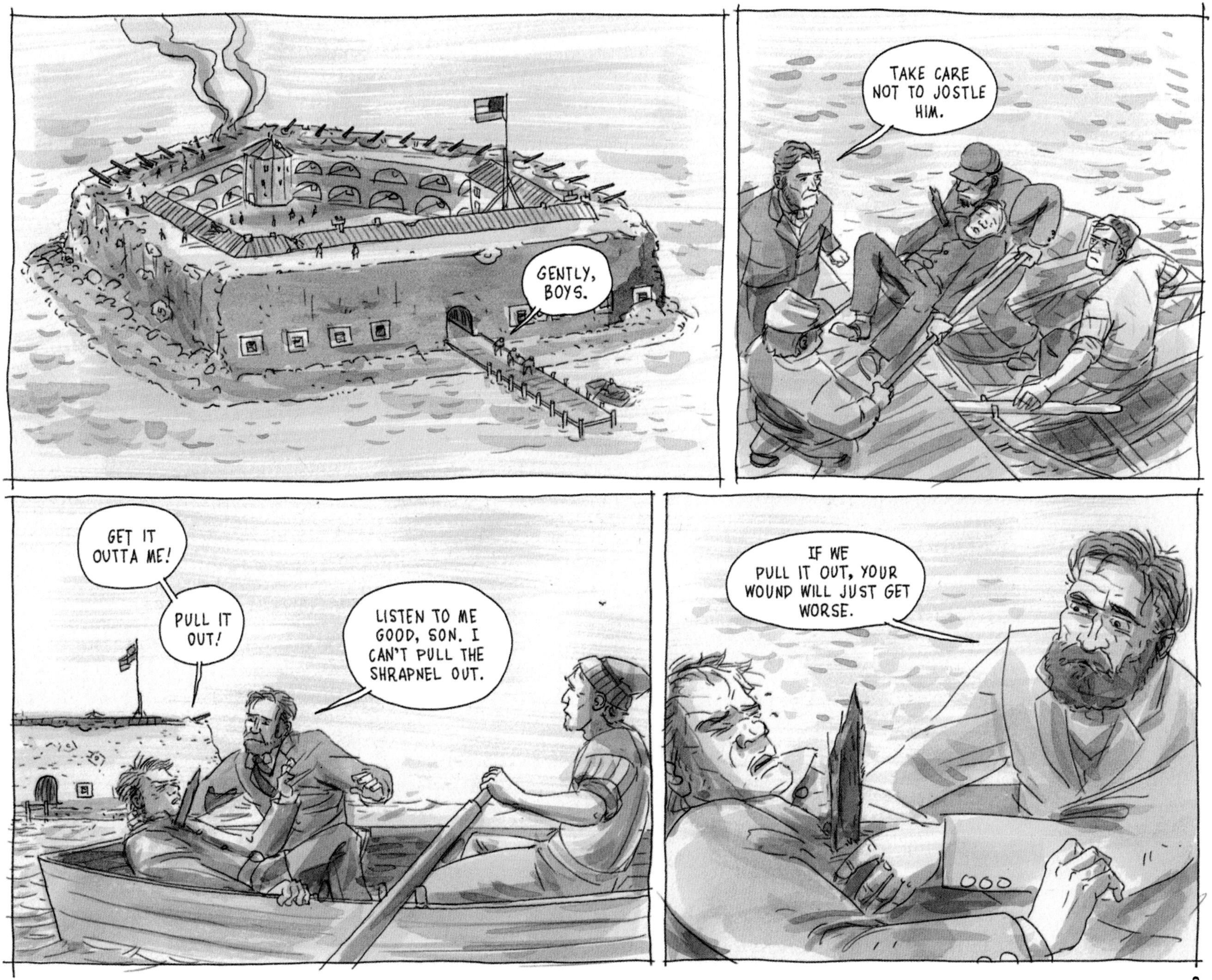
GENTLY, BOYS.
TAKE CARE NOT TO JOSTLE HIM.
GET IT OUTTA ME!
PULL IT OUT!
LISTEN TO ME GOOD, SON. I CAN'T PULL THE SHRAPNEL OUT.
IF WE PULL IT OUT, YOUR WOUND WILL JUST GET WORSE.

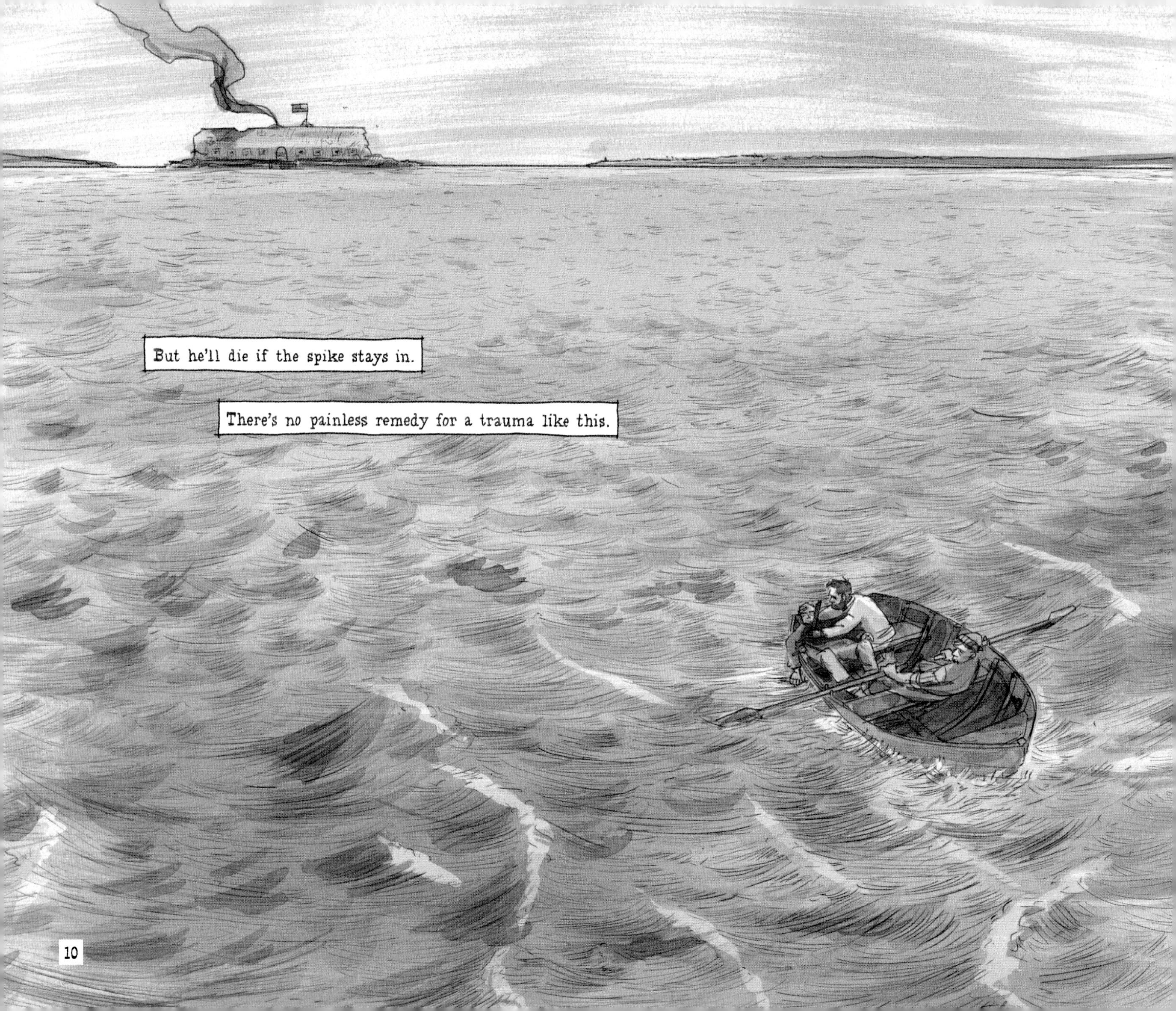
But he'll die if the spike stays in.
There's no painless remedy for a trauma like this.

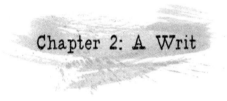

Chapter 2: A Writ

Baltimore Banner

April 20, 1861

SUMTER FALLS
Prompts Lincoln's Call for Troops

With Fort Sumter lost, President Lincoln reckoned that war had become inevitable. Still, he hoped to avoid a massive conflict that would transform the nation. He wanted instead to preserve the Union, to return things to the way they had been prior to his election, shedding as little blood and destroying as little property as possible in the process.

Observing that the North boasted huge advantages in population, industrial and manufacturing capacities, and transportation networks, it seemed to Lincoln that the war would be brief and to other observers that it might be glorious. Accordingly, the President called for 75,000 volunteers to serve for a period of just ninety days.

Southerners agreed that the fighting would not take long. Their section of the country counted among its citizens many of the nation's experienced fighting men. Effete Northerners, some rebels insisted, would run screaming at the first sign of blood, leaving the Confederacy in peace.

The violence at Sumter, though, released a flood tide of patriotism in both North and South, leaving recruiting offices awash in volunteer soldiers. In the Union, state after state asked President Lincoln to increase the quota of volunteers who could muster into the Federal Army. And in the Confederacy, state militias swelled to bursting with men ready to fight.

THE UPPER SOUTH SITS ON THE FENCE

As the Union and Confederacy prepared for war in the late spring of 1861, the Upper South seemed to control the fate of the nation. Eight undecided states--Arkansas, Delaware, Kentucky, Maryland, Missouri, North Carolina, Tennessee, and Virginia--contained more than 50 percent of the South's population, some 60 percent of its food crops and livestock, and roughly 75 percent of its industrial capacity.

Less than a week after the fall of Fort Sumter, Virginia's militia marked the state's unofficial decision to join the Confederacy by seizing control of the federal arsenal at Harpers Ferry, the site of John Brown's raid in 1859. Virginia provided the rebellion with an industrial base, a capital city in Richmond, and its most important hero, the gentleman warrior Robert E. Lee.

By the end of June, Arkansas, North Carolina, and Tennessee had also seceded. Of the remaining states, Delaware never considered leaving the Union, and Kentucky, Maryland, and Missouri split internally into pro-Confederate and pro-Union camps. Maryland ultimately remained loyal to the United States. Kentucky attempted to maintain its neutrality during the war but fell under Union control. Missouri found itself divided throughout the conflict, a violent borderland where guerrilla bands thrived. By the fall of 1861, the battle lines were drawn.

RUMORS FROM THE FRONT ☞

Violent Mobs in Baltimore Clash with Sixth Massachusetts Regiment on Way to Washington, D.C.

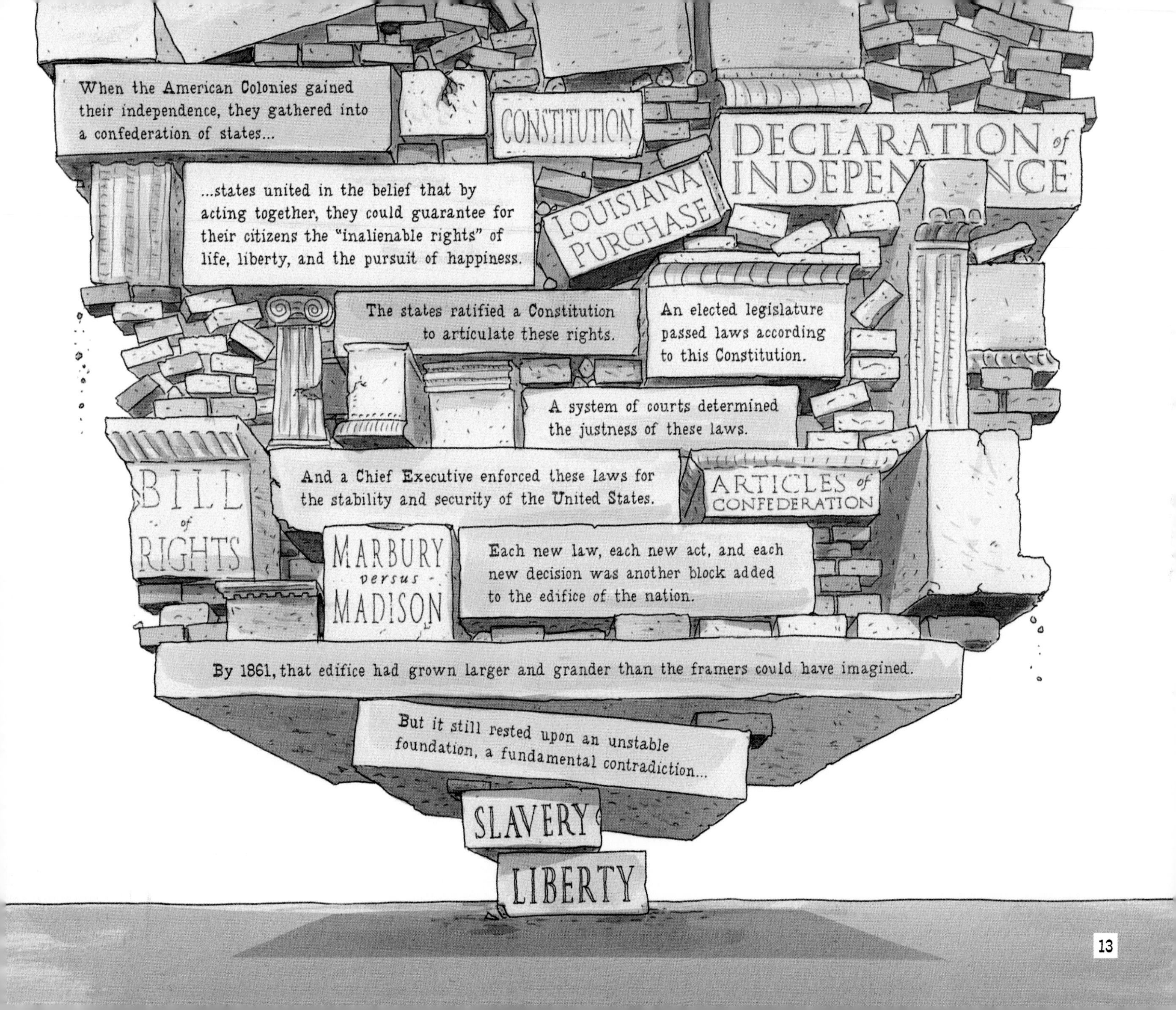
When the American Colonies gained their independence, they gathered into a confederation of states...
CONSTITUTION
DECLARATION of INDEPENDENCE
...states united in the belief that by acting together, they could guarantee for their citizens the "inalienable rights" of life, liberty, and the pursuit of happiness.
LOUISIANA PURCHASE
The states ratified a Constitution to articulate these rights.
An elected legislature passed laws according to this Constitution.
A system of courts determined the justness of these laws.
BILL of RIGHTS
And a Chief Executive enforced these laws for the stability and security of the United States.
ARTICLES of CONFEDERATION
MARBURY versus MADISON
Each new law, each new act, and each new decision was another block added to the edifice of the nation.
By 1861, that edifice had grown larger and grander than the framers could have imagined.
But it still rested upon an unstable foundation, a fundamental contradiction...
SLAVERY
LIBERTY

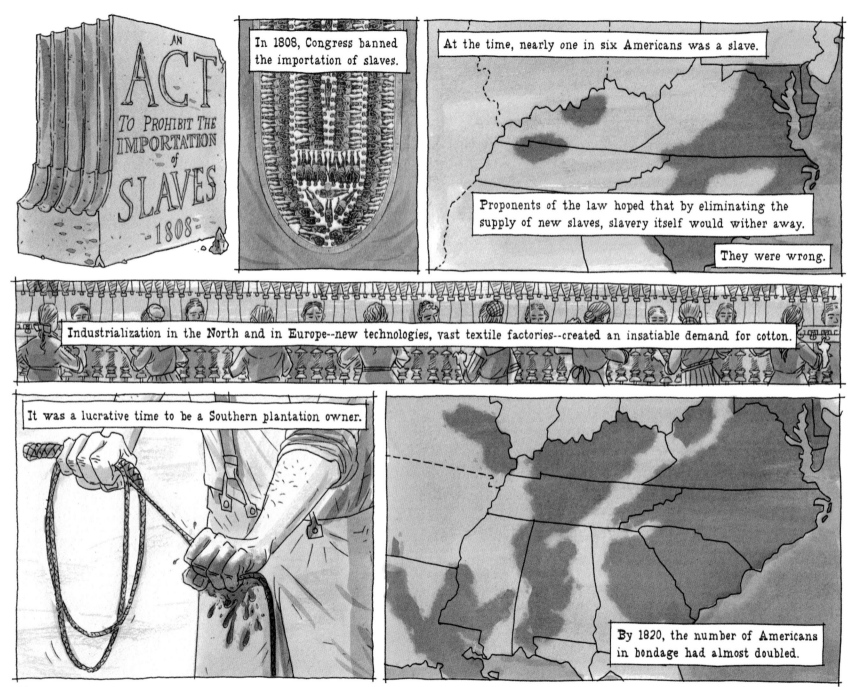

AN ACT
TO PROHIBIT THE IMPORTATION of SLAVES
-1808-

In 1808, Congress banned the importation of slaves.

At the time, nearly one in six Americans was a slave.

Proponents of the law hoped that by eliminating the supply of new slaves, slavery itself would wither away.

They were wrong.

Industrialization in the North and in Europe--new technologies, vast textile factories--created an insatiable demand for cotton.

It was a lucrative time to be a Southern plantation owner.

By 1820, the number of Americans in bondage had almost doubled.

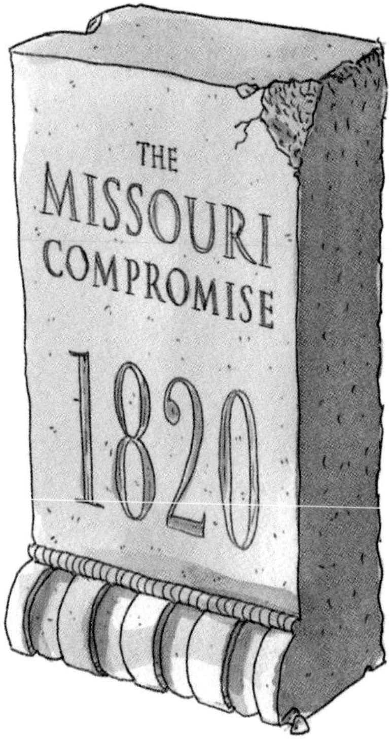
THE
MISSOURI
COMPROMISE
1820

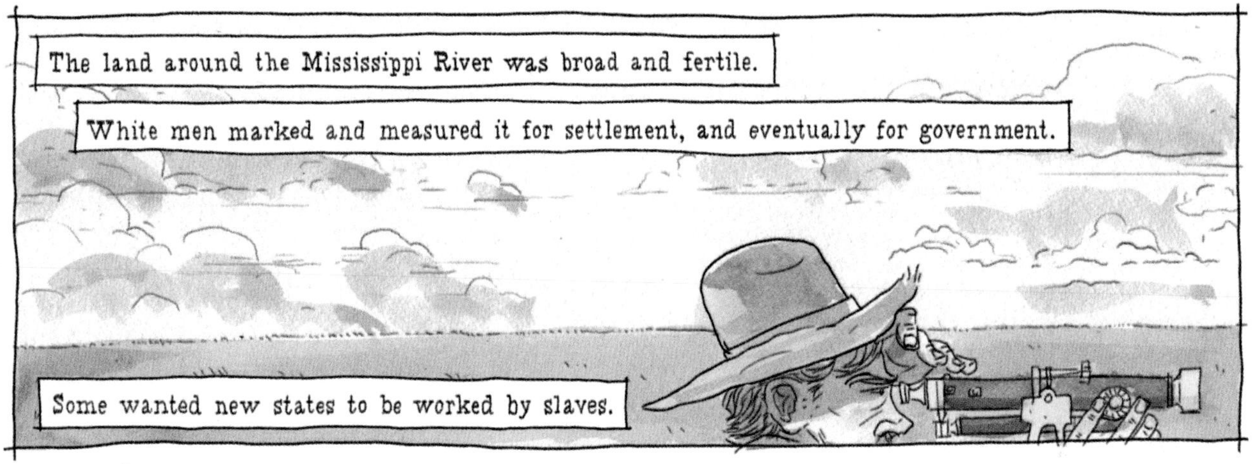
The land around the Mississippi River was broad and fertile.
White men marked and measured it for settlement, and eventually for government.
Some wanted new states to be worked by slaves.

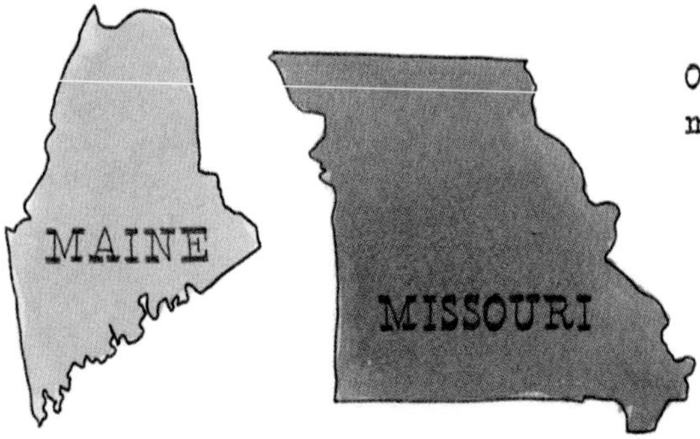
MAINE
MISSOURI

Others feared what would happen if too many states depended on slavery.

In 1820, a compromise was negotiated between the federal government and two new states being considered for entry into the Union.

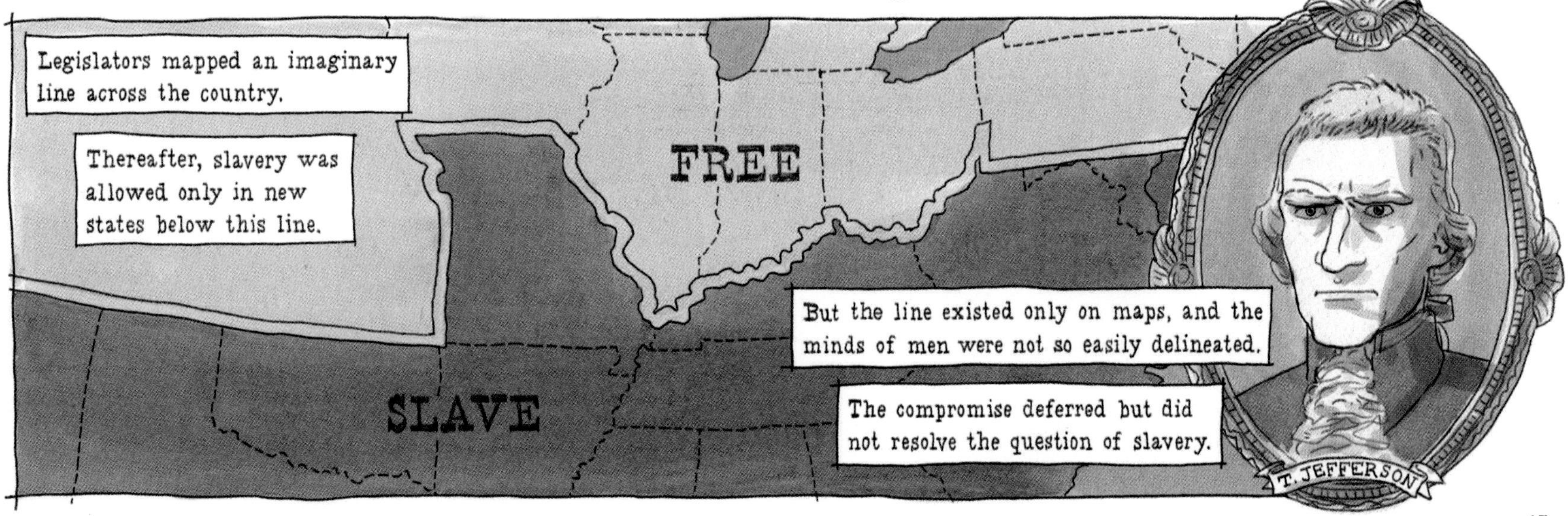
Legislators mapped an imaginary line across the country.
Thereafter, slavery was allowed only in new states below this line.
FREE
SLAVE
But the line existed only on maps, and the minds of men were not so easily delineated.
The compromise deferred but did not resolve the question of slavery.
T. JEFFERSON

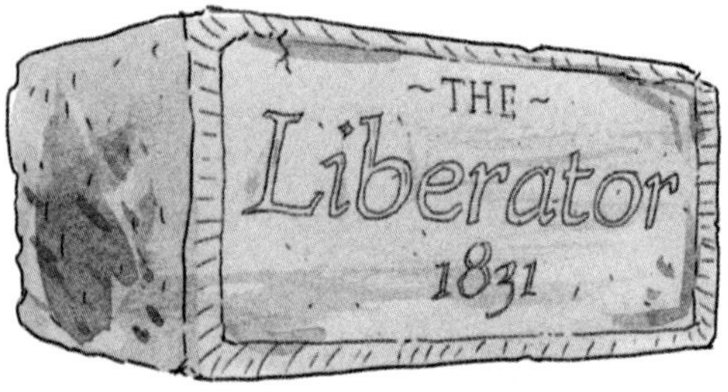
~THE~
Liberator
1831

In the 1830s, a spirit of religious reform animated the country. Some of the most radical of these reformers, calling themselves abolitionists, rallied to end slavery.

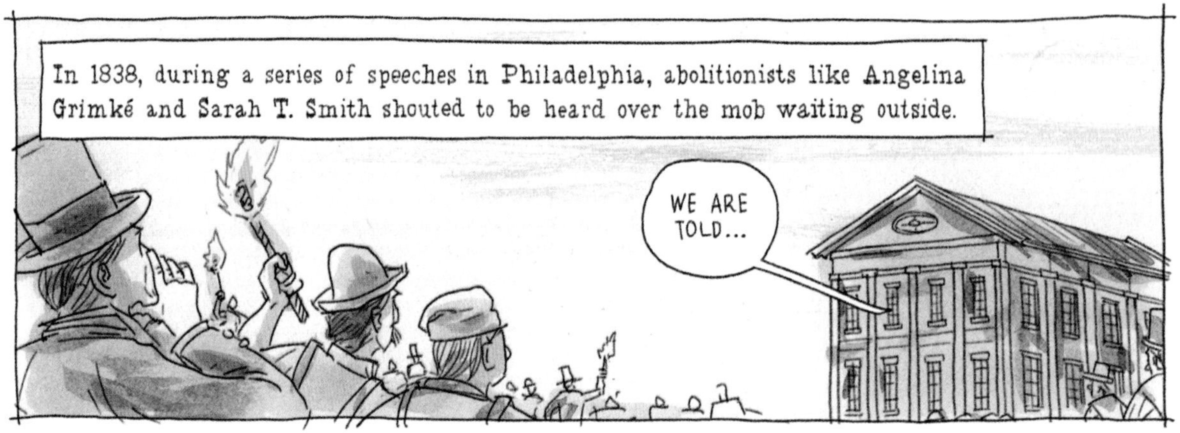
In 1838, during a series of speeches in Philadelphia, abolitionists like Angelina Grimké and Sarah T. Smith shouted to be heard over the mob waiting outside.
WE ARE TOLD...

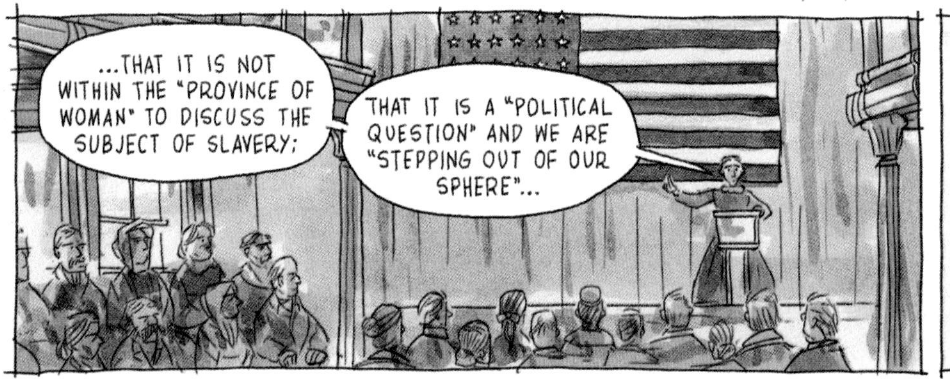
...THAT IT IS NOT WITHIN THE "PROVINCE OF WOMAN" TO DISCUSS THE SUBJECT OF SLAVERY;
THAT IT IS A "POLITICAL QUESTION" AND WE ARE "STEPPING OUT OF OUR SPHERE"...

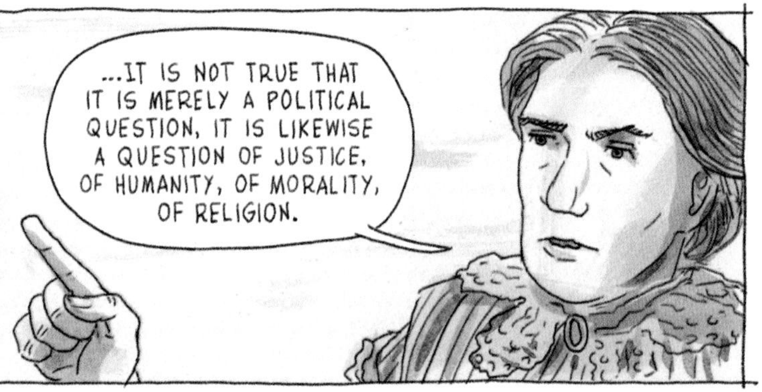
...IT IS NOT TRUE THAT IT IS MERELY A POLITICAL QUESTION, IT IS LIKEWISE A QUESTION OF JUSTICE, OF HUMANITY, OF MORALITY, OF RELIGION.

These voices joined with those of William Lloyd Garrison and James Forten to form a chorus of indignation.

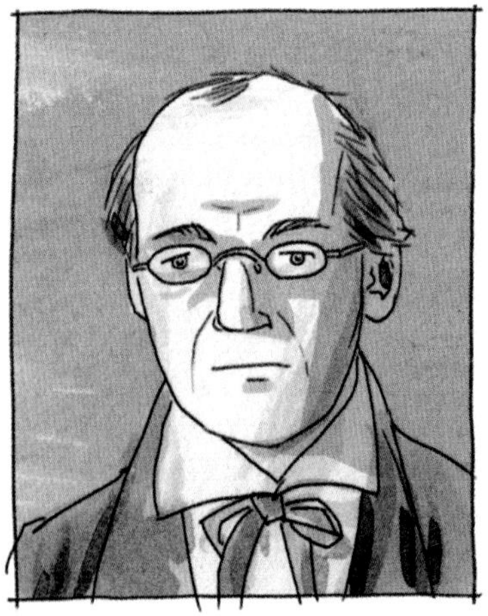

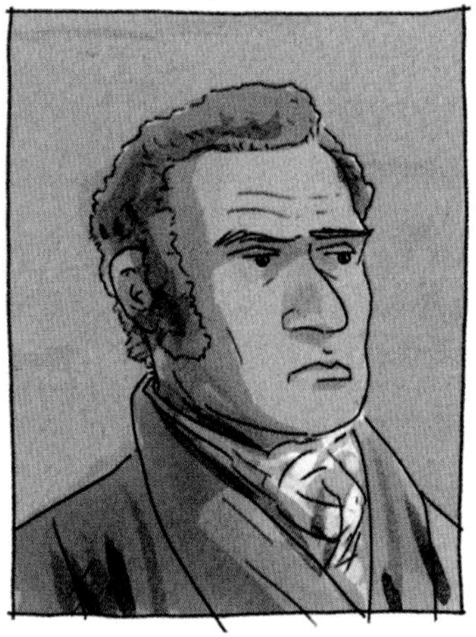

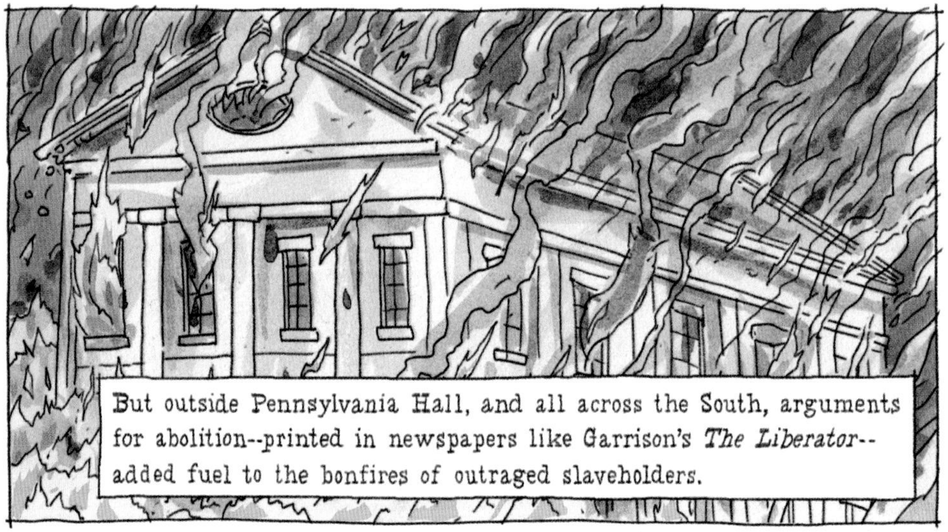
But outside Pennsylvania Hall, and all across the South, arguments for abolition--printed in newspapers like Garrison's *The Liberator*--added fuel to the bonfires of outraged slaveholders.

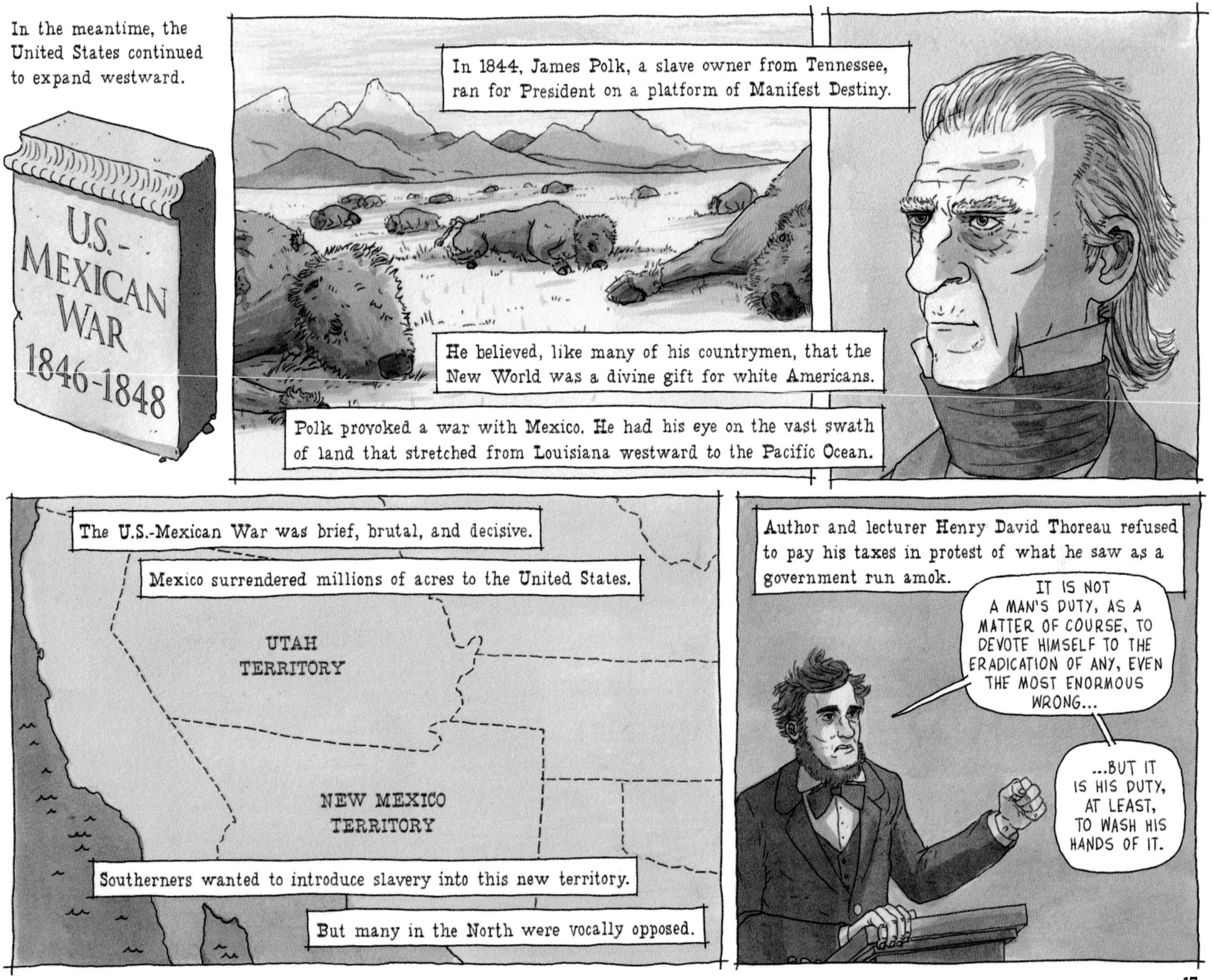
In the meantime, the United States continued to expand westward.
U.S.-MEXICAN WAR 1846-1848
In 1844, James Polk, a slave owner from Tennessee, ran for President on a platform of Manifest Destiny.
He believed, like many of his countrymen, that the New World was a divine gift for white Americans.
Polk provoked a war with Mexico. He had his eye on the vast swath of land that stretched from Louisiana westward to the Pacific Ocean.
The U.S.-Mexican War was brief, brutal, and decisive.
Mexico surrendered millions of acres to the United States.
UTAH TERRITORY
NEW MEXICO TERRITORY
Southerners wanted to introduce slavery into this new territory.
But many in the North were vocally opposed.
Author and lecturer Henry David Thoreau refused to pay his taxes in protest of what he saw as a government run amok.
IT IS NOT A MAN'S DUTY, AS A MATTER OF COURSE, TO DEVOTE HIMSELF TO THE ERADICATION OF ANY, EVEN THE MOST ENORMOUS WRONG...
...BUT IT IS HIS DUTY, AT LEAST, TO WASH HIS HANDS OF IT.

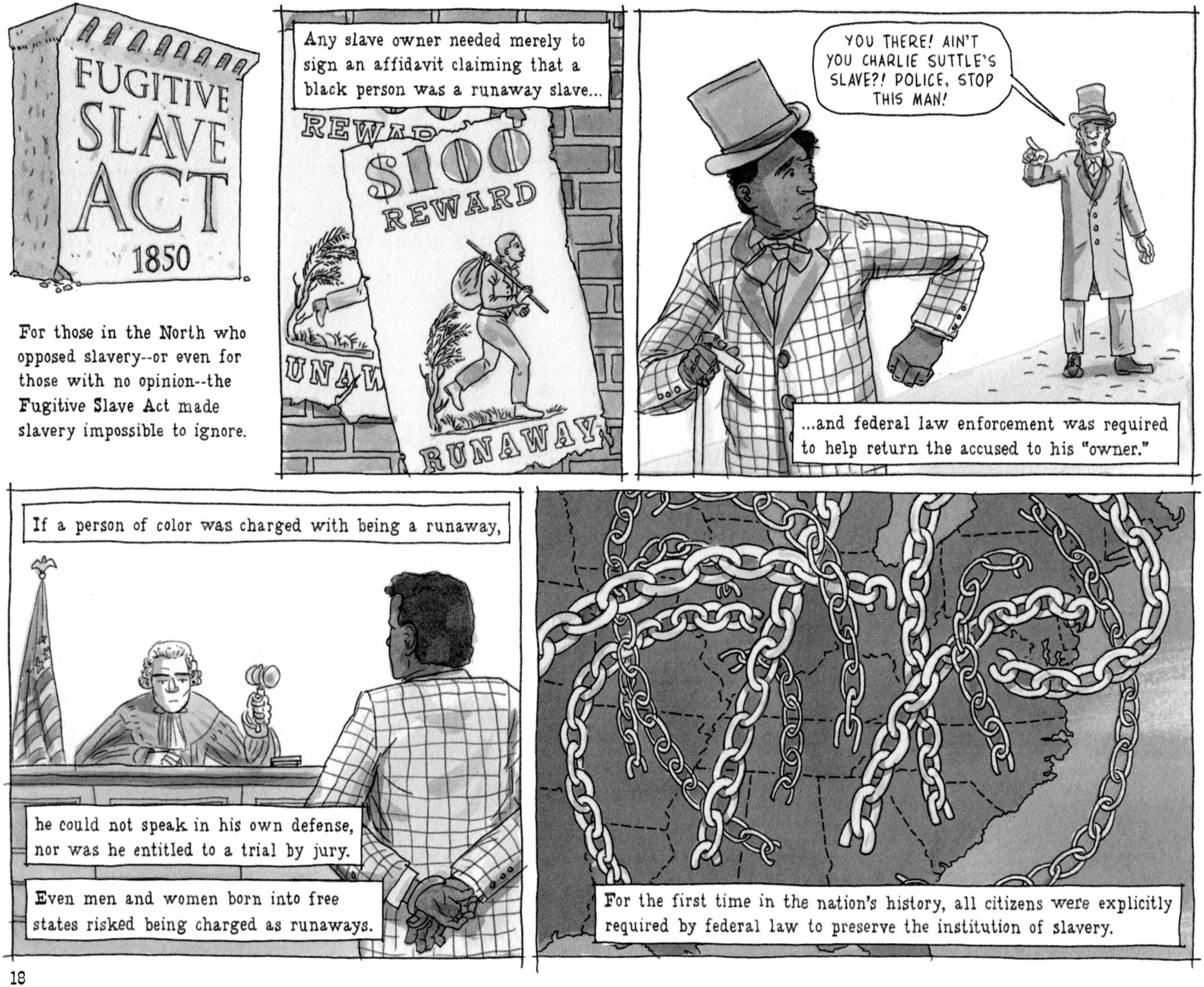
FUGITIVE SLAVE ACT 1850
For those in the North who opposed slavery--or even for those with no opinion--the Fugitive Slave Act made slavery impossible to ignore.
Any slave owner needed merely to sign an affidavit claiming that a black person was a runaway slave...
$100 REWARD
RUNAWAY
YOU THERE! AIN'T YOU CHARLIE SUTTLE'S SLAVE?! POLICE, STOP THIS MAN!
...and federal law enforcement was required to help return the accused to his "owner."
If a person of color was charged with being a runaway,
he could not speak in his own defense, nor was he entitled to a trial by jury.
Even men and women born into free states risked being charged as runaways.
For the first time in the nation's history, all citizens were explicitly required by federal law to preserve the institution of slavery.

Railroads, businesses, speculators, and homesteaders kept moving westward. But which of these new states, once it was admitted to the Union, would allow slavery?

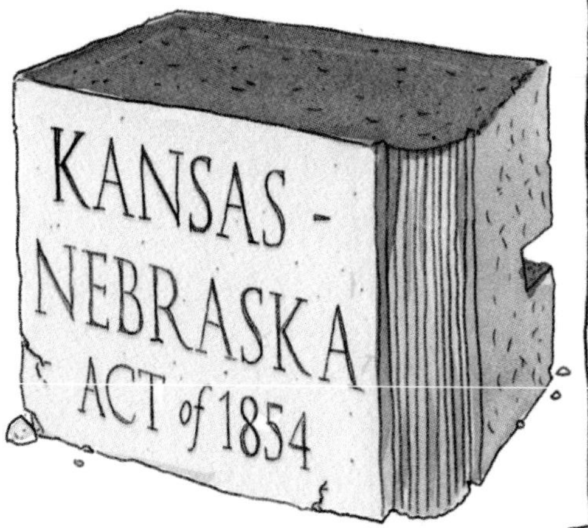
KANSAS - NEBRASKA ACT of 1854

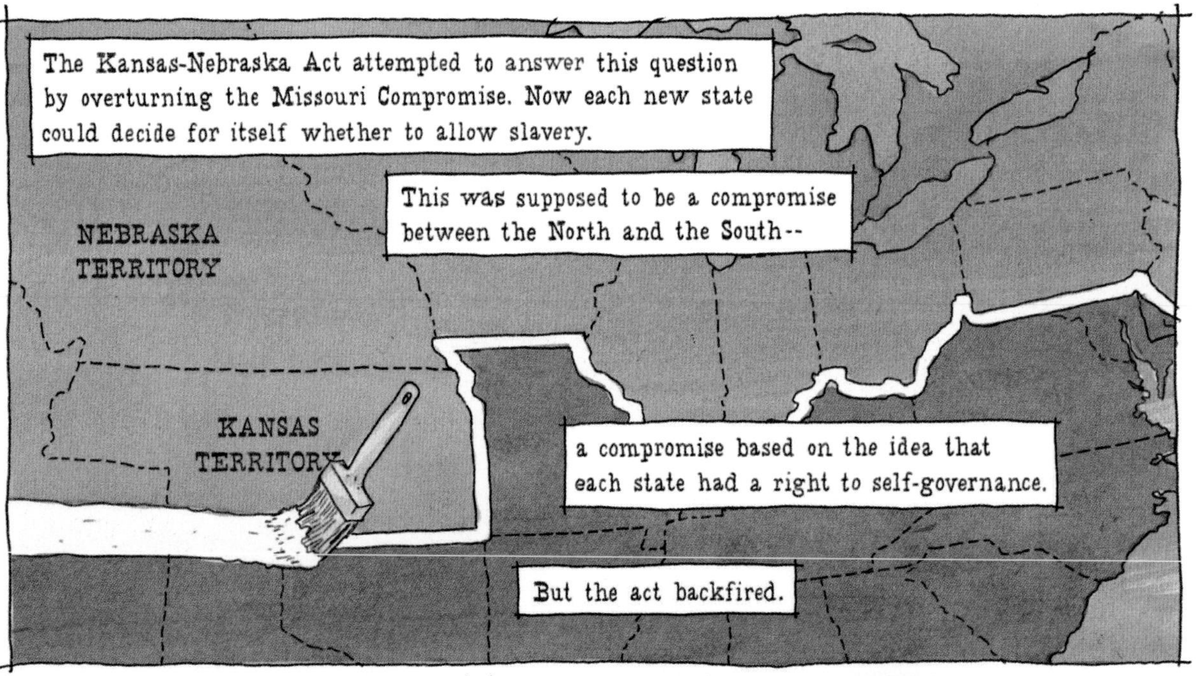
The Kansas-Nebraska Act attempted to answer this question by overturning the Missouri Compromise. Now each new state could decide for itself whether to allow slavery.
This was supposed to be a compromise between the North and the South--
NEBRASKA TERRITORY
KANSAS TERRITORY
a compromise based on the idea that each state had a right to self-governance.
But the act backfired.

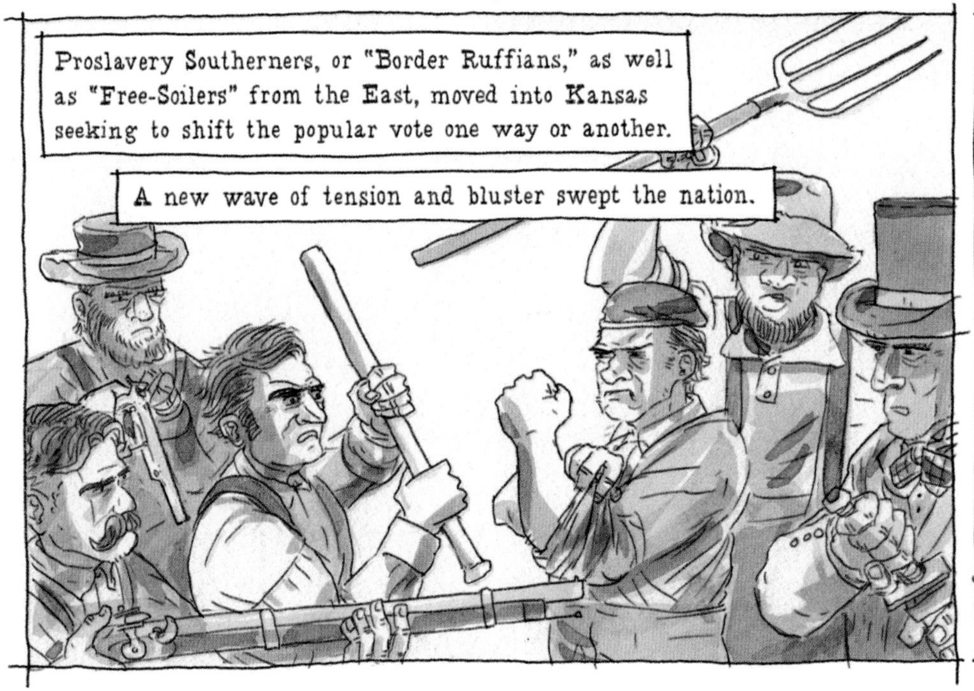
Proslavery Southerners, or "Border Ruffians," as well as "Free-Soilers" from the East, moved into Kansas seeking to shift the popular vote one way or another.
A new wave of tension and bluster swept the nation.

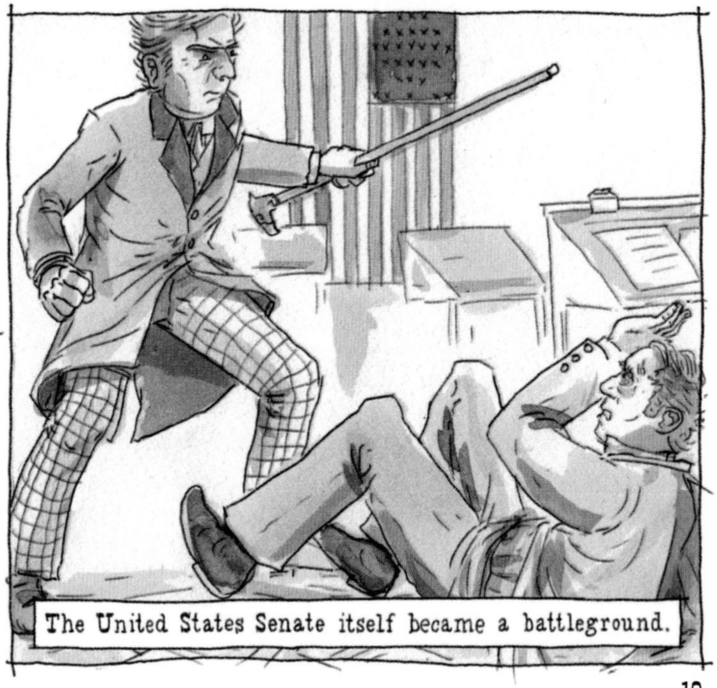
The United States Senate itself became a battleground.

BLEEDING KANSAS 1856 to 1858

In 1856, an abolitionist from New England filled a wagon with as many weapons and supplies as he could muster and headed off to Kansas.

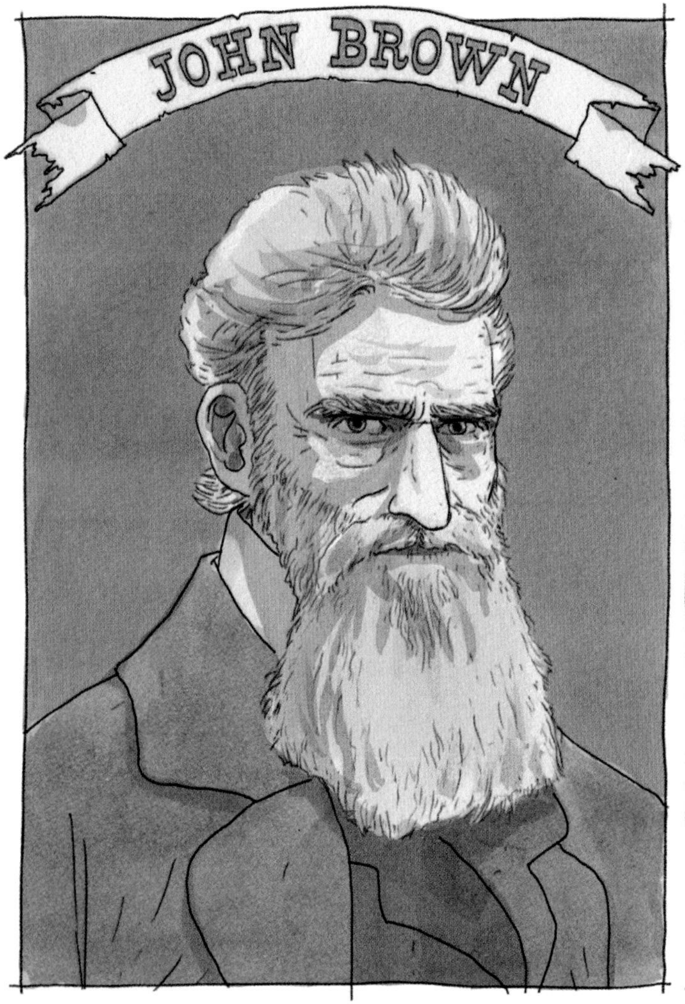
JOHN BROWN

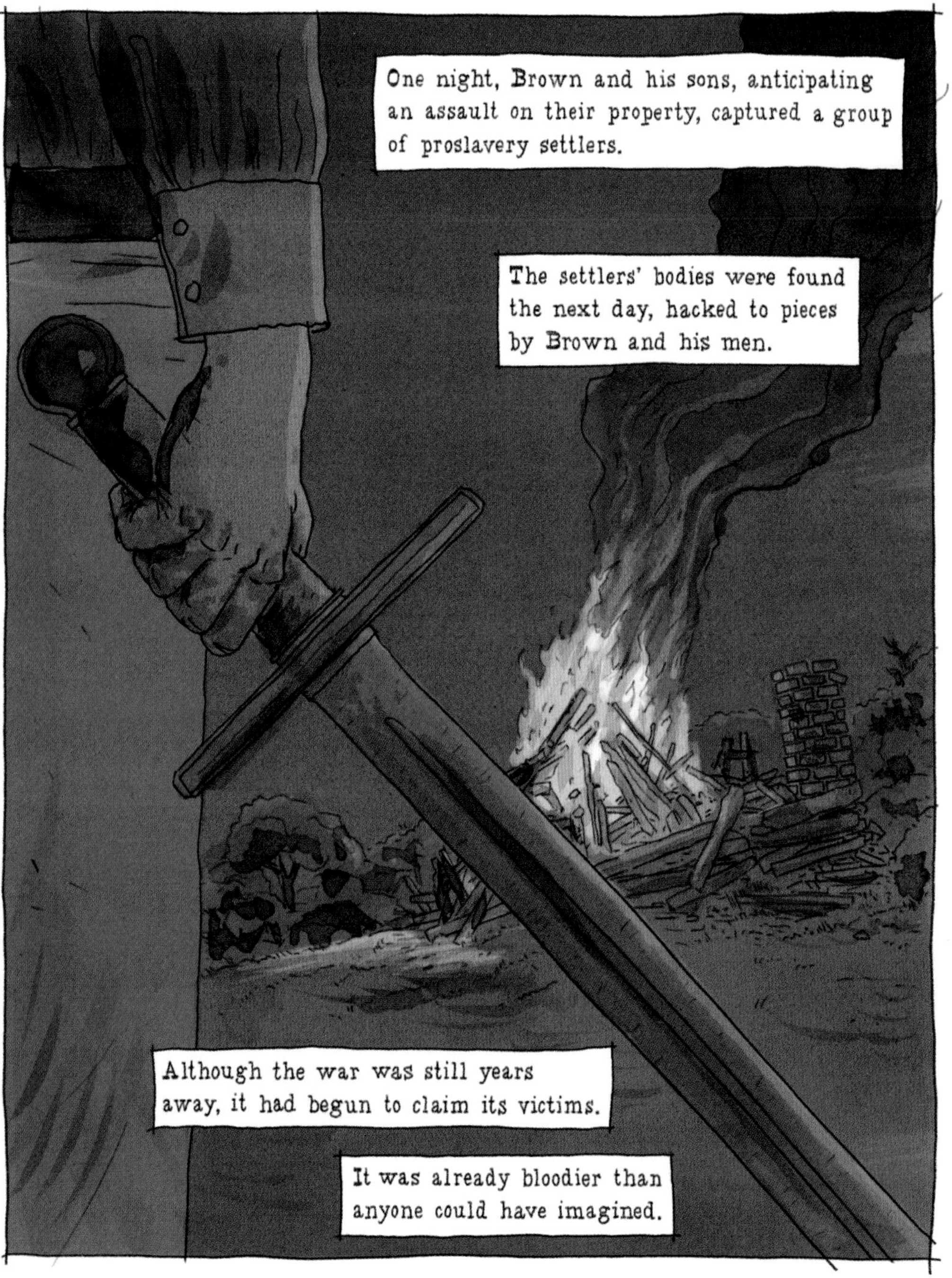
One night, Brown and his sons, anticipating an assault on their property, captured a group of proslavery settlers.
The settlers' bodies were found the next day, hacked to pieces by Brown and his men.
Although the war was still years away, it had begun to claim its victims.
It was already bloodier than anyone could have imagined.

Dred Scott was a slave owned by a surgeon in the U.S. Army.

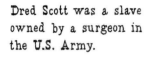

Scott had accompanied his owner to military forts throughout the country, including forts in states that prohibited slavery.

After his owner died, Scott sued for his freedom, claiming that by living in places where slavery was illegal, he had technically been emancipated.

The Supreme Court disagreed.

Chief Justice Roger Taney, a former slave owner, wrote the decision.

He asserted that any African American who was a slave or a descendant of slaves was not protected by the Constitution, could not be a U.S. citizen, and could not sue in court.

"BLACKS ARE SO FAR INFERIOR THAT THEY HAVE NO RIGHTS WHICH THE WHITE MAN IS BOUND TO RESPECT."

If Scott was to secure his freedom through the courts, Taney argued, African Americans in general would desire equality.

A month after Lincoln's inauguration and about the same time as the surrender of Fort Sumter, Federal troops gathered in Washington, D.C., to secure the nation's capital.

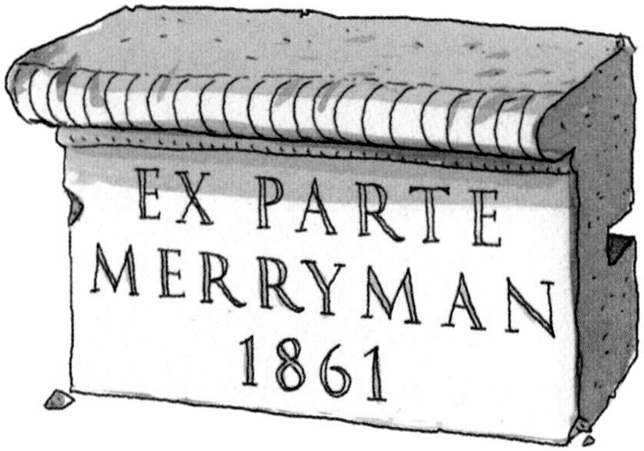
EX PARTE
MERRYMAN
1861

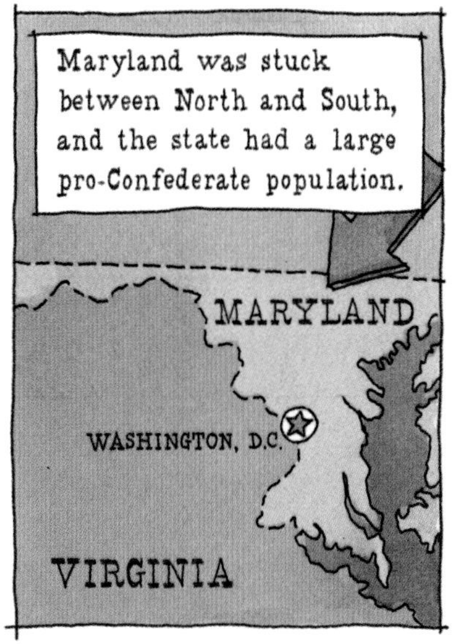
Maryland was stuck between North and South, and the state had a large pro-Confederate population.
MARYLAND
WASHINGTON, D.C.
VIRGINIA

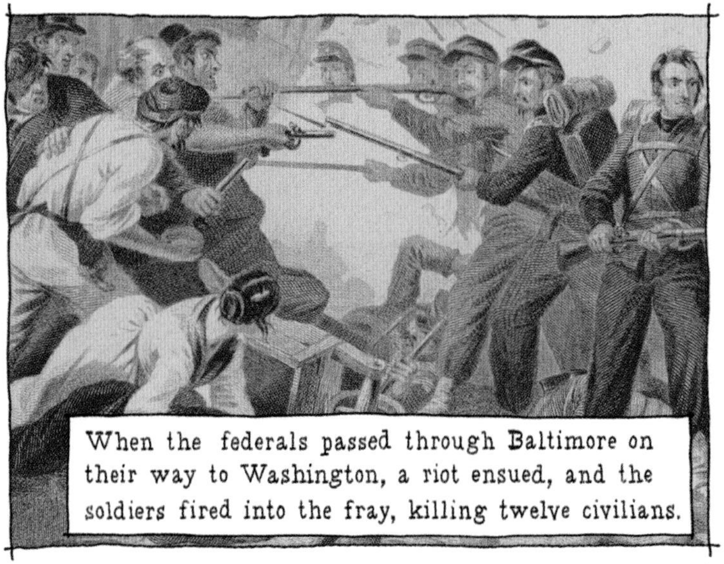
When the federals passed through Baltimore on their way to Washington, a riot ensued, and the soldiers fired into the fray, killing twelve civilians.

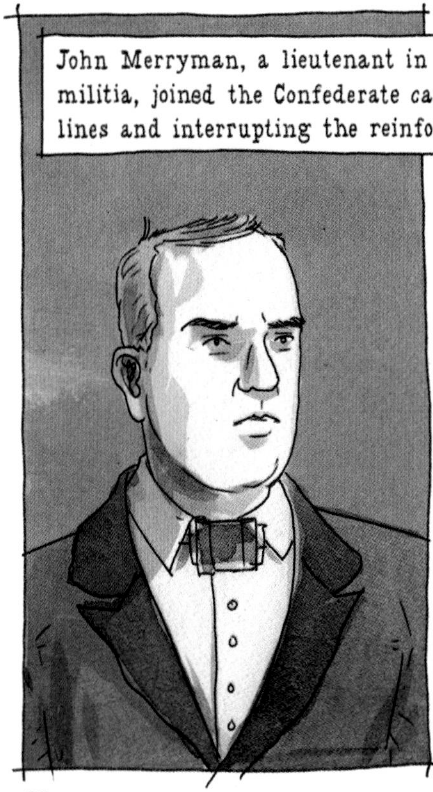
John Merryman, a lieutenant in the Maryland state militia, joined the Confederate cause by sabotaging rail lines and interrupting the reinforcement of Washington.

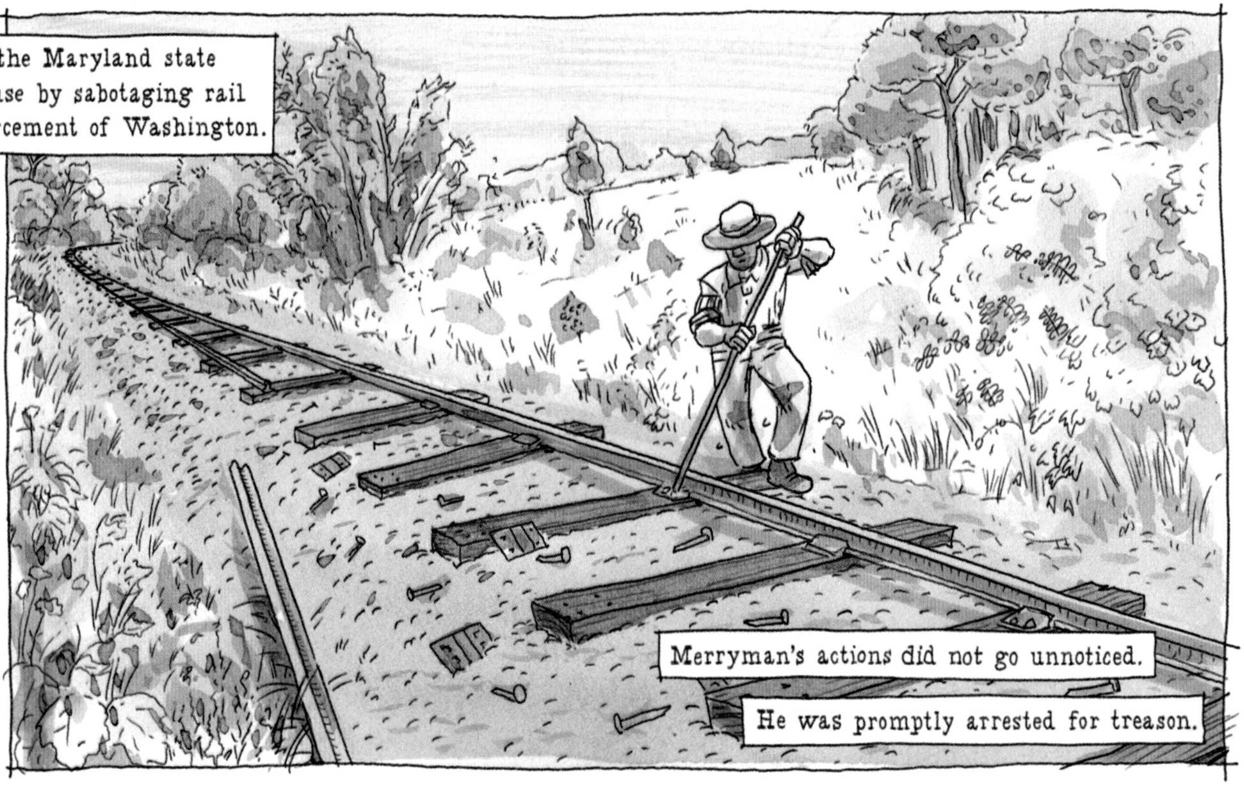
Merryman's actions did not go unnoticed.
He was promptly arrested for treason.

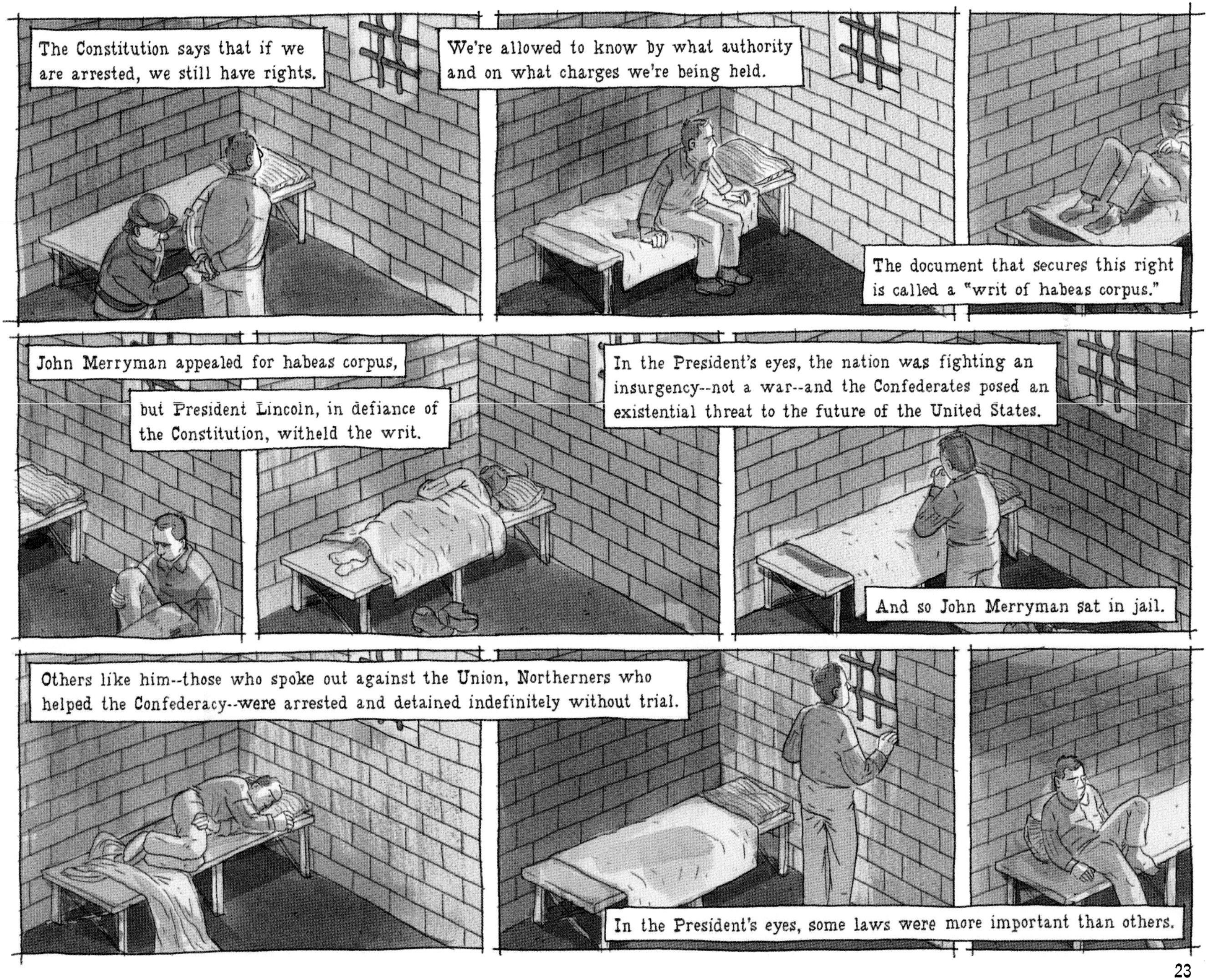
The Constitution says that if we are arrested, we still have rights.
We're allowed to know by what authority and on what charges we're being held.
The document that secures this right is called a "writ of habeas corpus."
John Merryman appealed for habeas corpus,
but President Lincoln, in defiance of the Constitution, witheld the writ.
In the President's eyes, the nation was fighting an insurgency--not a war--and the Confederates posed an existential threat to the future of the United States.
And so John Merryman sat in jail.
Others like him--those who spoke out against the Union, Northerners who helped the Confederacy--were arrested and detained indefinitely without trial.
In the President's eyes, some laws were more important than others.

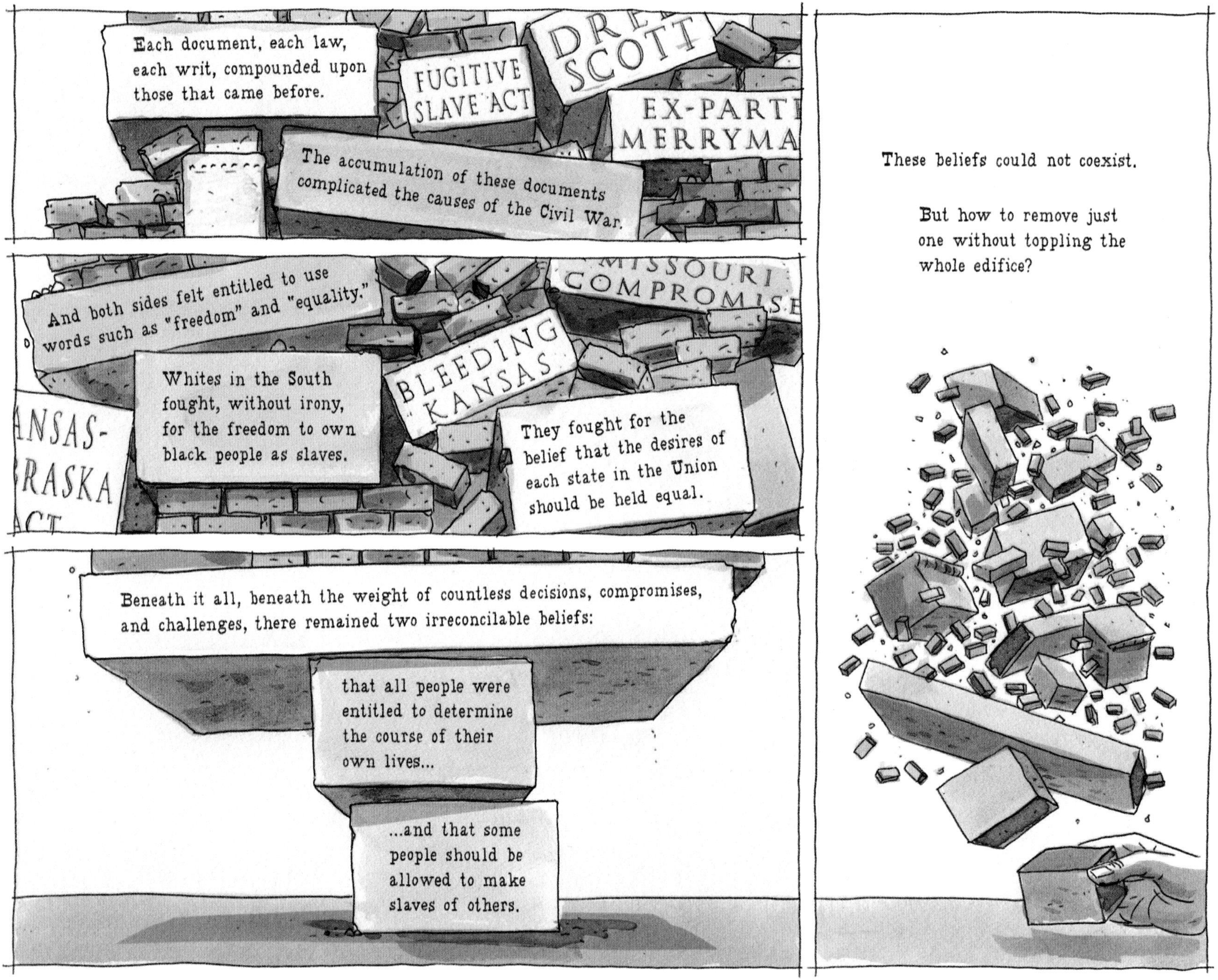

Each document, each law, each writ, compounded upon those that came before.
FUGITIVE SLAVE ACT
DRE SCOTT
EX-PART MERRYMA
The accumulation of these documents complicated the causes of the Civil War.
And both sides felt entitled to use words such as "freedom" and "equality."
MISSOURI COMPROMISE
BLEEDING KANSAS
ANSAS- BRASKA ACT
Whites in the South fought, without irony, for the freedom to own black people as slaves.
They fought for the belief that the desires of each state in the Union should be held equal.
Beneath it all, beneath the weight of countless decisions, compromises, and challenges, there remained two irreconcilable beliefs:
that all people were entitled to determine the course of their own lives...
...and that some people should be allowed to make slaves of others.
These beliefs could not coexist.
But how to remove just one without toppling the whole edifice?

Chapter 3: Opera Glasses

CENTREVILLE BLAZE

July 20, 1861

CALL TO ARMS!

CONFEDERATE CONGRESS AUTHORIZES AN ARMY OF 100,000

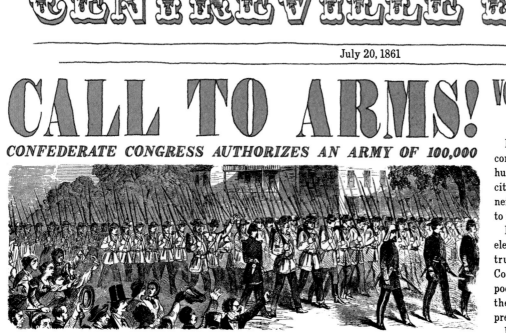

Still convinced that the war would be brief and glorious, the Confederate Congress, on March 6, 1861, called for 100,000 volunteers to augment the South's state militias for a period of twelve months.

The result was a ragtag army that would fight for a cash-strapped region crippled by its limited industrial capacity--in 1860, the North manufactured more than 95 percent of the nation's firearms, in excess of 90 percent of its cloth, and approximately 90 percent of its boots and shoes--and frequently march to war in homespun outfits. Consequently, though the Confederacy selected gray as its uniform color, soldiers arrived from throughout the South clad in an array of hues, sometimes resulting in tragic confusion once the fighting began in earnest.

Just a few months later, in May, the Confederacy would authorize the enlistment of another 400,000 troops for a term of three years. With the arrival of these new recruits, the South's equipment problems continued and never entirely abated throughout the conflict.

VOLUNTEER REGIMENTS
Show Local Spirit

In both the North and the South, Civil War companies were composed of approximately one hundred volunteers, often from a single town or city. Ten companies, occasionally drawn from neighboring communities, would then combine to form a regiment.

Early in the war, enlisted men sometimes elected their own officers, choosing people they trusted or admired to lead them into battle. Consequently, citizen soldiers, no matter how poorly trained or green they might have been at the start of the conflict, felt extraordinary pressure to perform courageously under fire.

Knowing that they would return home at the end of their term of enlistment with their surviving comrades-in-arms, even the most inexperienced troops usually displayed courage and fought hard to win approval from the men who, once they mustered out of the military and made their way back to their hometown, might be in a position to offer them a job, a bank loan, or the right to court their daughter.

RUMORS FROM THE FRONT ☞

*Armies Converge on Manassas Junction,
Outside Centreville, VA*

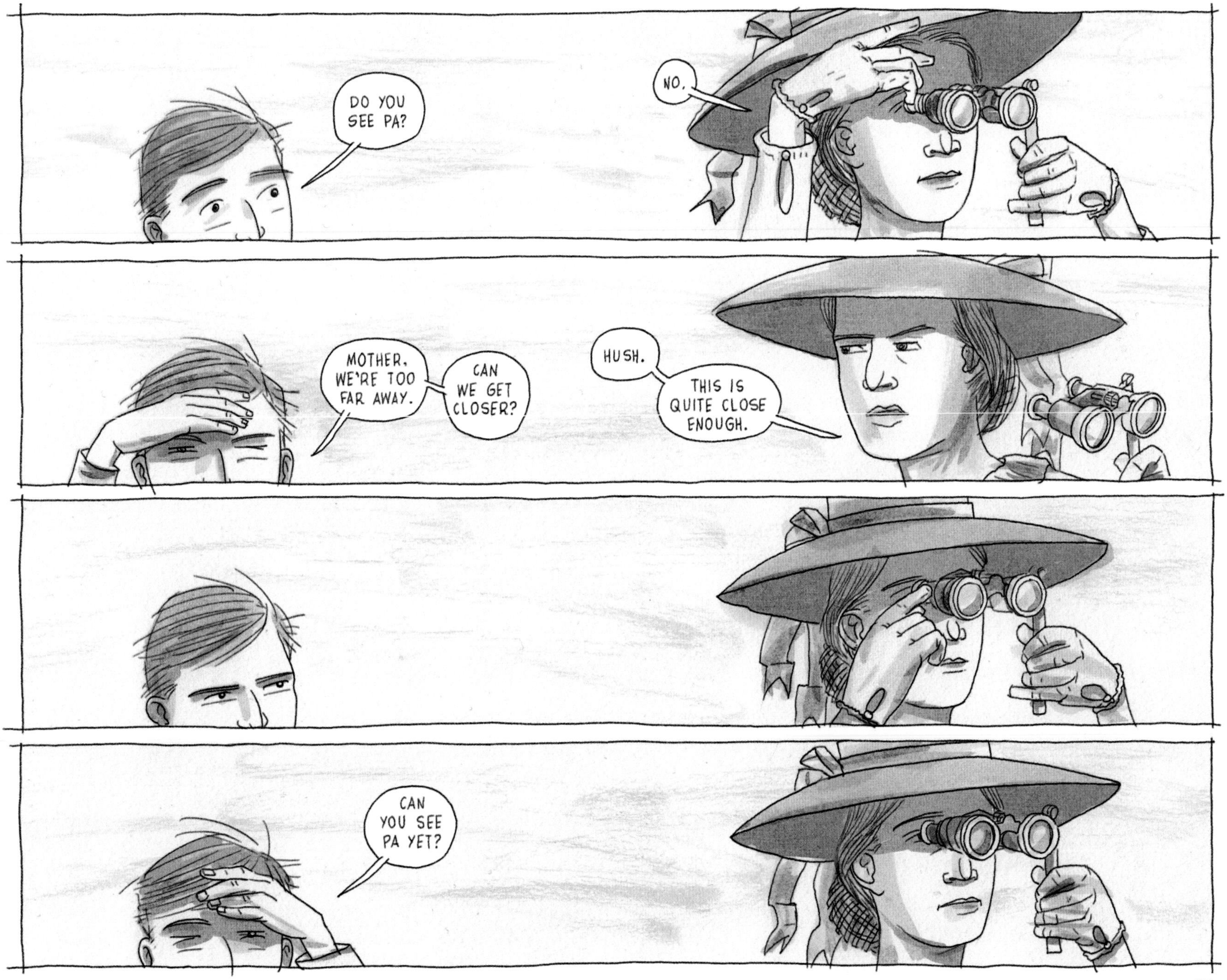
DO YOU SEE PA?
NO.
MOTHER, WE'RE TOO FAR AWAY.
CAN WE GET CLOSER?
HUSH.
THIS IS QUITE CLOSE ENOUGH.
CAN YOU SEE PA YET?

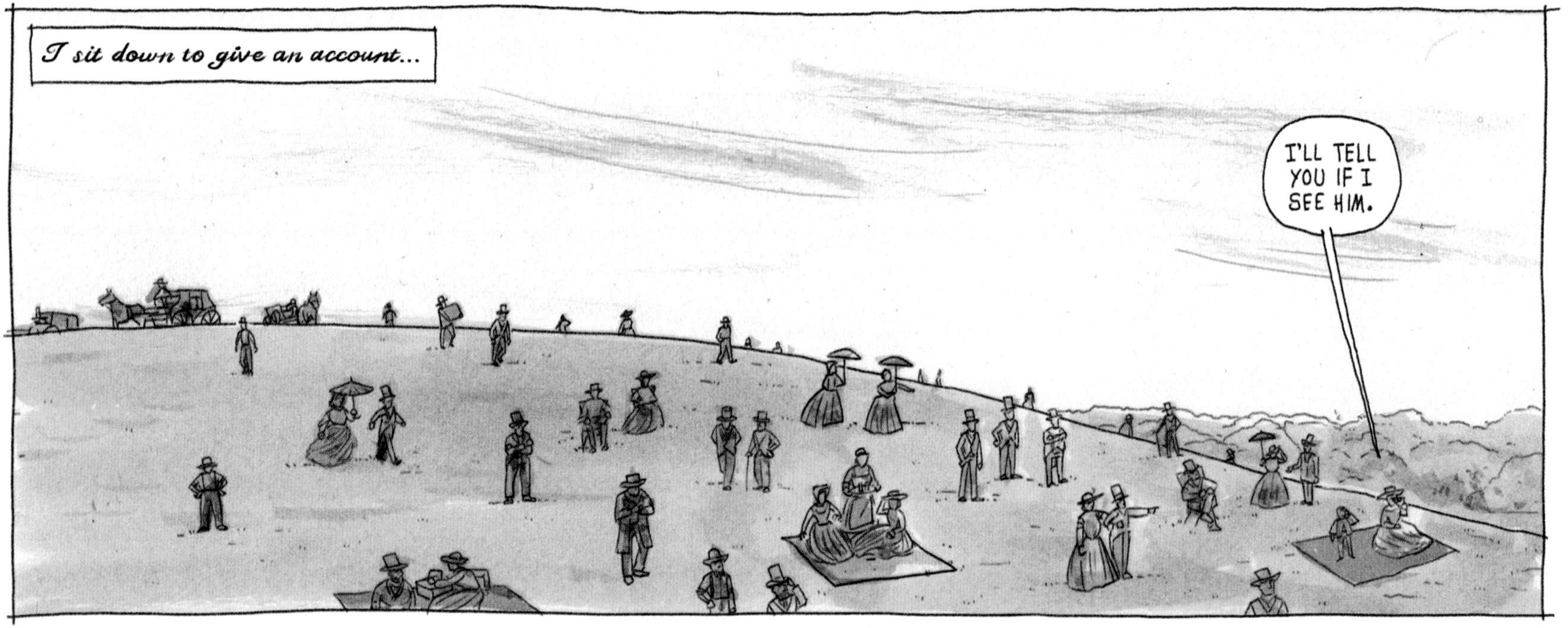
I sit down to give an account...
I'LL TELL YOU IF I SEE HIM.

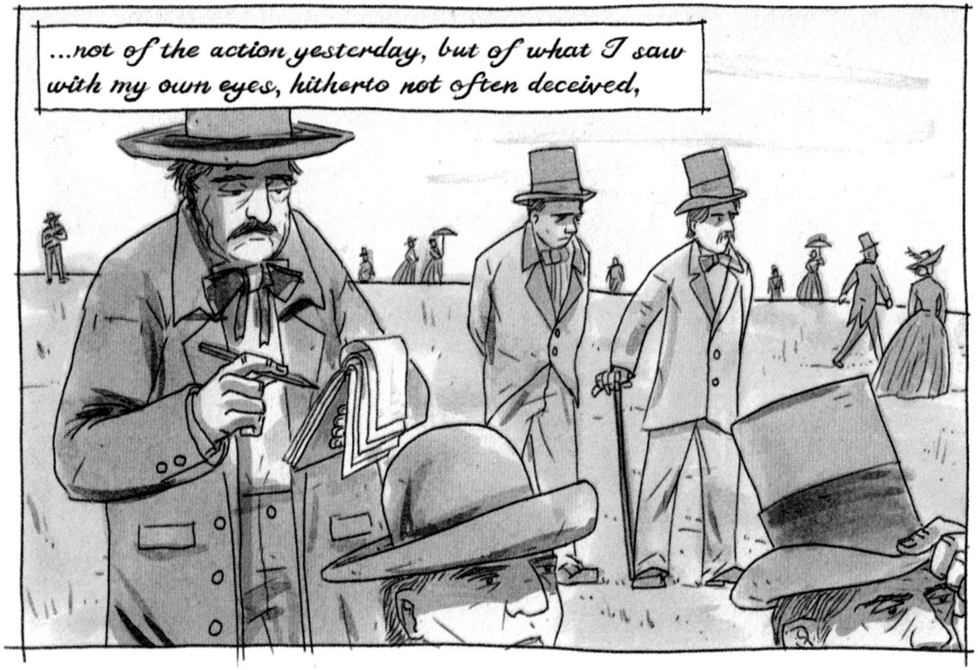
...not of the action yesterday, but of what I saw with my own eyes, hitherto not often deceived,

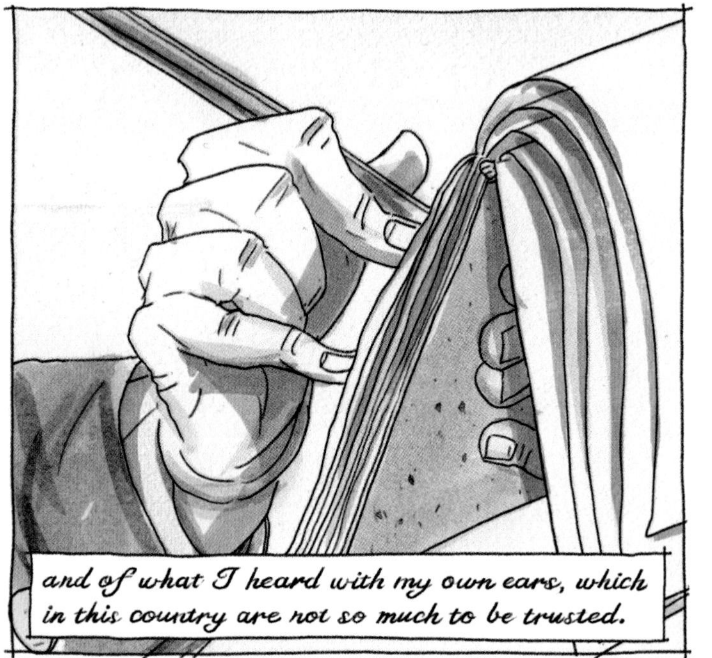
and of what I heard with my own ears, which in this country are not so much to be trusted.

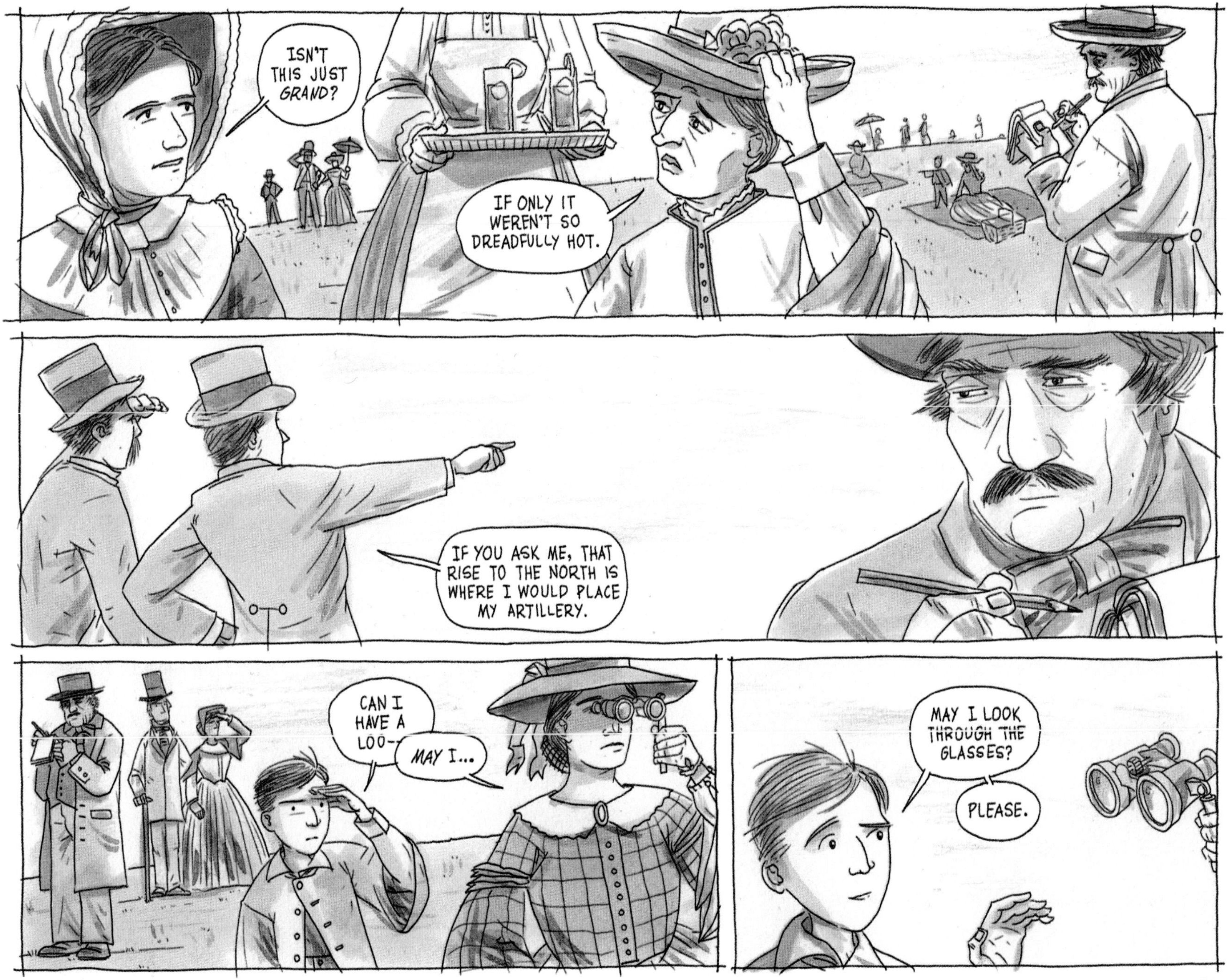
ISN'T THIS JUST GRAND?
IF ONLY IT WEREN'T SO DREADFULLY HOT.
IF YOU ASK ME, THAT RISE TO THE NORTH IS WHERE I WOULD PLACE MY ARTILLERY.
CAN I HAVE A LOO--
MAY I...
MAY I LOOK THROUGH THE GLASSES?
PLEASE.

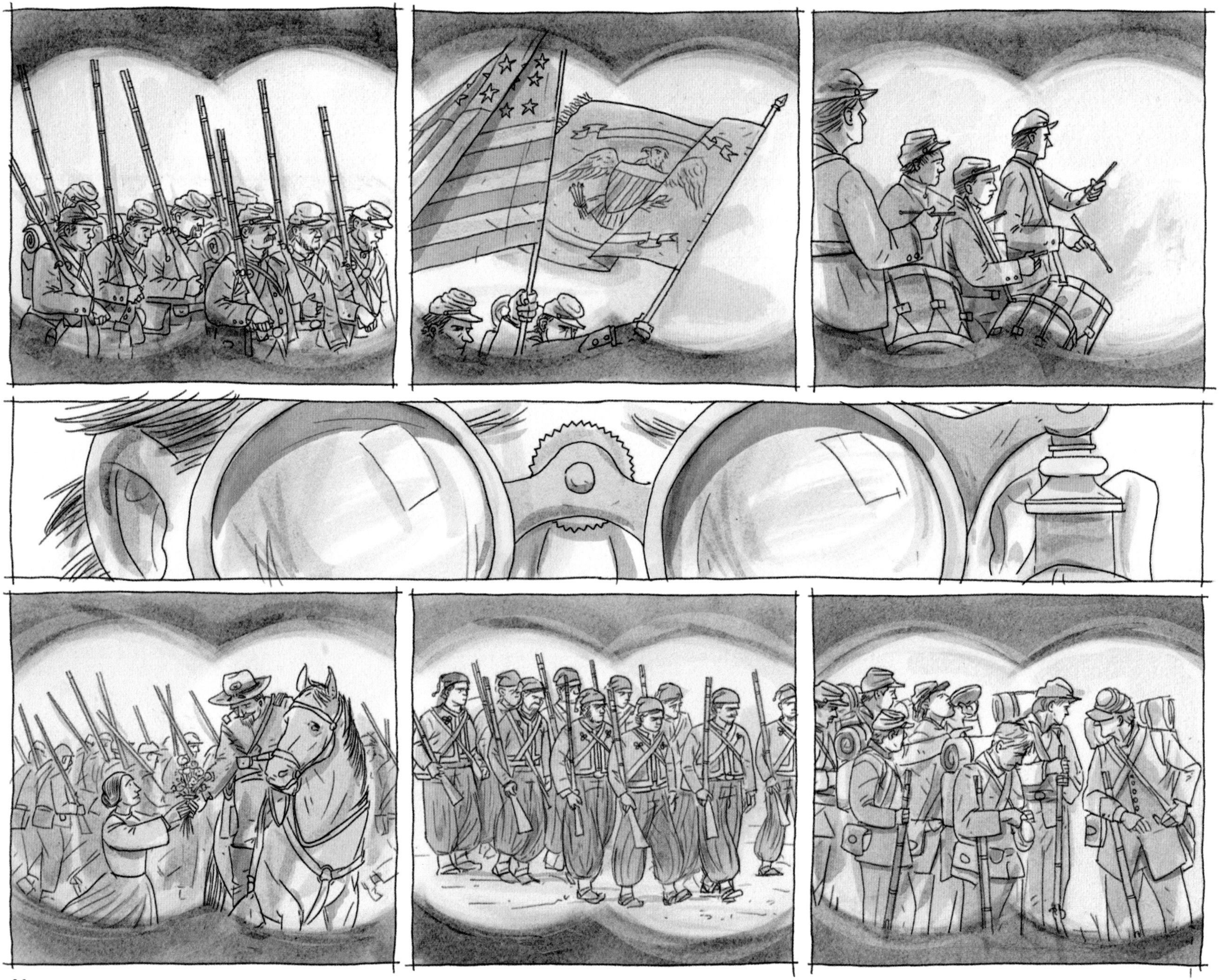

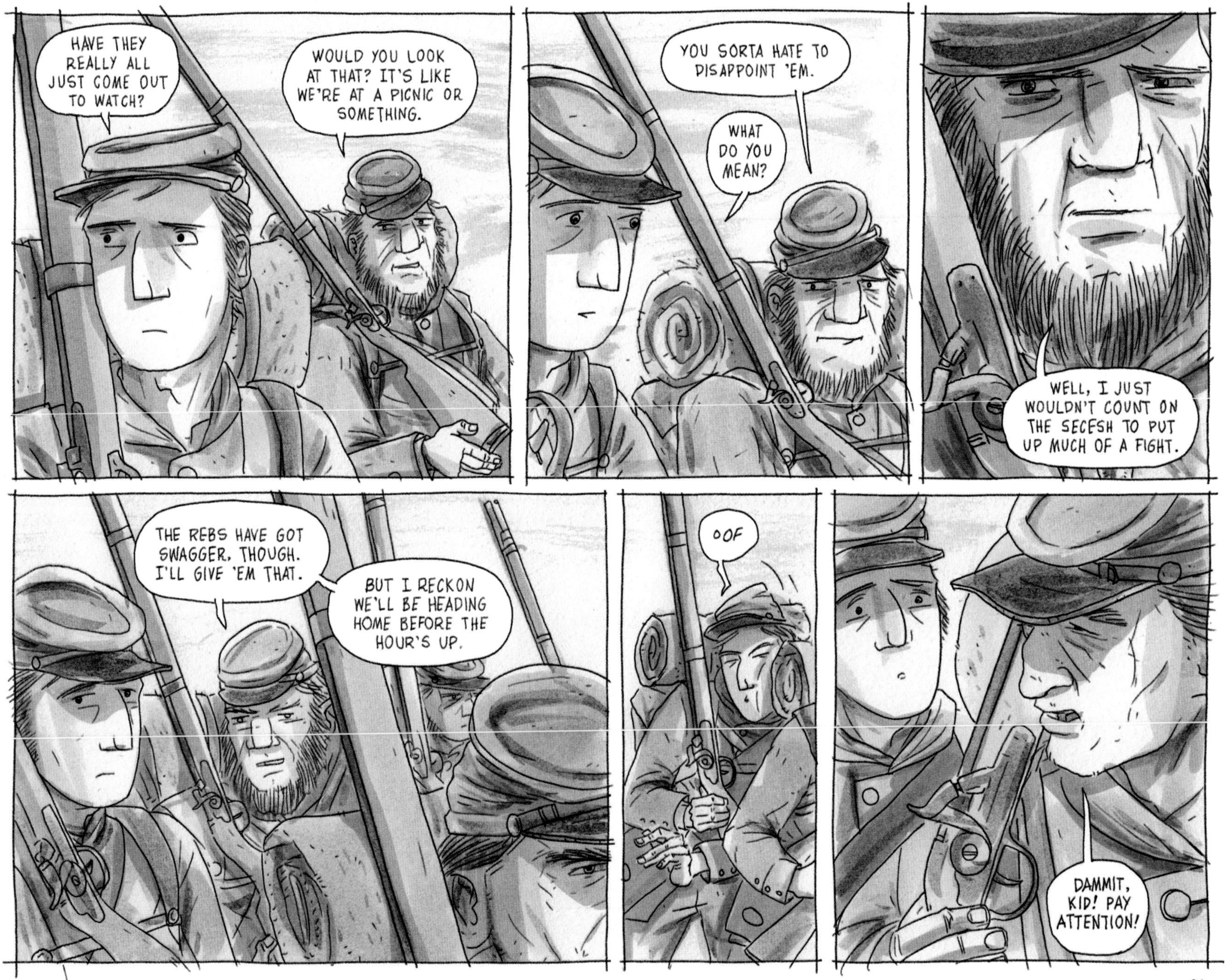

HAVE THEY REALLY ALL JUST COME OUT TO WATCH?
WOULD YOU LOOK AT THAT? IT'S LIKE WE'RE AT A PICNIC OR SOMETHING.
YOU SORTA HATE TO DISAPPOINT 'EM.
WHAT DO YOU MEAN?
WELL, I JUST WOULDN'T COUNT ON THE SECESH TO PUT UP MUCH OF A FIGHT.
THE REBS HAVE GOT SWAGGER, THOUGH. I'LL GIVE 'EM THAT.
BUT I RECKON WE'LL BE HEADING HOME BEFORE THE HOUR'S UP.
OOF
DAMMIT, KID! PAY ATTENTION!

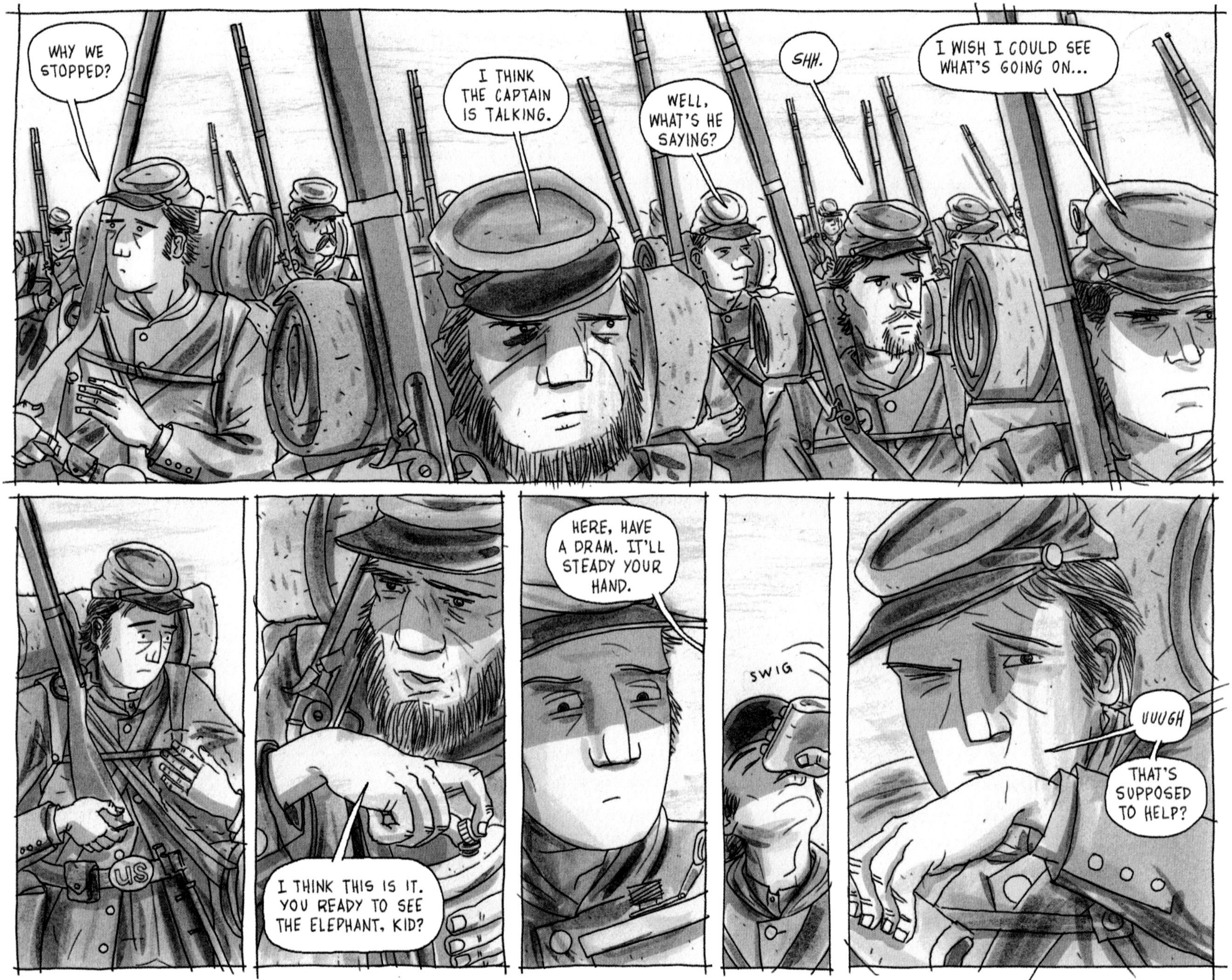
WHY WE STOPPED?
I THINK THE CAPTAIN IS TALKING.
WELL, WHAT'S HE SAYING?
SHH.
I WISH I COULD SEE WHAT'S GOING ON...
US
I THINK THIS IS IT. YOU READY TO SEE THE ELEPHANT, KID?
HERE, HAVE A DRAM. IT'LL STEADY YOUR HAND.
SWIG
UUUGH
THAT'S SUPPOSED TO HELP?

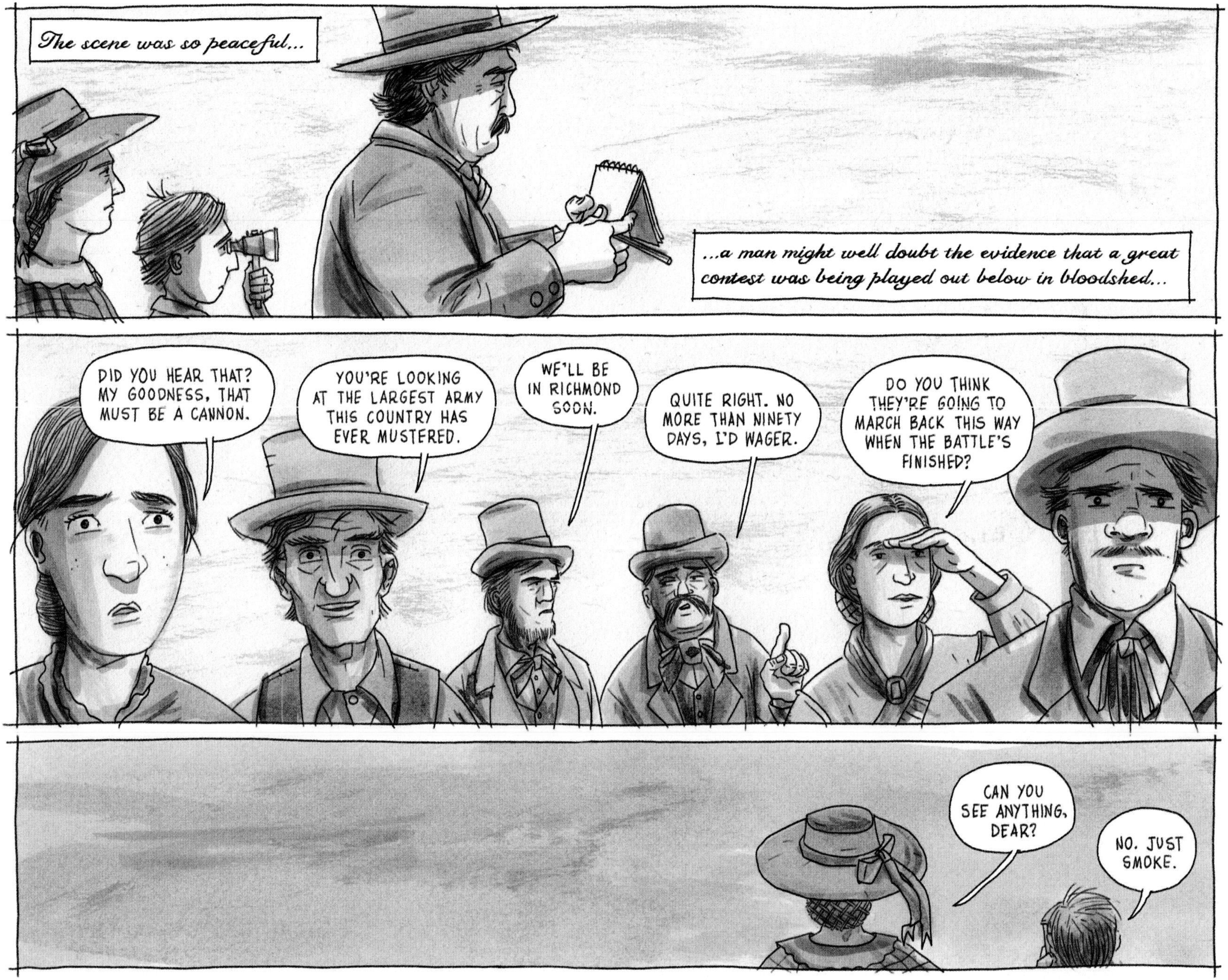
The scene was so peaceful...
...a man might well doubt the evidence that a great contest was being played out below in bloodshed...
DID YOU HEAR THAT? MY GOODNESS, THAT MUST BE A CANNON.
YOU'RE LOOKING AT THE LARGEST ARMY THIS COUNTRY HAS EVER MUSTERED.
WE'LL BE IN RICHMOND SOON.
QUITE RIGHT. NO MORE THAN NINETY DAYS, I'D WAGER.
DO YOU THINK THEY'RE GOING TO MARCH BACK THIS WAY WHEN THE BATTLE'S FINISHED?
CAN YOU SEE ANYTHING, DEAR?
NO. JUST SMOKE.

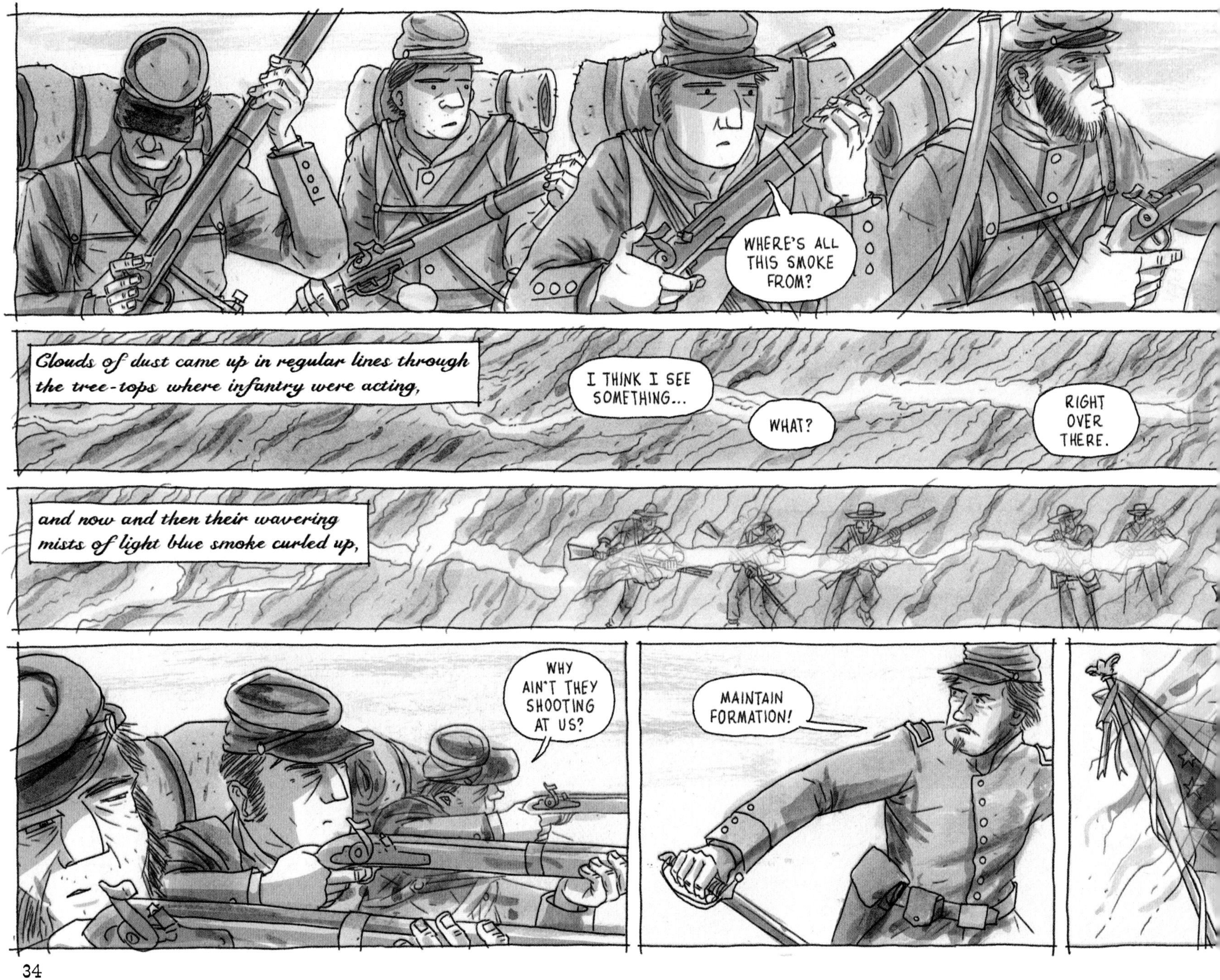
WHERE'S ALL THIS SMOKE FROM?
Clouds of dust came up in regular lines through the tree-tops where infantry were acting,
I THINK I SEE SOMETHING...
WHAT?
RIGHT OVER THERE.
and now and then their wavering mists of light blue smoke curled up,
WHY AIN'T THEY SHOOTING AT US?
MAINTAIN FORMATION!

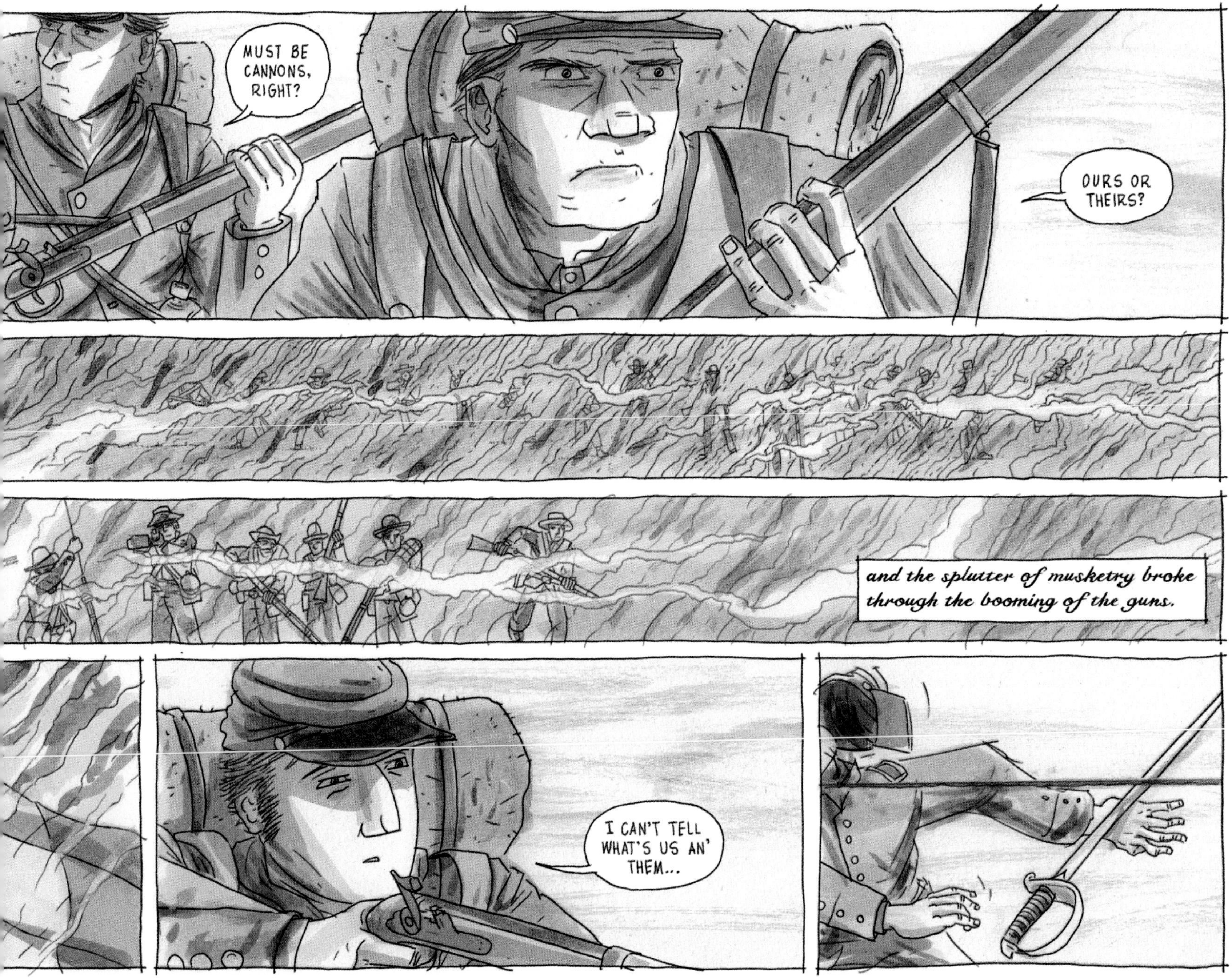
MUST BE CANNONS, RIGHT?
OURS OR THEIRS?
and the splutter of musketry broke through the booming of the guns.
I CAN'T TELL WHAT'S US AN' THEM...

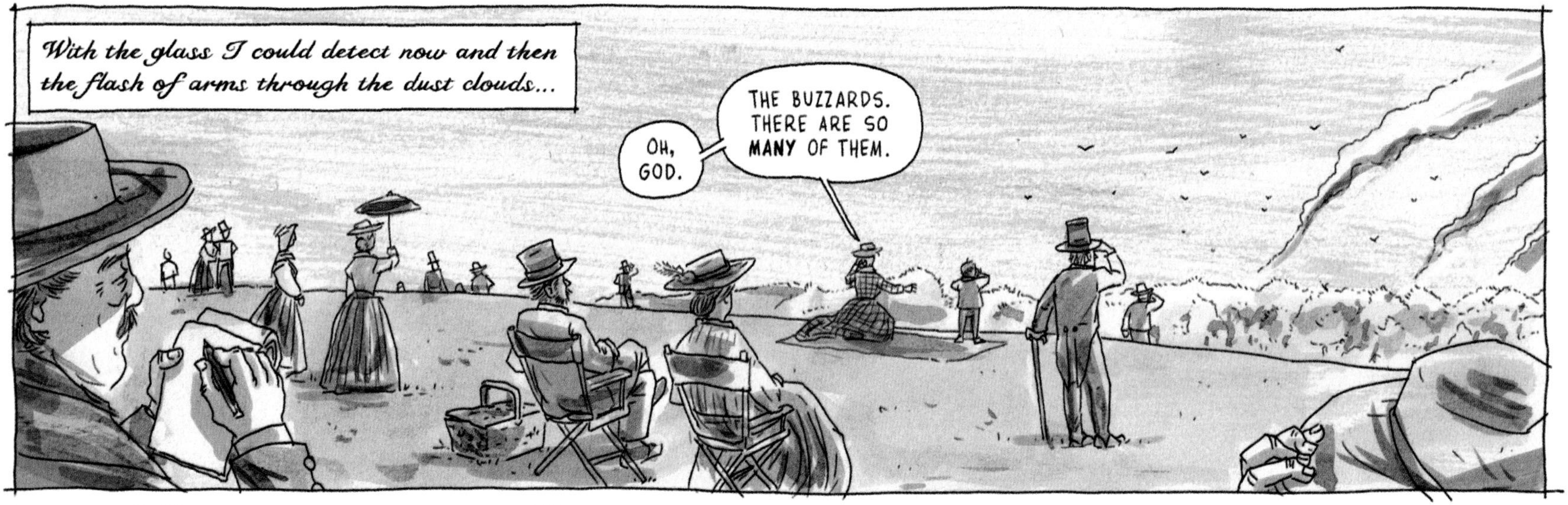
With the glass I could detect now and then the flash of arms through the dust clouds...
OH, GOD.
THE BUZZARDS. THERE ARE SO MANY OF THEM.

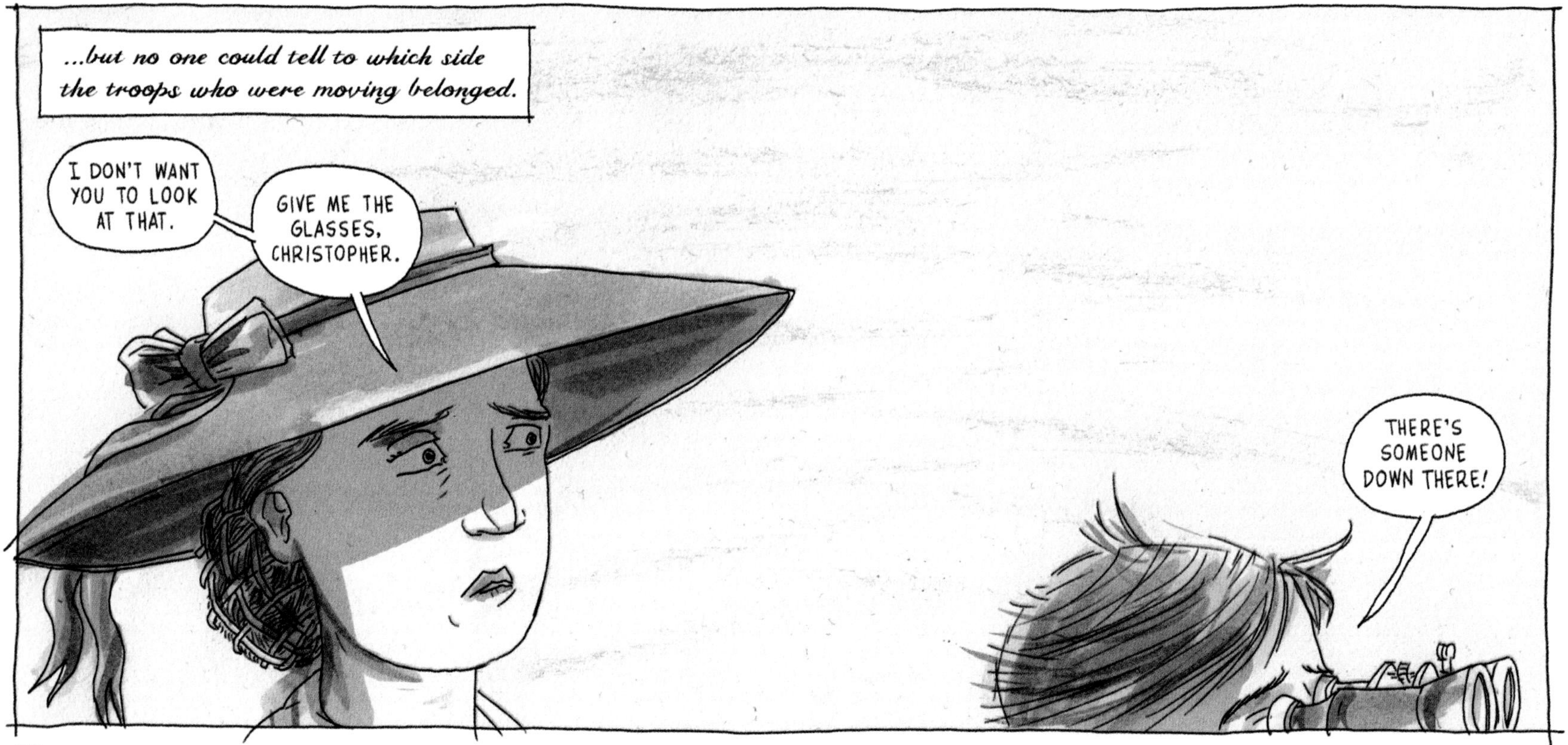
...but no one could tell to which side the troops who were moving belonged.
I DON'T WANT YOU TO LOOK AT THAT.
GIVE ME THE GLASSES, CHRISTOPHER.
THERE'S SOMEONE DOWN THERE!

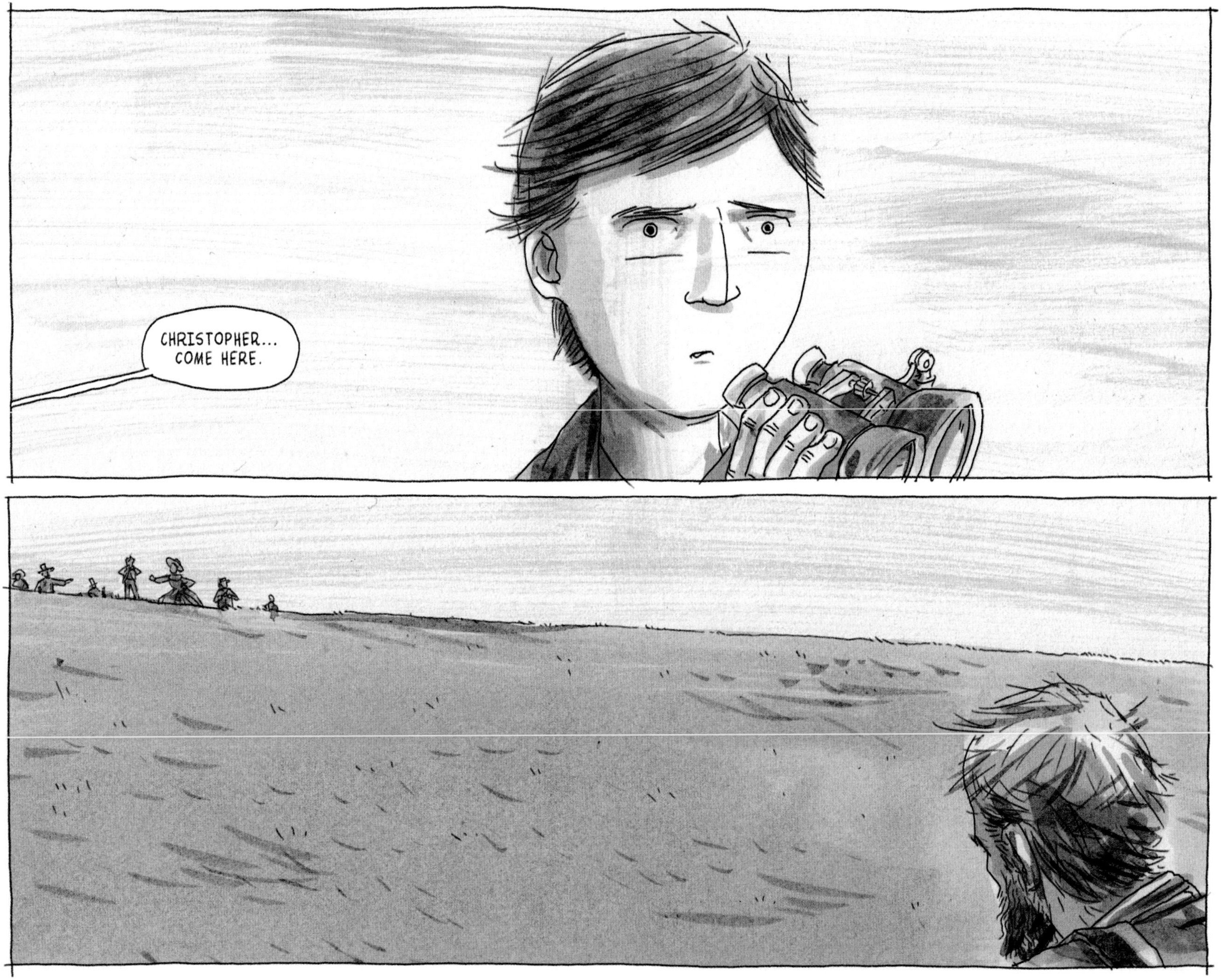
CHRISTOPHER...
COME HERE.

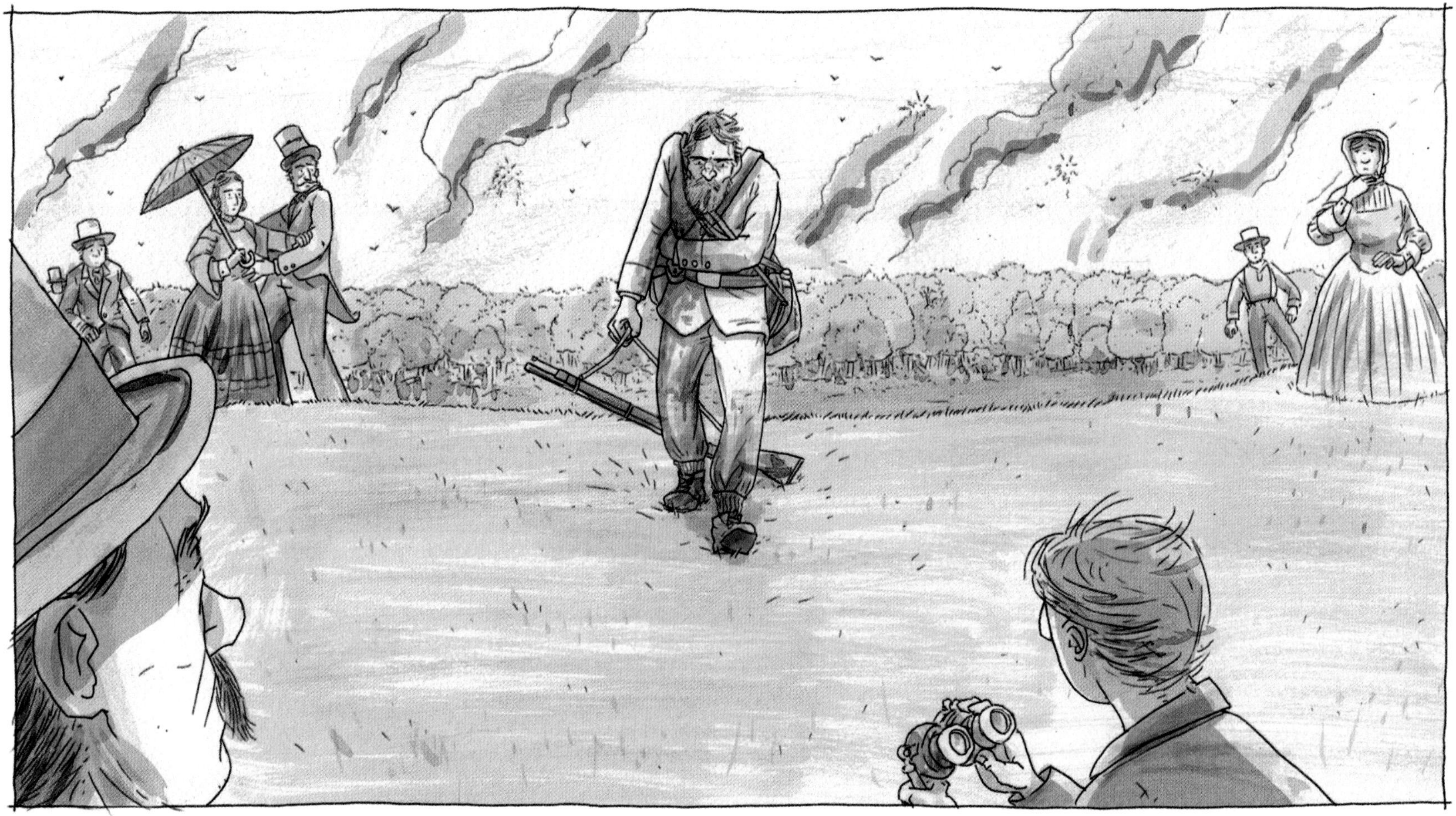

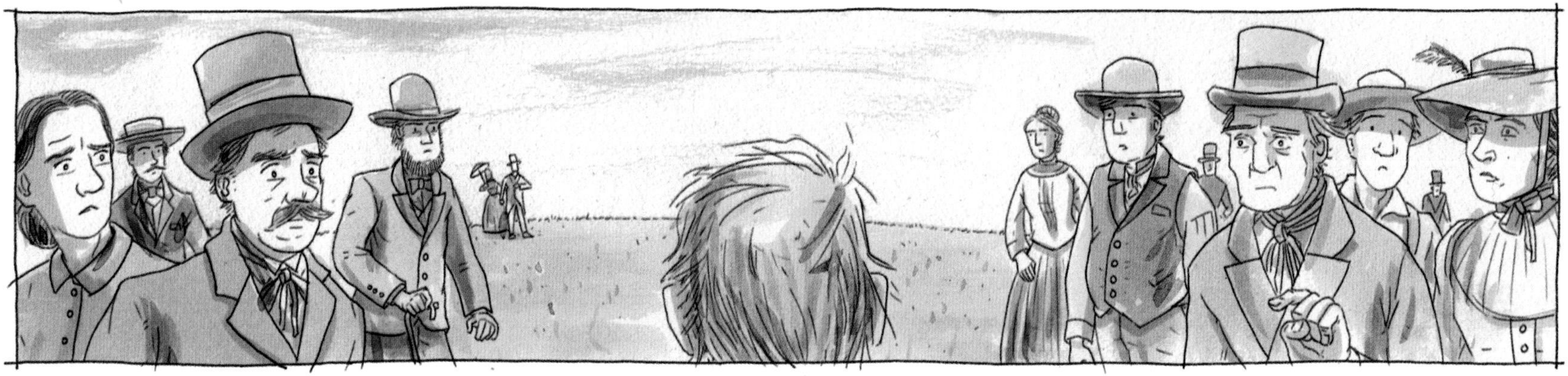

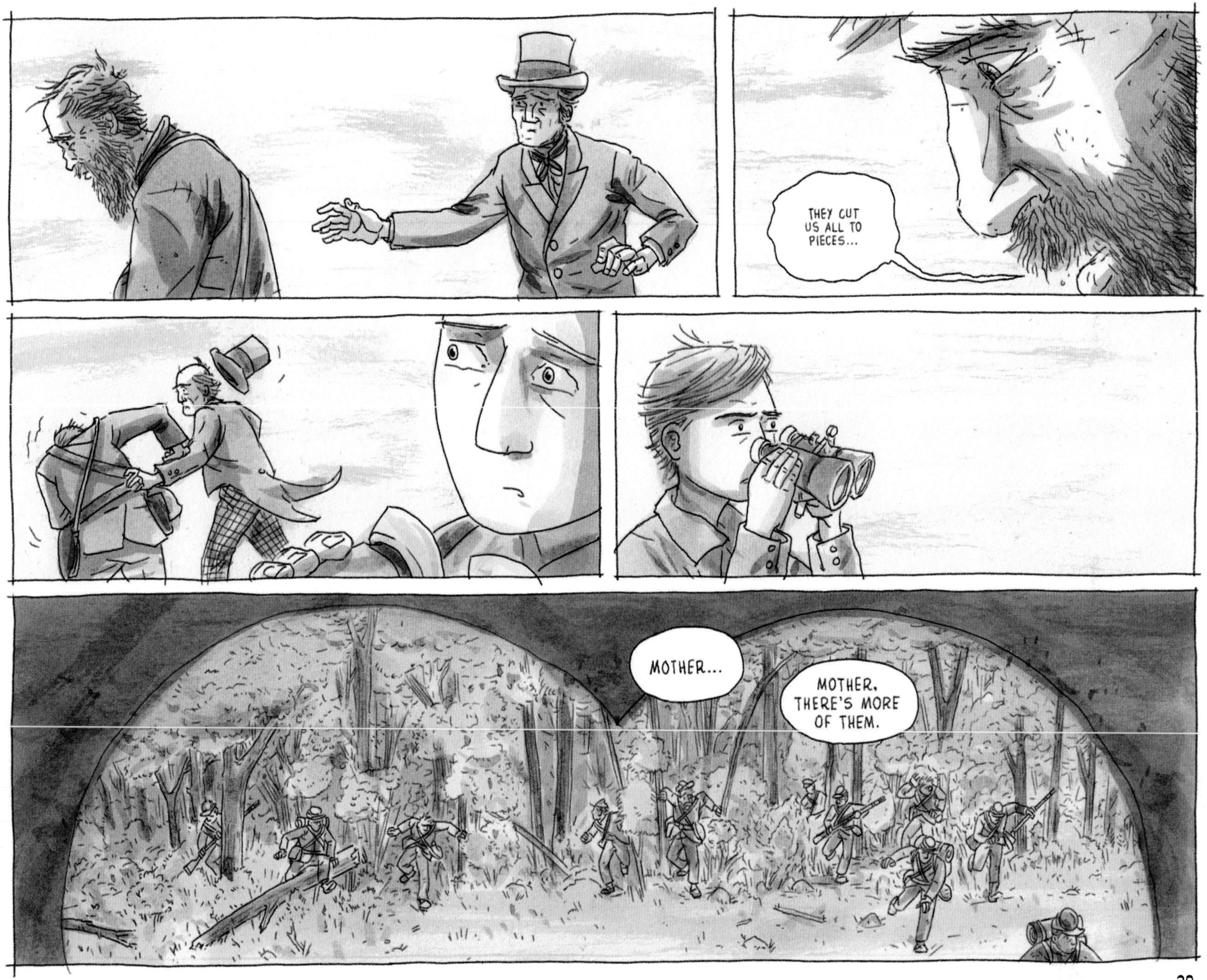
THEY CUT US ALL TO PIECES...
MOTHER...
MOTHER. THERE'S MORE OF THEM.

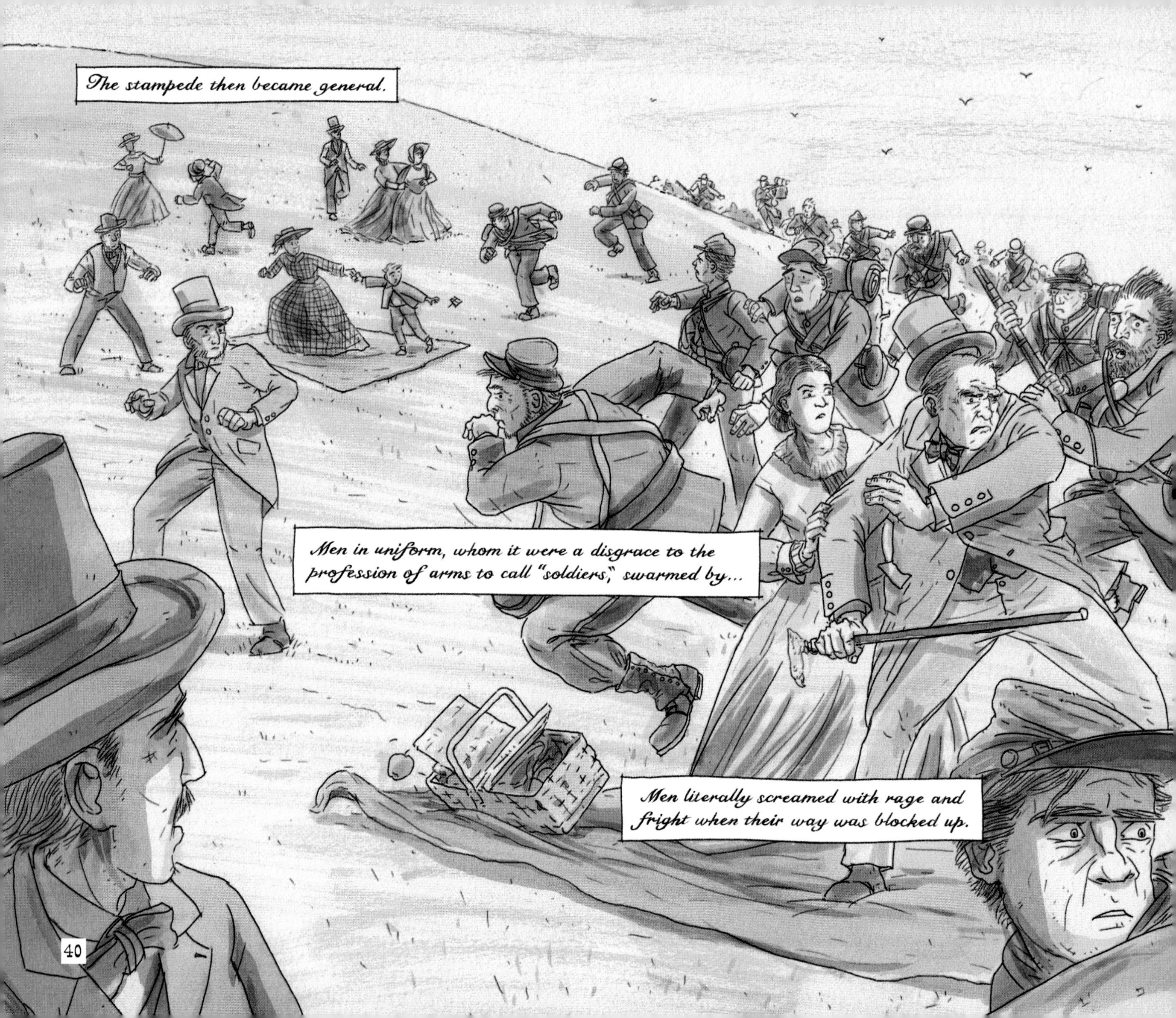
The stampede then became general.
Men in uniform, whom it were a disgrace to the profession of arms to call "soldiers," swarmed by...
Men literally screamed with rage and fright when their way was blocked up.

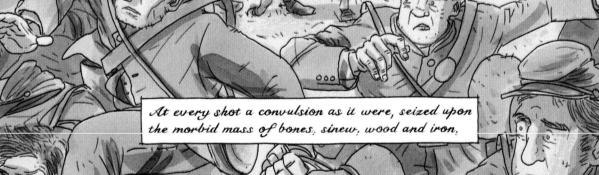

At every shot a convulsion as it were, seized upon the morbid mass of bones, sinew, wood and iron,

and thrilled through it, giving new energy and action to its desperate efforts to get free from itself.

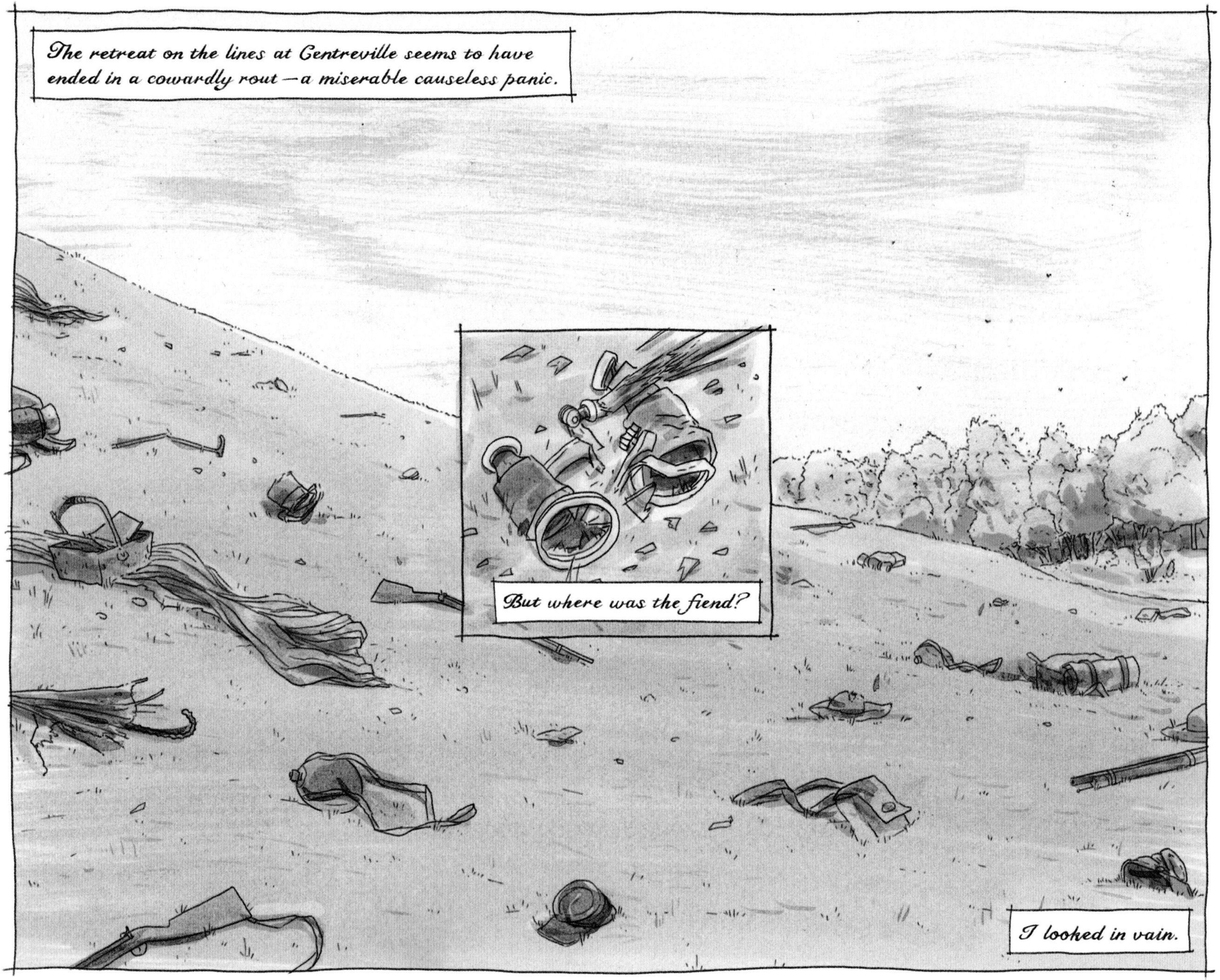
The retreat on the lines at Centreville seems to have ended in a cowardly rout—a miserable causeless panic.
But where was the fiend?
I looked in vain.

Chapter 4: Leg Irons

NEWPORT NEWS TIMES

September 30, 1861

LINCOLN'S WOES CONTINUE
Forced to Recall GENERAL FRÉMONT

In the immediate aftermath of the Union's humiliating defeat at First Bull Run (Manassas), President Lincoln hoped for good news from the Western Theater of the war, where General John C. Frémont served as department commander. Although renowned before the war as a politician and explorer of the American West, the "Great Pathfinder" quickly found himself overmatched by the task of working in divided Missouri.

After his subordinate, Nathaniel Lyon, lost the war's first major battle in the Western Theater, along the banks of Wilson's Creek on August 10, 1861, Frémont tried to bolster his flagging reputation by cracking down on disloyal Missourians. He declared martial law, warned that Confederate guerrillas found behind Union lines would be executed, and summarily freed the slaves belonging to leading secessionists in the state.

President Lincoln, still wary of offending the Border States, warned Frémont that he had gone too far with his impolitic orders. Frémont ignored his Commander in Chief, and Lincoln removed him from command.

ABOLITIONISTS & RADICAL REPUBLICANS
Pressure Reluctant President to Embrace Emancipation

Many abolitionists, including such prominent figures as Frederick Douglass, responded to the loss at First Bull Run by shifting tactics. Rather than continuing to rely on "moral suasion" to win adherents to their cause, they began asserting that emancipation was also a military necessity--that the war would be harder to win so long as the South could rely on slaves to do its heavy lifting.

General Butler

At the same time, many abolitionists also insisted that slaveholders, in a state of open rebellion against the Union, had forsaken the United States Constitution, including protections it offered private property holders. Accordingly, abolitionists argued, Federal soldiers in the field could and should begin seizing slaves as the spoils of victory--what Union General Benjamin Butler labeled "contraband of war."

The Lincoln administration reluctantly allowed Butler to put this plan into action. By August 1861, hundreds of slaves had crossed the Union lines. Their legal status remained ambiguous. Had they freed themselves, or were they still enslaved, still property, but without any obvious owner?

The political weight of the contrabands, however, was entirely clear: they pushed the Union, and a still-cautious President Lincoln, toward emancipation.

RUMORS FROM THE FRONT ☞
*Slaves Roam the Virginia Countryside
Seeking Freedom Behind Union Lines
at Fortress Monroe*

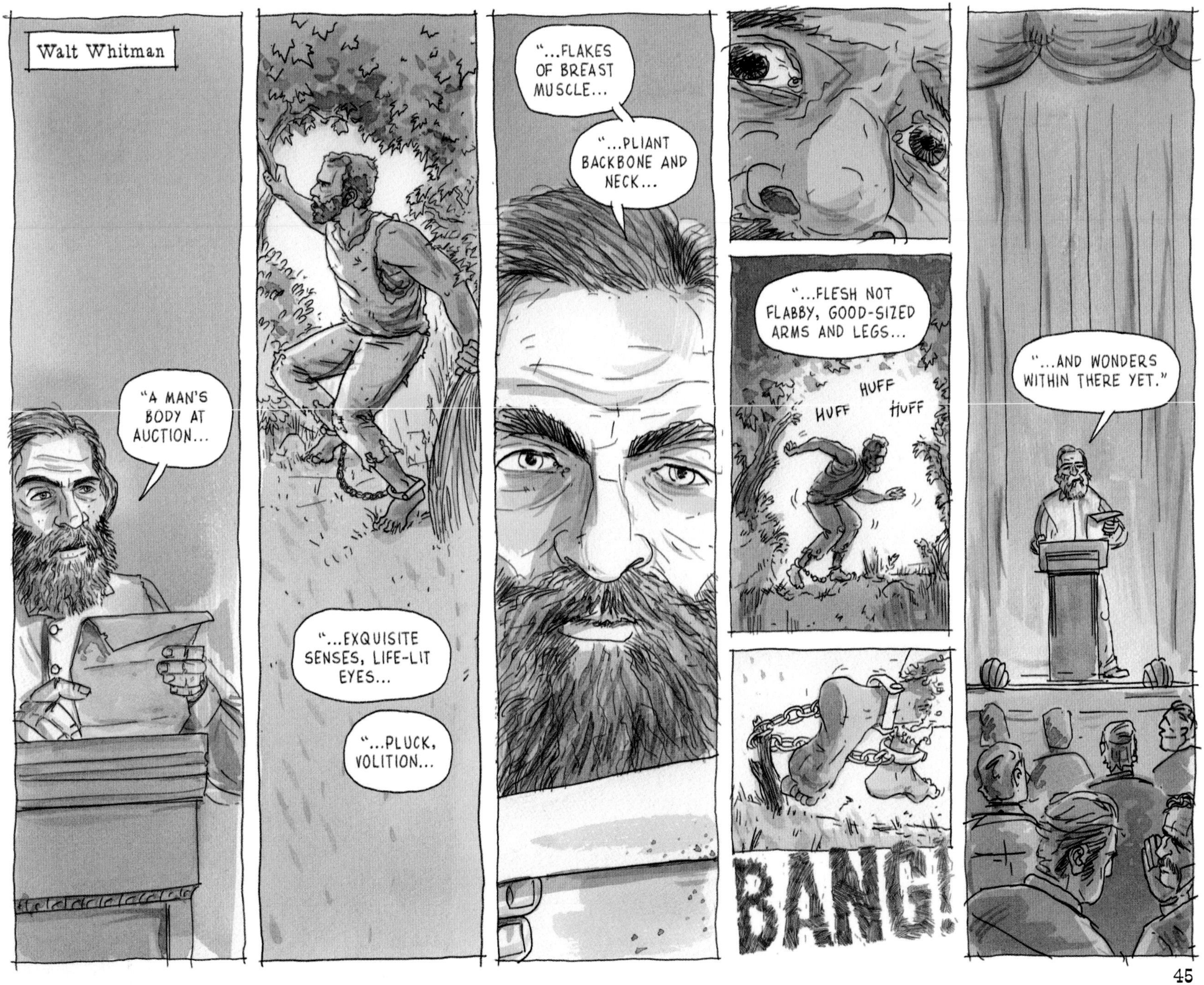
Walt Whitman
"A MAN'S BODY AT AUCTION...
"...EXQUISITE SENSES, LIFE-LIT EYES...
"...PLUCK, VOLITION...
"...FLAKES OF BREAST MUSCLE...
"...PLIANT BACKBONE AND NECK...
"...FLESH NOT FLABBY, GOOD-SIZED ARMS AND LEGS...
HUFF
HUFF
HUFF
BANG!
"...AND WONDERS WITHIN THERE YET."

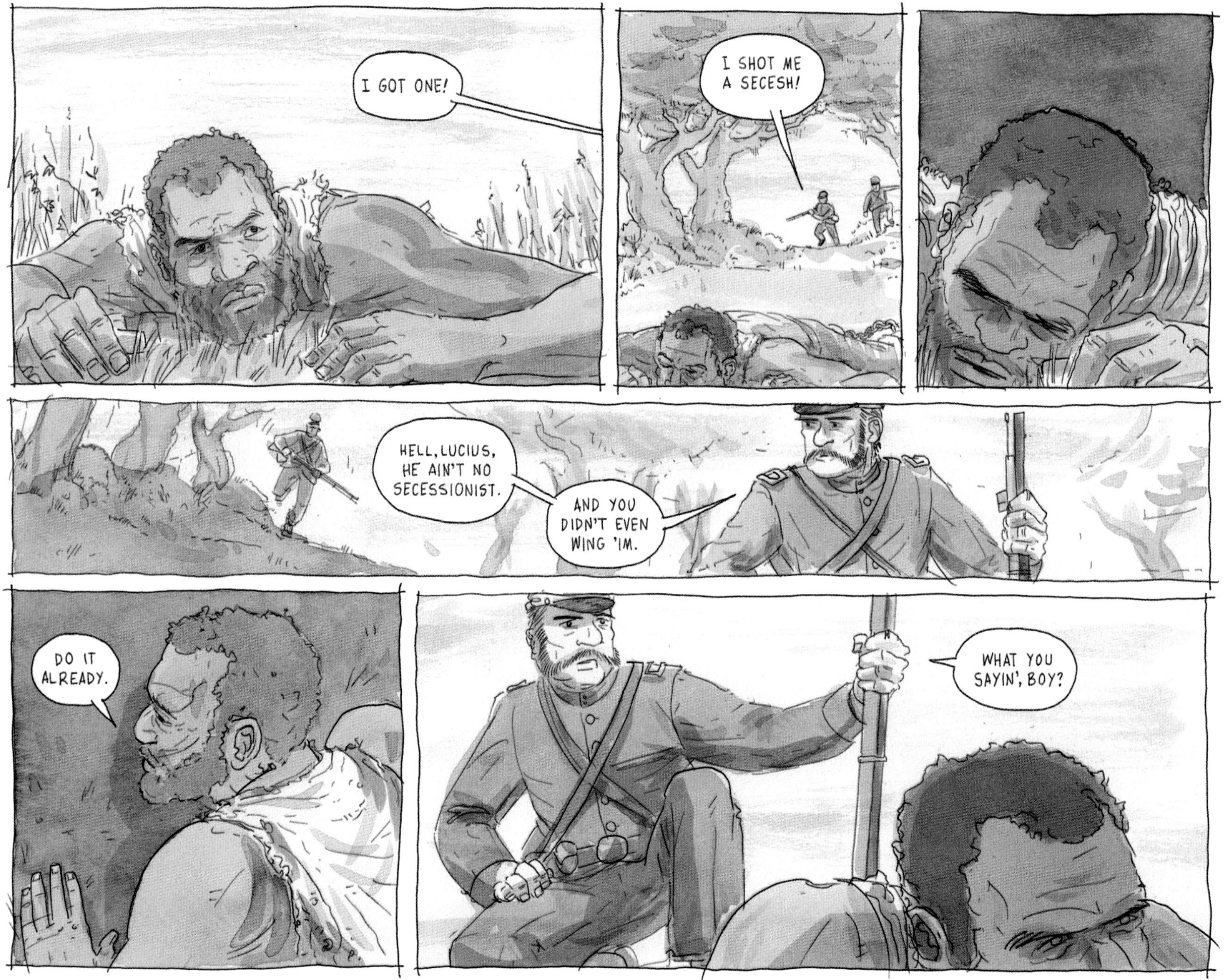
I GOT ONE!
I SHOT ME A SECESH!
HELL, LUCIUS, HE AIN'T NO SECESSIONIST.
AND YOU DIDN'T EVEN WING 'IM.
DO IT ALREADY.
WHAT YOU SAYIN', BOY?

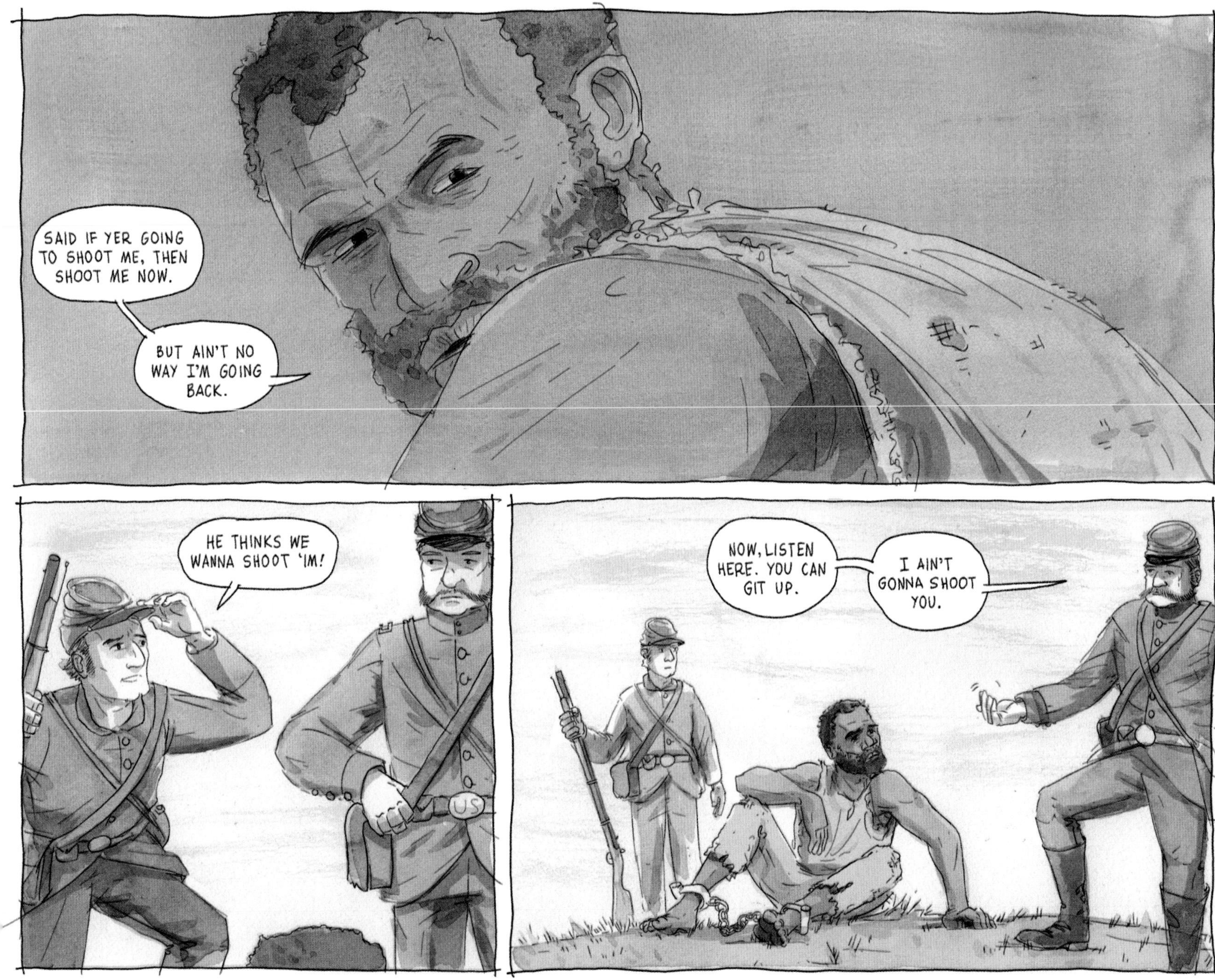
SAID IF YER GOING TO SHOOT ME, THEN SHOOT ME NOW.
BUT AIN'T NO WAY I'M GOING BACK.
HE THINKS WE WANNA SHOOT 'IM!
US
NOW, LISTEN HERE. YOU CAN GIT UP.
I AIN'T GONNA SHOOT YOU.

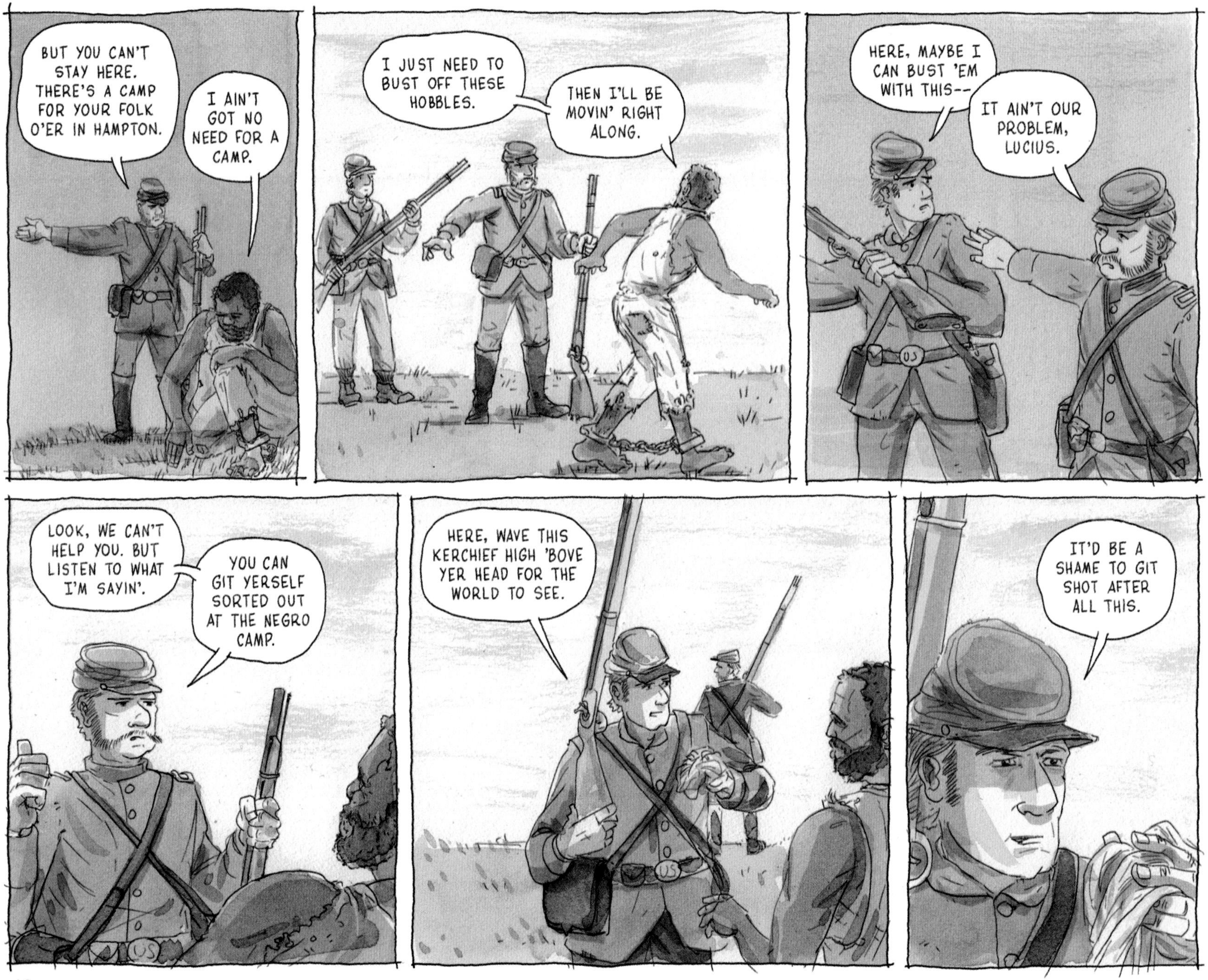
BUT YOU CAN'T STAY HERE. THERE'S A CAMP FOR YOUR FOLK O'ER IN HAMPTON.
I AIN'T GOT NO NEED FOR A CAMP.
I JUST NEED TO BUST OFF THESE HOBBLES.
THEN I'LL BE MOVIN' RIGHT ALONG.
HERE, MAYBE I CAN BUST 'EM WITH THIS--
IT AIN'T OUR PROBLEM, LUCIUS.
LOOK, WE CAN'T HELP YOU. BUT LISTEN TO WHAT I'M SAYIN'.
YOU CAN GIT YERSELF SORTED OUT AT THE NEGRO CAMP.
HERE, WAVE THIS KERCHIEF HIGH 'BOVE YER HEAD FOR THE WORLD TO SEE.
IT'D BE A SHAME TO GIT SHOT AFTER ALL THIS.

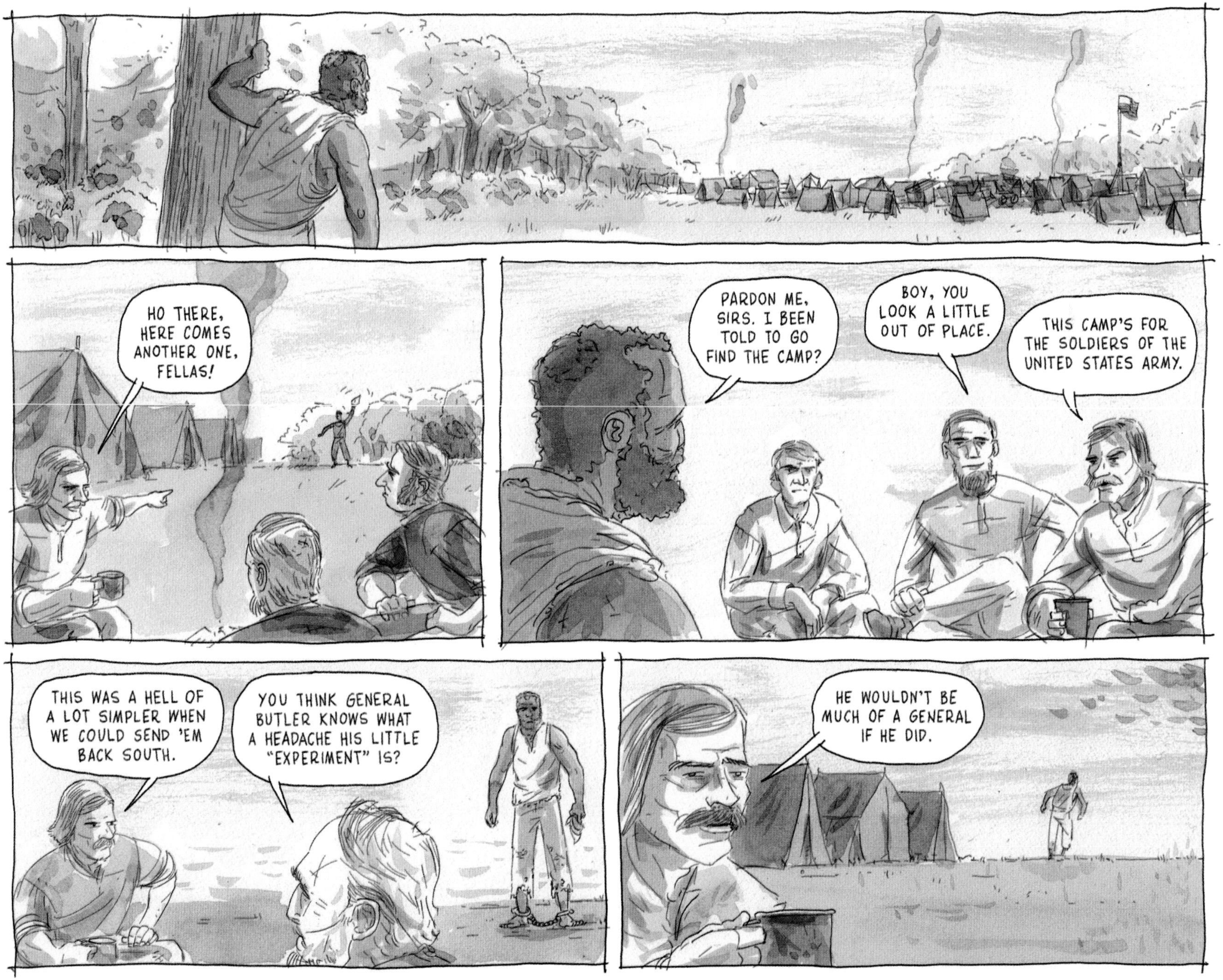
HO THERE, HERE COMES ANOTHER ONE, FELLAS!
PARDON ME, SIRS. I BEEN TOLD TO GO FIND THE CAMP?
BOY, YOU LOOK A LITTLE OUT OF PLACE.
THIS CAMP'S FOR THE SOLDIERS OF THE UNITED STATES ARMY.
THIS WAS A HELL OF A LOT SIMPLER WHEN WE COULD SEND 'EM BACK SOUTH.
YOU THINK GENERAL BUTLER KNOWS WHAT A HEADACHE HIS LITTLE "EXPERIMENT" IS?
HE WOULDN'T BE MUCH OF A GENERAL IF HE DID.

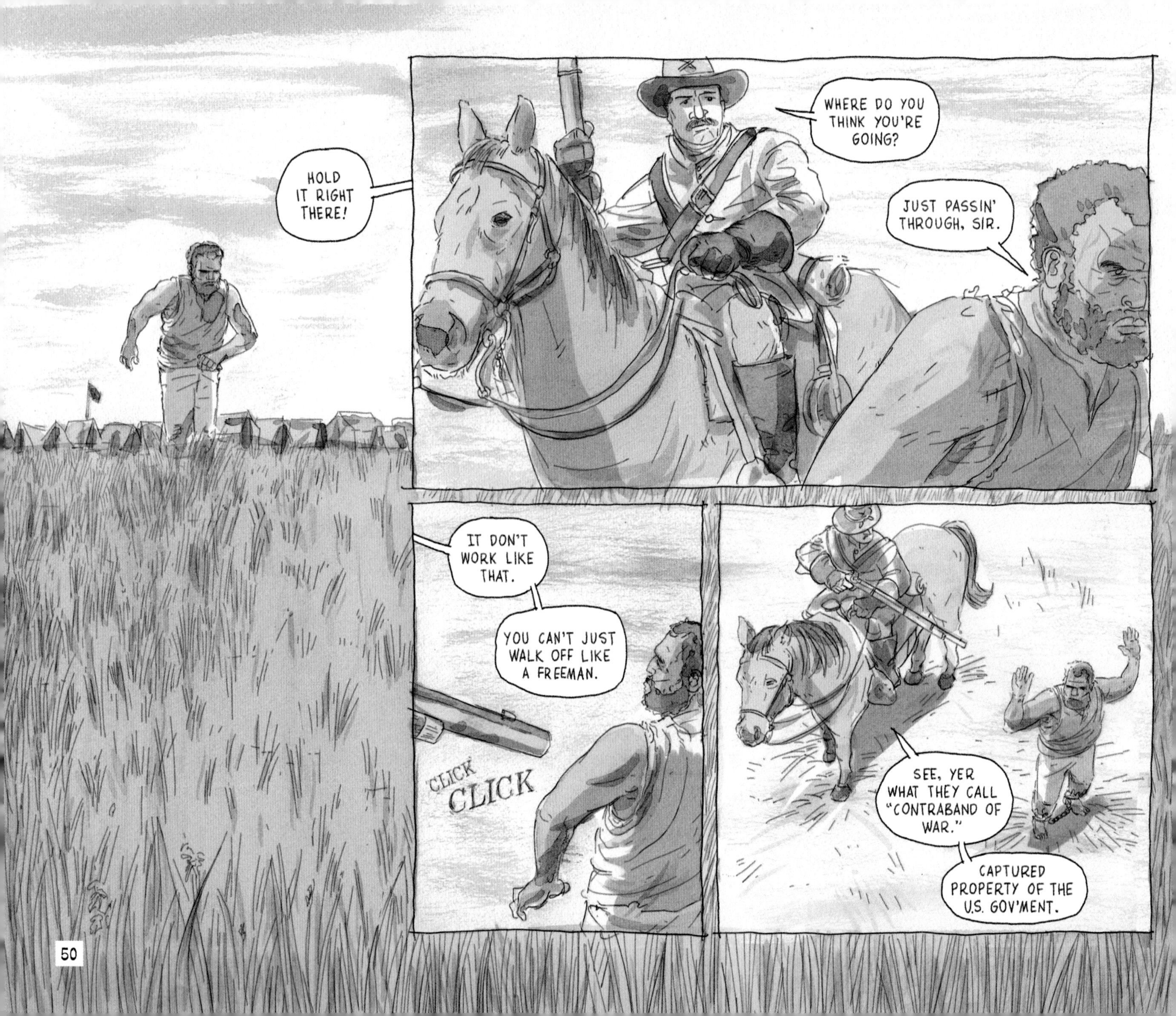
HOLD IT RIGHT THERE!
WHERE DO YOU THINK YOU'RE GOING?
JUST PASSIN' THROUGH, SIR.
IT DON'T WORK LIKE THAT.
YOU CAN'T JUST WALK OFF LIKE A FREEMAN.
CLICK
CLICK
SEE, YER WHAT THEY CALL "CONTRABAND OF WAR."
CAPTURED PROPERTY OF THE U.S. GOV'MENT.

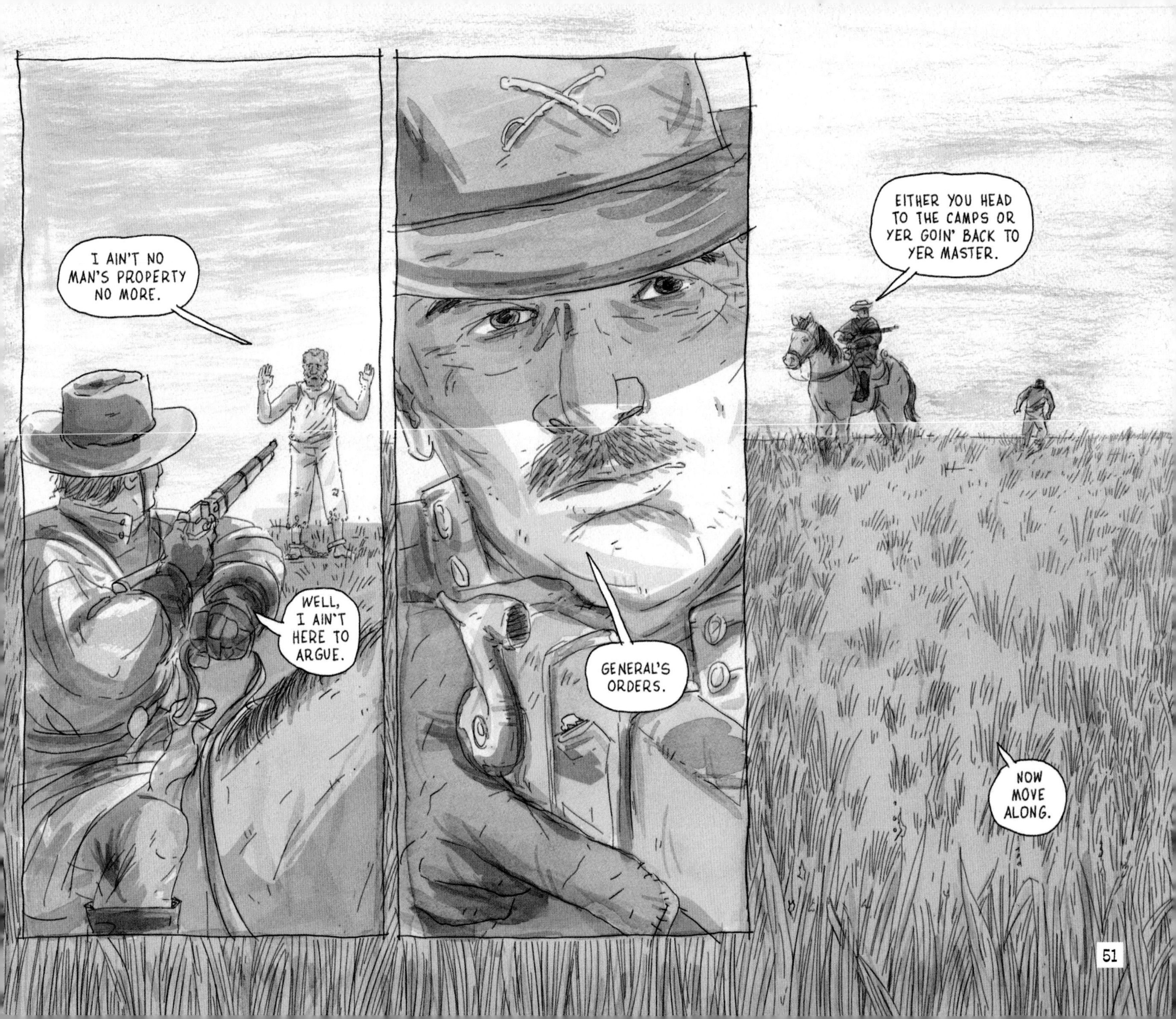
I AIN'T NO MAN'S PROPERTY NO MORE.
WELL, I AIN'T HERE TO ARGUE.
GENERAL'S ORDERS.
EITHER YOU HEAD TO THE CAMPS OR YER GOIN' BACK TO YER MASTER.
NOW MOVE ALONG.

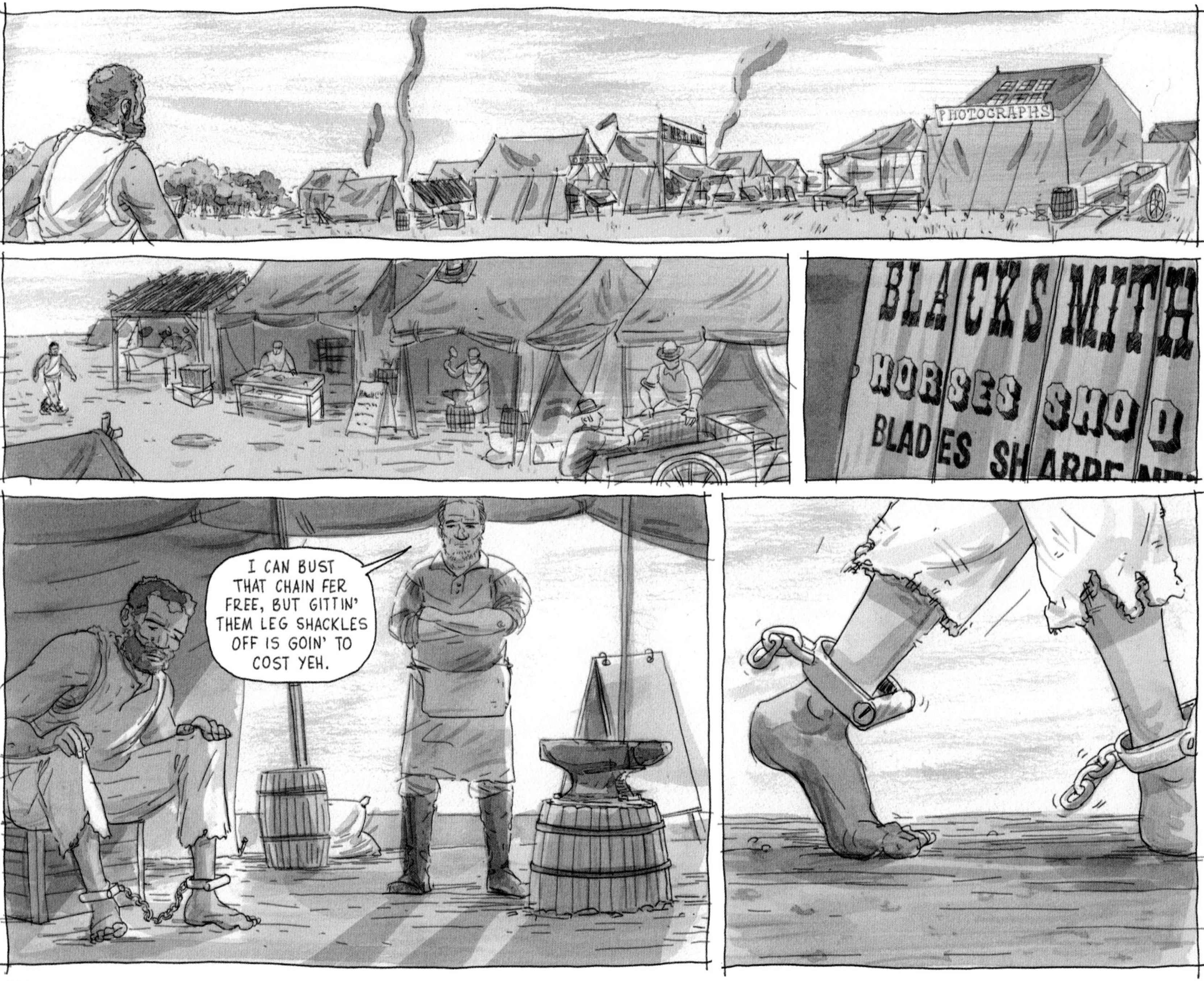
PHOTOGRAPHS
BLACKSMITH
HORSES SHOD
I CAN BUST THAT CHAIN FER FREE, BUT GITTIN' THEM LEG SHACKLES OFF IS GOIN' TO COST YEH.

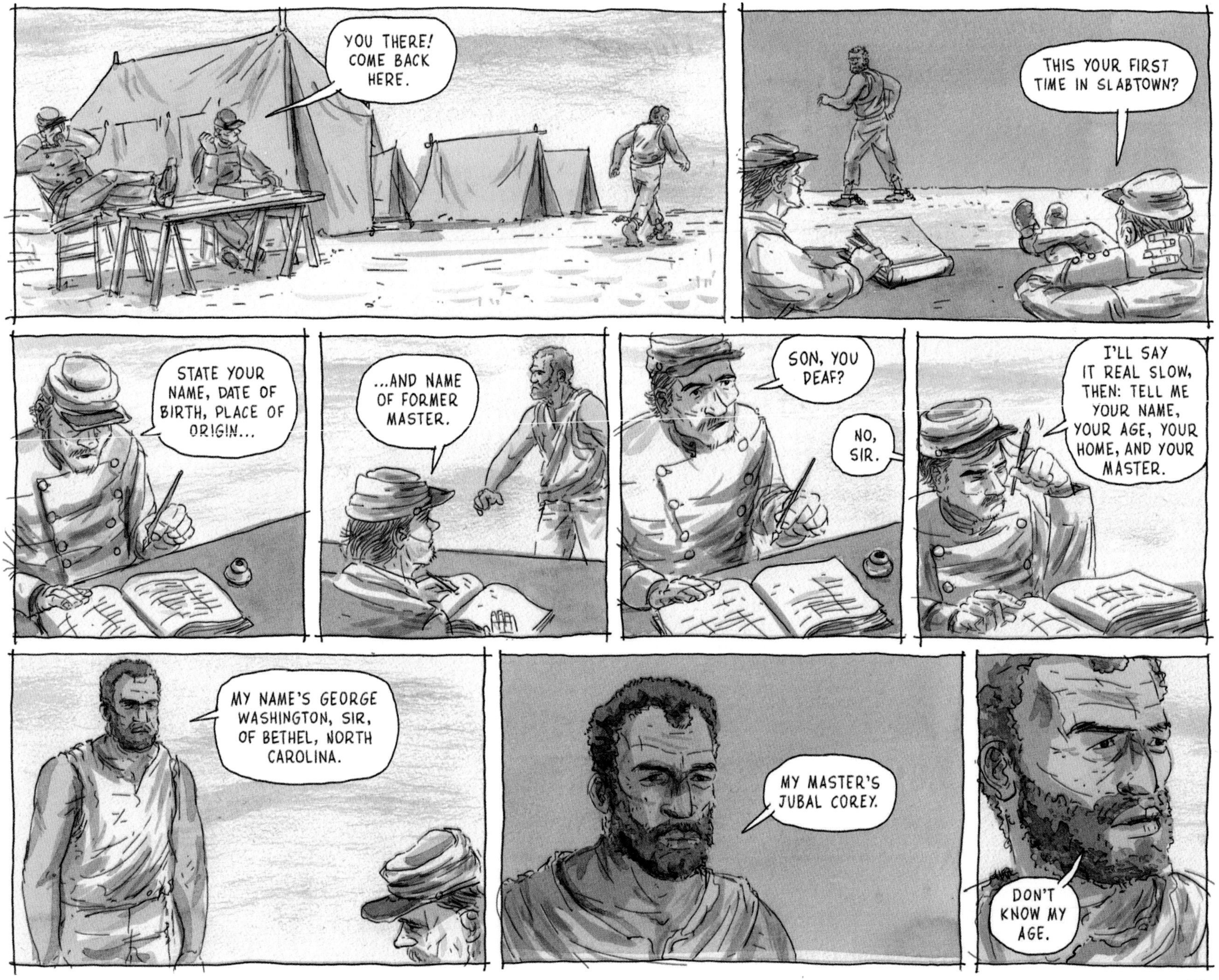
YOU THERE! COME BACK HERE.
THIS YOUR FIRST TIME IN SLABTOWN?
STATE YOUR NAME, DATE OF BIRTH, PLACE OF ORIGIN...
...AND NAME OF FORMER MASTER.
SON, YOU DEAF?
NO, SIR.
I'LL SAY IT REAL SLOW, THEN: TELL ME YOUR NAME, YOUR AGE, YOUR HOME, AND YOUR MASTER.
MY NAME'S GEORGE WASHINGTON, SIR, OF BETHEL, NORTH CAROLINA.
MY MASTER'S JUBAL COREY.
DON'T KNOW MY AGE.

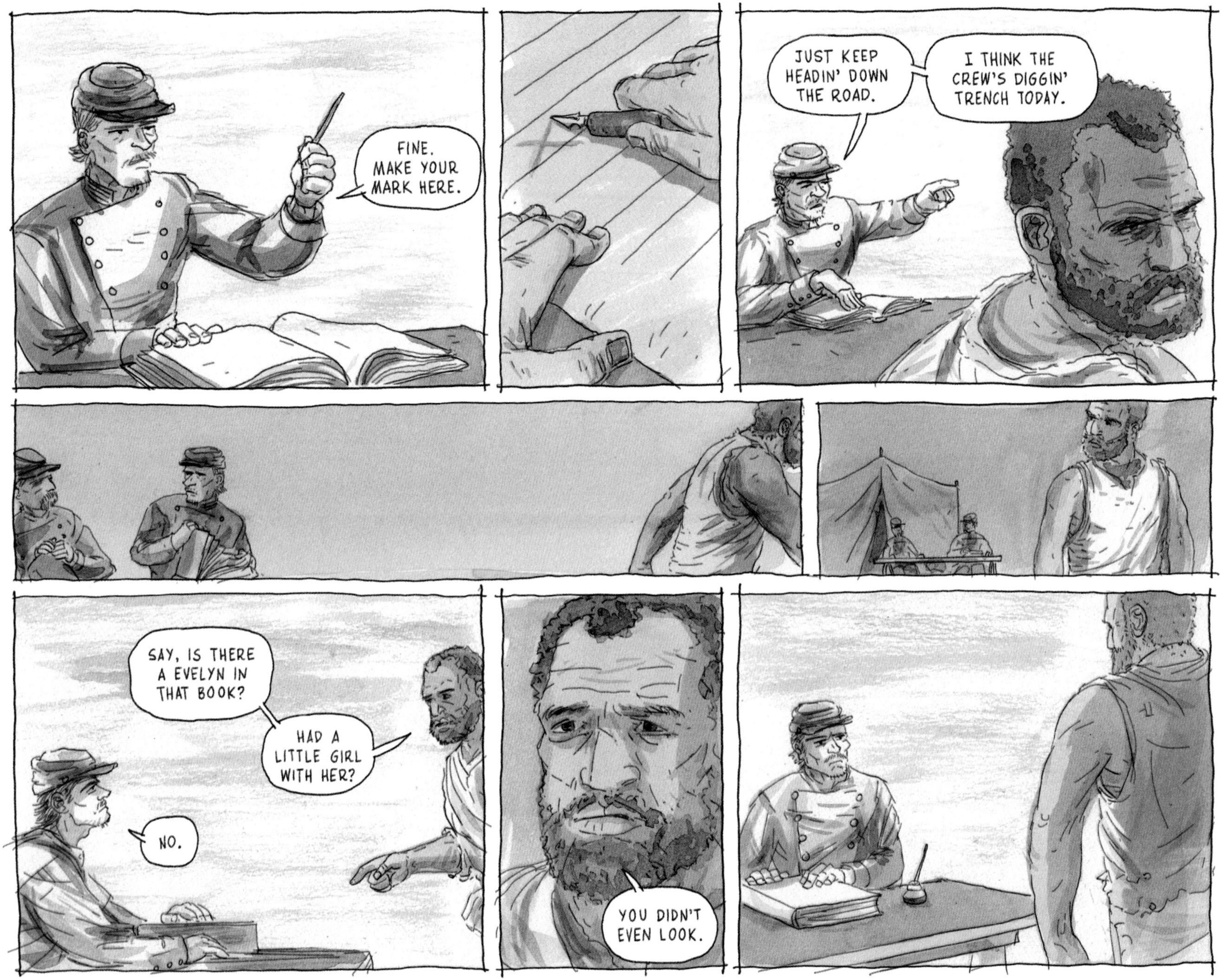
FINE. MAKE YOUR MARK HERE.
JUST KEEP HEADIN' DOWN THE ROAD.
I THINK THE CREW'S DIGGIN' TRENCH TODAY.
SAY, IS THERE A EVELYN IN THAT BOOK?
HAD A LITTLE GIRL WITH HER?
NO.
YOU DIDN'T EVEN LOOK.

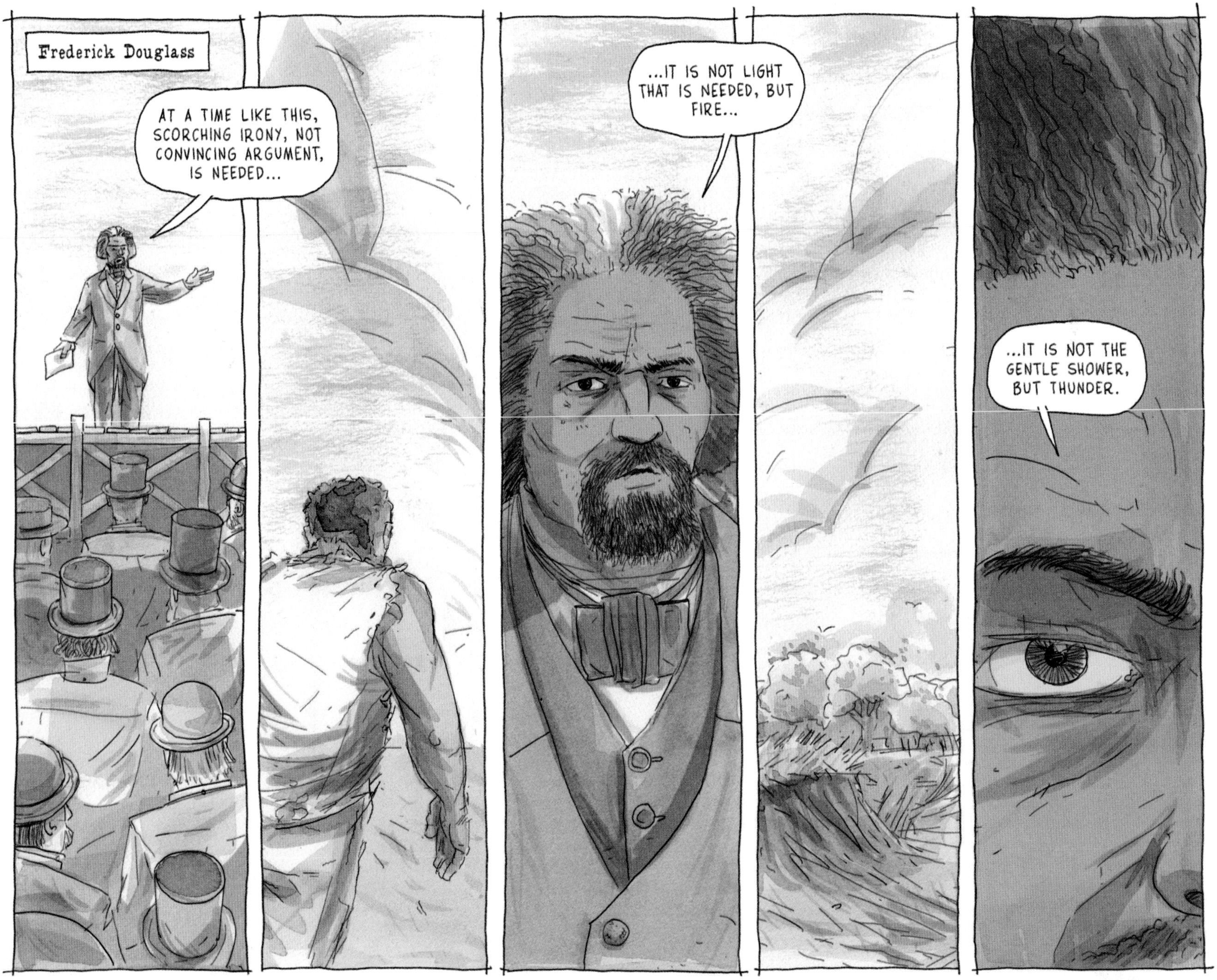
Frederick Douglass
AT A TIME LIKE THIS, SCORCHING IRONY, NOT CONVINCING ARGUMENT, IS NEEDED...
...IT IS NOT LIGHT THAT IS NEEDED, BUT FIRE...
...IT IS NOT THE GENTLE SHOWER, BUT THUNDER.

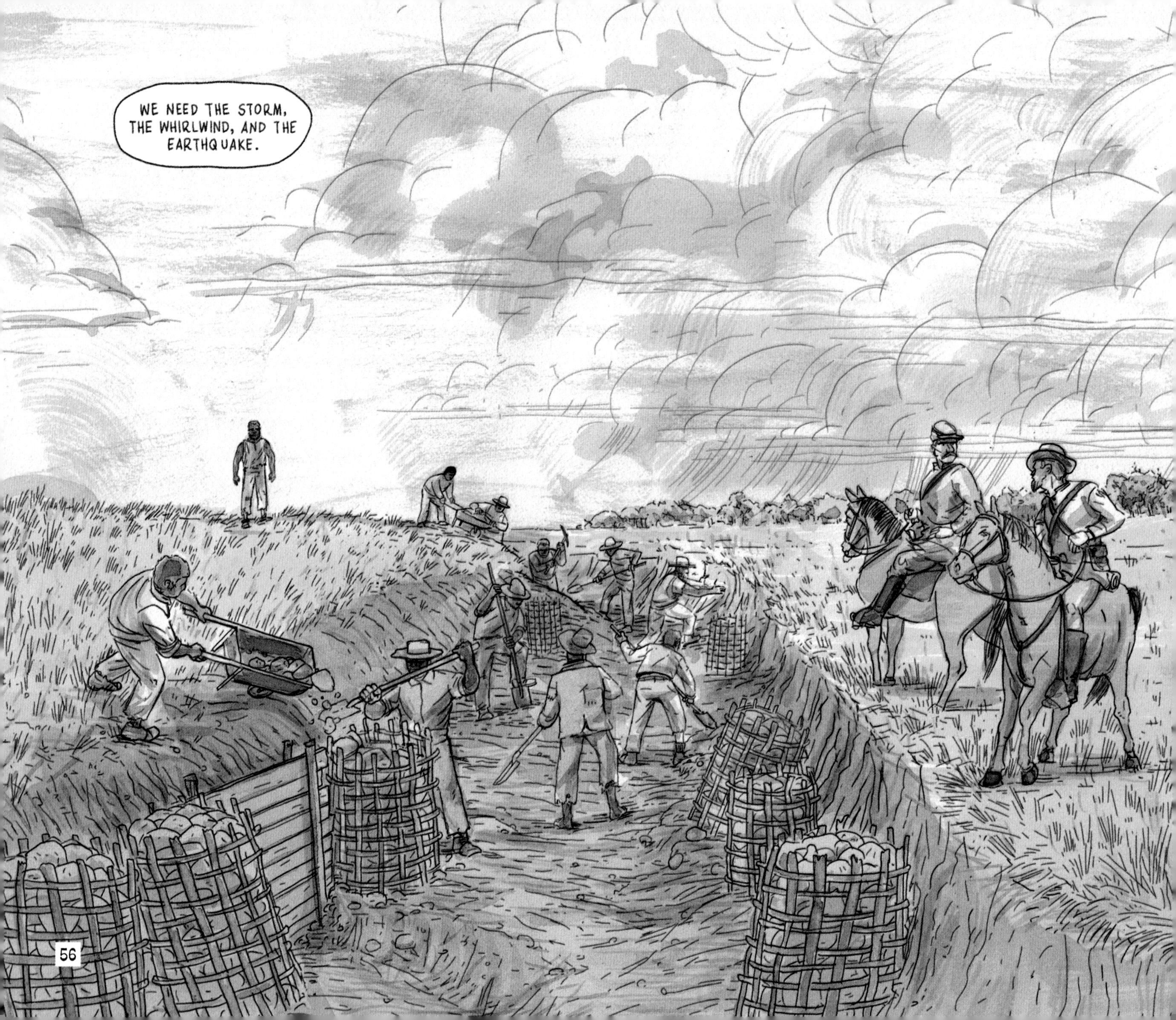
WE NEED THE STORM, THE WHIRLWIND, AND THE EARTHQUAKE.

Chapter 5: The Magic Bullet

September 16, 1862

TIDE OF WAR TURNS!

UNPRECEDENTED CARNAGE AT SHILOH USHERS IN NEW ERA FOR WAR

The twenty thousand killed and wounded at Shiloh in early April 1862 exceeded the combined casualties from all of the war's major battles to that point--Bull Run, Wilson's Creek, Fort Donelson, and Pea Ridge.

The rivers of blood flowing from Shiloh washed away any lingering claims, in both the North and the South, that the war would be brief and glorious. Now rebels and Union men alike understood that the struggle would instead be long and grim.

Shiloh also continued the rise of General Ulysses S. Grant, who, two months earlier, had provided the Union with much-needed good news from the Western Theater when his forces captured Forts Henry and Donelson in Tennessee. With General McClellan still bungling operations back east--complaining incessantly that his superiors, including President Lincoln, constantly undermined him; that, no matter the truth, his enemy vastly outnumbered him; and that, because of weather or other excuses, it was never a good day to fight--Lincoln began to keep a close eye on Grant, watching for proof that he might be the fighting general the President had long sought.

Despite McClellan's paranoia and dithering, outnumbered rebels withdrew before him, consolidating their forces, in the spring of 1862. By May, the Army of the Potomac could hear Richmond's church bells.

LEE HUMILIATES McCLELLAN IN SEVEN DAYS; JACKSON MAKES MAYHEM IN SHENANDOAH

Even as the Confederacy reached a low ebb, General Thomas "Stonewall" Jackson's seventeen thousand men began striking at Union outposts in the Shenandoah Valley. In just over a month, Jackson's troops marched what seemed impossible distances impossibly fast, won several battles, and earned themselves and their commander a reputation for invincibility. Union forces had to pursue them, taking pressure off Richmond.

As Jackson's men wreaked havoc, Jefferson Davis elevated Robert E. Lee to command of what became known as the Army of Northern Virginia. To that point in the war, Lee's reputation had suffered, but he quickly redeemed himself. Taking McClellan's measure, he ordered a series of relentless attacks on the Union invaders. From June 25 through July 1, Lee's and McClellan's armies clashed. More than thirty thousand men were killed or wounded during the Seven Days' Battles, and though the fighting ended in a stalemate, McClellan's brittle confidence had shattered.

After the rebels won again late in August at Second Bull Run, Lee began contemplating an even bolder move: an invasion of the Union that he hoped would foster antiwar sentiment in the North and convince the British to forge an alliance with the Confederacy.

RUMORS FROM THE FRONT ☞
General Lee's Army on the March near Sharpsburg!

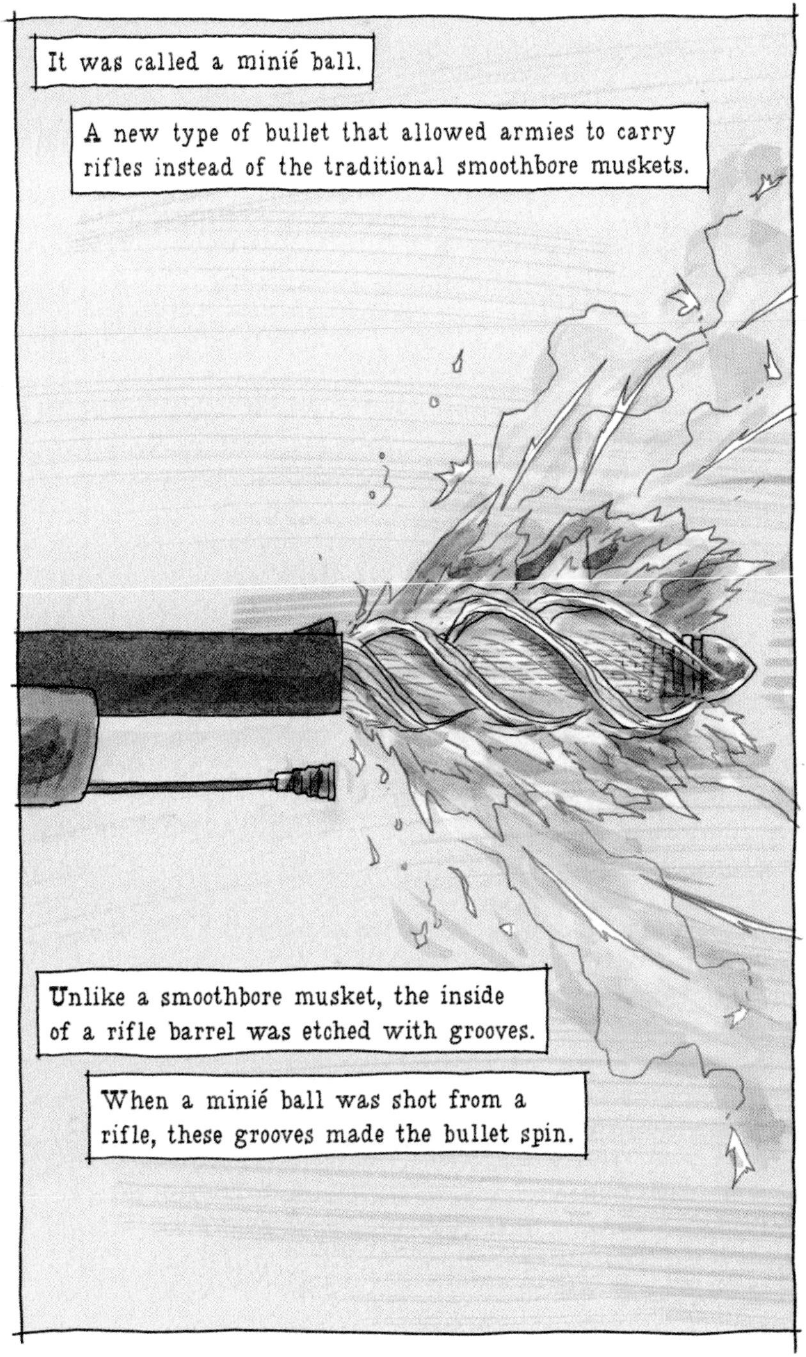
It was called a minié ball.
A new type of bullet that allowed armies to carry rifles instead of the traditional smoothbore muskets.
Unlike a smoothbore musket, the inside of a rifle barrel was etched with grooves.
When a minié ball was shot from a rifle, these grooves made the bullet spin.

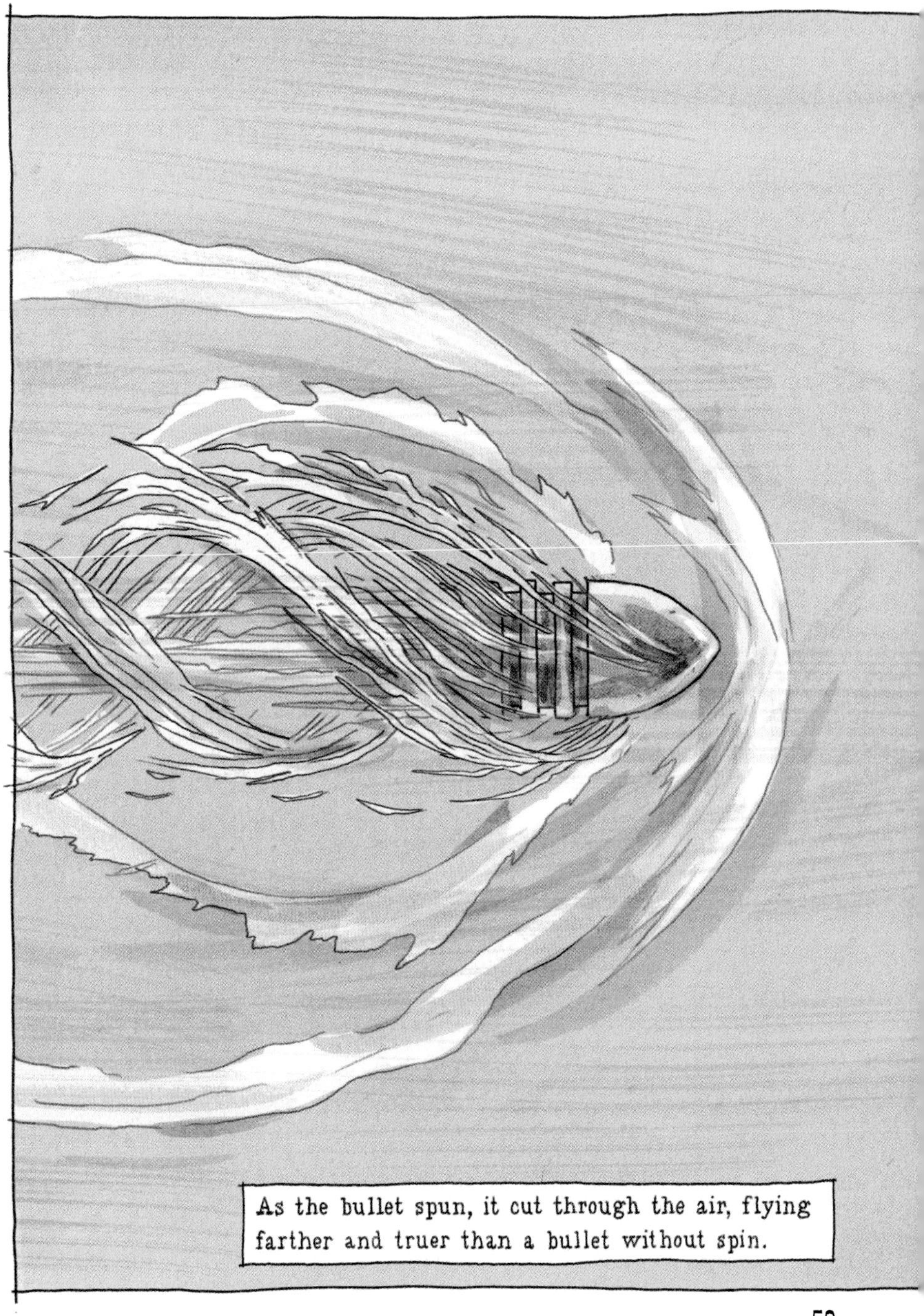
As the bullet spun, it cut through the air, flying farther and truer than a bullet without spin.

The military technology of the Civil War was new,

the weapons were more lethal than ever before,

but the military *tactics* deployed on the battlefield were those of an earlier age.

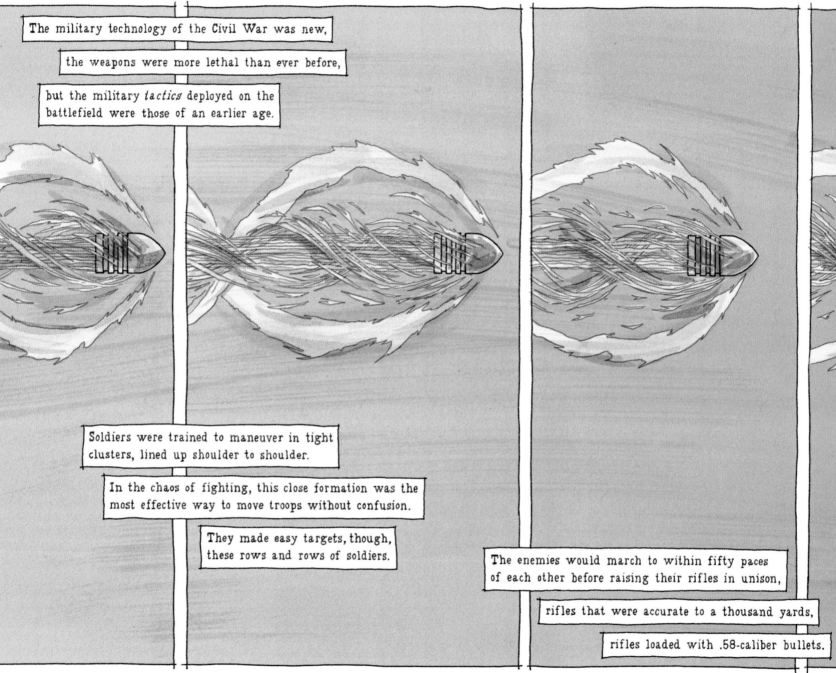

Soldiers were trained to maneuver in tight clusters, lined up shoulder to shoulder.

In the chaos of fighting, this close formation was the most effective way to move troops without confusion.

They made easy targets, though, these rows and rows of soldiers.

The enemies would march to within fifty paces of each other before raising their rifles in unison,

rifles that were accurate to a thousand yards,

rifles loaded with .58-caliber bullets.

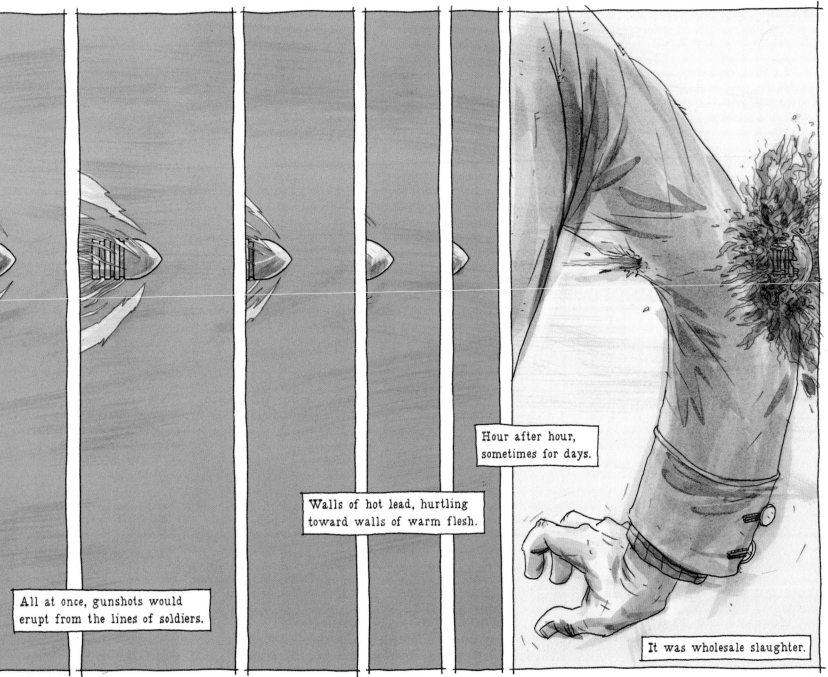

All at once, gunshots would erupt from the lines of soldiers.

Walls of hot lead, hurtling toward walls of warm flesh.

Hour after hour, sometimes for days.

It was wholesale slaughter.

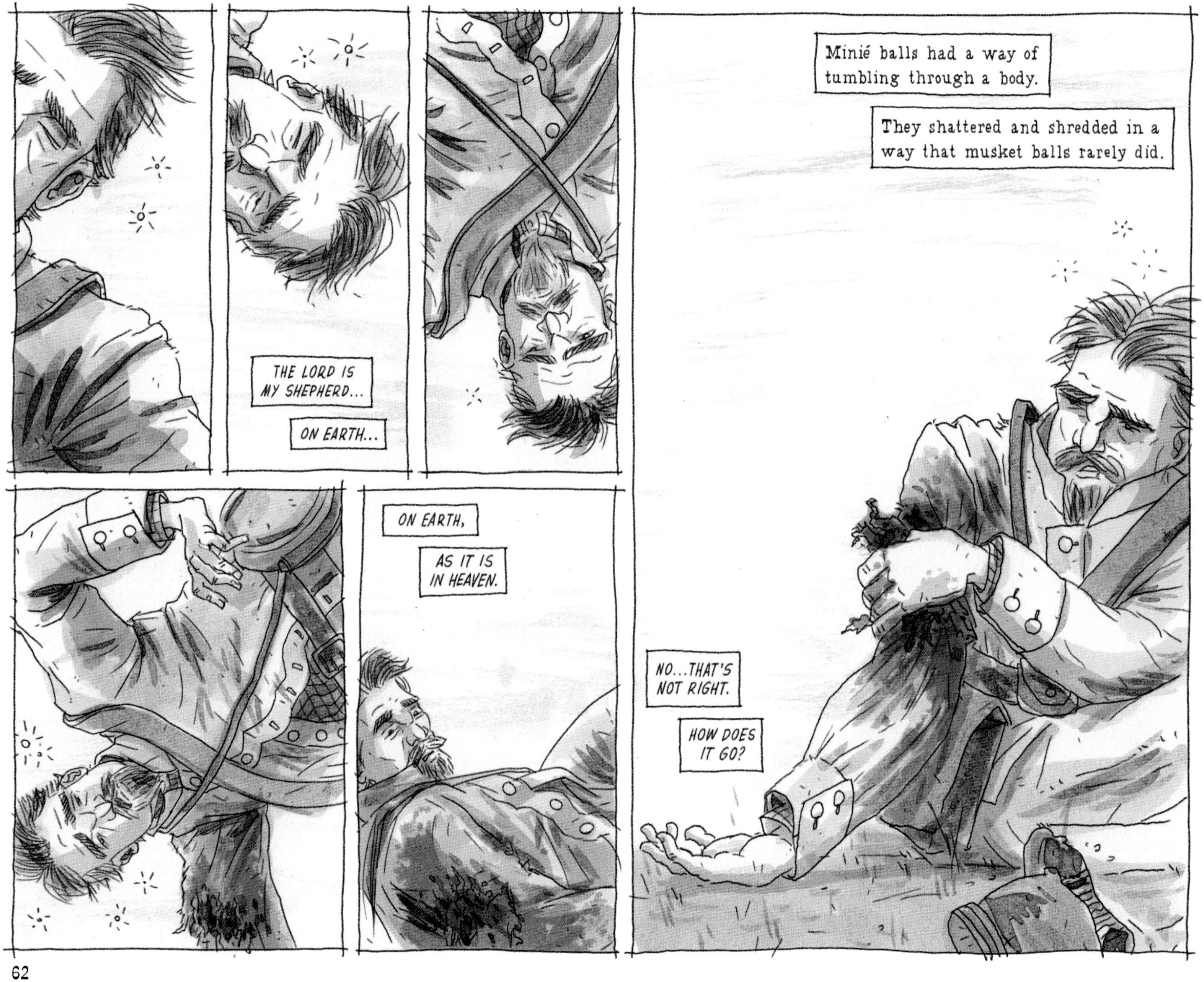
THE LORD IS MY SHEPHERD...
ON EARTH...
ON EARTH,
AS IT IS IN HEAVEN.
Minié balls had a way of tumbling through a body.
They shattered and shredded in a way that musket balls rarely did.
NO...THAT'S NOT RIGHT.
HOW DOES IT GO?

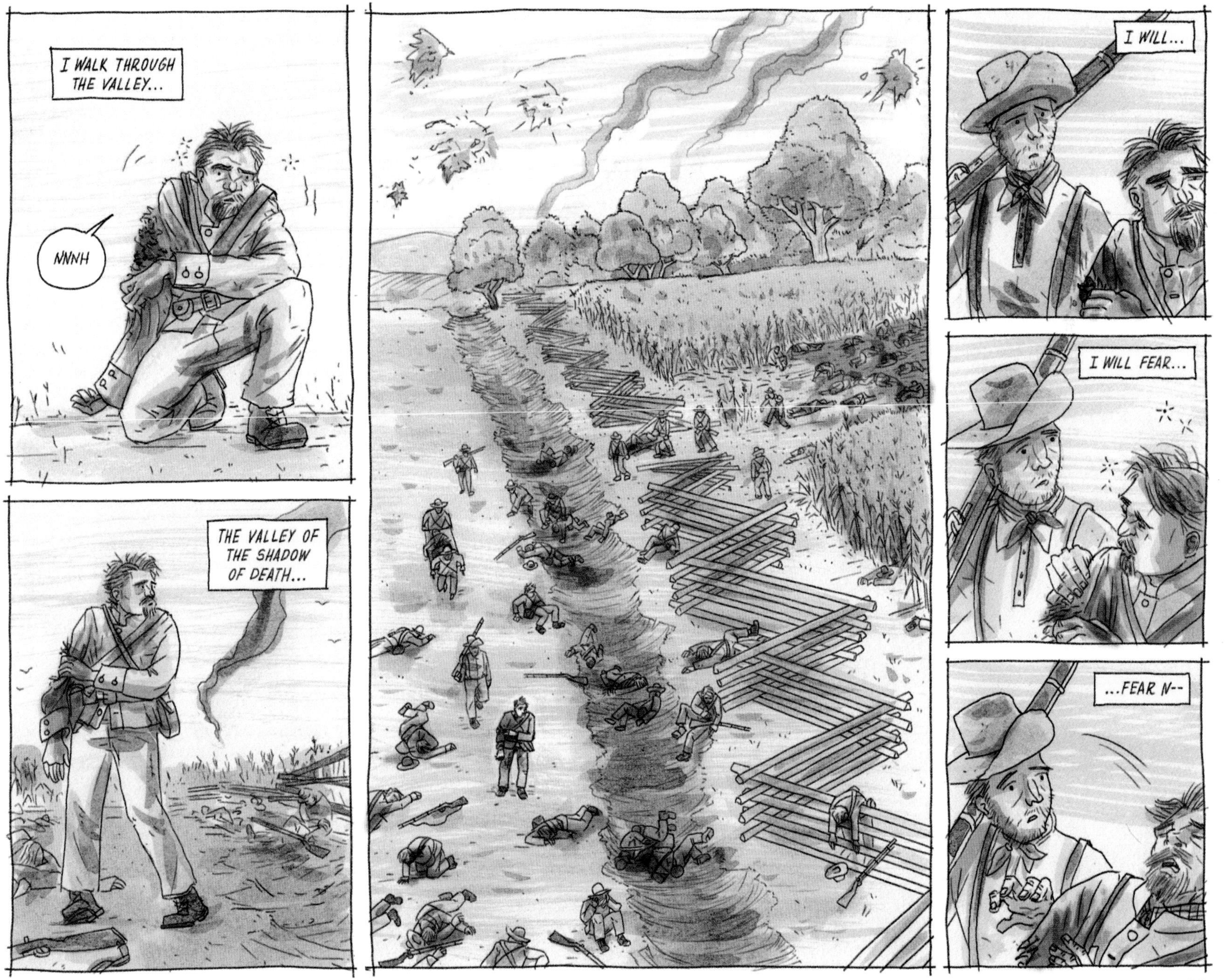
I WALK THROUGH THE VALLEY...
NNNH
THE VALLEY OF THE SHADOW OF DEATH...
I WILL...
I WILL FEAR...
...FEAR N--

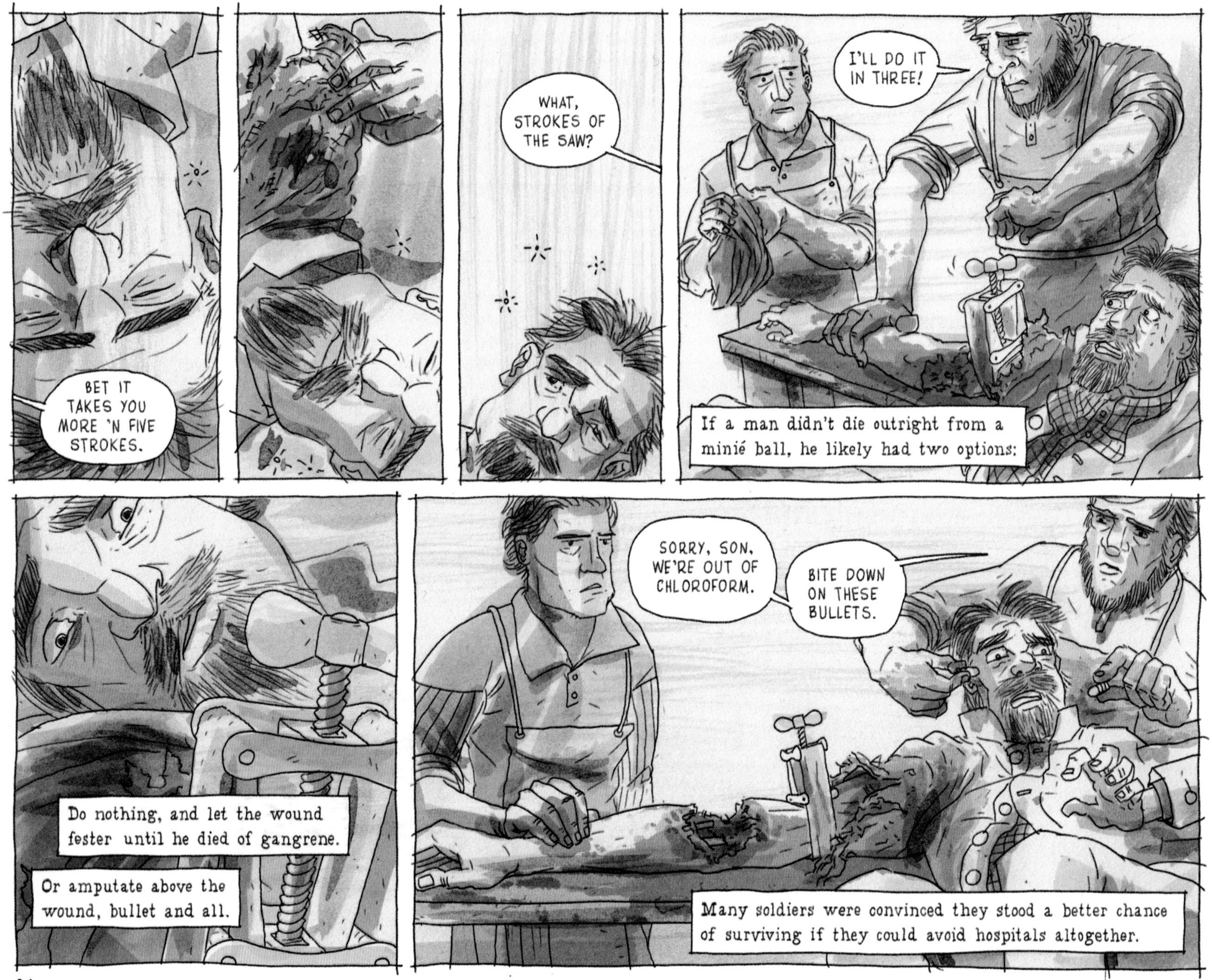
BET IT TAKES YOU MORE 'N FIVE STROKES.
WHAT, STROKES OF THE SAW?
I'LL DO IT IN THREE!
If a man didn't die outright from a minié ball, he likely had two options:
Do nothing, and let the wound fester until he died of gangrene.
Or amputate above the wound, bullet and all.
SORRY, SON, WE'RE OUT OF CHLOROFORM.
BITE DOWN ON THESE BULLETS.
Many soldiers were convinced they stood a better chance of surviving if they could avoid hospitals altogether.

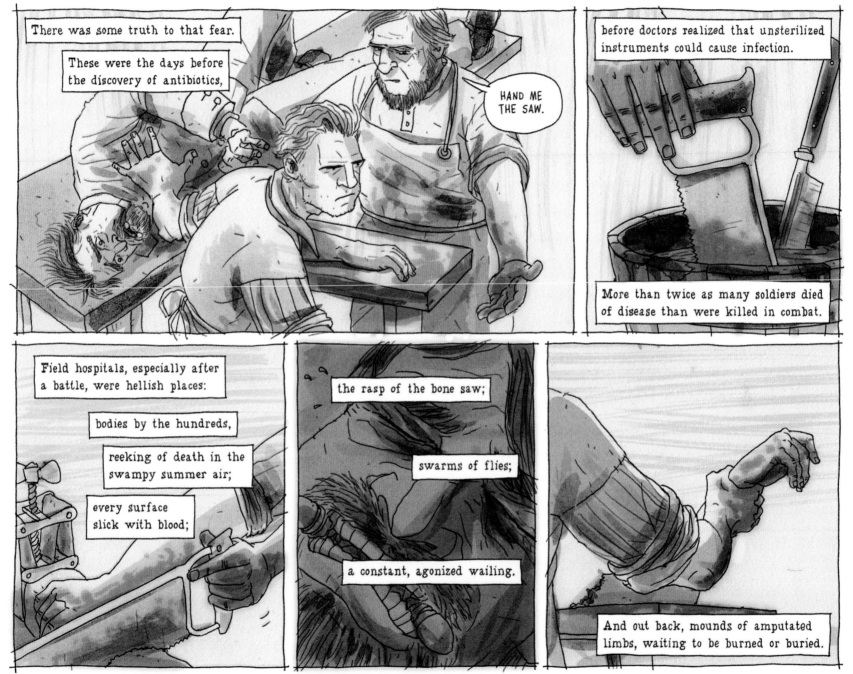

There was some truth to that fear.

These were the days before the discovery of antibiotics,

HAND ME THE SAW.

before doctors realized that unsterilized instruments could cause infection.

More than twice as many soldiers died of disease than were killed in combat.

Field hospitals, especially after a battle, were hellish places:

bodies by the hundreds,

reeking of death in the swampy summer air;

every surface slick with blood;

the rasp of the bone saw;

swarms of flies;

a constant, agonized wailing.

And out back, mounds of amputated limbs, waiting to be burned or buried.

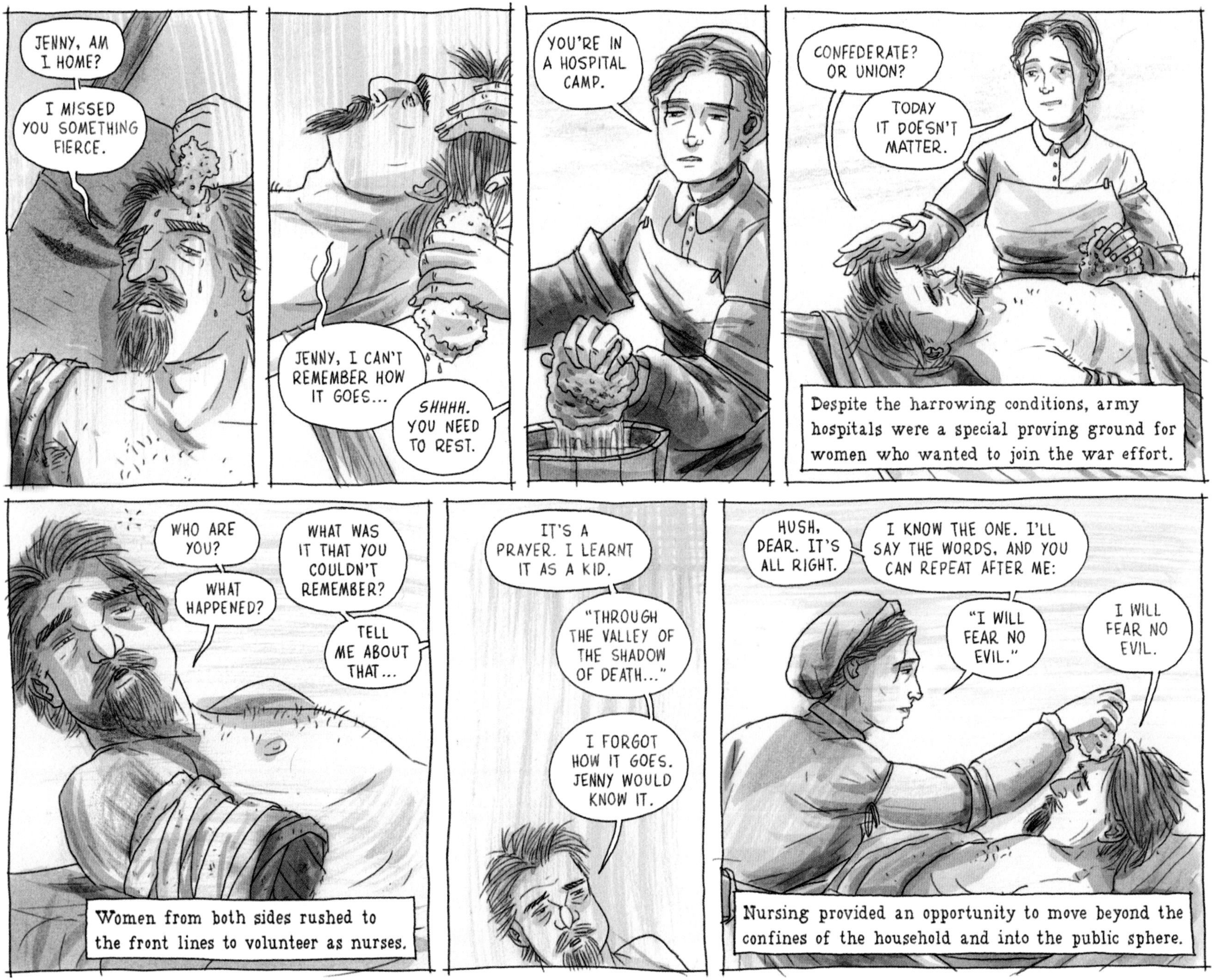
JENNY, AM I HOME?
I MISSED YOU SOMETHING FIERCE.
JENNY, I CAN'T REMEMBER HOW IT GOES...
SHHHH. YOU NEED TO REST.
YOU'RE IN A HOSPITAL CAMP.
CONFEDERATE? OR UNION?
TODAY IT DOESN'T MATTER.
Despite the harrowing conditions, army hospitals were a special proving ground for women who wanted to join the war effort.
WHO ARE YOU?
WHAT HAPPENED?
WHAT WAS IT THAT YOU COULDN'T REMEMBER?
TELL ME ABOUT THAT...
Women from both sides rushed to the front lines to volunteer as nurses.
IT'S A PRAYER. I LEARNT IT AS A KID.
"THROUGH THE VALLEY OF THE SHADOW OF DEATH..."
I FORGOT HOW IT GOES. JENNY WOULD KNOW IT.
HUSH, DEAR. IT'S ALL RIGHT.
I KNOW THE ONE. I'LL SAY THE WORDS, AND YOU CAN REPEAT AFTER ME:
"I WILL FEAR NO EVIL."
I WILL FEAR NO EVIL.
Nursing provided an opportunity to move beyond the confines of the household and into the public sphere.

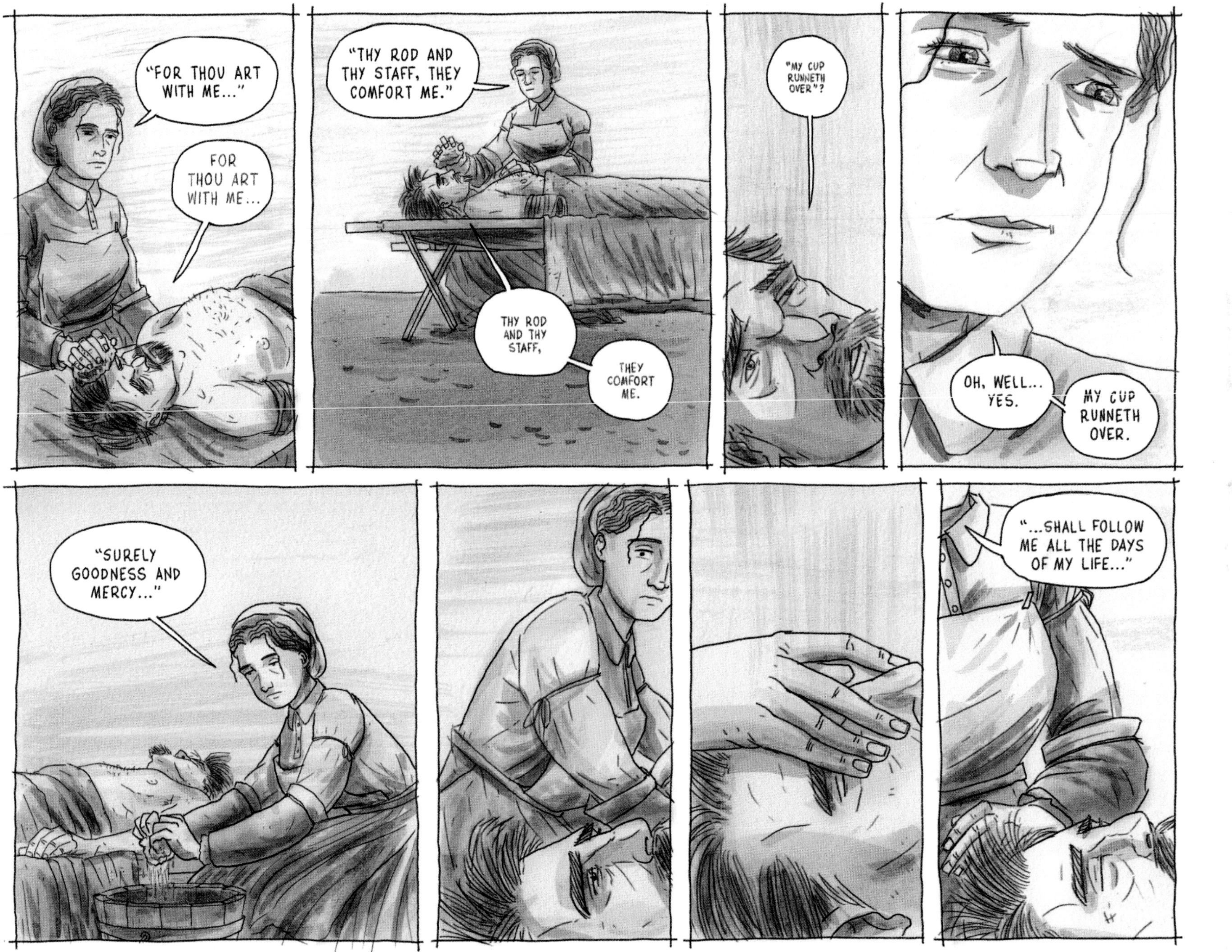
"FOR THOU ART WITH ME..."
FOR THOU ART WITH ME...
"THY ROD AND THY STAFF, THEY COMFORT ME."
THY ROD AND THY STAFF,
THEY COMFORT ME.
"MY CUP RUNNETH OVER"?
OH, WELL... YES.
MY CUP RUNNETH OVER.
"SURELY GOODNESS AND MERCY..."
"...SHALL FOLLOW ME ALL THE DAYS OF MY LIFE..."

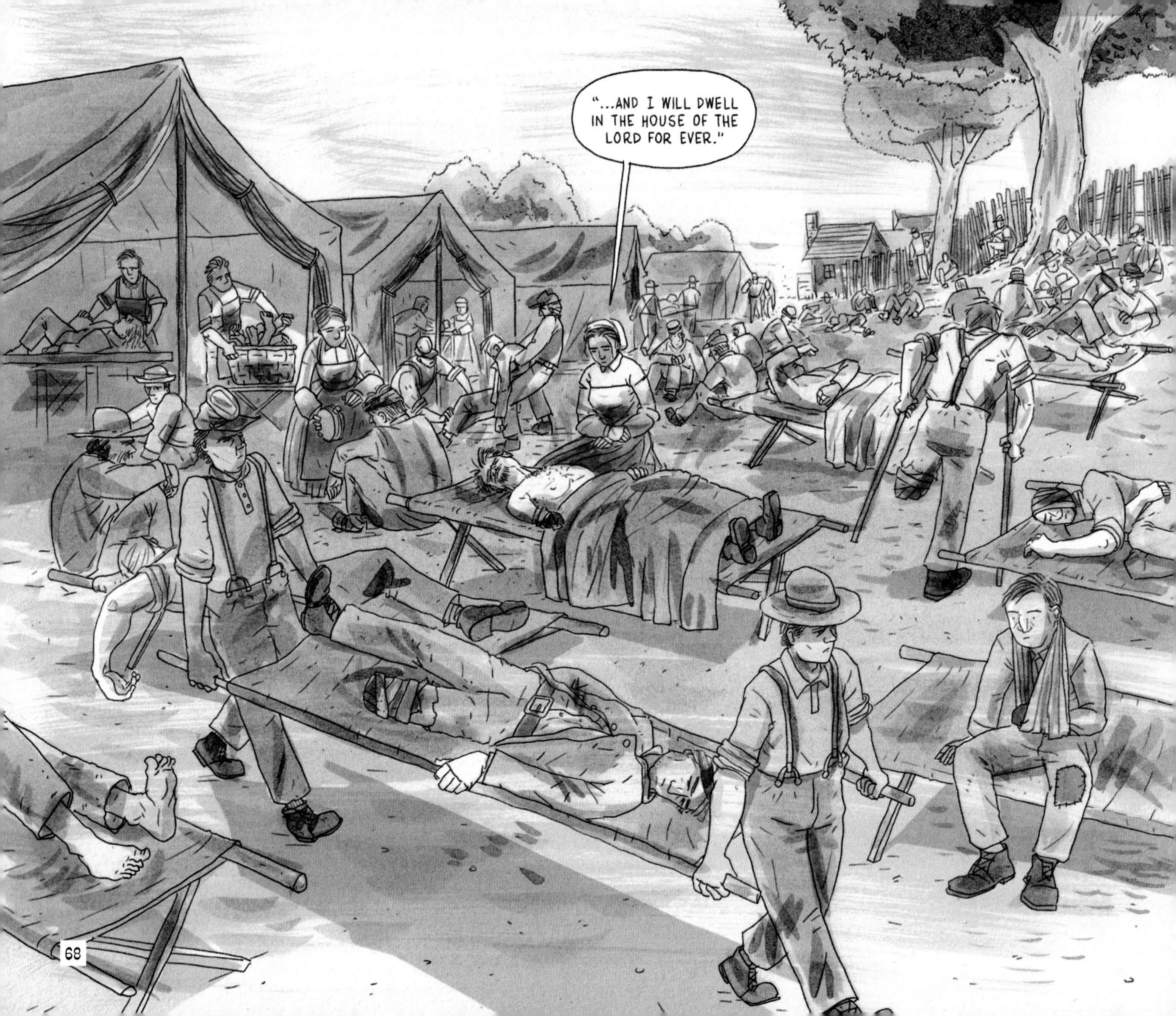
"...AND I WILL DWELL IN THE HOUSE OF THE LORD FOR EVER."

Chapter 6: A Brick

CAPITAL CITY HERALD

April 3, 1863

Lincoln Issues EMANCIPATION PROCLAMATION

In the wake of the carnage during the Seven Days' Battles, the federal government moved toward a strategy of total war. Because much of the Confederacy's strength came from its ability to exploit slaves, Union war planners recognized that in order to defeat the South, slavery would first have to be destroyed.

In July 1862, President Lincoln approached representatives from the Border States to discuss compensated emancipation, offering to pay slaveholders for their human chattel. After receiving a frosty reply, he shifted to a more radical position: he would wait until a Union victory, when morale was at its highest, and then issue a proclamation freeing the slaves.

The President had a long wait, as bad news kept coming from the front. Then, after the Battle of Antietam, Lincoln finally issued his Proclamation. It seemed to some observers like a half measure. The Proclamation would go into effect only in states still rebelling against federal authority on January 1, 1863. These were states, skeptics noted, in which the Lincoln administration would actually have no power to enforce the Proclamation. The President, meanwhile, insisted that the Constitution did not give him the authority to free slaves in states loyal to the Union.

In part, he issued his Proclamation as a signal to all onlookers that if the Union prevailed, the nation would be transformed, and to African Americans that they could help that cause by withholding their labor in the South or, in the North, by enlisting to fight for the Union.

EMANCIPATION OF THE SLAVES.

In less than two years, the President's views on slavery had changed. Before the Civil War began, Lincoln had assured Southerners and Northerners alike that he had no interest in freeing the slaves. But by the summer of 1862, Lincoln had come to see emancipation as both a moral and military imperative. The Civil War was evolving into a war of liberation.

CONFEDERATE HOME FRONT
Groans Beneath Weight of War

As early as spring 1862, some Confederate citizens, confronting the realities of a bloody and protracted conflict, saw their enthusiasm for secession and war begin to wane.

Rebel forces in the East and West faced long odds, and in April the Confederate Congress enacted a conscription law. The new law infuriated an electorate steeped in small-government bromides, especially because it contained a "substitute clause": drafted men of means could hire stand-ins to serve in their place. Critics howled that the conflict had become a rich man's war but a poor man's fight.

Adding insult to injury, with the South's economy foundering, its government struggled to finance the war. Most of the region's capital was tied up in illiquid assets: land and slaves.

Taxes might have solved the problem--in the North, Congress instituted the nation's first income tax and created a Bureau of Internal Revenue in 1862--but again, the South's commitment to limited government complicated its ability to prosecute the war. The Confederacy took on debt and printed money, leading to runaway inflation: more than 10 percent monthly in early 1862. By the start of the following year, it took $7 to purchase what had cost $1 at the beginning of the war.

RUMORS FROM THE FRONT ☞

Richmond's Women Riot for Bread

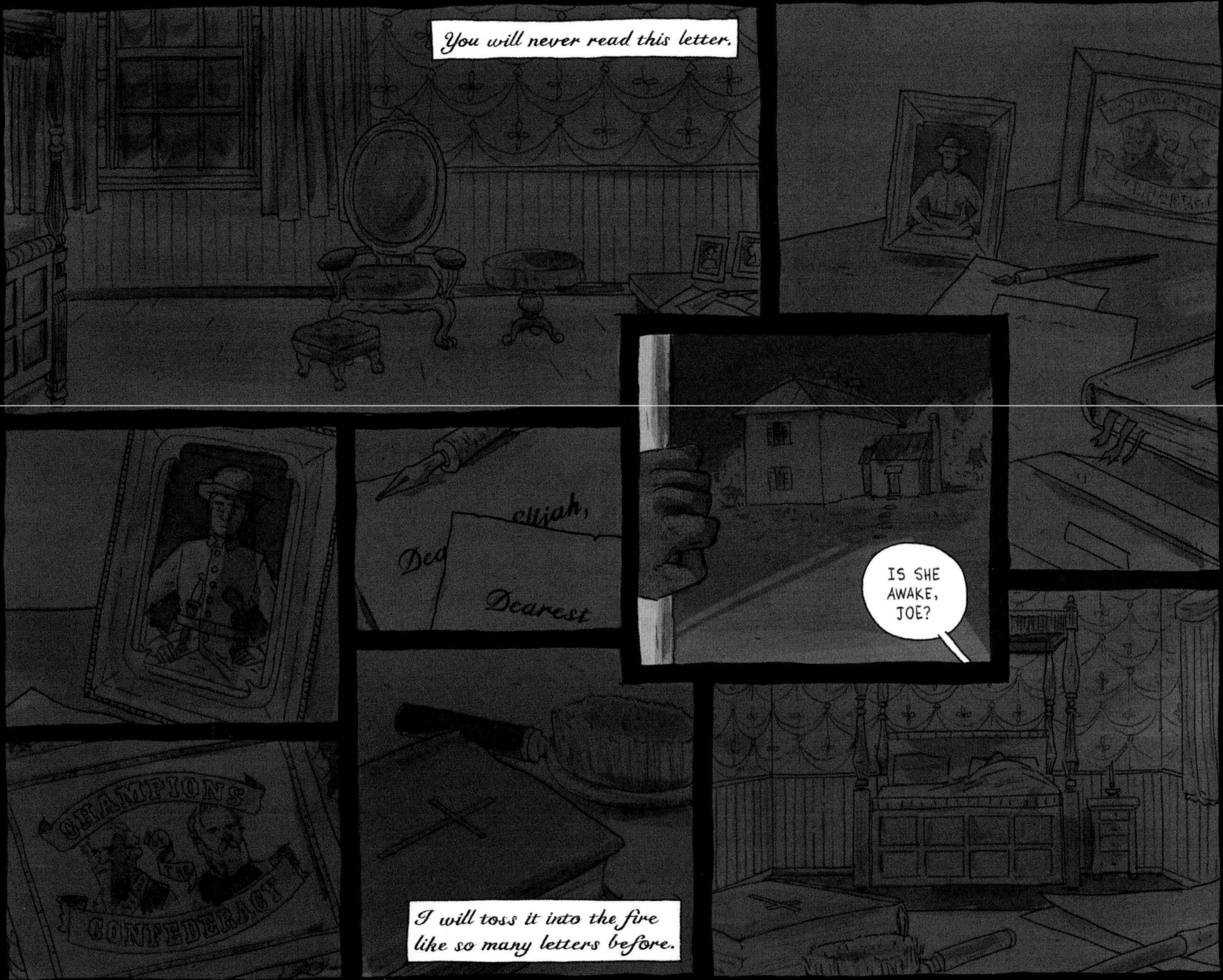
You will never read this letter.
Dearest
Elijah,
Dearest
IS SHE AWAKE, JOE?
CHAMPIONS
CONFEDERACY
I will toss it into the fire like so many letters before.

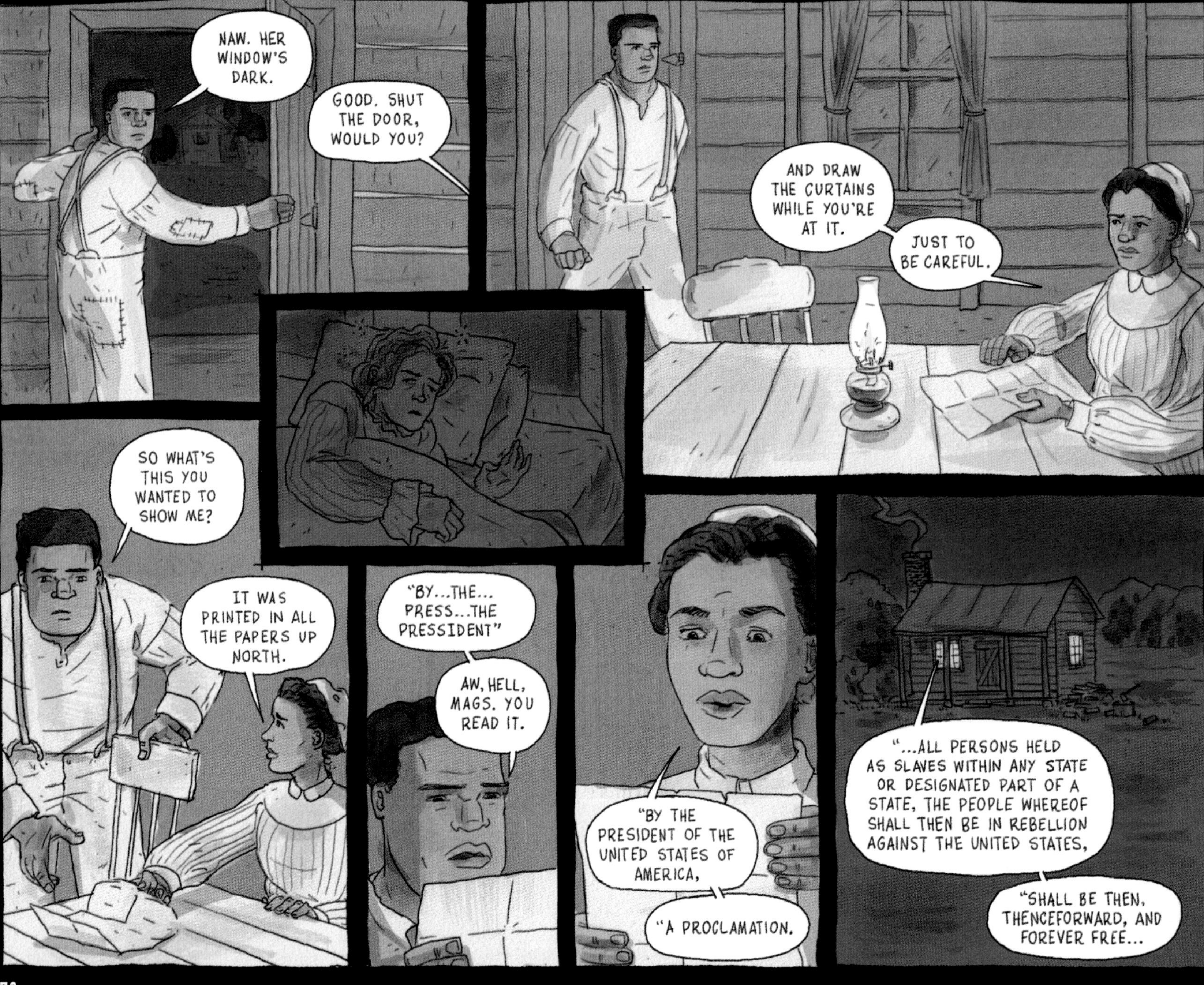
NAW. HER WINDOW'S DARK.
GOOD. SHUT THE DOOR, WOULD YOU?
AND DRAW THE CURTAINS WHILE YOU'RE AT IT.
JUST TO BE CAREFUL.
SO WHAT'S THIS YOU WANTED TO SHOW ME?
IT WAS PRINTED IN ALL THE PAPERS UP NORTH.
"BY...THE... PRESS...THE PRESSIDENT"
AW, HELL, MAGS. YOU READ IT.
"BY THE PRESIDENT OF THE UNITED STATES OF AMERICA,
"A PROCLAMATION.
"...ALL PERSONS HELD AS SLAVES WITHIN ANY STATE OR DESIGNATED PART OF A STATE, THE PEOPLE WHEREOF SHALL THEN BE IN REBELLION AGAINST THE UNITED STATES,
"SHALL BE THEN, THENCEFORWARD, AND FOREVER FREE...

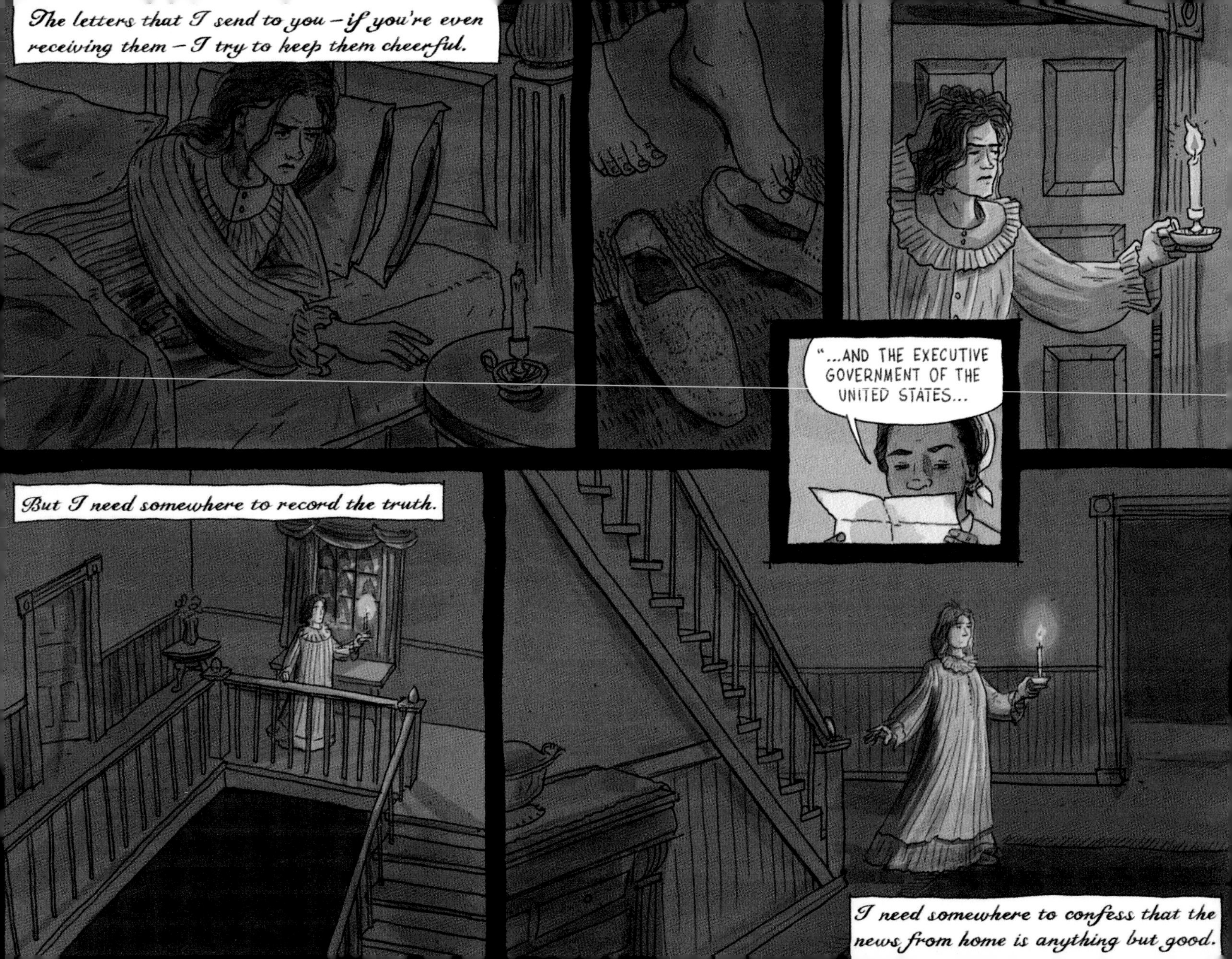
The letters that I send to you – if you're even receiving them – I try to keep them cheerful.
"...AND THE EXECUTIVE GOVERNMENT OF THE UNITED STATES...
But I need somewhere to record the truth.
I need somewhere to confess that the news from home is anything but good.

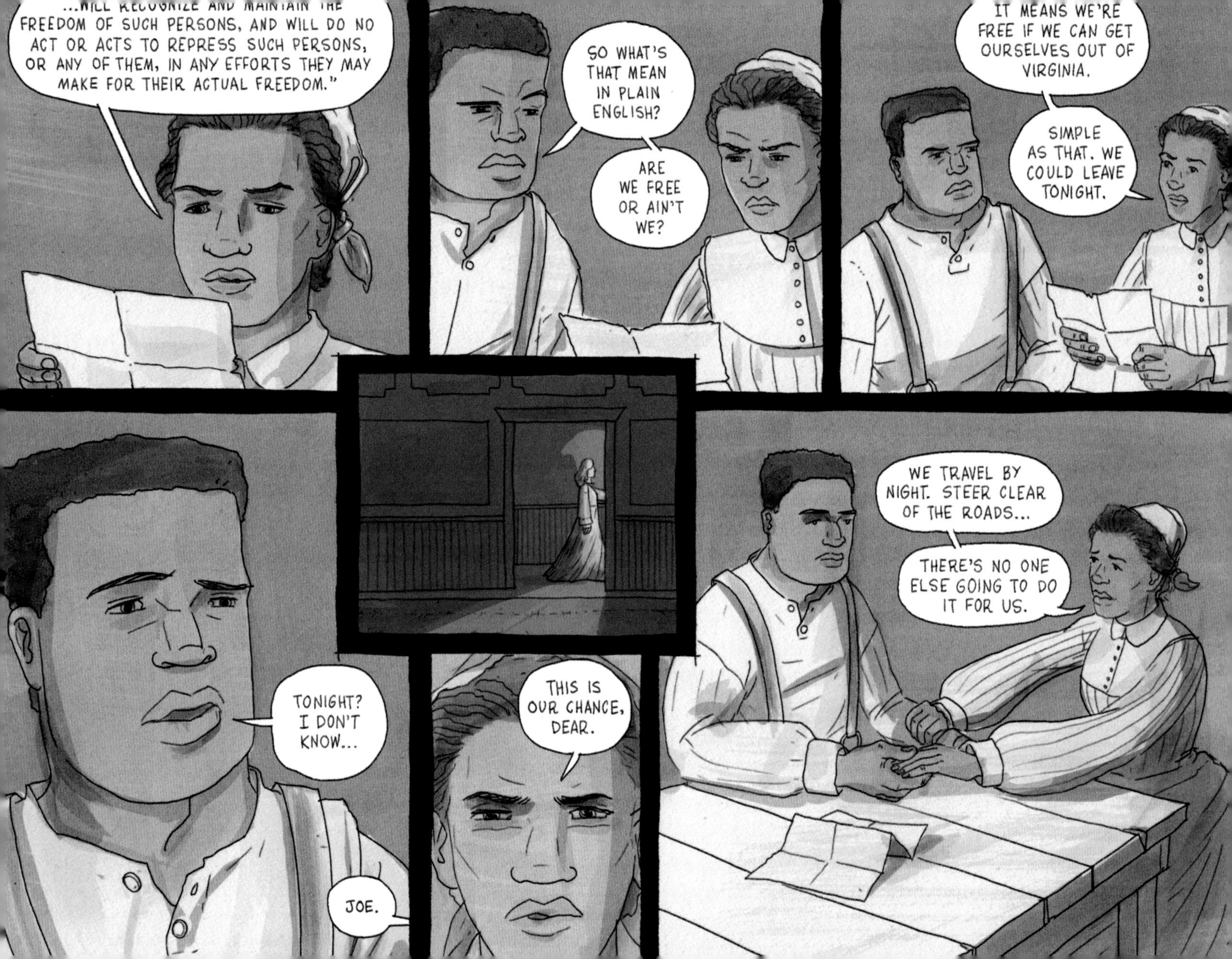
...WILL RECOGNIZE AND MAINTAIN THE FREEDOM OF SUCH PERSONS, AND WILL DO NO ACT OR ACTS TO REPRESS SUCH PERSONS, OR ANY OF THEM, IN ANY EFFORTS THEY MAY MAKE FOR THEIR ACTUAL FREEDOM."
SO WHAT'S THAT MEAN IN PLAIN ENGLISH?
ARE WE FREE OR AIN'T WE?
IT MEANS WE'RE FREE IF WE CAN GET OURSELVES OUT OF VIRGINIA.
SIMPLE AS THAT. WE COULD LEAVE TONIGHT.
TONIGHT? I DON'T KNOW...
JOE.
THIS IS OUR CHANCE, DEAR.
WE TRAVEL BY NIGHT. STEER CLEAR OF THE ROADS...
THERE'S NO ONE ELSE GOING TO DO IT FOR US.

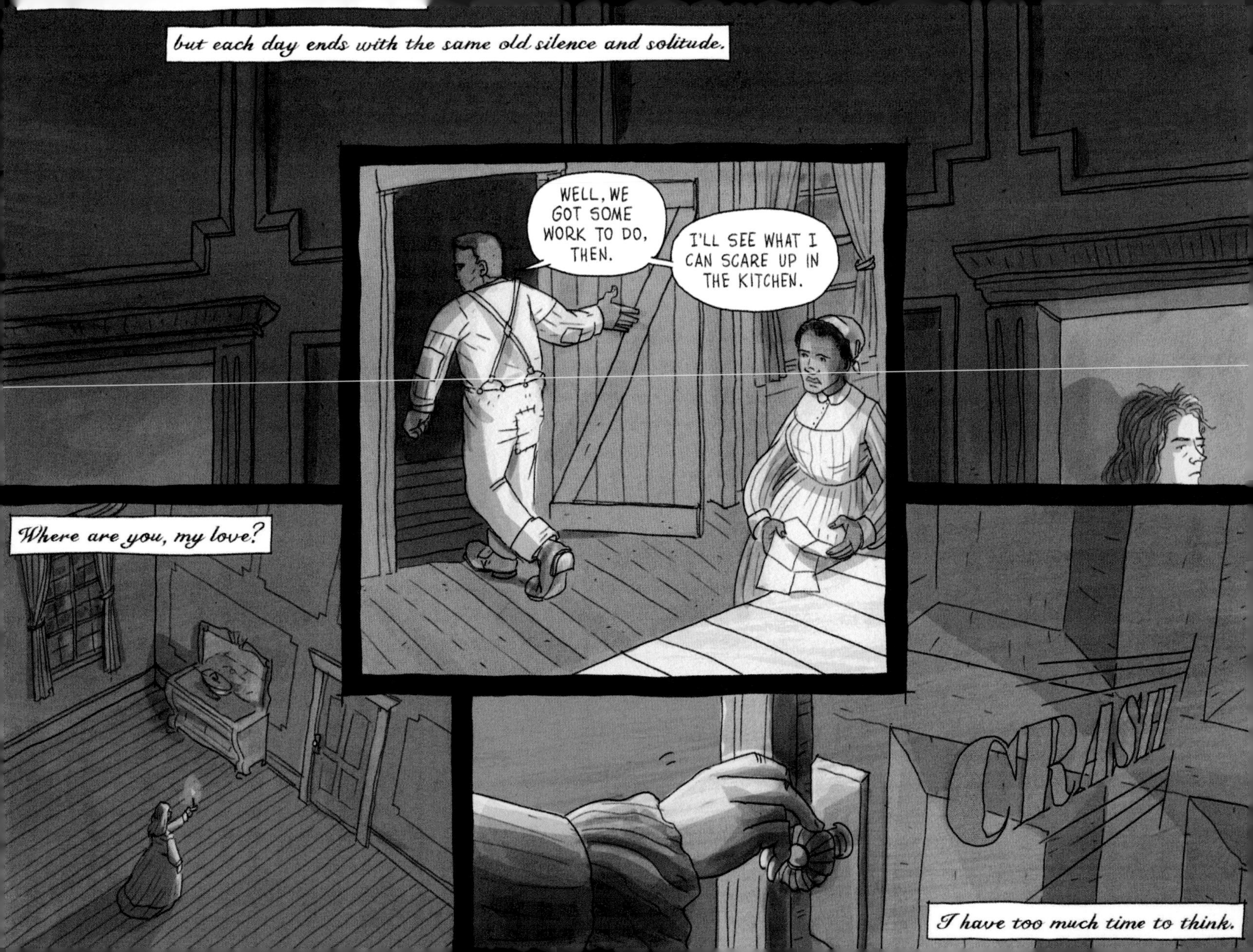
but each day ends with the same old silence and solitude.
WELL, WE GOT SOME WORK TO DO, THEN.
I'LL SEE WHAT I CAN SCARE UP IN THE KITCHEN.
Where are you, my love?
CRASH
I have too much time to think.

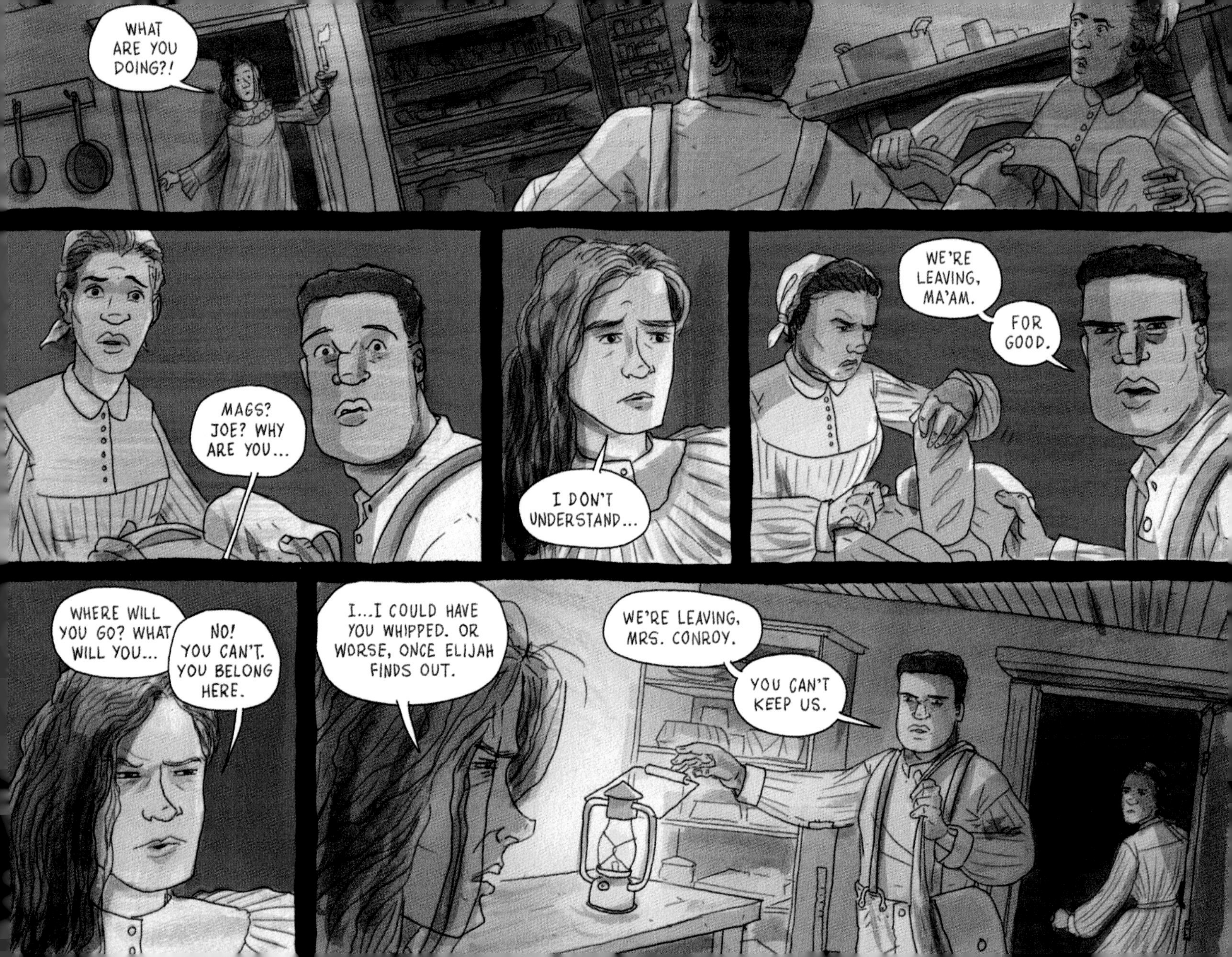
WHAT ARE YOU DOING?!
MAGS? JOE? WHY ARE YOU...
I DON'T UNDERSTAND...
WE'RE LEAVING, MA'AM.
FOR GOOD.
WHERE WILL YOU GO? WHAT WILL YOU...
NO! YOU CAN'T. YOU BELONG HERE.
I...I COULD HAVE YOU WHIPPED. OR WORSE, ONCE ELIJAH FINDS OUT.
WE'RE LEAVING, MRS. CONROY.
YOU CAN'T KEEP US.

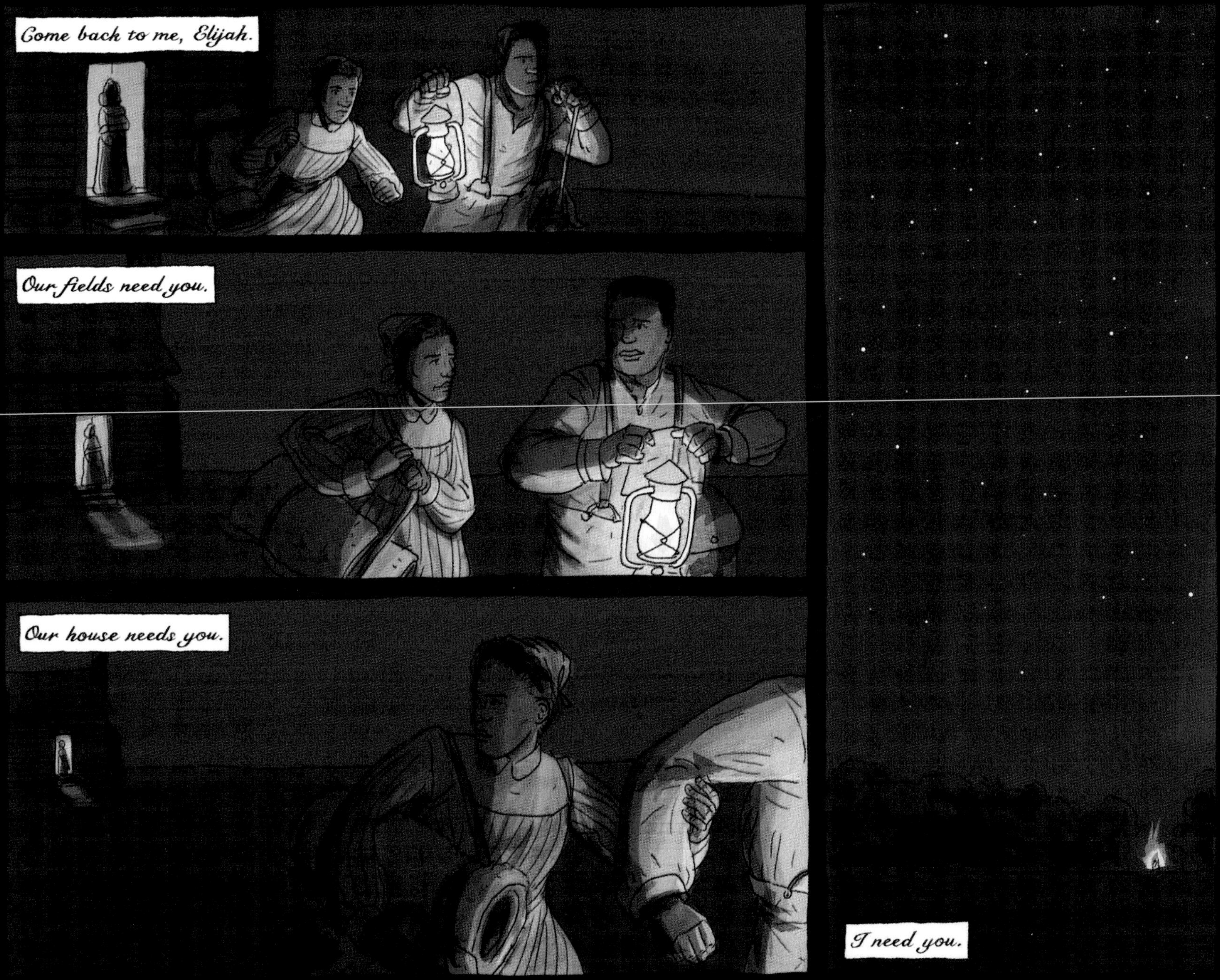
Come back to me, Elijah.
Our fields need you.
Our house needs you.
I need you.

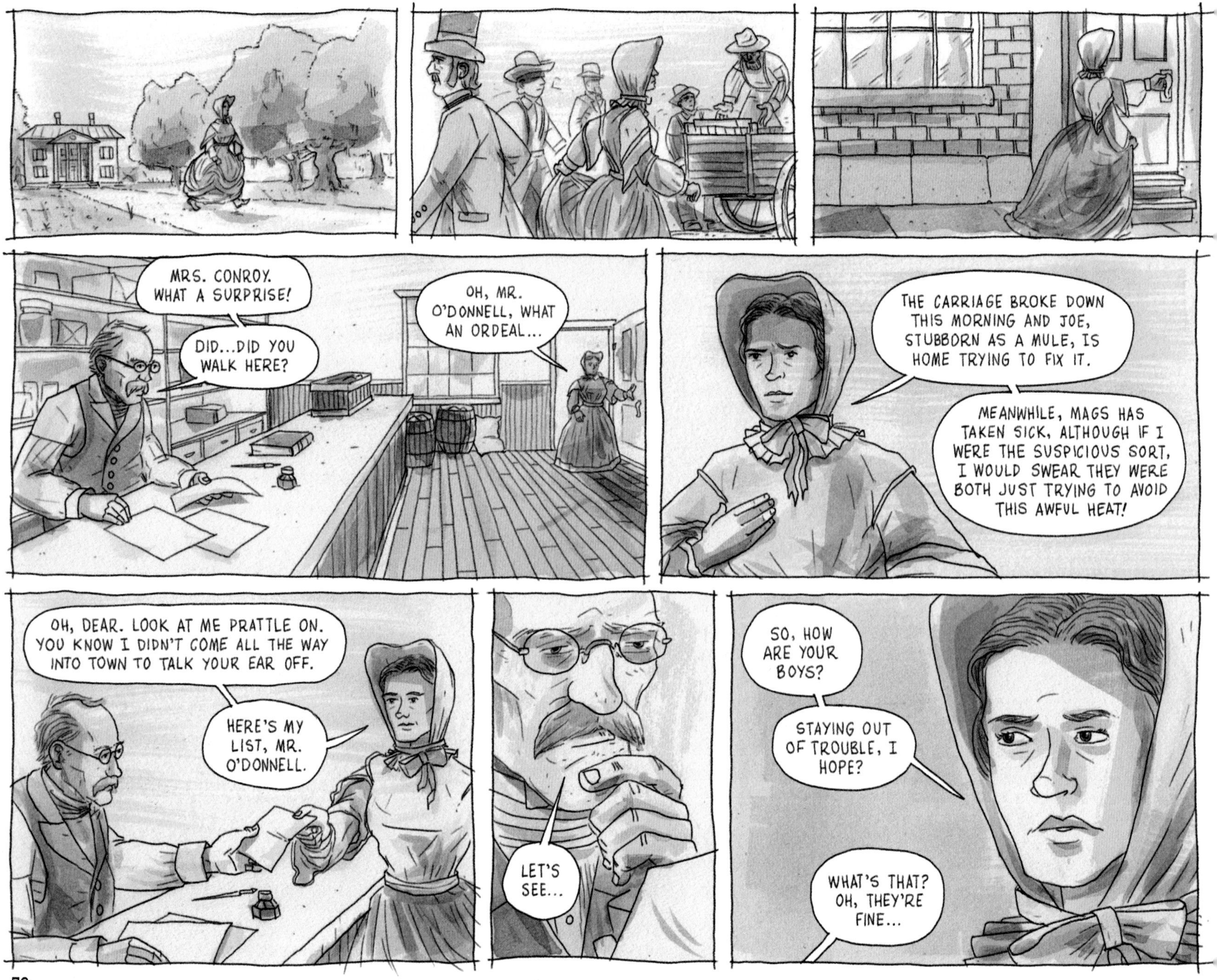
MRS. CONROY. WHAT A SURPRISE!
DID...DID YOU WALK HERE?
OH, MR. O'DONNELL, WHAT AN ORDEAL...
THE CARRIAGE BROKE DOWN THIS MORNING AND JOE, STUBBORN AS A MULE, IS HOME TRYING TO FIX IT.
MEANWHILE, MAGS HAS TAKEN SICK, ALTHOUGH IF I WERE THE SUSPICIOUS SORT, I WOULD SWEAR THEY WERE BOTH JUST TRYING TO AVOID THIS AWFUL HEAT!
OH, DEAR. LOOK AT ME PRATTLE ON. YOU KNOW I DIDN'T COME ALL THE WAY INTO TOWN TO TALK YOUR EAR OFF.
HERE'S MY LIST, MR. O'DONNELL.
LET'S SEE...
SO, HOW ARE YOUR BOYS?
STAYING OUT OF TROUBLE, I HOPE?
WHAT'S THAT? OH, THEY'RE FINE...

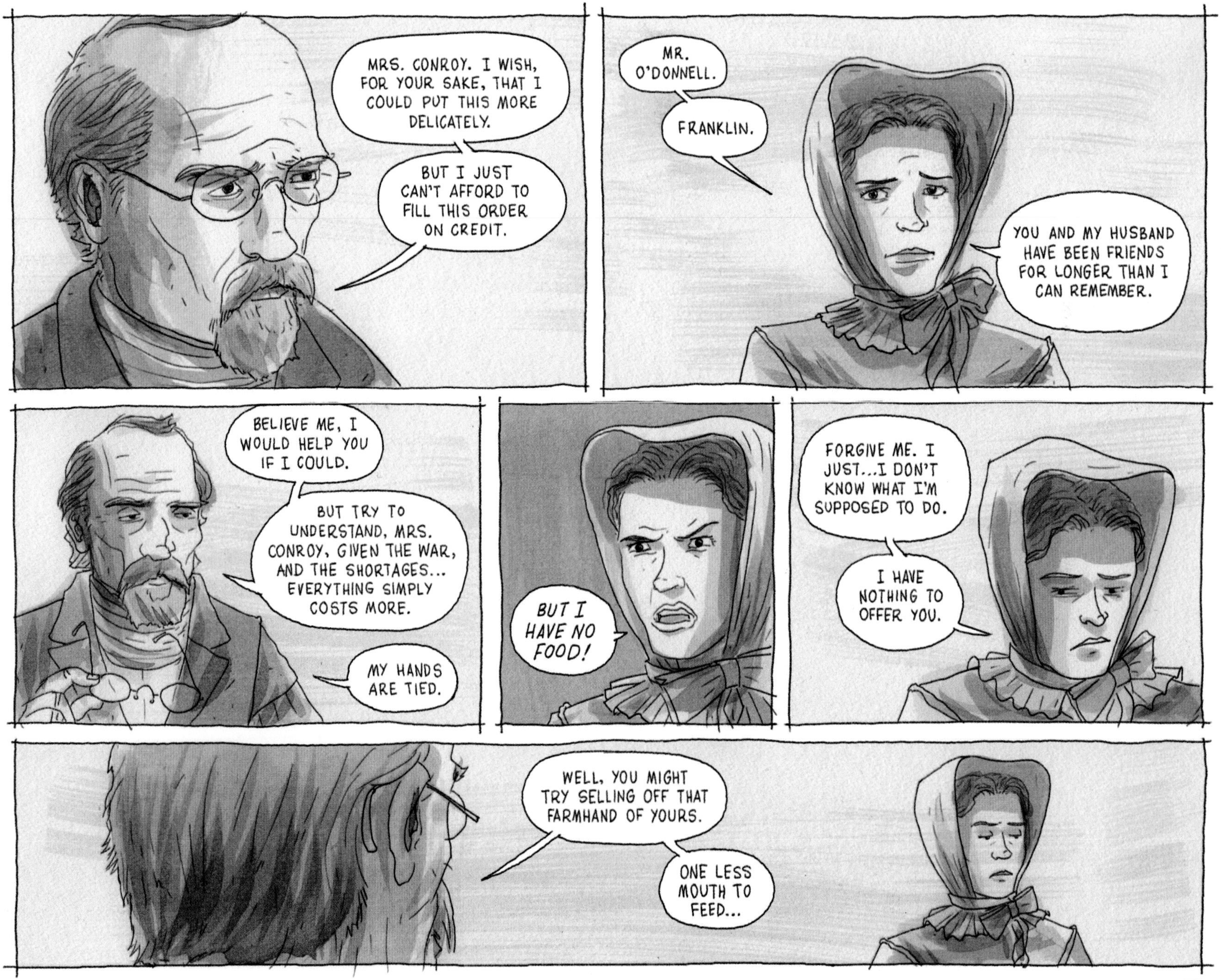
MRS. CONROY. I WISH, FOR YOUR SAKE, THAT I COULD PUT THIS MORE DELICATELY.
BUT I JUST CAN'T AFFORD TO FILL THIS ORDER ON CREDIT.
MR. O'DONNELL.
FRANKLIN.
YOU AND MY HUSBAND HAVE BEEN FRIENDS FOR LONGER THAN I CAN REMEMBER.
BELIEVE ME, I WOULD HELP YOU IF I COULD.
BUT TRY TO UNDERSTAND, MRS. CONROY, GIVEN THE WAR, AND THE SHORTAGES... EVERYTHING SIMPLY COSTS MORE.
MY HANDS ARE TIED.
BUT I HAVE NO FOOD!
FORGIVE ME. I JUST...I DON'T KNOW WHAT I'M SUPPOSED TO DO.
I HAVE NOTHING TO OFFER YOU.
WELL, YOU MIGHT TRY SELLING OFF THAT FARMHAND OF YOURS.
ONE LESS MOUTH TO FEED...

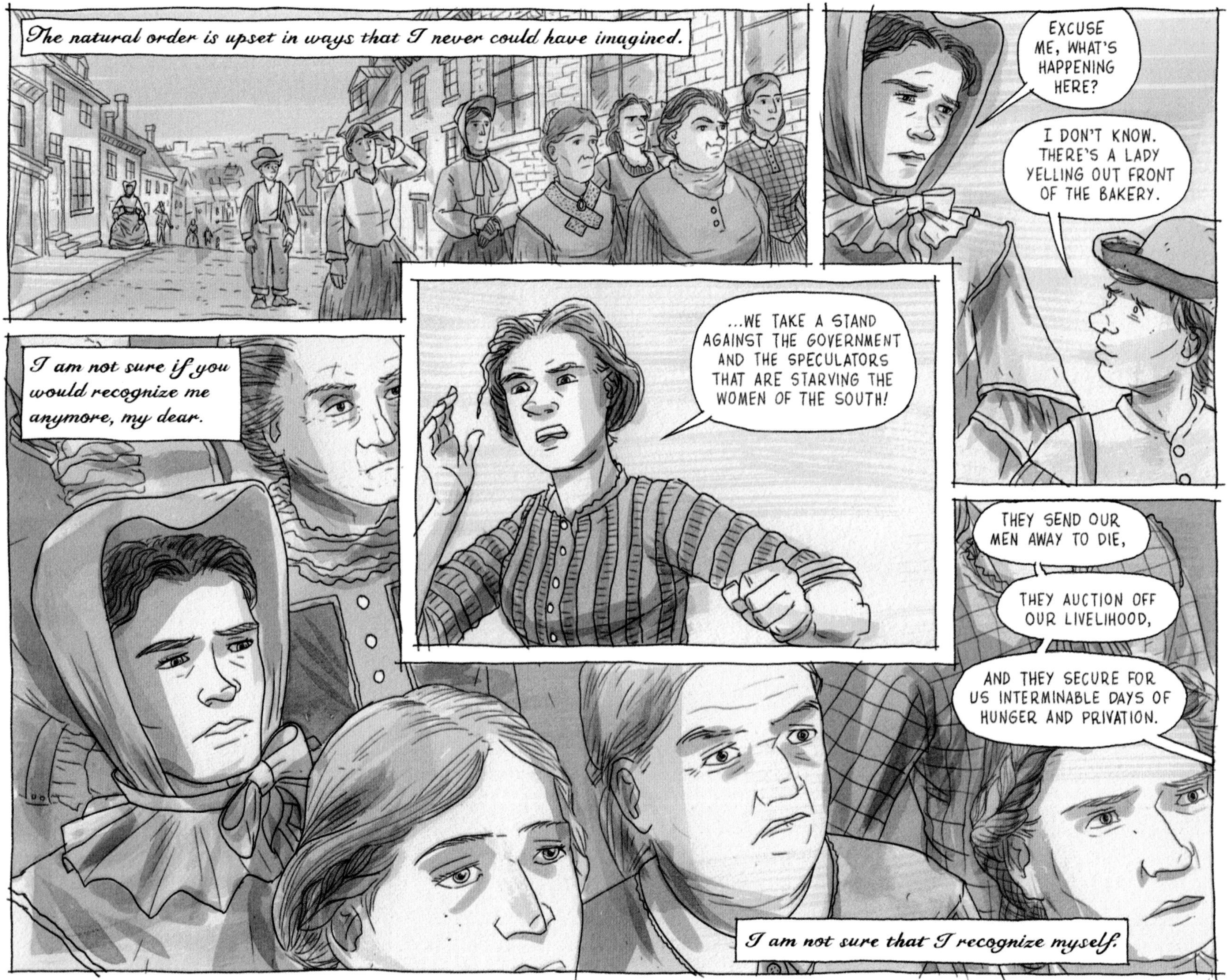
The natural order is upset in ways that I never could have imagined.
EXCUSE ME, WHAT'S HAPPENING HERE?
I DON'T KNOW. THERE'S A LADY YELLING OUT FRONT OF THE BAKERY.
I am not sure if you would recognize me anymore, my dear.
...WE TAKE A STAND AGAINST THE GOVERNMENT AND THE SPECULATORS THAT ARE STARVING THE WOMEN OF THE SOUTH!
THEY SEND OUR MEN AWAY TO DIE,
THEY AUCTION OFF OUR LIVELIHOOD,
AND THEY SECURE FOR US INTERMINABLE DAYS OF HUNGER AND PRIVATION.
I am not sure that I recognize myself.

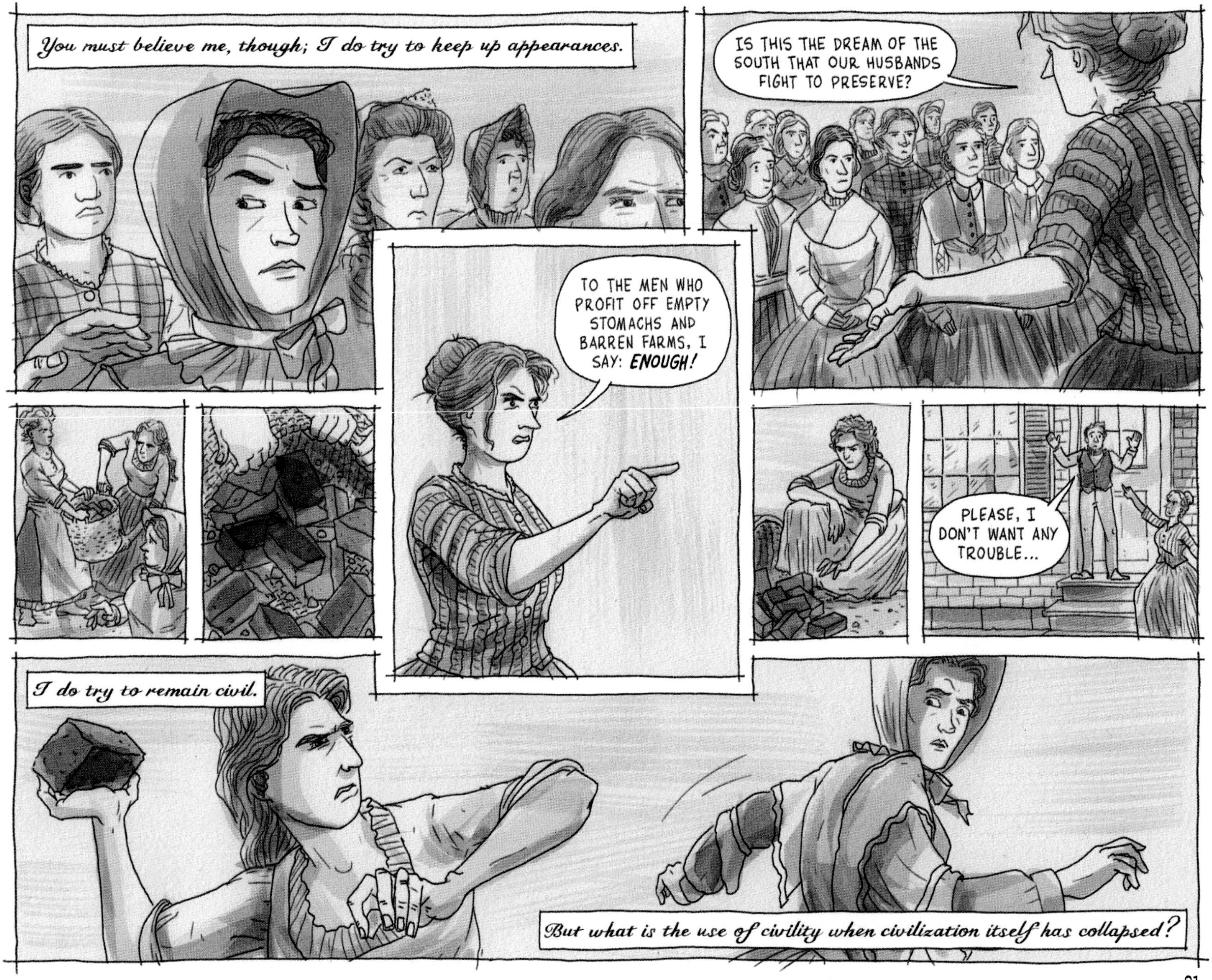
You must believe me, though; I do try to keep up appearances.
IS THIS THE DREAM OF THE SOUTH THAT OUR HUSBANDS FIGHT TO PRESERVE?
TO THE MEN WHO PROFIT OFF EMPTY STOMACHS AND BARREN FARMS, I SAY: ENOUGH!
PLEASE, I DON'T WANT ANY TROUBLE...
I do try to remain civil.
But what is the use of civility when civilization itself has collapsed?

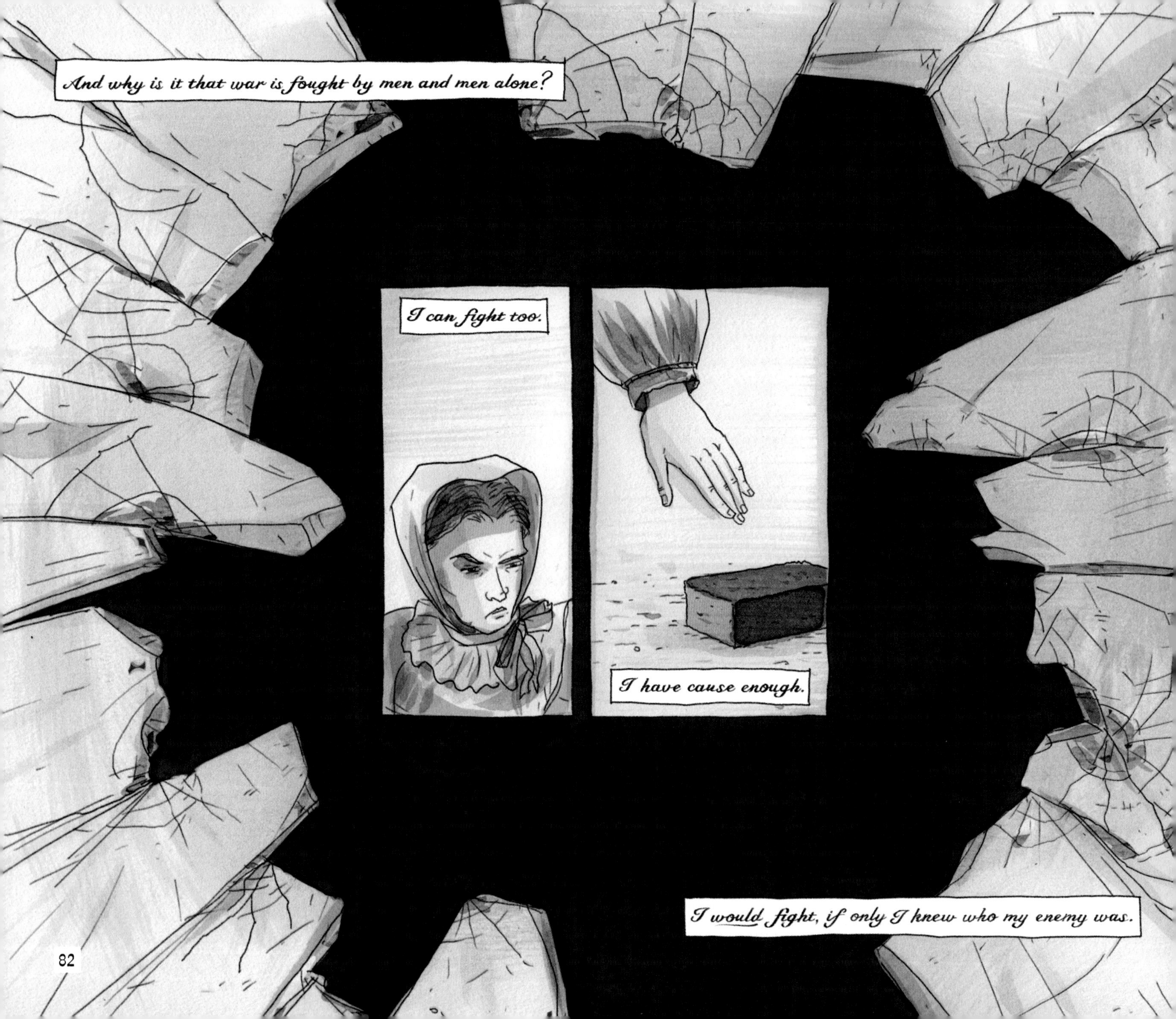
And why is it that war is fought by men and men alone?
I can fight too.
I have cause enough.
I would fight, if only I knew who my enemy was.

Chapter 7: The Bug

VICKSBURG COURANT

June 1, 1863

DEMOCRATS *Rally Against* Emancipation Proclamation

When President Lincoln issued the Emancipation Proclamation, he provided a tonic for a beleaguered Democratic Party in the North. Heading into the 1862 midterm elections, Northern Democrats pointed to Lincoln's stand on emancipation and his uneasy relationship with civil liberties as evidence that he was a tyrant intent on securing rights for African Americans at the expense of whites and immigrants who, in the coming years, would have to compete with freed slaves for jobs.

Antiwar Democrats went a step further, noting that the conflict had already dragged on for a year and a half; that despite recent Union victories at Antietam and Corinth, the rebellion was still in a strong position; and that tens of thousands of killed or wounded white men had fought for abolition by another name. It was time for a change, Democrats suggested, courting an electorate they hoped was weary of an increasingly brutal conflict.

The election, like so many battles in the war, very nearly ended as a draw. And in its aftermath President Lincoln replaced General McClellan with Ambrose Burnside. Then, on

January 1, 1863, the Emancipation Proclamation went into effect. The Democratic Party would not let go of that issue in the future, and the party's antiwar wing would only grow stronger as the bloodshed continued.

General Burnside

From the East to the West: UNION FORCES FOUNDER

Late in 1862, Ambrose Burnside, aware that his Commander in Chief longed for a fighting general, led the Army of the Potomac into a horrible slaughter at the Battle of Fredericksburg. After attacking entrenched Confederate forces, more than twelve thousand

Union men fell in the carnage. The rebels, by contrast, lost fewer than five thousand killed and wounded.

Morale in the North plumbed new depths.

Against that grim backdrop, Generals Ulysses Grant and William Sherman, Grant's trusted lieutenant in the Western Theater, assaulted the city of Vicksburg, Mississippi. Grant quickly found his long supply lines menaced by Confederate cavalry, including Nathan Bedford Forrest's men. With the new year approaching, Grant scuttled the operation.

As Grant's army retreated toward Tennessee, his men lived off the land, plundering the surrounding countryside--a tactic he and Sherman would remember later in the war. In the meantime, Grant prepared to redouble his attack on Vicksburg, planning to besiege the city in the spring of 1863.

RUMORS FROM THE FRONT ☞

Plague Prostrates Vexed Vicksburg

84

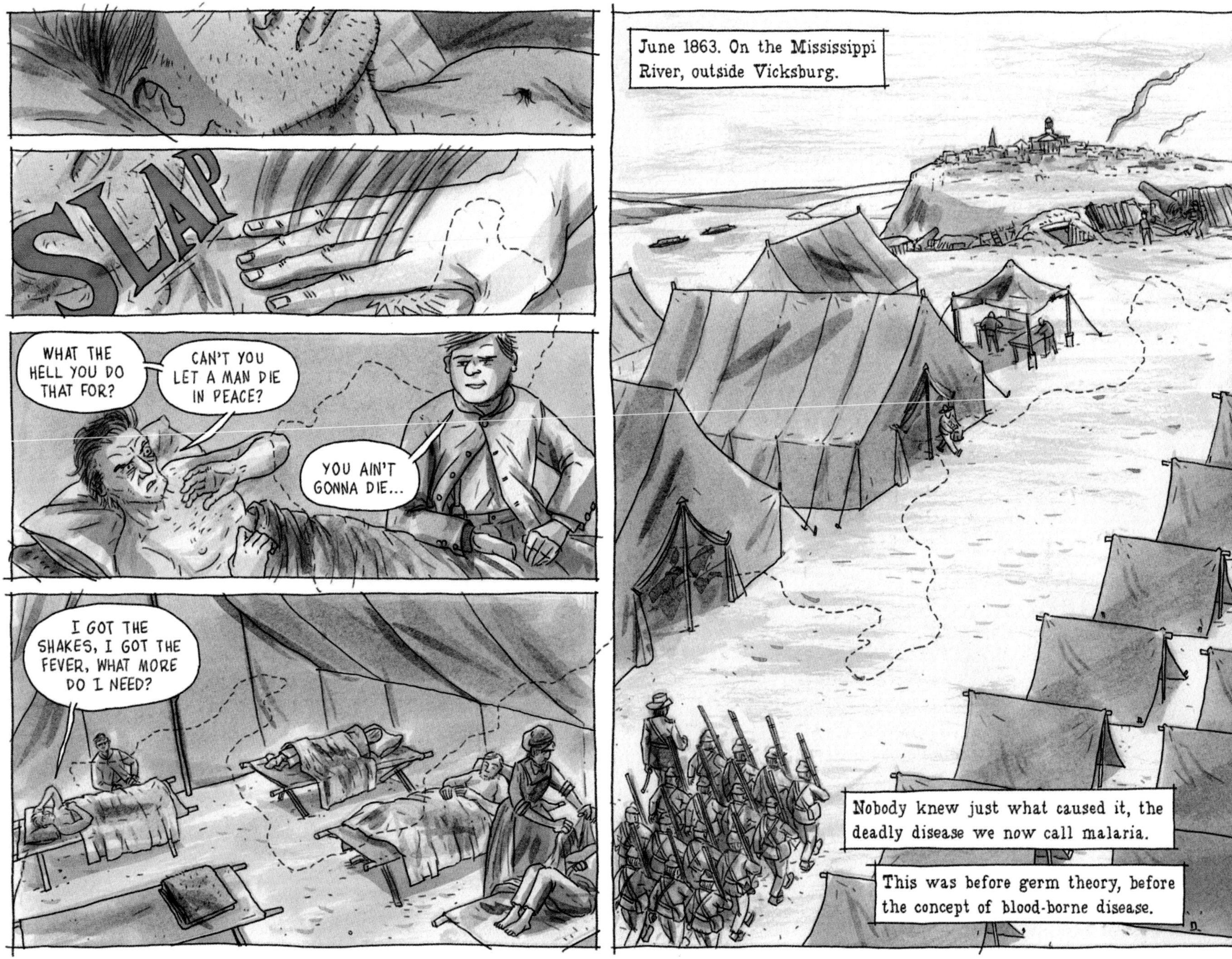
SLAP
WHAT THE HELL YOU DO THAT FOR?
CAN'T YOU LET A MAN DIE IN PEACE?
YOU AIN'T GONNA DIE...
I GOT THE SHAKES, I GOT THE FEVER, WHAT MORE DO I NEED?
June 1863. On the Mississippi River, outside Vicksburg.
Nobody knew just what caused it, the deadly disease we now call malaria.
This was before germ theory, before the concept of blood-borne disease.

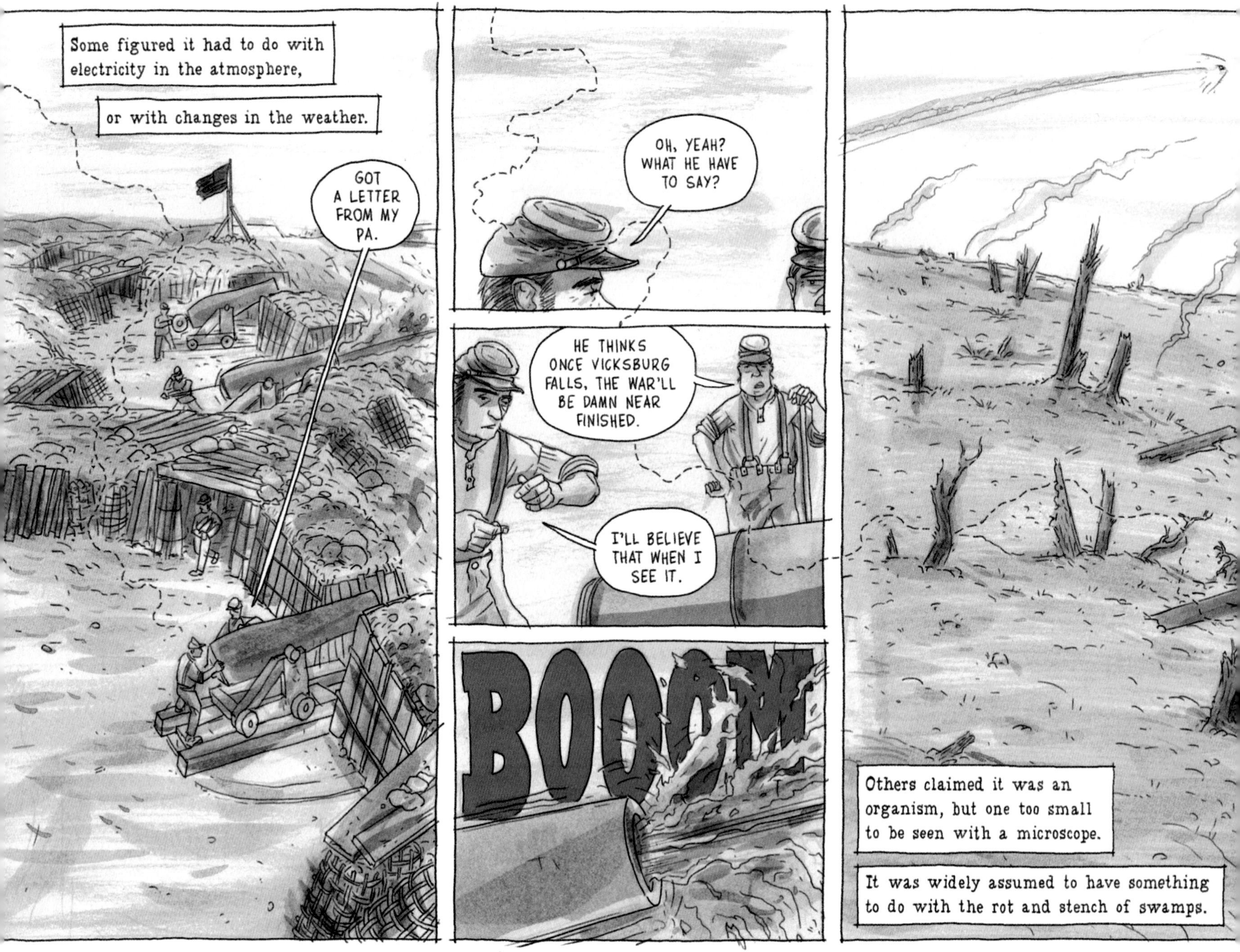
Some figured it had to do with electricity in the atmosphere,
or with changes in the weather.
GOT A LETTER FROM MY PA.
OH, YEAH? WHAT HE HAVE TO SAY?
HE THINKS ONCE VICKSBURG FALLS, THE WAR'LL BE DAMN NEAR FINISHED.
I'LL BELIEVE THAT WHEN I SEE IT.
BOOOM
Others claimed it was an organism, but one too small to be seen with a microscope.
It was widely assumed to have something to do with the rot and stench of swamps.

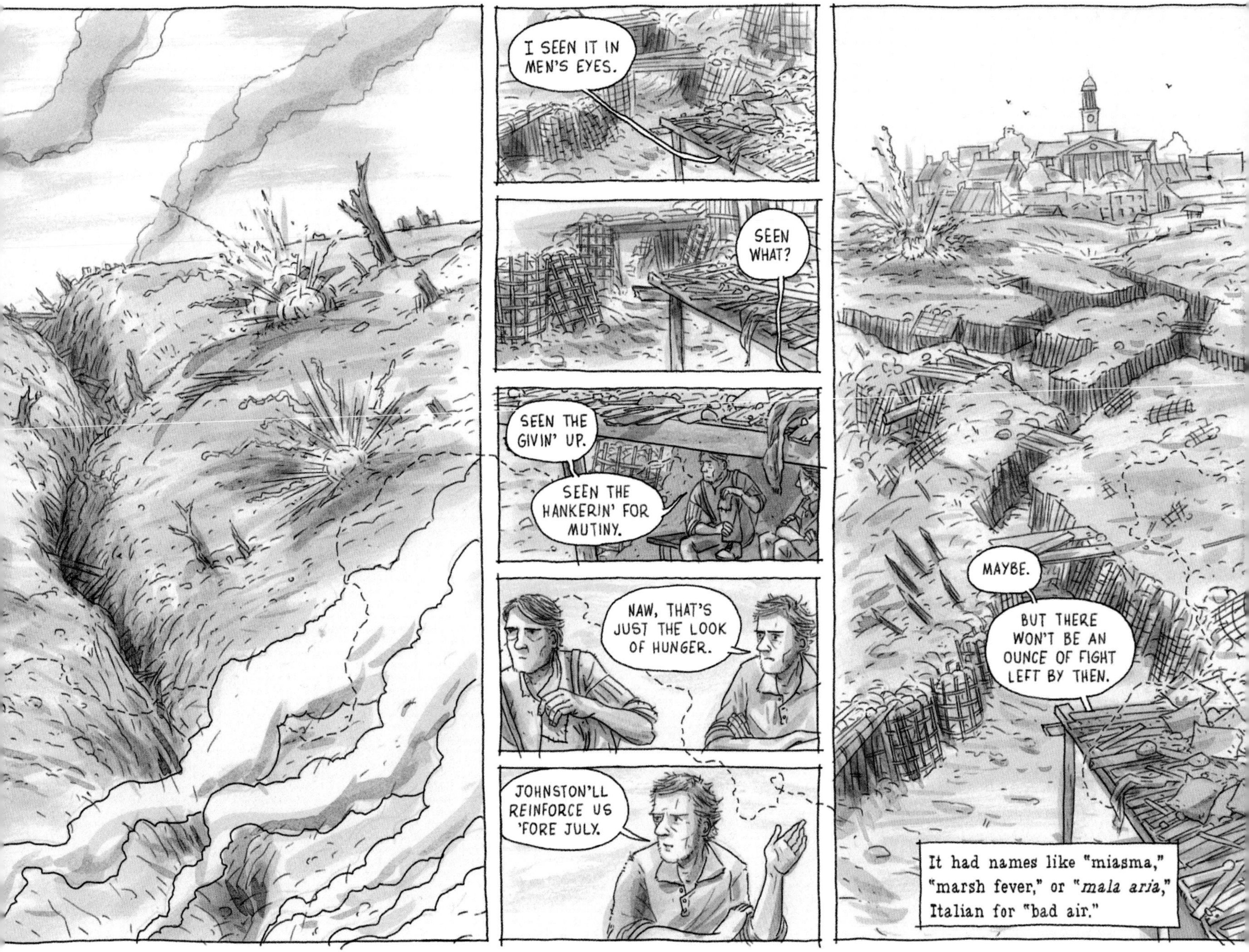

I SEEN IT IN MEN'S EYES.
SEEN WHAT?
SEEN THE GIVIN' UP.
SEEN THE HANKERIN' FOR MUTINY.
NAW, THAT'S JUST THE LOOK OF HUNGER.
JOHNSTON'LL REINFORCE US 'FORE JULY.
MAYBE.
BUT THERE WON'T BE AN OUNCE OF FIGHT LEFT BY THEN.
It had names like "miasma," "marsh fever," or "*mala aria*," Italian for "bad air."

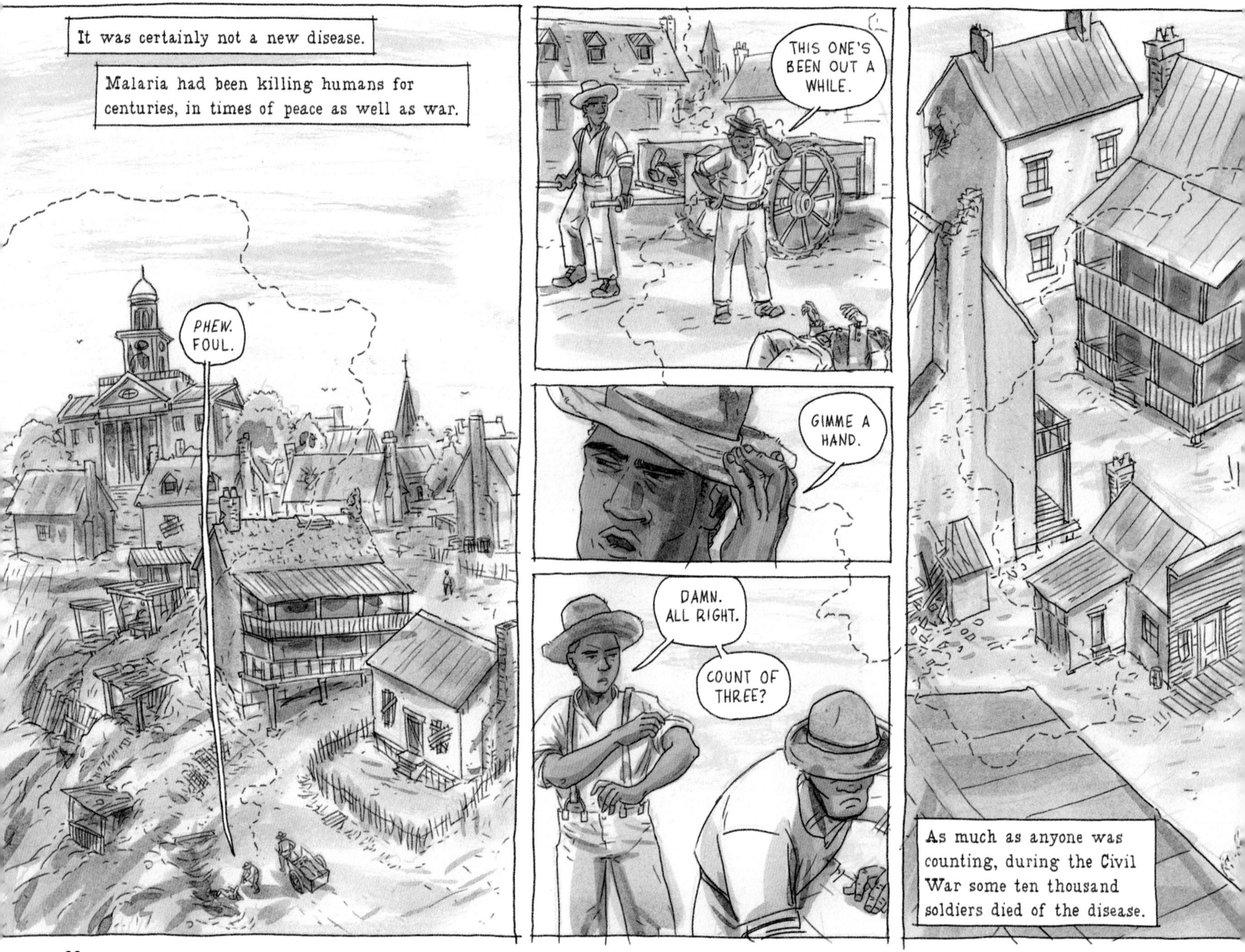

It was certainly not a new disease.
Malaria had been killing humans for centuries, in times of peace as well as war.
PHEW. FOUL.
THIS ONE'S BEEN OUT A WHILE.
GIMME A HAND.
DAMN. ALL RIGHT.
COUNT OF THREE?
As much as anyone was counting, during the Civil War some ten thousand soldiers died of the disease.

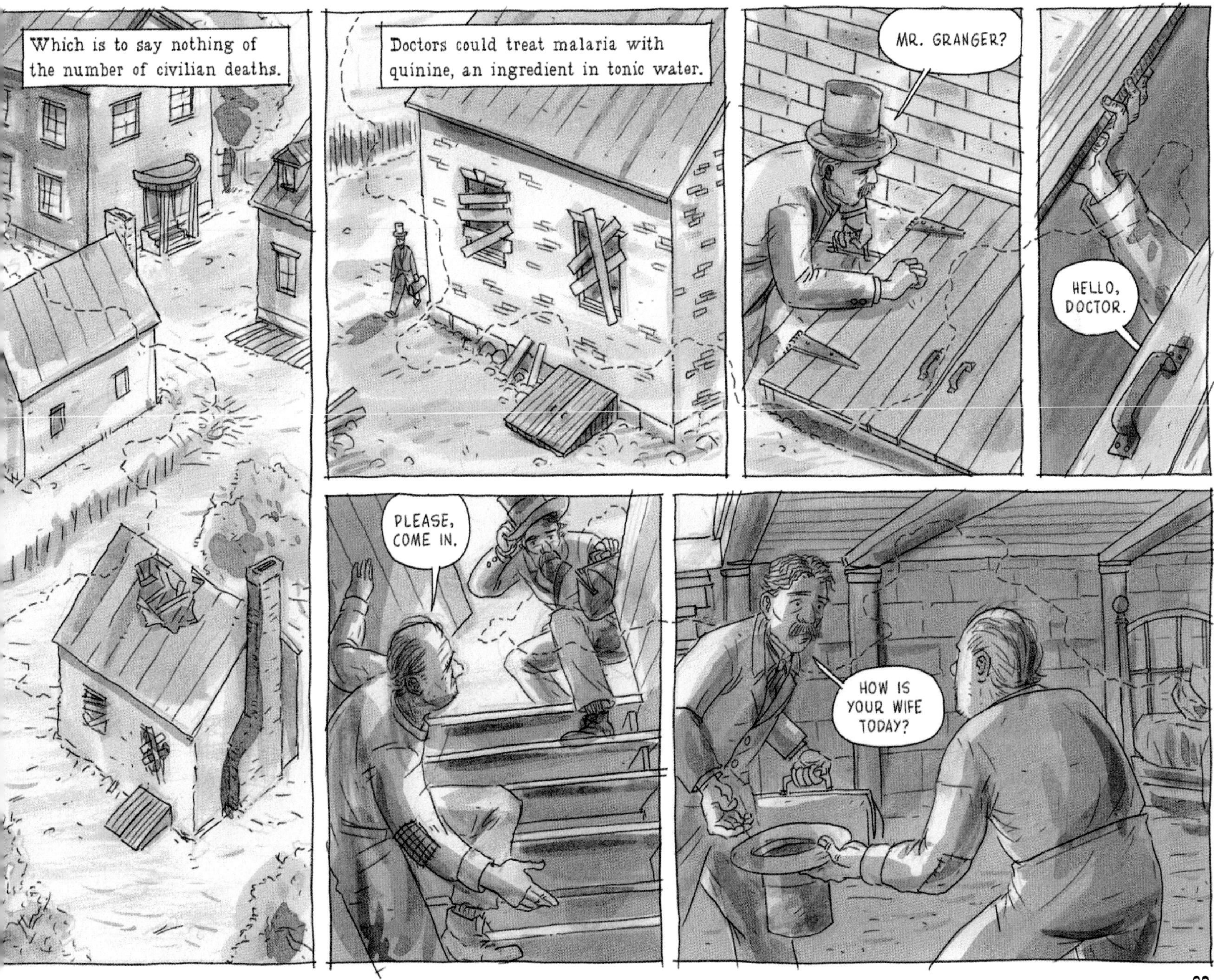
Which is to say nothing of the number of civilian deaths.
Doctors could treat malaria with quinine, an ingredient in tonic water.
MR. GRANGER?
HELLO, DOCTOR.
PLEASE, COME IN.
HOW IS YOUR WIFE TODAY?

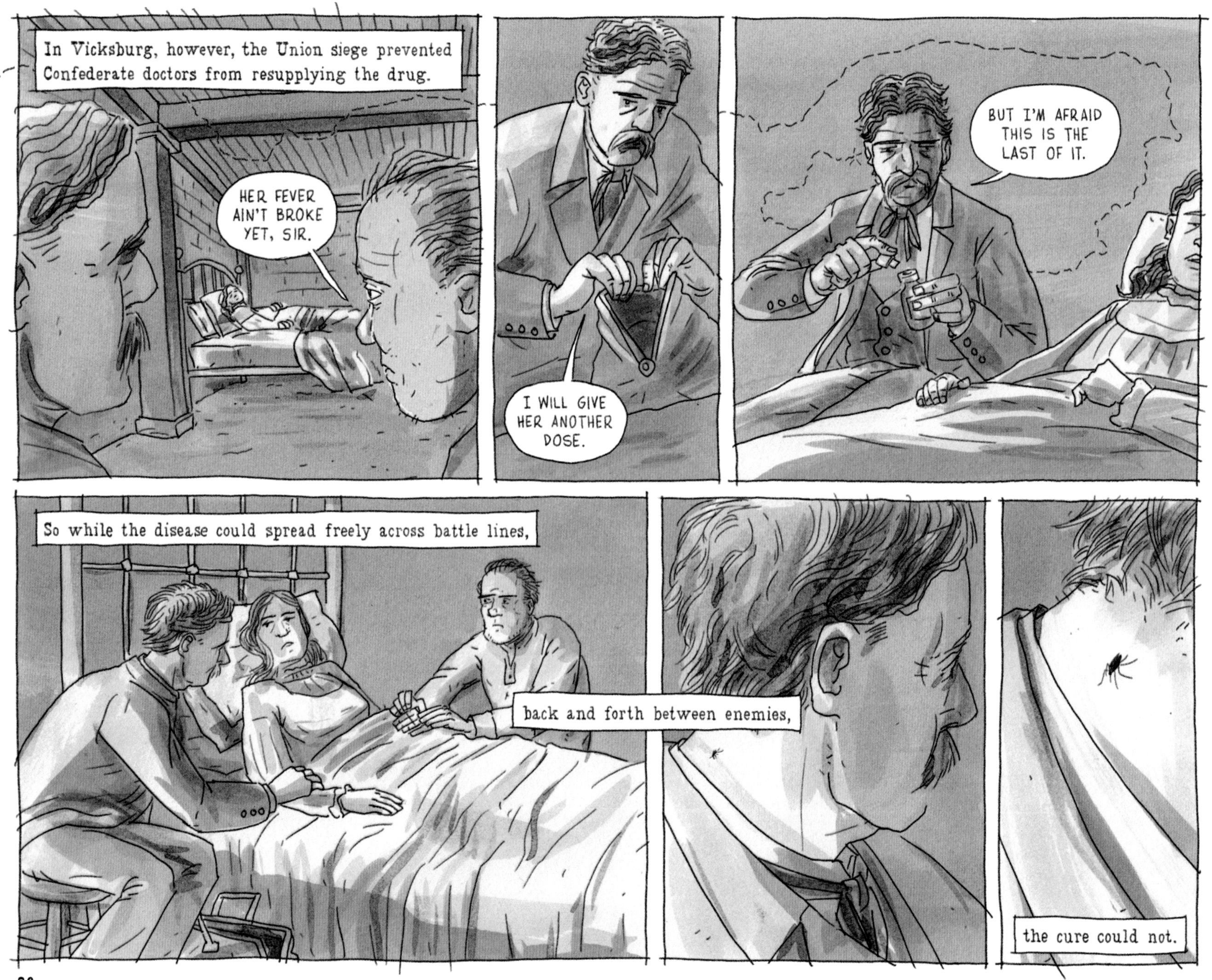
In Vicksburg, however, the Union siege prevented Confederate doctors from resupplying the drug.
HER FEVER AIN'T BROKE YET, SIR.
I WILL GIVE HER ANOTHER DOSE.
BUT I'M AFRAID THIS IS THE LAST OF IT.
So while the disease could spread freely across battle lines,
back and forth between enemies,
the cure could not.

Chapter 8: A Photograph

HARRISBURG BULLETIN

June 30, 1863

LINCOLN STILL LOOKING FOR RIGHT MAN TO LEAD ARMY OF THE POTOMAC

Ambrose Burnside, despite the majesty of his side-whiskers, lost the confidence of his men at Fredericksburg. President Lincoln then turned to Joseph Hooker to command the Army of the Potomac. In April 1863, Hooker's men executed a series of daring maneuvers designed to lure General Lee's Army of Northern Virginia from the trenches.

But early in May, Hooker found himself tactically overmatched by Lee and his trusted subordinates, cavalry commander Jeb Stuart and Lieutenant General Stonewall Jackson, at the Battle of Chancellorsville. Across four terrible days, more than thirty thousand soldiers were killed or wounded: some seventeen thousand Union men and approximately thirteen thousand rebels. General Lee won a resounding victory over Hooker but lost one of his most important assets in the battle: a wounded Stonewall Jackson died of pneumonia less than a week later.

Shortly afterward, in mid-May, Lee conferred with Jefferson Davis and his cabinet. The Confederate high command hoped to provide aid and comfort to antiwar Democrats in the North by invading the Union for a second time (the invasion of Maryland, culminating in the Battle of Antietam, being the first). Lincoln realized that public opinion of his presidency rose and fell with news from the front lines, and he grew increasingly despondent as General Hooker continued to blunder. Three days before the Battle of Gettysburg, Lincoln relieved Hooker of command, putting George Meade in charge of the Union army.

COPPERHEADS
Strike in the North

With the Army of the Potomac recovering from bloodlettings at Fredericksburg and Chancellorsville, and General Grant still trying to solve the riddle of Vicksburg, by spring 1863 many Northerners were tiring of war. Clement Vallandigham, a former congressman from Ohio, led the Democrats' peace wing, the Copperheads. Vallandigham was a vocal supporter of the idea of a negotiated settlement with the Confederacy. He argued that allowing the South to overturn emancipation would be a fair trade to end the war and prevent the continued slaughter of white soldiers from the North.

When, on May 1, military officials arrested Vallandigham on charges of disloyalty, President Lincoln faced a dilemma. He worried that antiwar rhetoric was gaining purchase among immigrants and working-class whites who had little interest in fighting to free the slaves. At the same time, he recognized that putting his opponent in prison would only make him a martyr to the Copperhead cause. Instead of keeping Vallandigham locked up, Lincoln banished him across the rebel lines.

Vallandigham then traveled to Ontario. From Canada, he campaigned to become governor of Ohio. Although he lost the election, the antiwar movement he led won new members.

Even as Lincoln challenged his critics by penning an open letter--asking, "Must I shoot a simple-minded soldier boy who deserts, while I must not touch a hair of the wily agitator who induces him to desert?"--more and more skeptics wondered if the war was still worth fighting.

RUMORS FROM THE FRONT ☞

Lee's Army on the March in Pennsylvania!

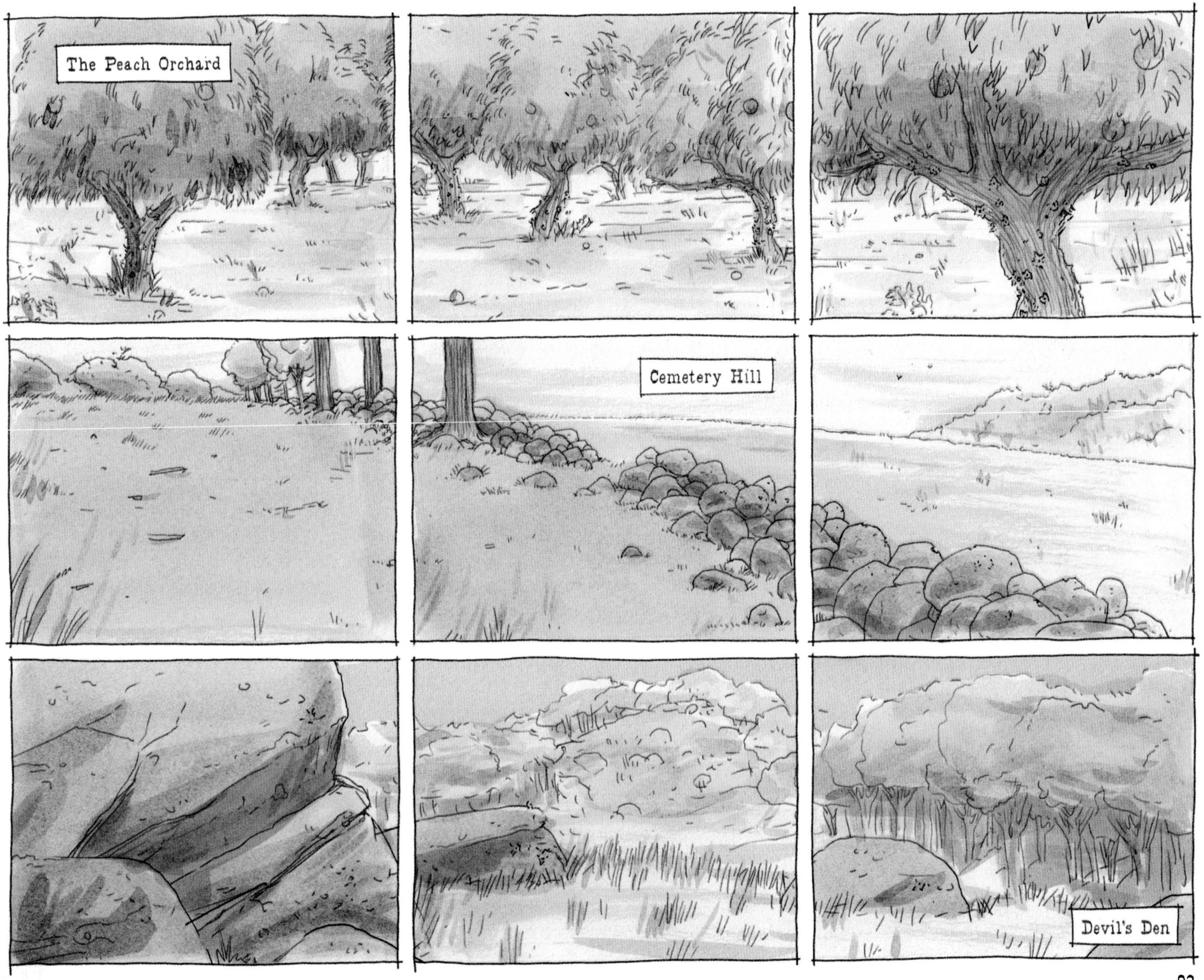
The Peach Orchard
Cemetery Hill
Devil's Den

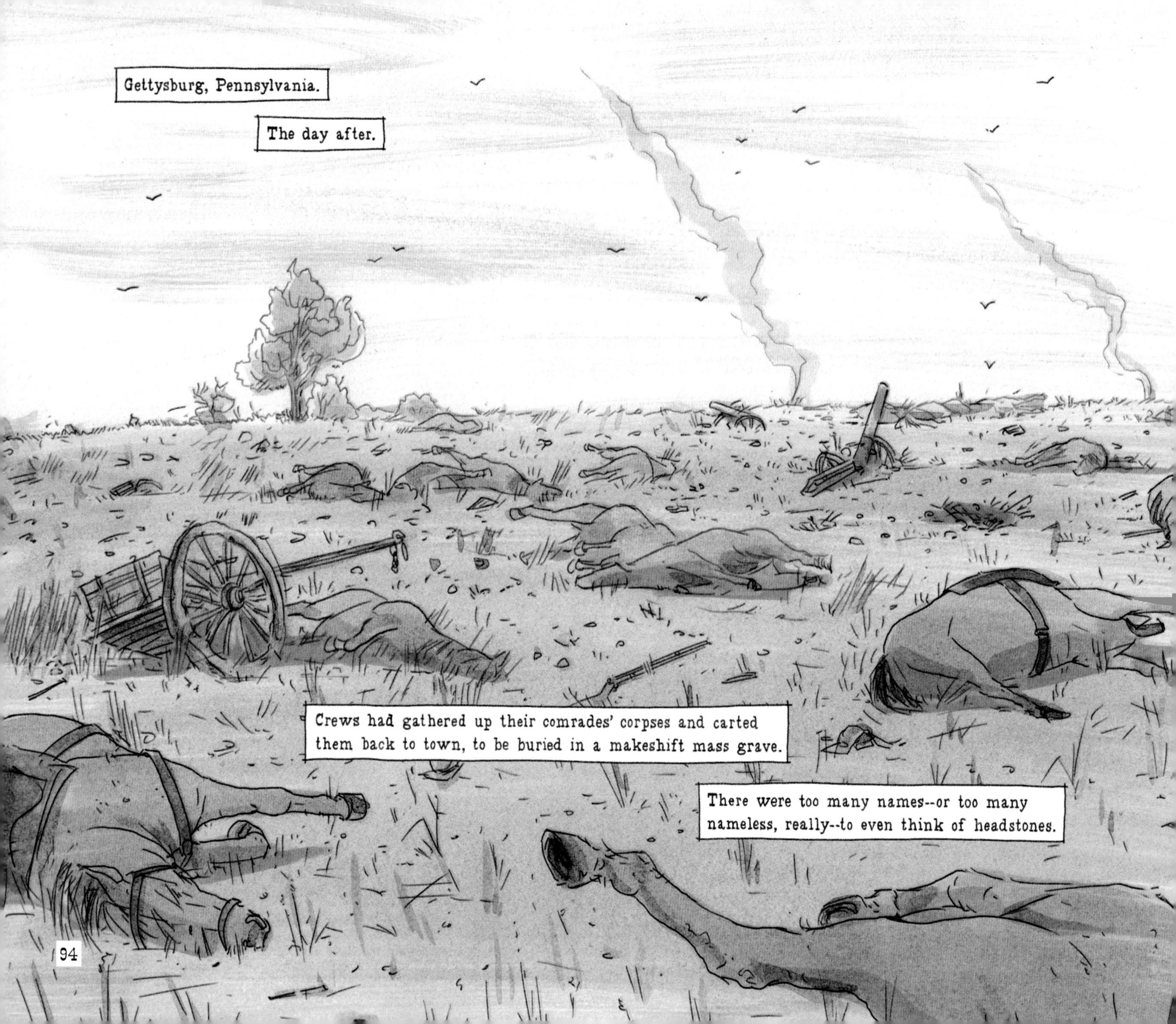
Gettysburg, Pennsylvania.
The day after.
Crews had gathered up their comrades' corpses and carted them back to town, to be buried in a makeshift mass grave.
There were too many names--or too many nameless, really--to even think of headstones.

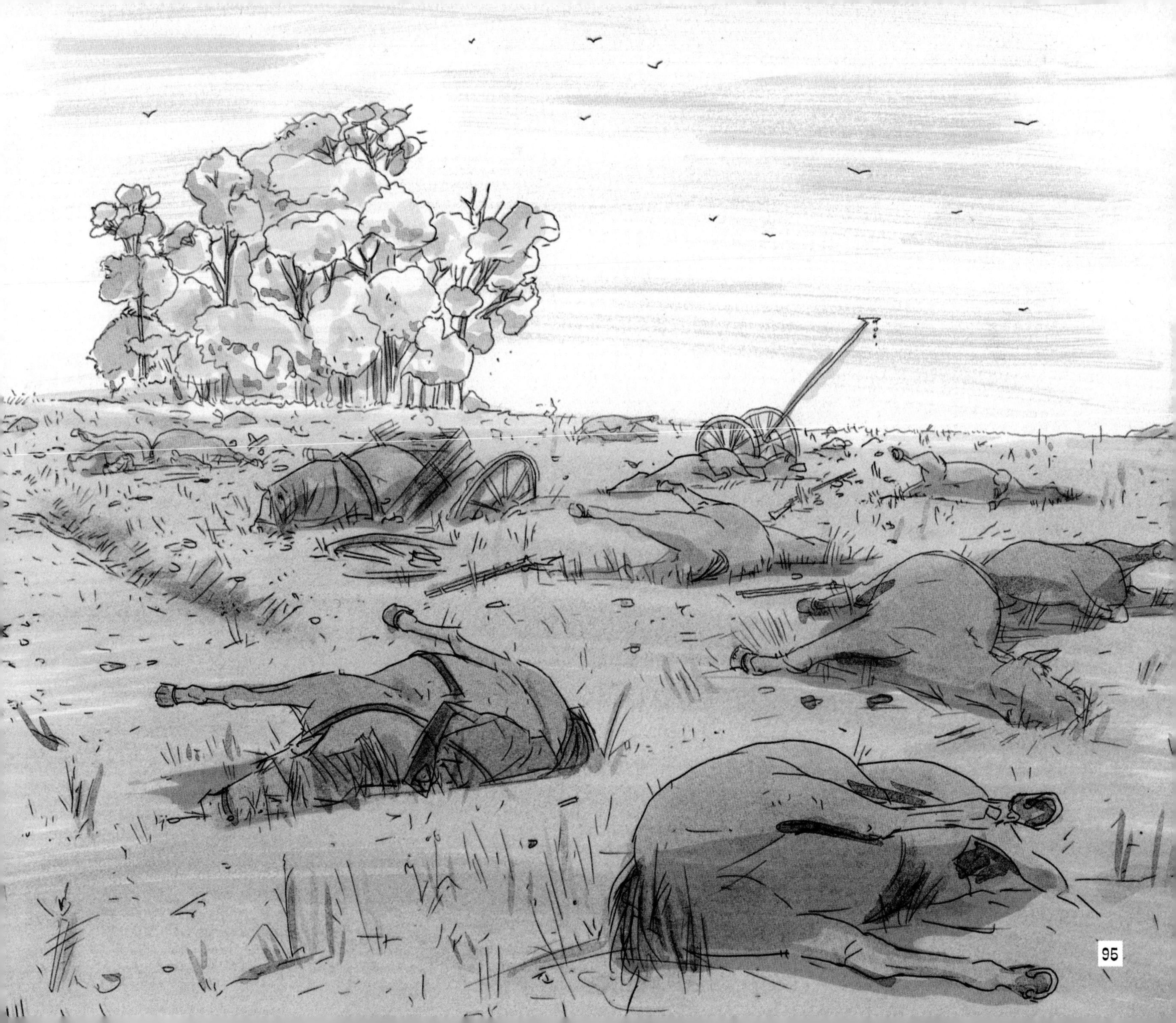

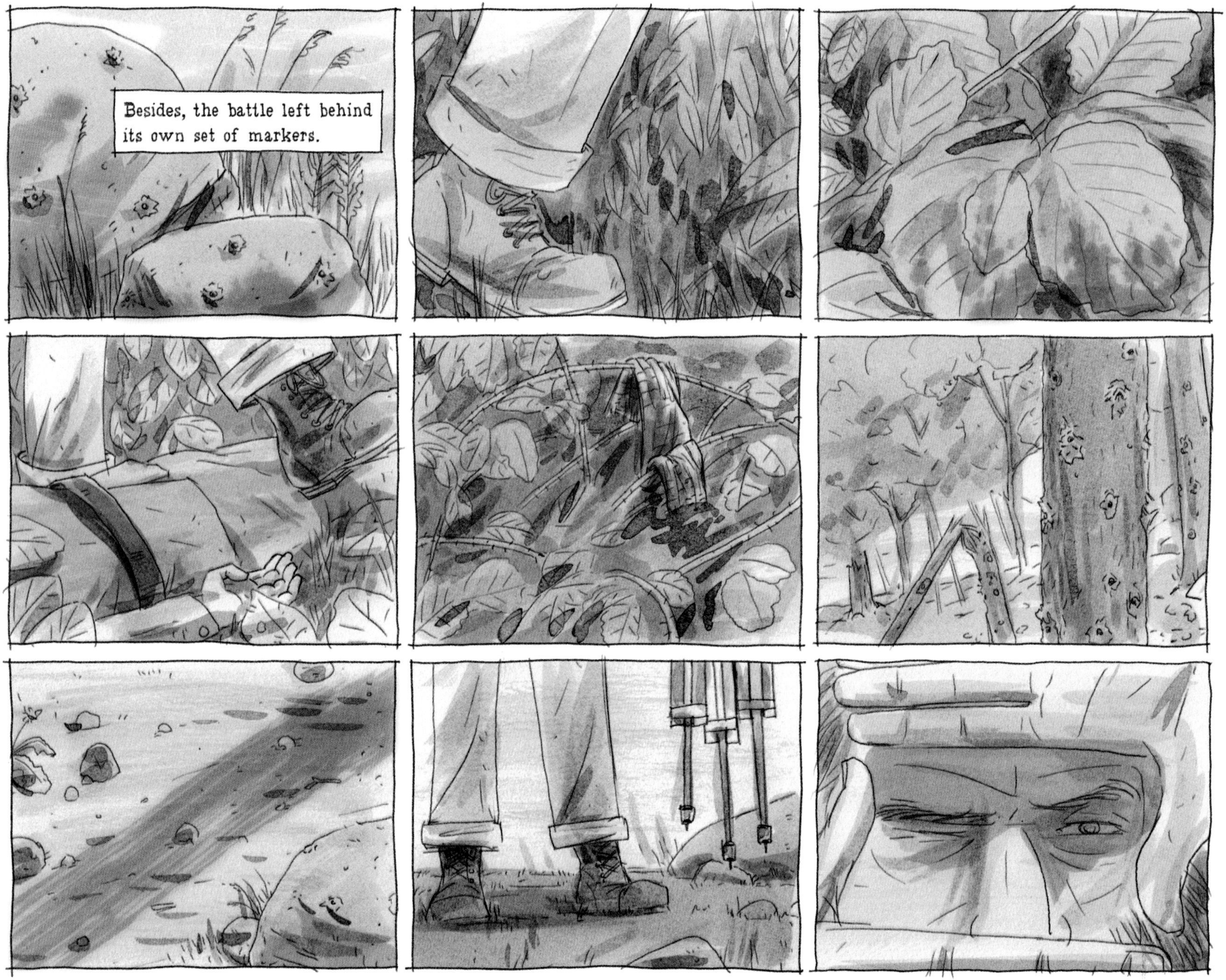
Besides, the battle left behind its own set of markers.

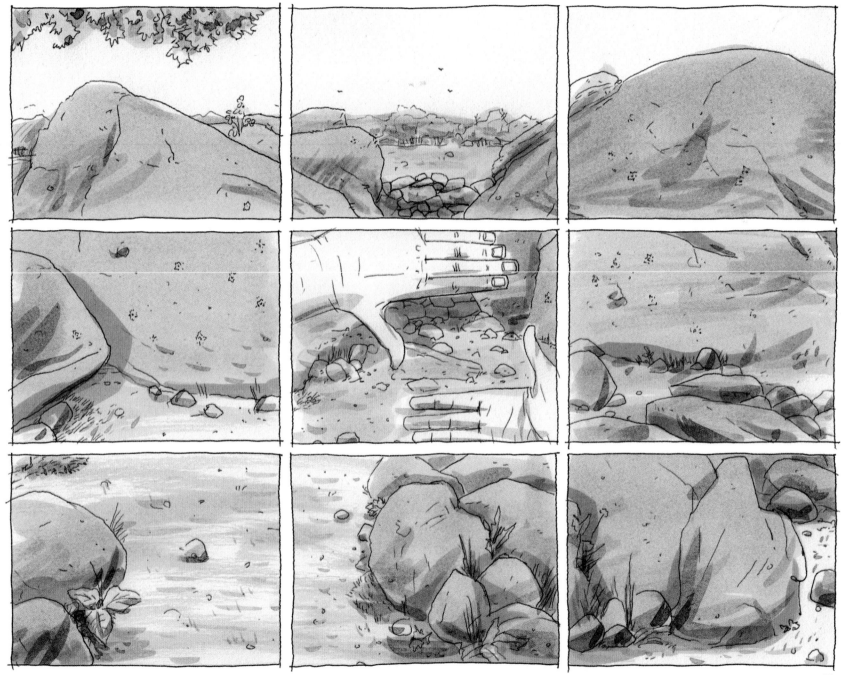

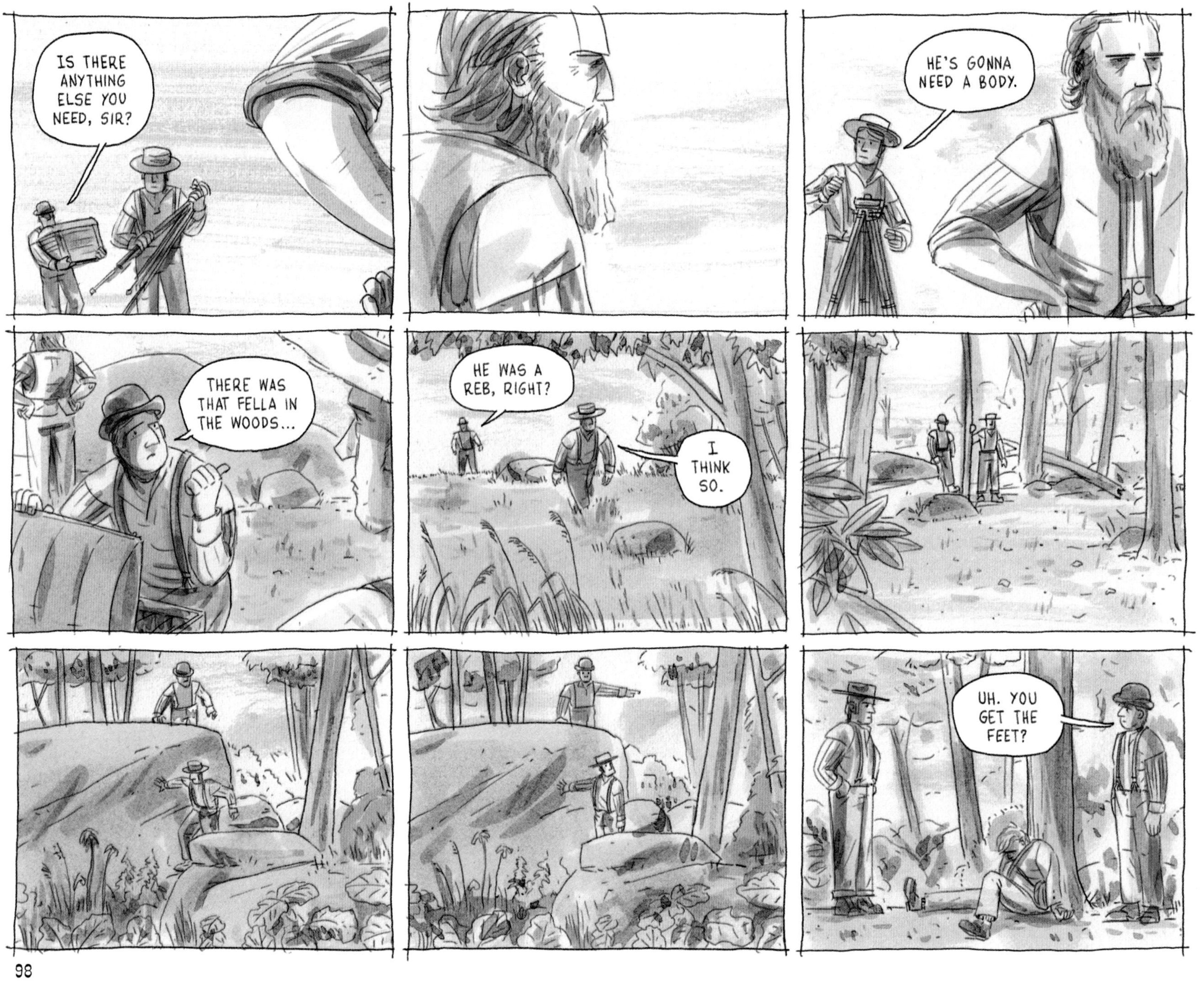
IS THERE ANYTHING ELSE YOU NEED, SIR?
HE'S GONNA NEED A BODY.
THERE WAS THAT FELLA IN THE WOODS...
HE WAS A REB, RIGHT?
I THINK SO.
UH. YOU GET THE FEET?

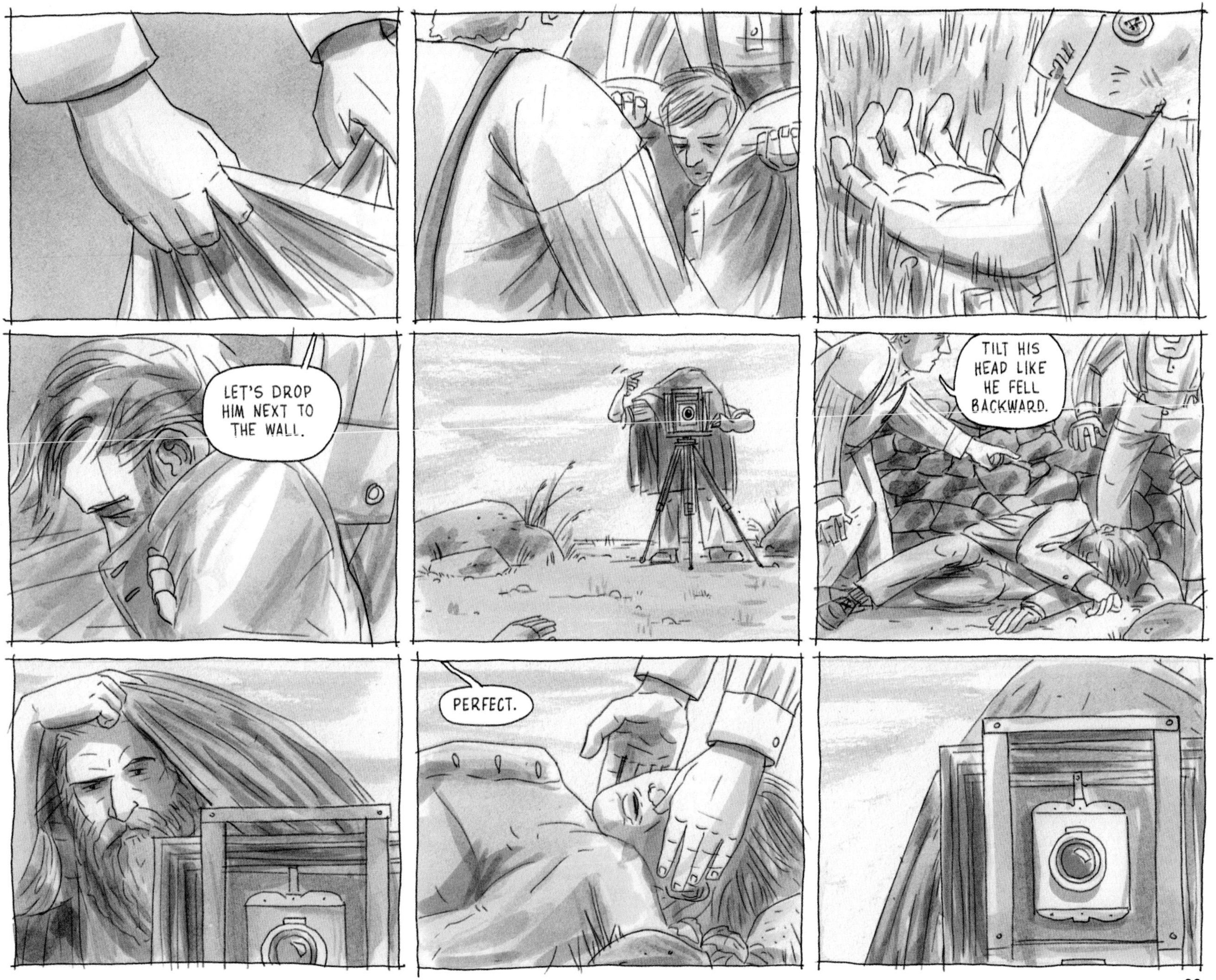
LET'S DROP HIM NEXT TO THE WALL.
TILT HIS HEAD LIKE HE FELL BACKWARD.
PERFECT.

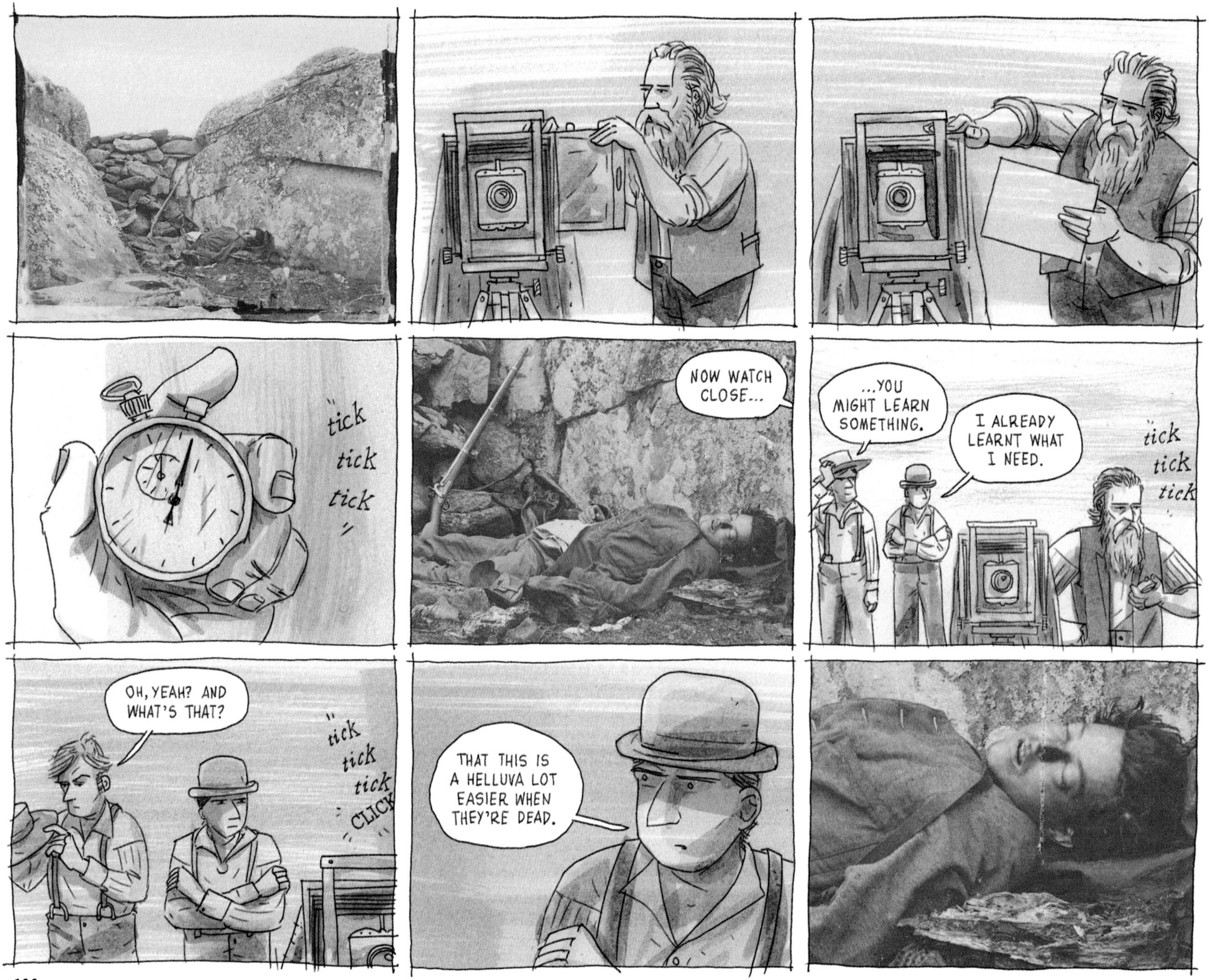
tick
tick
tick
NOW WATCH CLOSE...
...YOU MIGHT LEARN SOMETHING.
I ALREADY LEARNT WHAT I NEED.
tick
tick
tick
OH, YEAH? AND WHAT'S THAT?
tick
tick
tick
CLICK
THAT THIS IS A HELLUVA LOT EASIER WHEN THEY'RE DEAD.

Chapter 9: Draft Numbers

NEW YORK TELEGRAPH

July 17, 1863

UNION VICTORIES!

Gettysburg, Vicksburg, and Elsewhere

During the first three days of July 1863, in fields and orchards outside Gettysburg, Pennsylvania--a landscape that would, months later, be consecrated as hallowed ground by President Lincoln--the men of George Meade's Army of the Potomac turned back Robert E. Lee's invasion of the North. The victory came at a horrifying cost: some twenty-eight thousand Federal troops were killed and wounded alongside thirty-two thousand rebel casualties. It was the bloodiest confrontation of the war.

On the day after fighting ended, Independence Day, roughly a thousand miles to the southwest, Ulysses S. Grant's men took Vicksburg, the "Gibraltar of the West," thus ending a long and brutal campaign and siege. While Meade allowed the Army of Northern Virginia to escape, further prolonging the war, Grant occupied Vicksburg and then turned his attention elsewhere. Union soldiers in the West began driving Confederate forces out of Tennessee.

Despite losing the Western Theater's bloodiest battle at Chickamauga late in September--some sixteen thousand bluecoats were killed and wounded compared to more than eighteen thousand Southern troops--by year's end the Union would control most of the region.

With the momentum of Union victories in the West propelling him, General Sherman planned a campaign to take Atlanta the following spring.

Meanwhile, the Federal high command began the process of transforming its forces in the West from an army of conquest into an army of occupation. Confederate citizens resented the Yankees' presence, and Northern soldiers, in turn, came to realize that their role as occupiers brought with it a whole new set of challenges.

General Grant

CONGRESS AUTHORIZES DRAFT
For All Men Ages 20 to 45

On March 3, 1863, months in advance of the fall of Vicksburg and the Army of the Potomac's victory at Gettysburg, the U.S. Congress authorized a draft, mimicking a decision made by the Confederacy a year earlier.

Unlike in the South, though, the economy in the North was booming, so jobs outside military service were plentiful. At the same time, the grim realities of the war had become impossible to ignore, leaving recruiters frustrated by a lack of volunteers. Federal authorities hoped the threat of conscription would foster a surge of enlistments.

The draft did that, but it also offered Democrats more fodder for their attacks on the Lincoln administration and the Republican Party. And much as in the Confederacy, the implementation of the draft deepened class and ethnic antagonisms in the North. The fact that relatively well-heeled draftees could buy their way out of service--either by hiring a substitute or by paying a $300 commutation fee-- antagonized the working classes, immigrants especially, who often despised a war that Democratic leaders insisted was being fought only for abolition.

RUMORS FROM THE FRONT ☞

Riots in New York City!

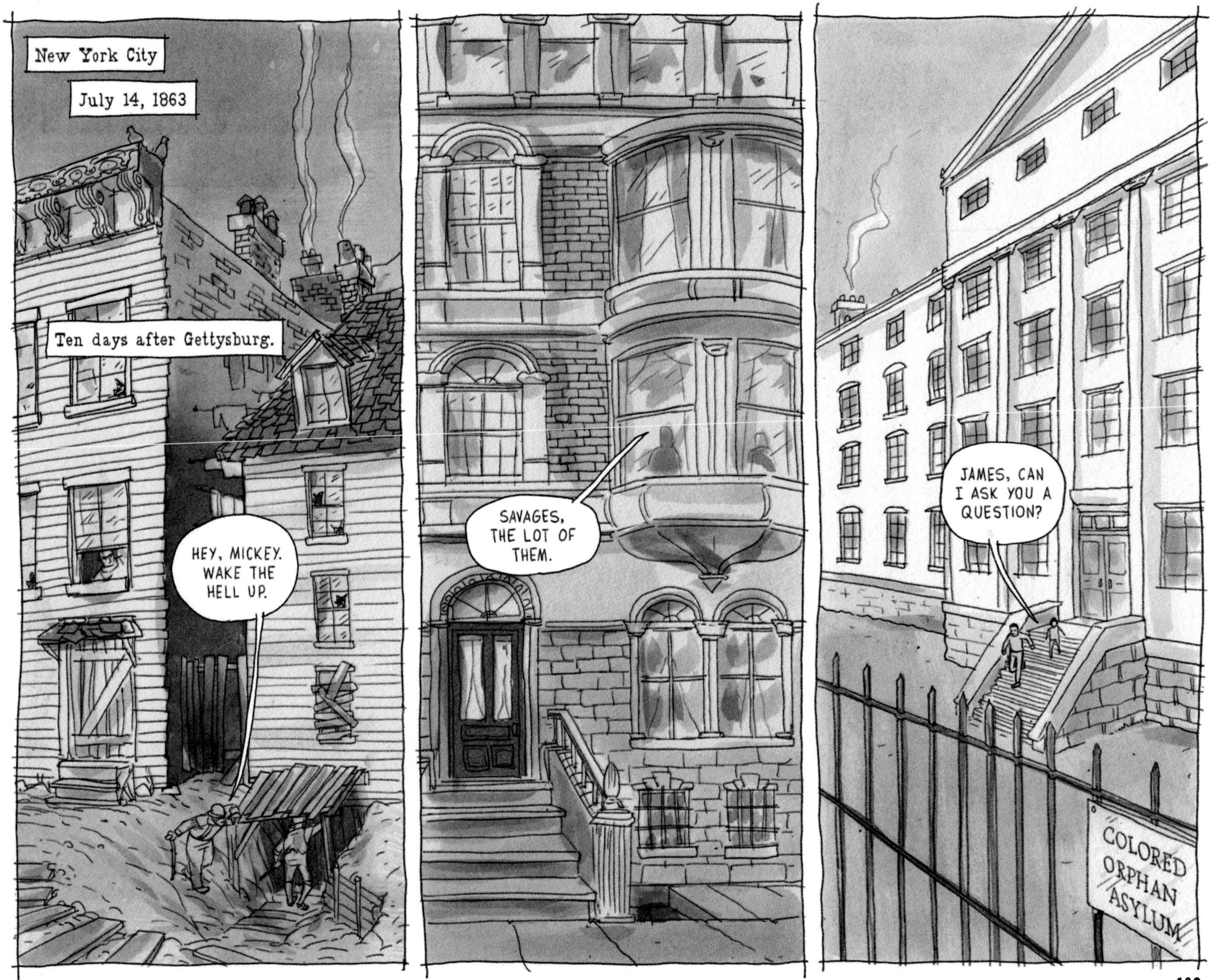

New York City
July 14, 1863
Ten days after Gettysburg.
HEY, MICKEY. WAKE THE HELL UP.
SAVAGES, THE LOT OF THEM.
JAMES, CAN I ASK YOU A QUESTION?
COLORED ORPHAN ASYLUM

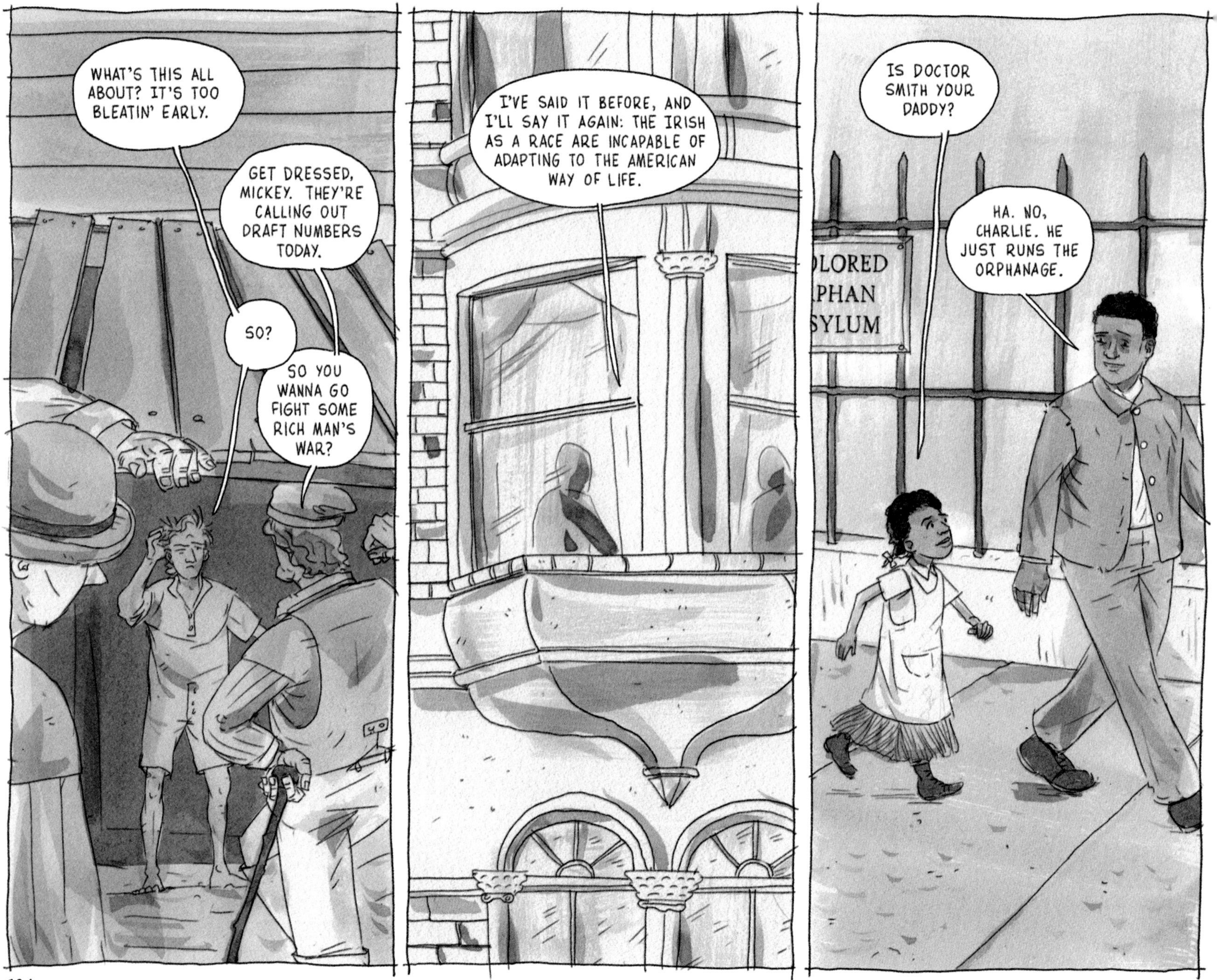
WHAT'S THIS ALL ABOUT? IT'S TOO BLEATIN' EARLY.
GET DRESSED, MICKEY. THEY'RE CALLING OUT DRAFT NUMBERS TODAY.
SO?
SO YOU WANNA GO FIGHT SOME RICH MAN'S WAR?
I'VE SAID IT BEFORE, AND I'LL SAY IT AGAIN: THE IRISH AS A RACE ARE INCAPABLE OF ADAPTING TO THE AMERICAN WAY OF LIFE.
OLORED
PHAN
SYLUM
IS DOCTOR SMITH YOUR DADDY?
HA. NO, CHARLIE. HE JUST RUNS THE ORPHANAGE.

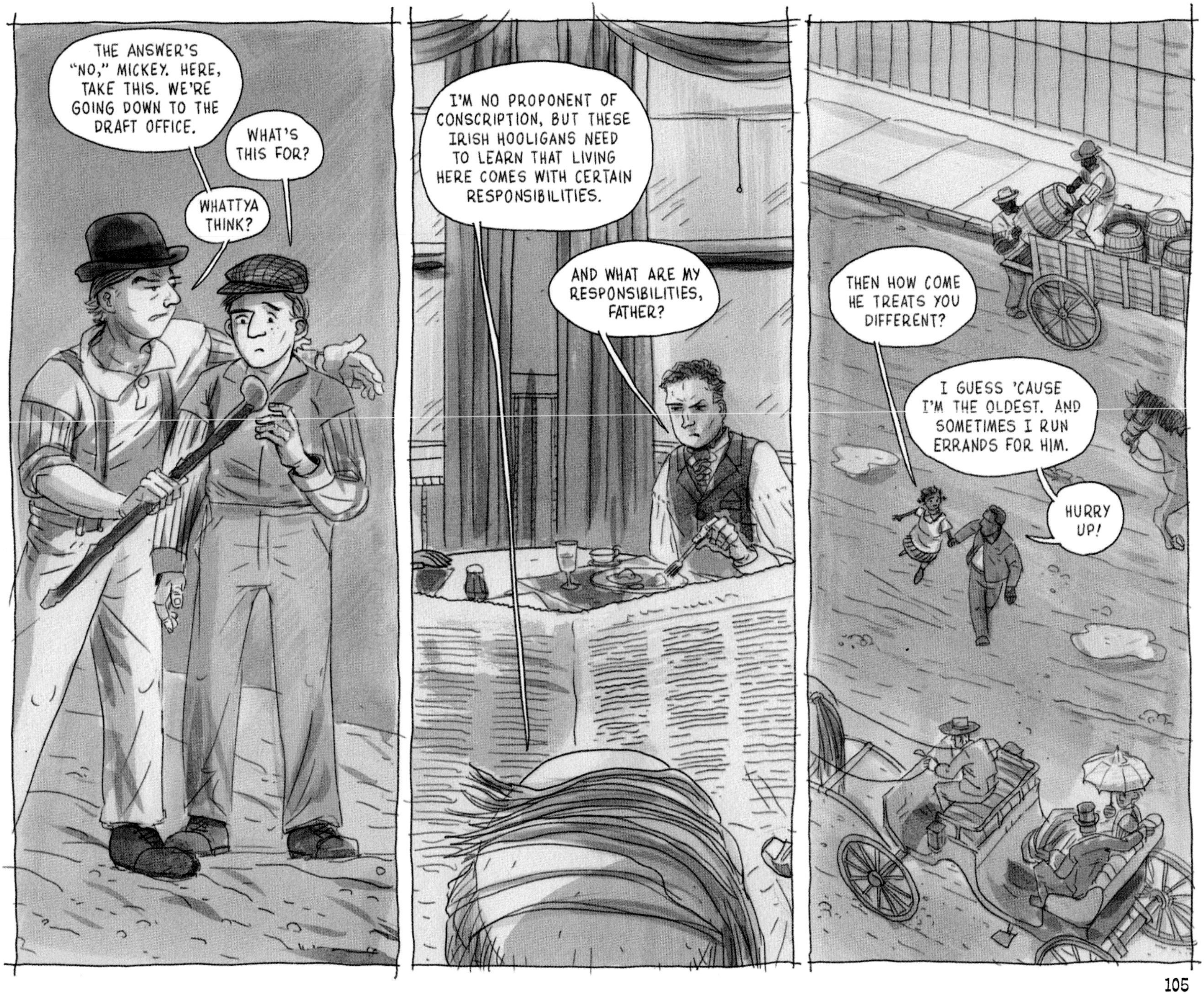
THE ANSWER'S "NO," MICKEY. HERE, TAKE THIS. WE'RE GOING DOWN TO THE DRAFT OFFICE.
WHAT'S THIS FOR?
WHATTYA THINK?
I'M NO PROPONENT OF CONSCRIPTION, BUT THESE IRISH HOOLIGANS NEED TO LEARN THAT LIVING HERE COMES WITH CERTAIN RESPONSIBILITIES.
AND WHAT ARE MY RESPONSIBILITIES, FATHER?
THEN HOW COME HE TREATS YOU DIFFERENT?
I GUESS 'CAUSE I'M THE OLDEST. AND SOMETIMES I RUN ERRANDS FOR HIM.
HURRY UP!

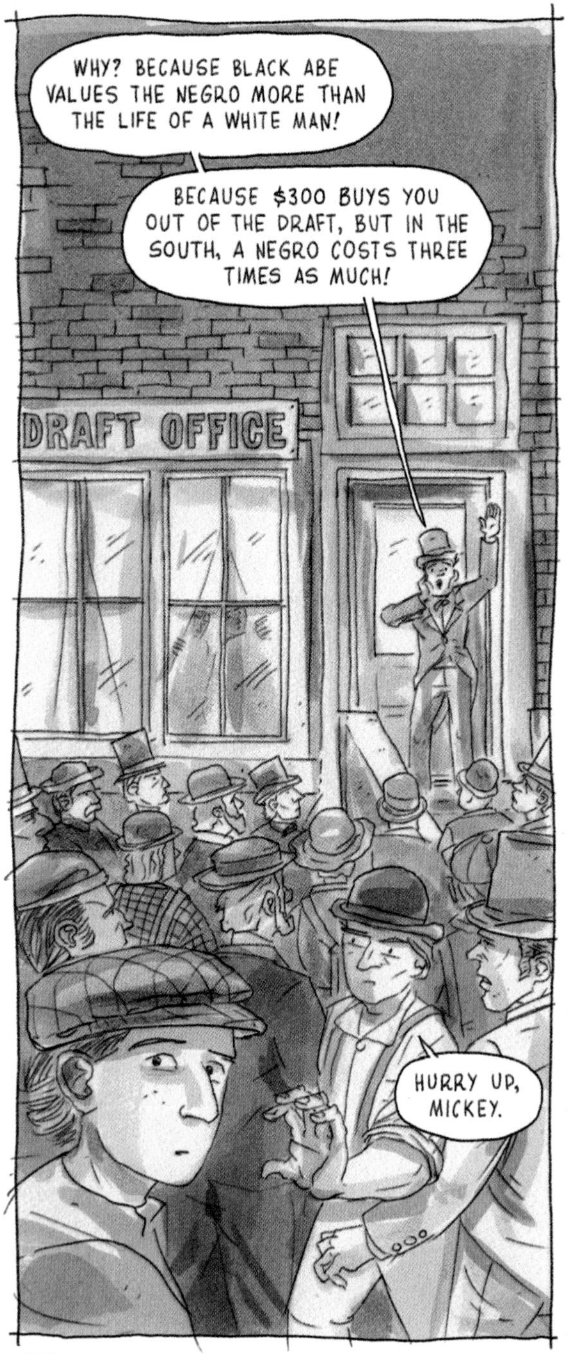
DRAFT OFFICE
WHY? BECAUSE BLACK ABE VALUES THE NEGRO MORE THAN THE LIFE OF A WHITE MAN!
BECAUSE $300 BUYS YOU OUT OF THE DRAFT, BUT IN THE SOUTH, A NEGRO COSTS THREE TIMES AS MUCH!
HURRY UP, MICKEY.
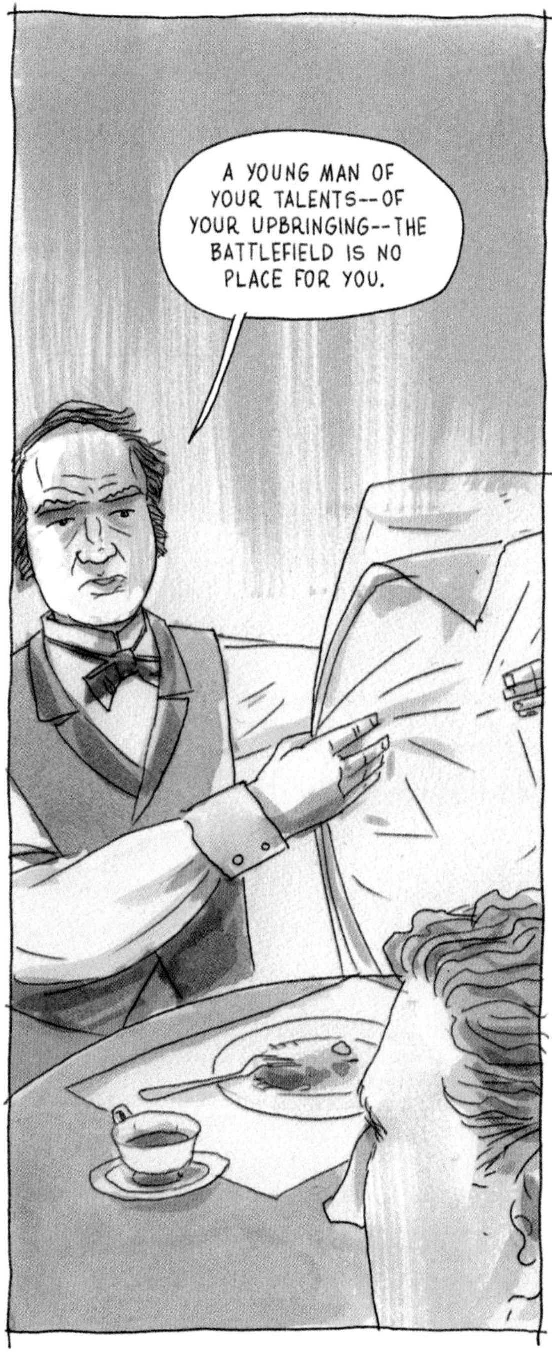
A YOUNG MAN OF YOUR TALENTS--OF YOUR UPBRINGING--THE BATTLEFIELD IS NO PLACE FOR YOU.
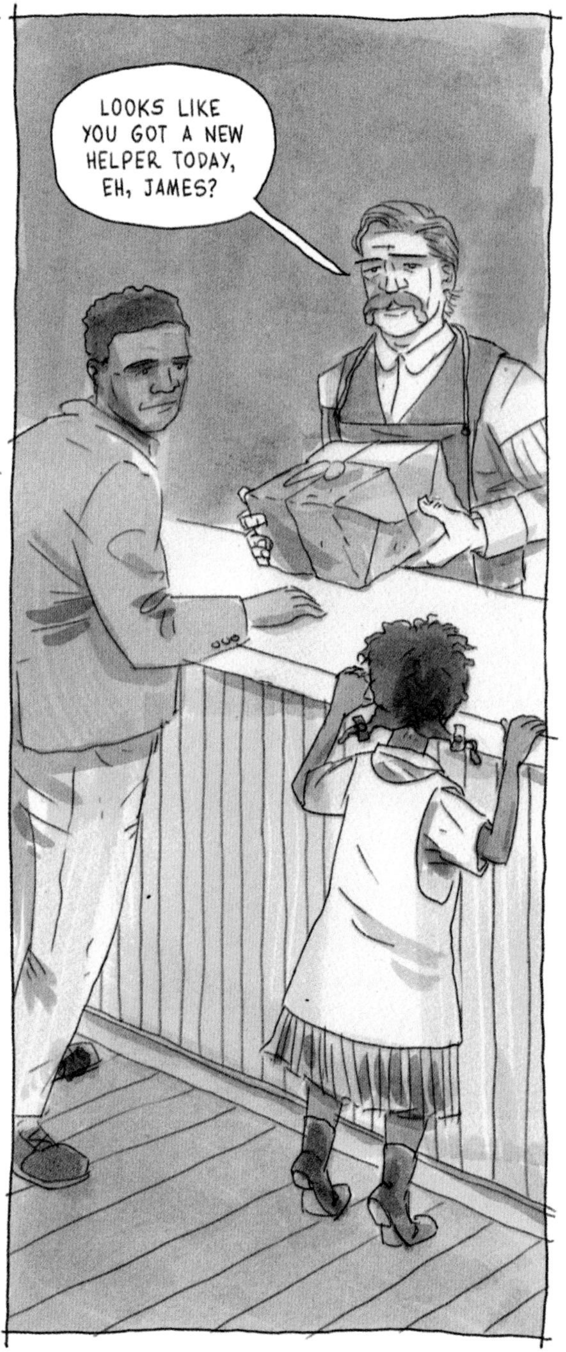
LOOKS LIKE YOU GOT A NEW HELPER TODAY, EH, JAMES?

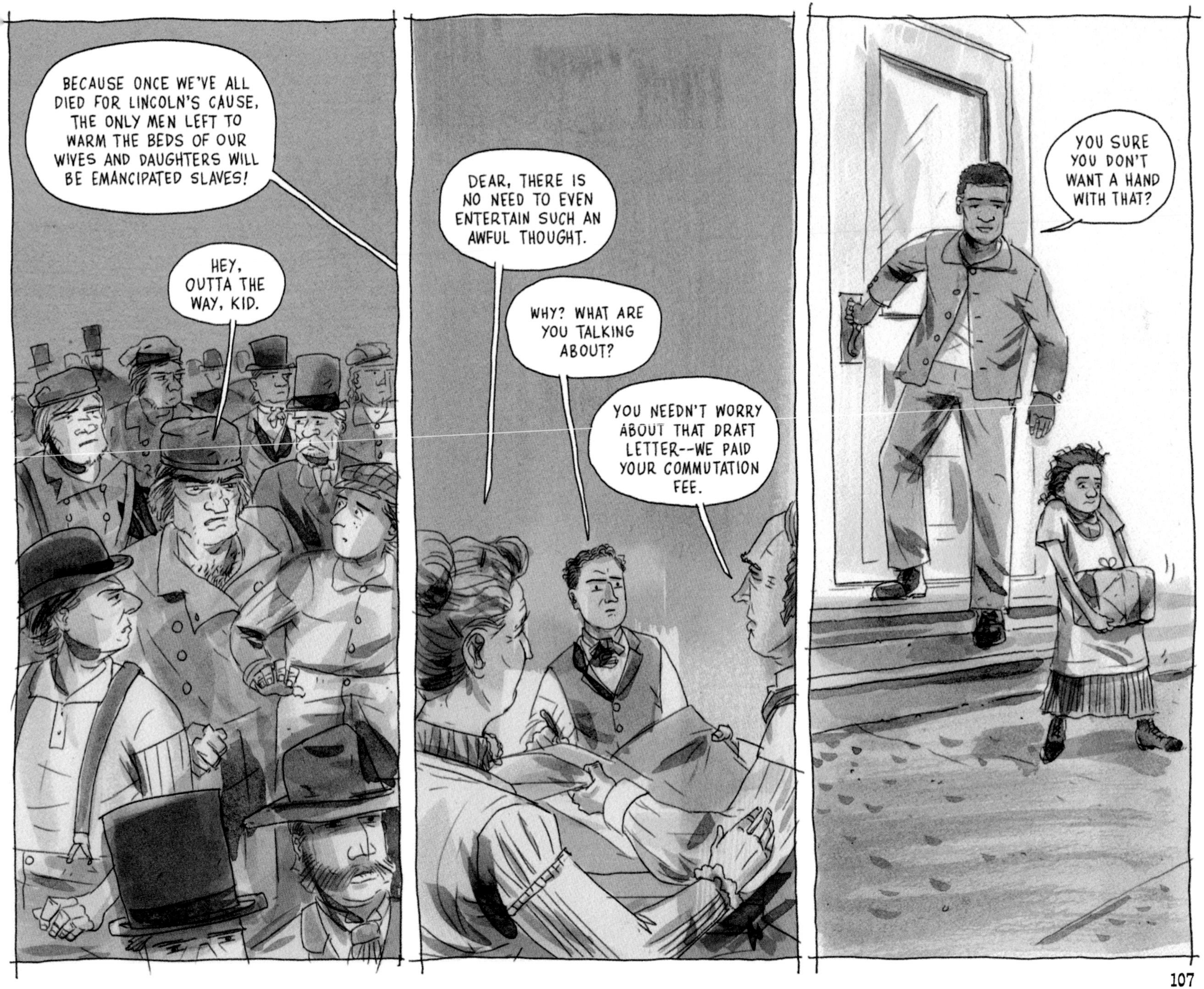
BECAUSE ONCE WE'VE ALL DIED FOR LINCOLN'S CAUSE, THE ONLY MEN LEFT TO WARM THE BEDS OF OUR WIVES AND DAUGHTERS WILL BE EMANCIPATED SLAVES!
HEY, OUTTA THE WAY, KID.
DEAR, THERE IS NO NEED TO EVEN ENTERTAIN SUCH AN AWFUL THOUGHT.
WHY? WHAT ARE YOU TALKING ABOUT?
YOU NEEDN'T WORRY ABOUT THAT DRAFT LETTER--WE PAID YOUR COMMUTATION FEE.
YOU SURE YOU DON'T WANT A HAND WITH THAT?

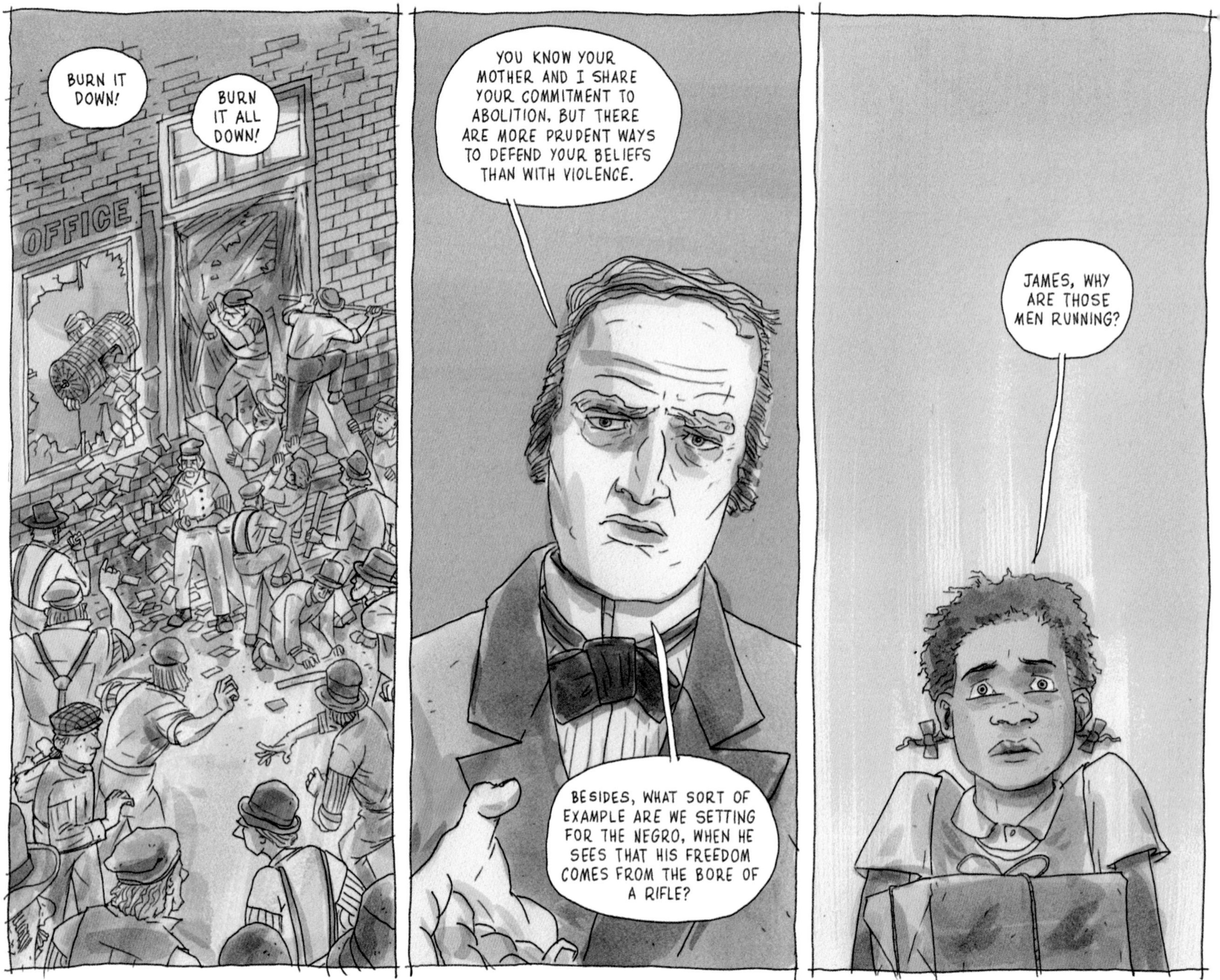
BURN IT DOWN!
BURN IT ALL DOWN!
OFFICE
YOU KNOW YOUR MOTHER AND I SHARE YOUR COMMITMENT TO ABOLITION, BUT THERE ARE MORE PRUDENT WAYS TO DEFEND YOUR BELIEFS THAN WITH VIOLENCE.
BESIDES, WHAT SORT OF EXAMPLE ARE WE SETTING FOR THE NEGRO, WHEN HE SEES THAT HIS FREEDOM COMES FROM THE BORE OF A RIFLE?
JAMES, WHY ARE THOSE MEN RUNNING?

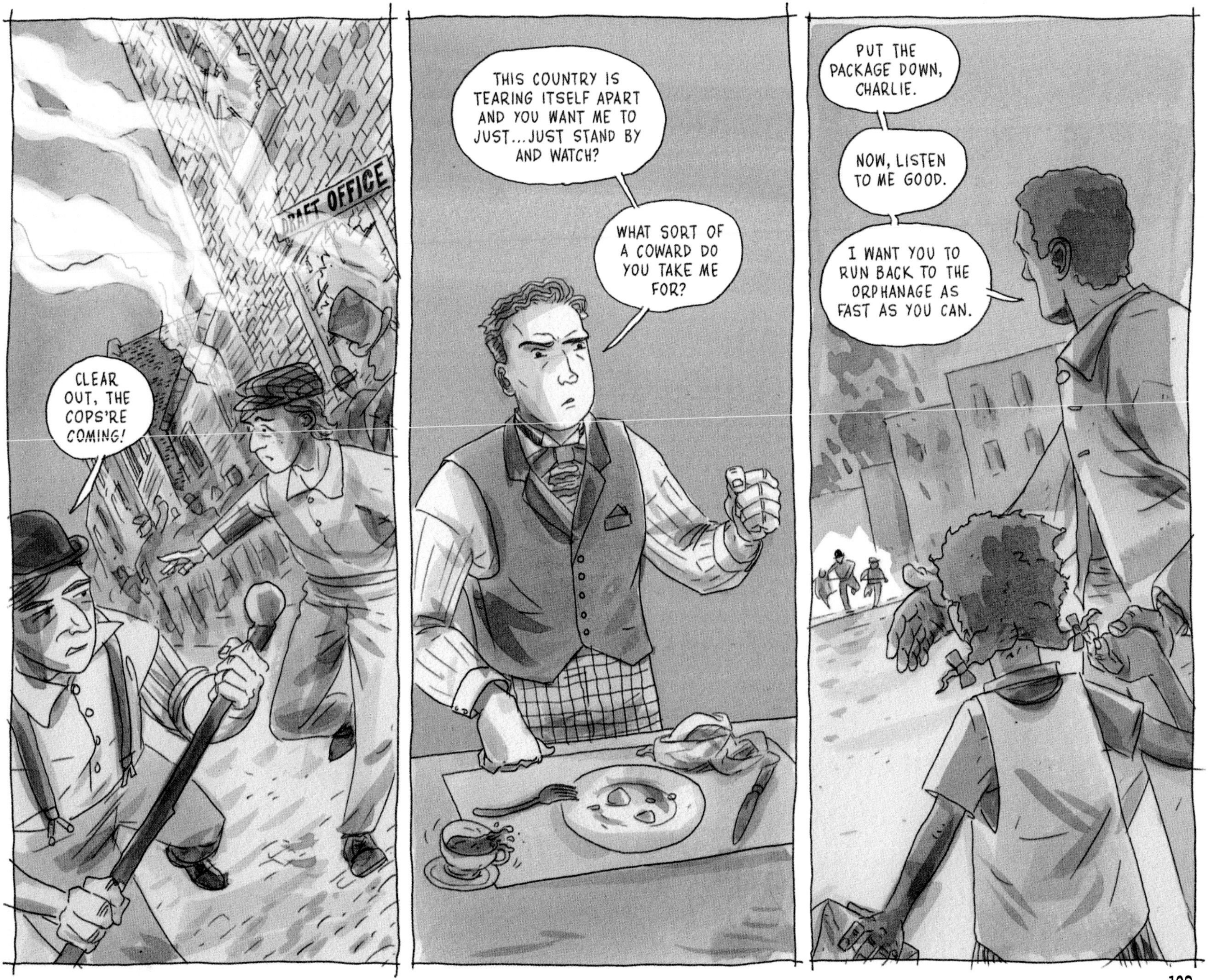
DRAFT OFFICE
CLEAR OUT, THE COPS'RE COMING!
THIS COUNTRY IS TEARING ITSELF APART AND YOU WANT ME TO JUST...JUST STAND BY AND WATCH?
WHAT SORT OF A COWARD DO YOU TAKE ME FOR?
PUT THE PACKAGE DOWN, CHARLIE.
NOW, LISTEN TO ME GOOD.
I WANT YOU TO RUN BACK TO THE ORPHANAGE AS FAST AS YOU CAN.

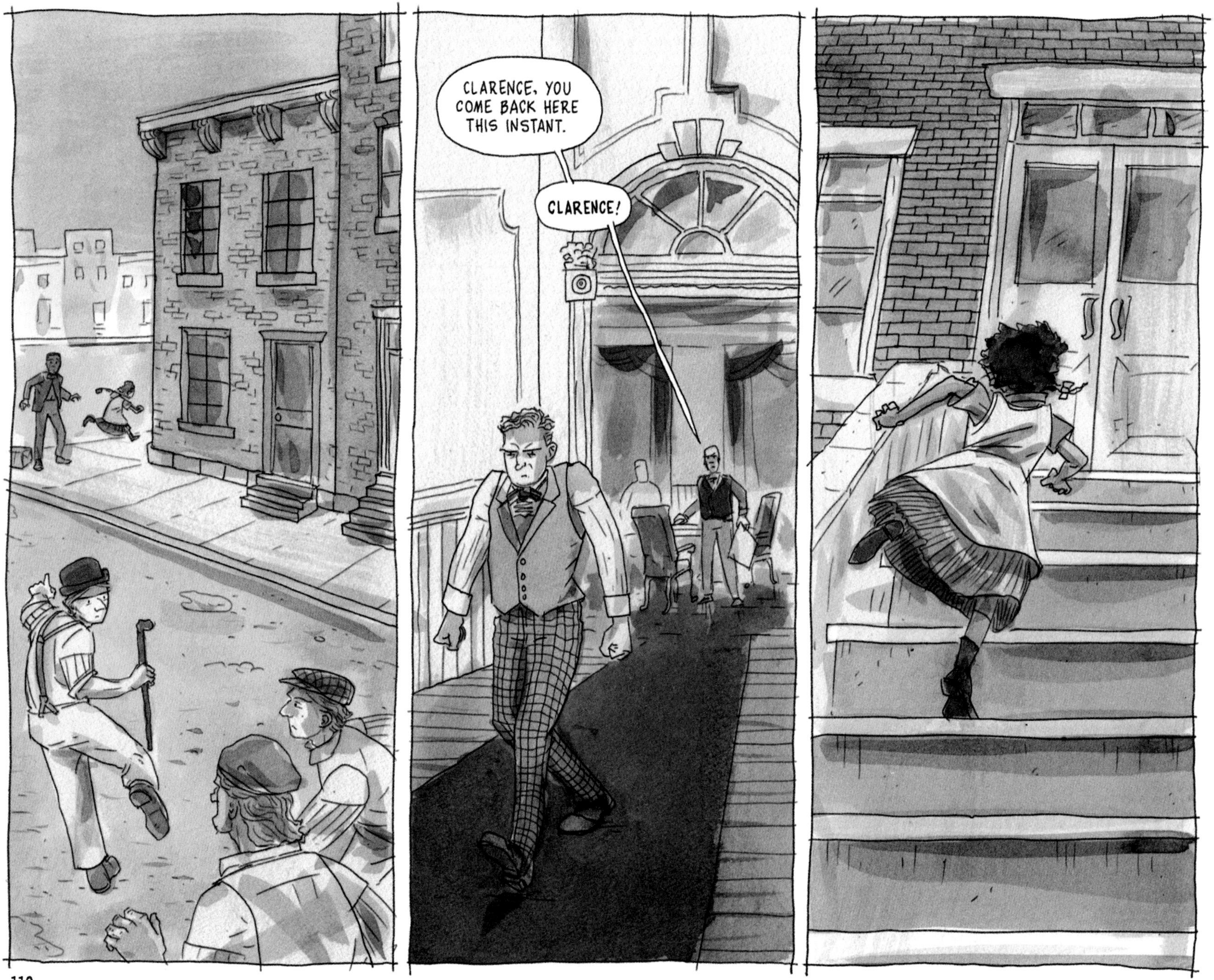
CLARENCE, YOU COME BACK HERE THIS INSTANT.
CLARENCE!

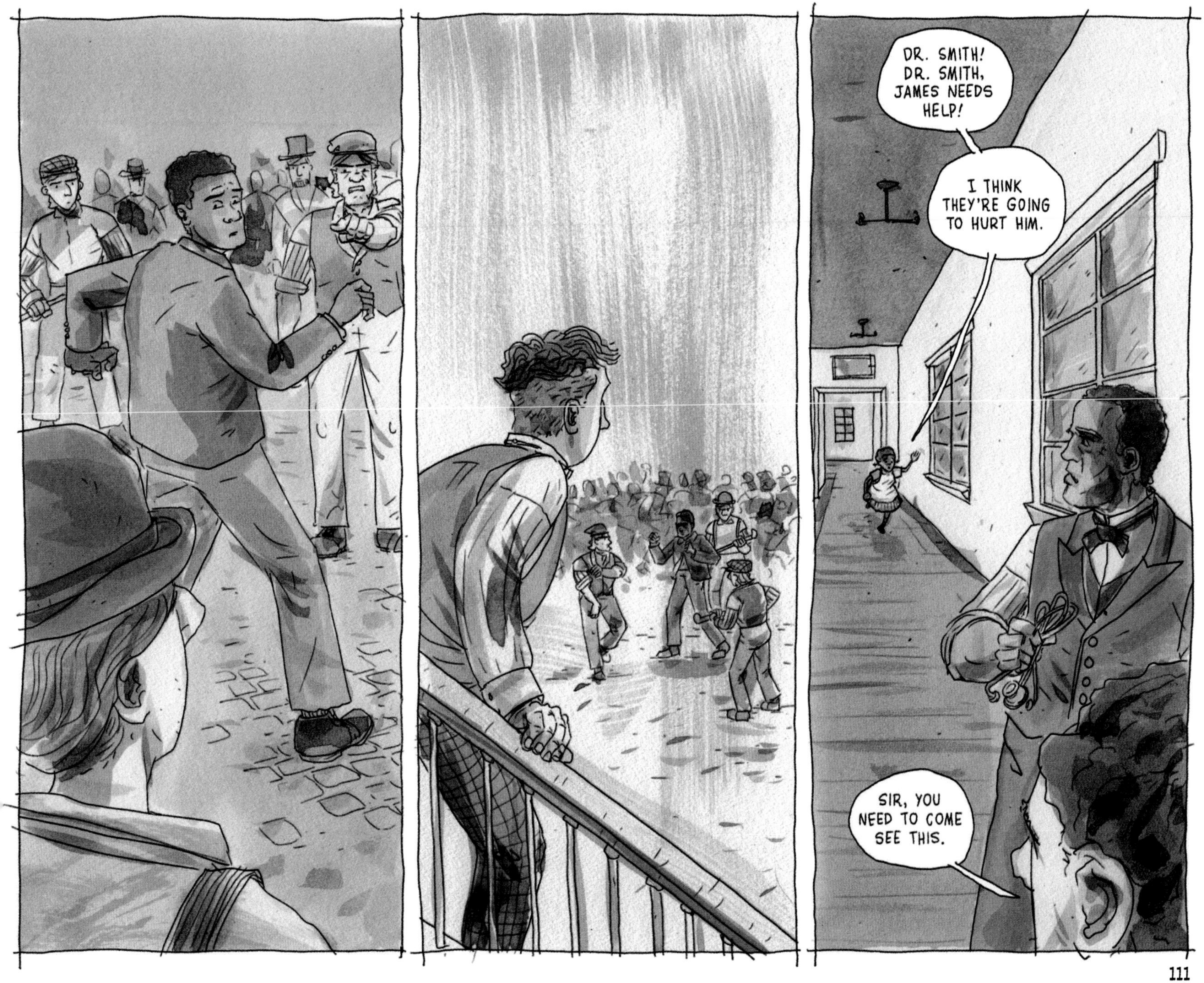
DR. SMITH! DR. SMITH, JAMES NEEDS HELP!
I THINK THEY'RE GOING TO HURT HIM.
SIR, YOU NEED TO COME SEE THIS.

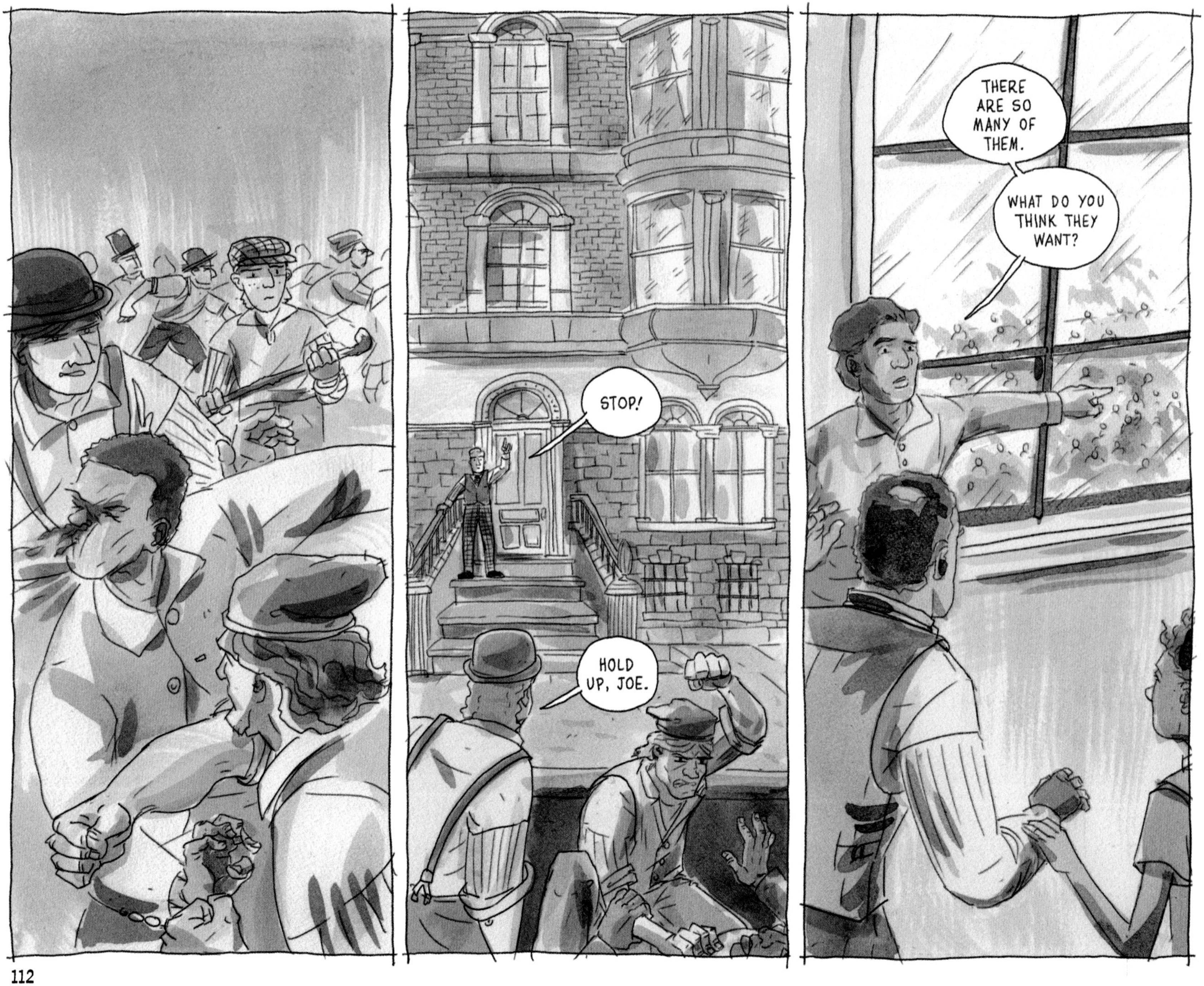
STOP!
HOLD UP, JOE.
THERE ARE SO MANY OF THEM.
WHAT DO YOU THINK THEY WANT?

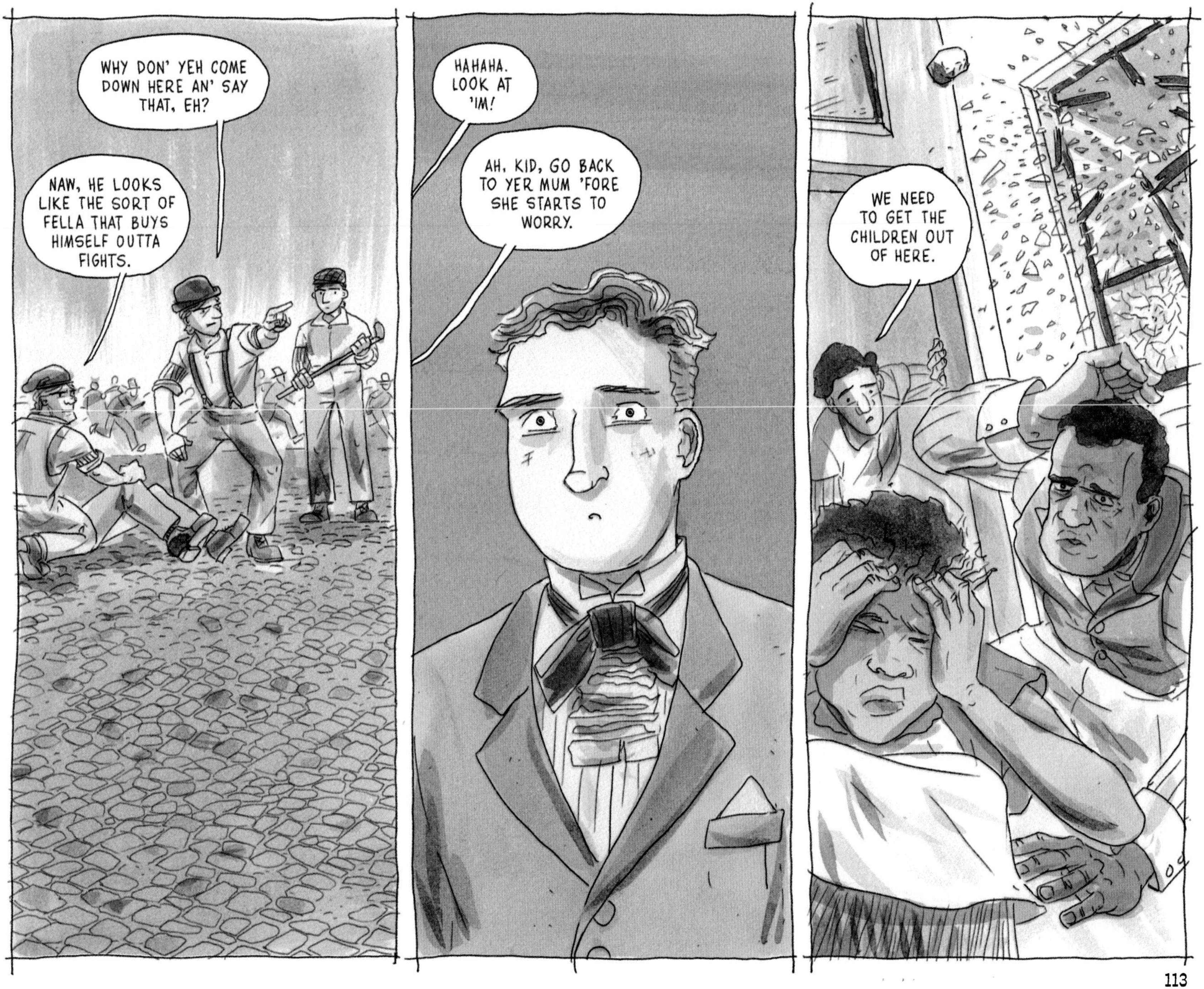
WHY DON' YEH COME DOWN HERE AN' SAY THAT, EH?
NAW, HE LOOKS LIKE THE SORT OF FELLA THAT BUYS HIMSELF OUTTA FIGHTS.
HAHAHA. LOOK AT 'IM!
AH, KID, GO BACK TO YER MUM 'FORE SHE STARTS TO WORRY.
WE NEED TO GET THE CHILDREN OUT OF HERE.

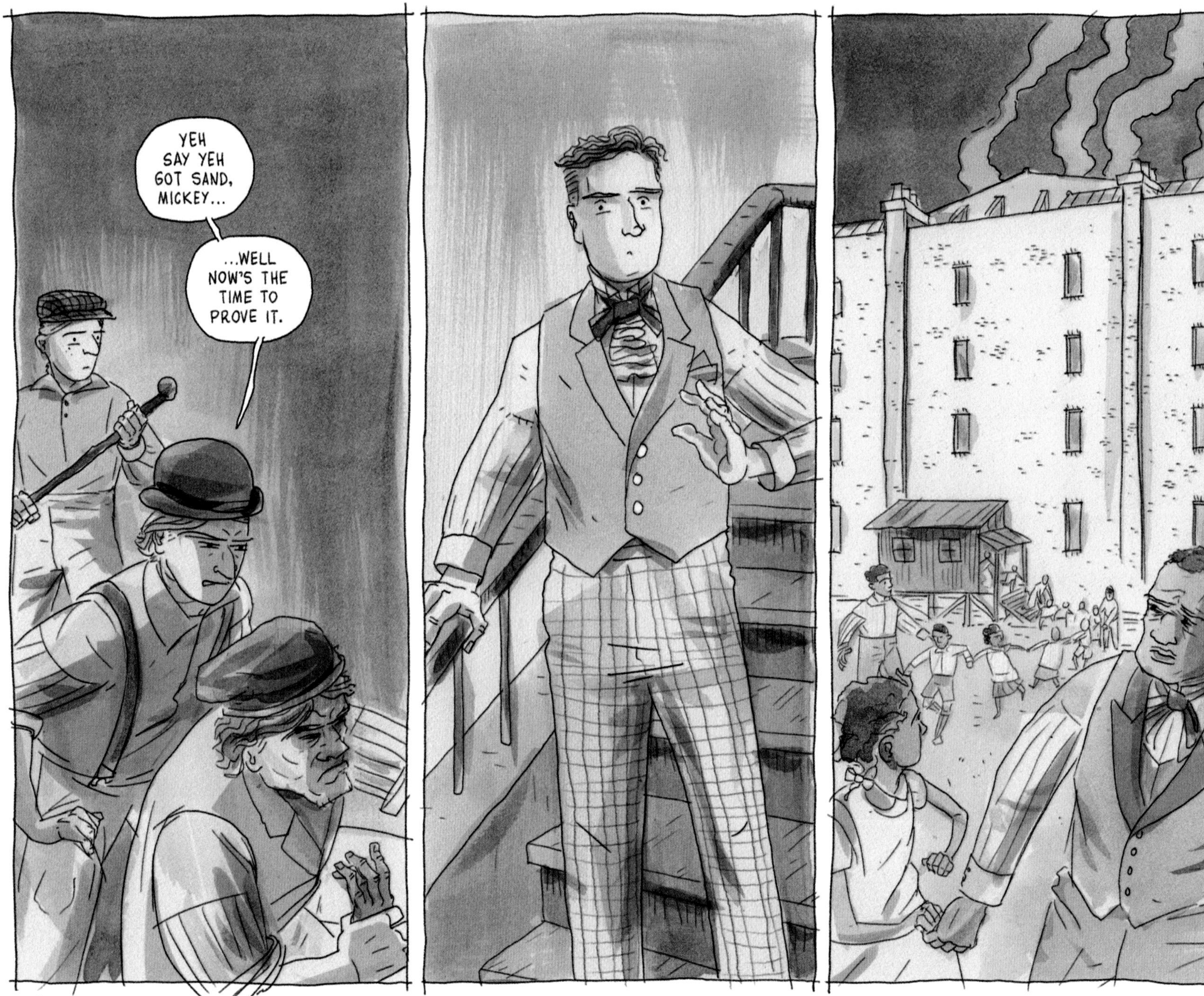
YEH SAY YEH GOT SAND, MICKEY...
...WELL NOW'S THE TIME TO PROVE IT.

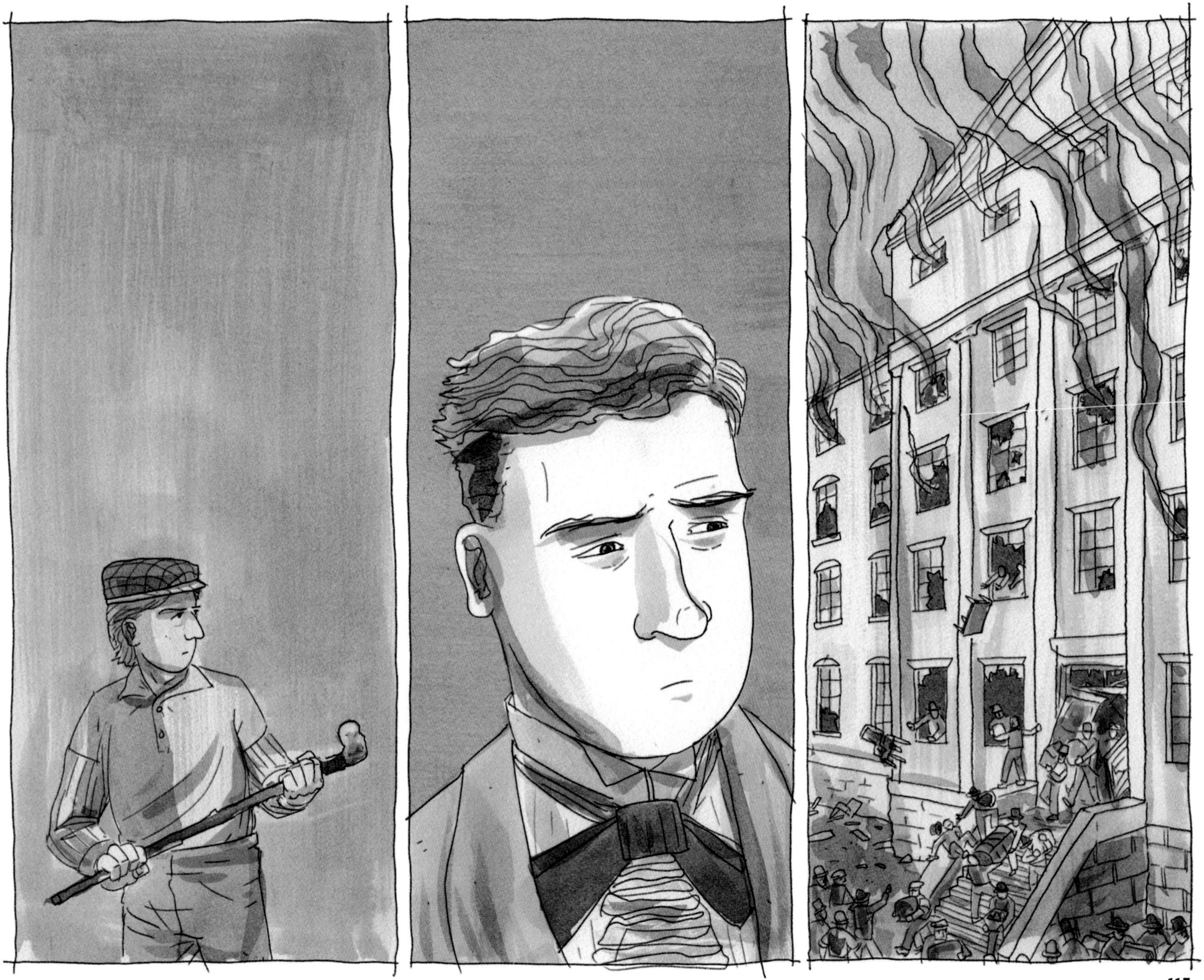

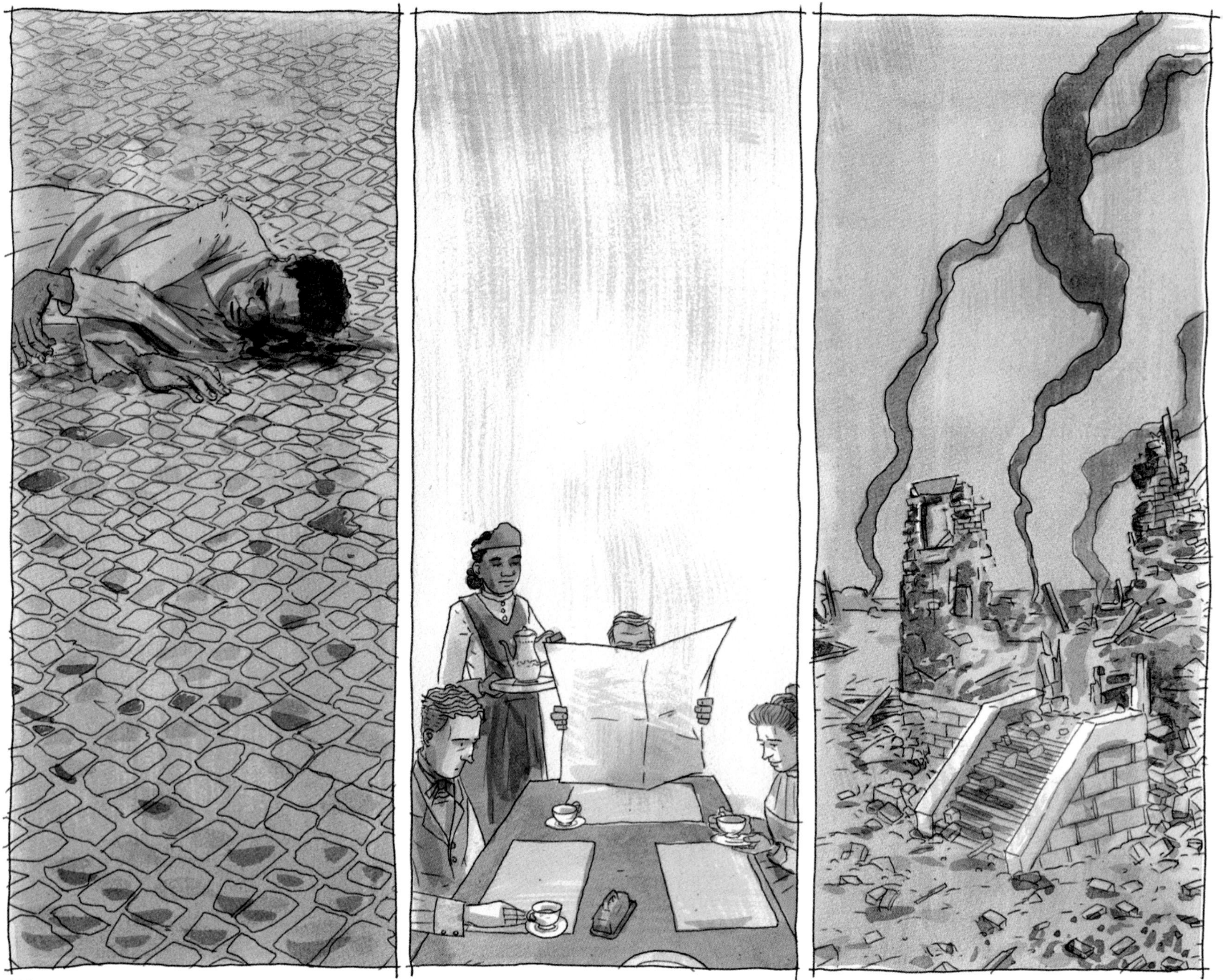

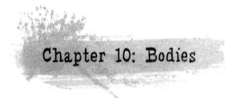

Chapter 10: Bodies

CHARLESTON JOURNAL

July 19, 1863

NEW YORK SMOLDERS

SOLDIERS CALLED IN TO QUELL RIOTS

On the evening of July 12, 1863, little more than a week after the Union victories at Gettysburg and Vicksburg, a crowd of laborers, mostly Irish immigrants, gathered in Manhattan to protest the federal draft. By the next morning, July 13, the crowd had transformed into an angry mob, menacing officials who tried to draw numbers for the draft, burning buildings--especially structures associated with federal authority and the Republican Party--and targeting African Americans for special abuse, including lynchings.

For three more days, as local law enforcement found itself overwhelmed by the violence, the draft riots raged. Finally, on July 16, some four thousand Union soldiers, diverted from the aftermath of the Battle of Gettysburg, arrived in New York City to put down the uprising and attempt to keep a fragile peace.

By that time, more than a hundred people--the overwhelming majority of whom were African American--had been killed, another two thousand or so had been injured, and millions of dollars of property had been destroyed. The draft riots were the worst civil insurrection in U.S. history.

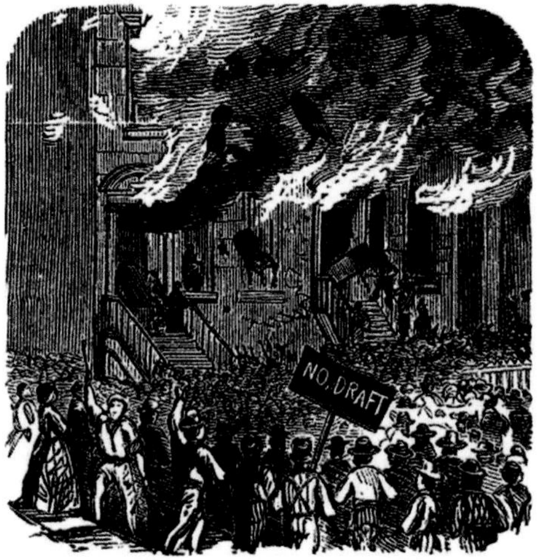
NO DRAFT

UNION VICTORIES

CRIPPLE CONFEDERATE DIPLOMATIC EFFORTS

The Confederacy's long-standing dream of winning the British over to its side was among the casualties of the fall of Vicksburg and the Battle of Gettysburg.

Even before the war started, Southern politicians believed they could forge an alliance with Great Britain. After all, England's textile industry thrived by spinning Dixie's cotton into finished cloth. And so when, during the summer of 1862, Robert E. Lee racked up a series of victories in Virginia at the same time that a so-called cotton famine began starving Lancaster's mills of raw materials, it appeared that the British Parliament would throw its lot in with the South. Indeed, Liverpool's shipyards began producing vessels that soon flew the Confederate flag.

But then the Union's victory at Antietam and President Lincoln's decision to hand down the Emancipation Proclamation blunted Great Britain's enthusiasm for the Confederate cause. The English prided themselves on being the greatest champions of liberty that the world had ever seen. At the same time, British politicians were only interested in backing a winner in a bloody conflict abroad.

The following spring, though, Ulysses S. Grant's troubles outside Vicksburg and General Lee's invasion of the North revived Confederate hopes for a British alliance. Early in July, those hopes died in the Pennsylvania countryside and on bluffs overlooking the Mississippi River. The Confederacy would have to go it alone, as Great Britain maintained its neutrality for the remainder of the Civil War.

RUMORS FROM THE FRONT ☞

African American Troops Prove Their Mettle During Assault on Fort Wagner

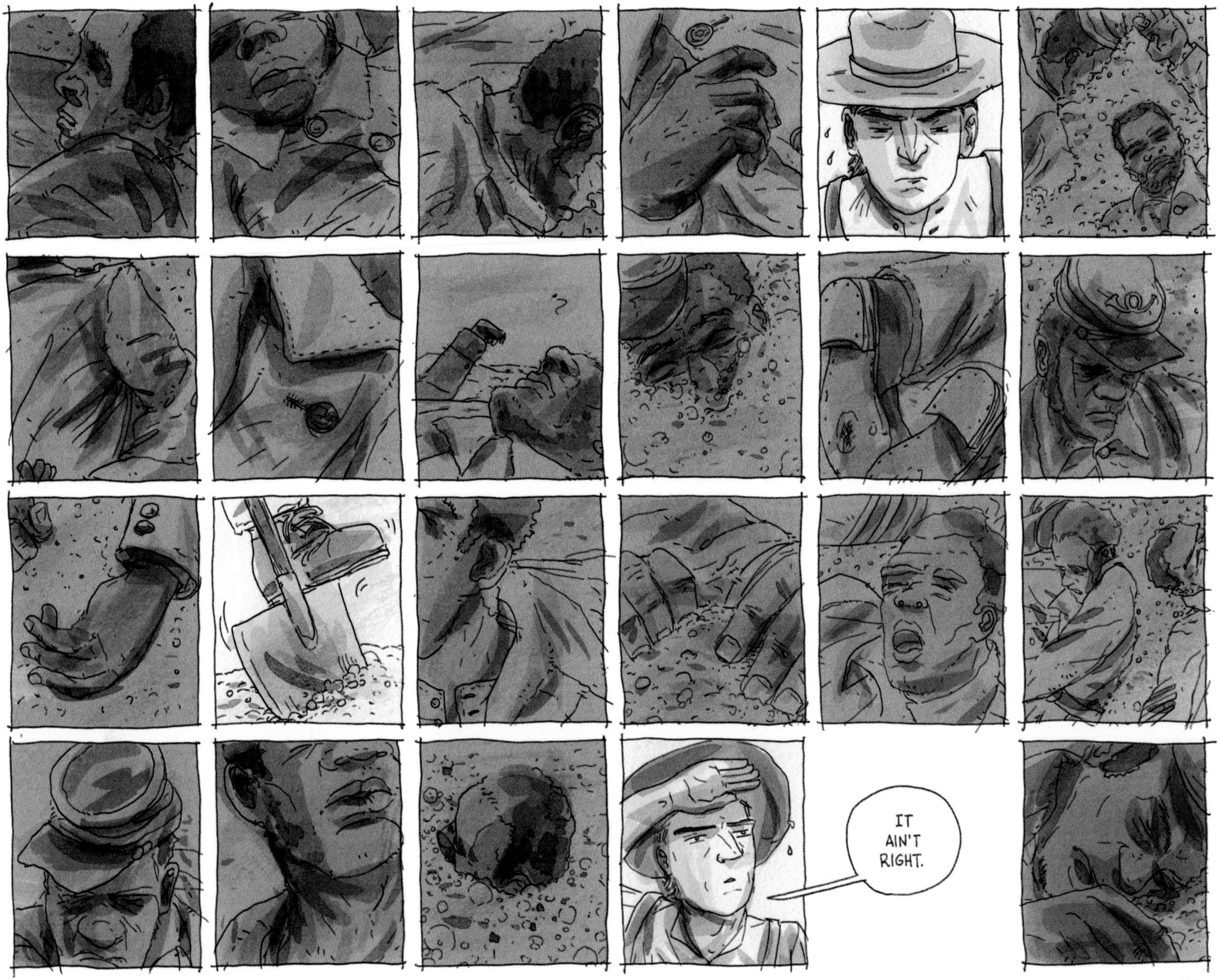
IT AIN'T RIGHT.

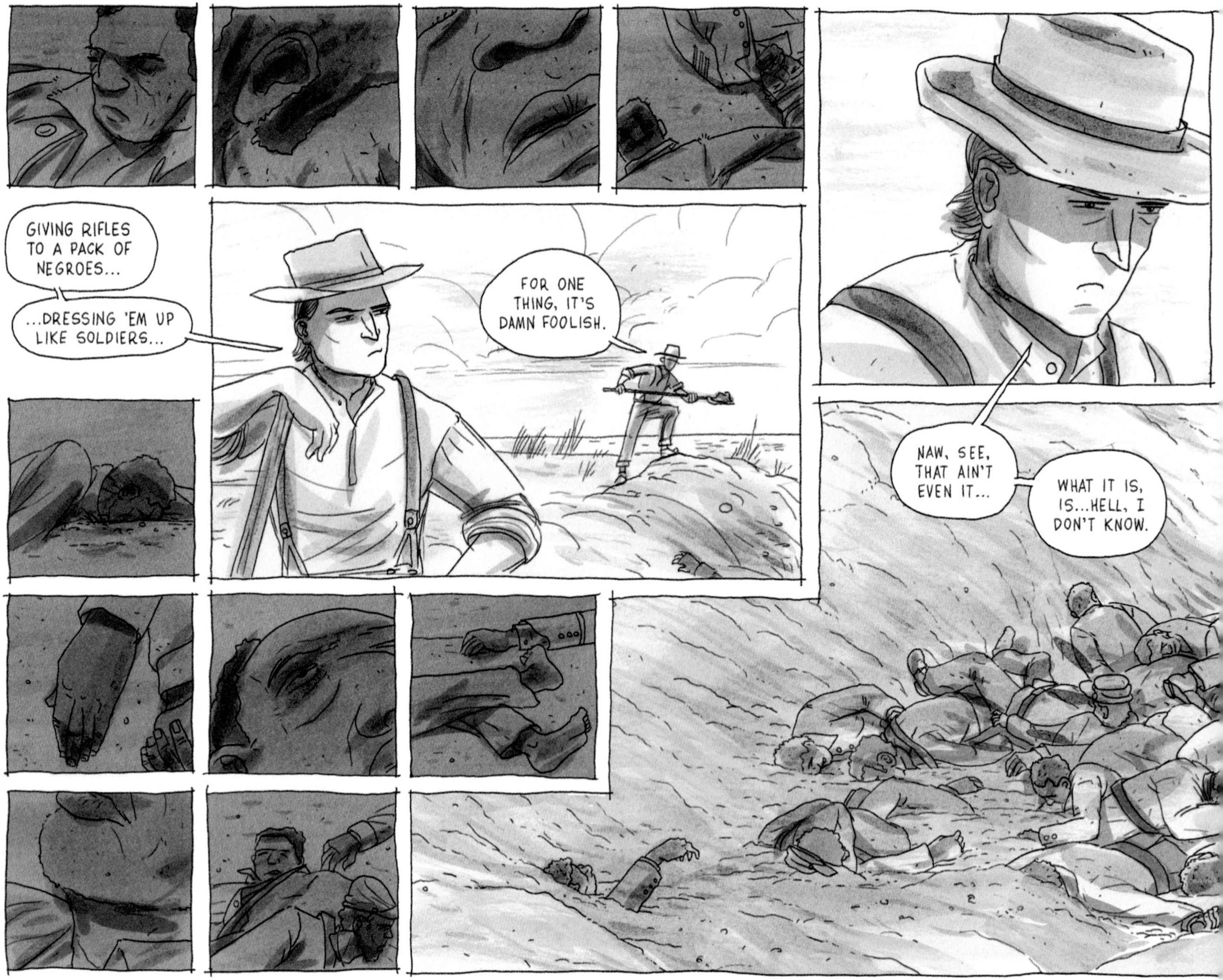
GIVING RIFLES TO A PACK OF NEGROES...
...DRESSING 'EM UP LIKE SOLDIERS...
FOR ONE THING, IT'S DAMN FOOLISH.
NAW, SEE, THAT AIN'T EVEN IT...
WHAT IT IS, IS...HELL, I DON'T KNOW.

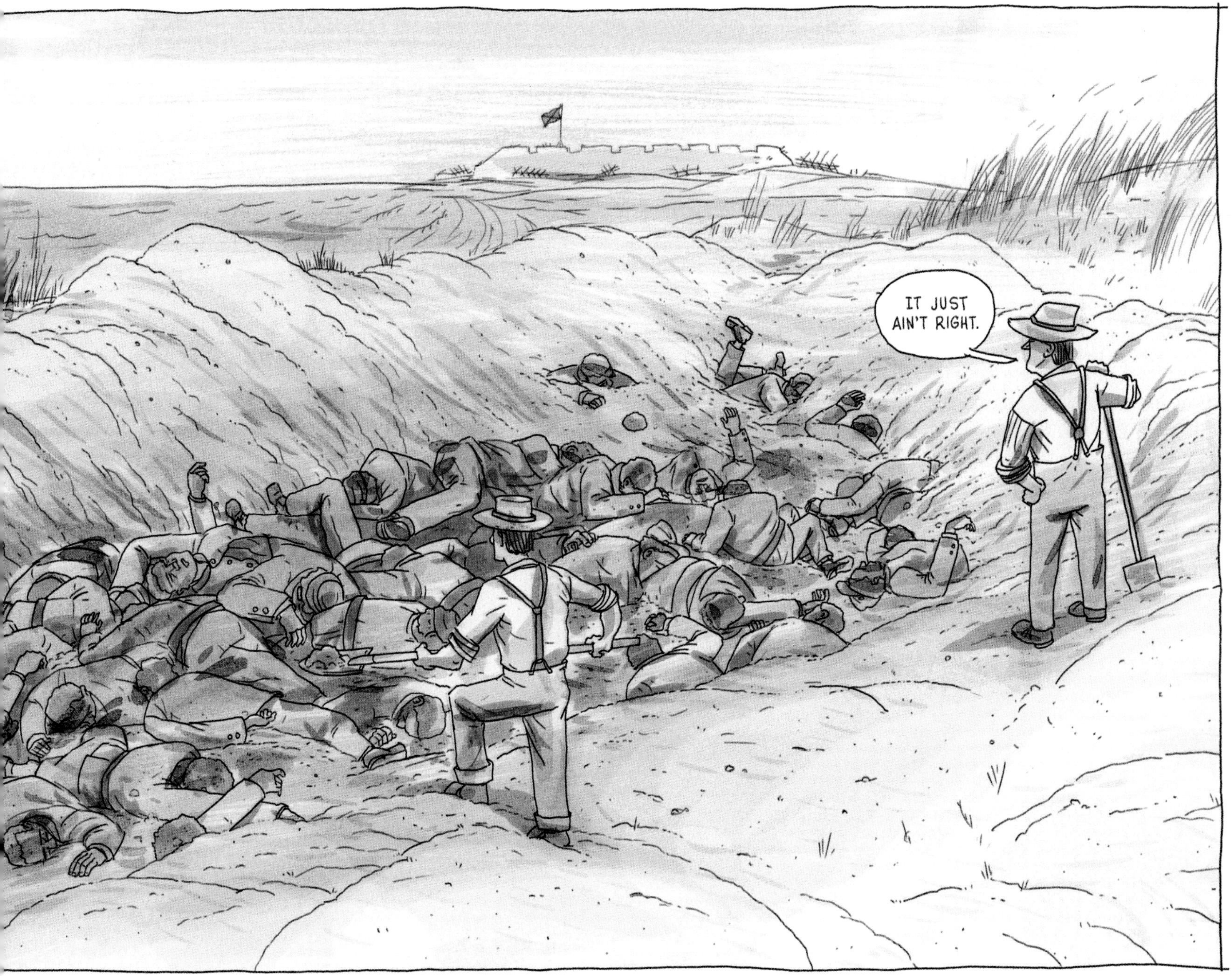
IT JUST AIN'T RIGHT.

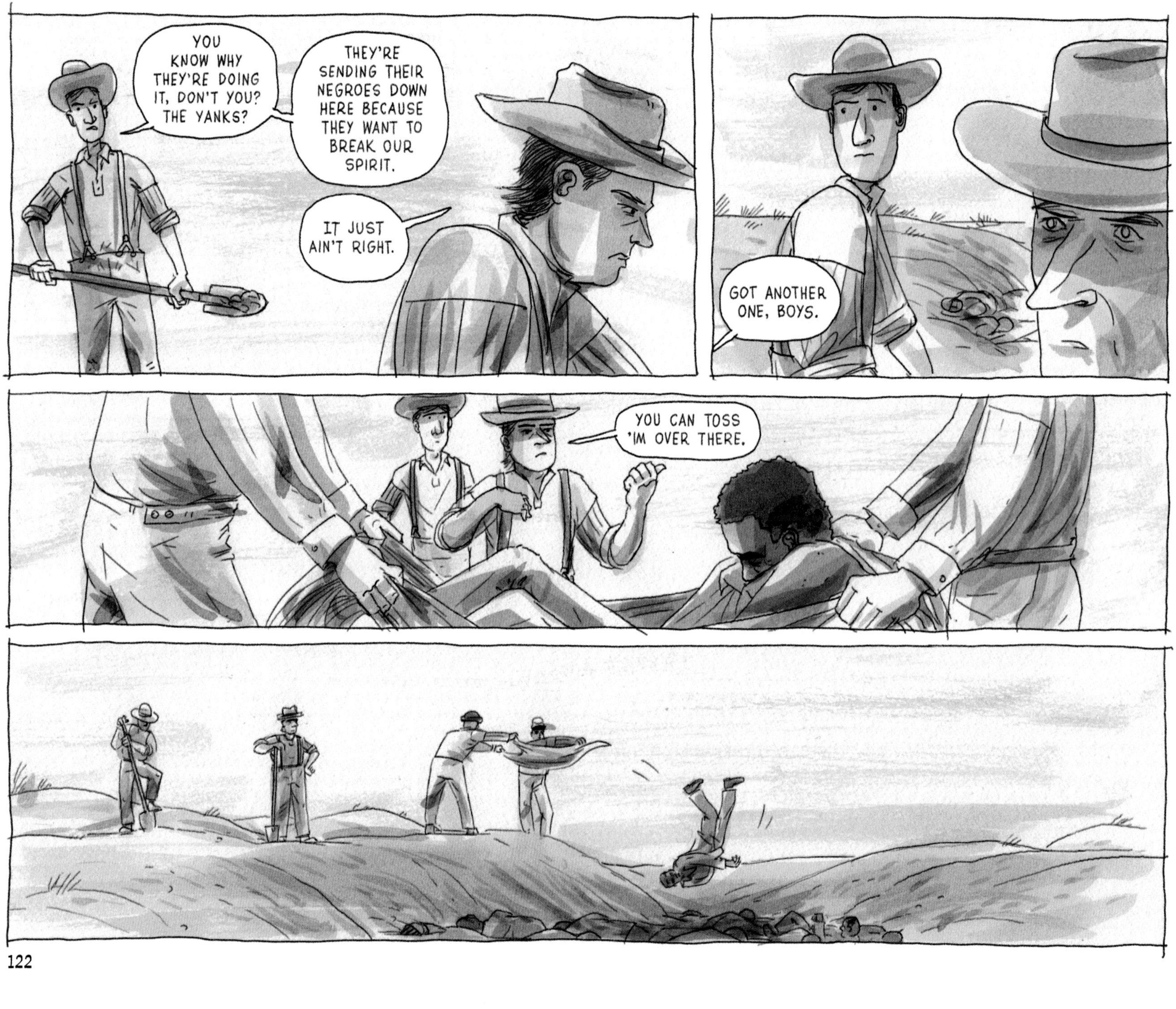
YOU KNOW WHY THEY'RE DOING IT, DON'T YOU? THE YANKS?
THEY'RE SENDING THEIR NEGROES DOWN HERE BECAUSE THEY WANT TO BREAK OUR SPIRIT.
IT JUST AIN'T RIGHT.
GOT ANOTHER ONE, BOYS.
YOU CAN TOSS 'IM OVER THERE.

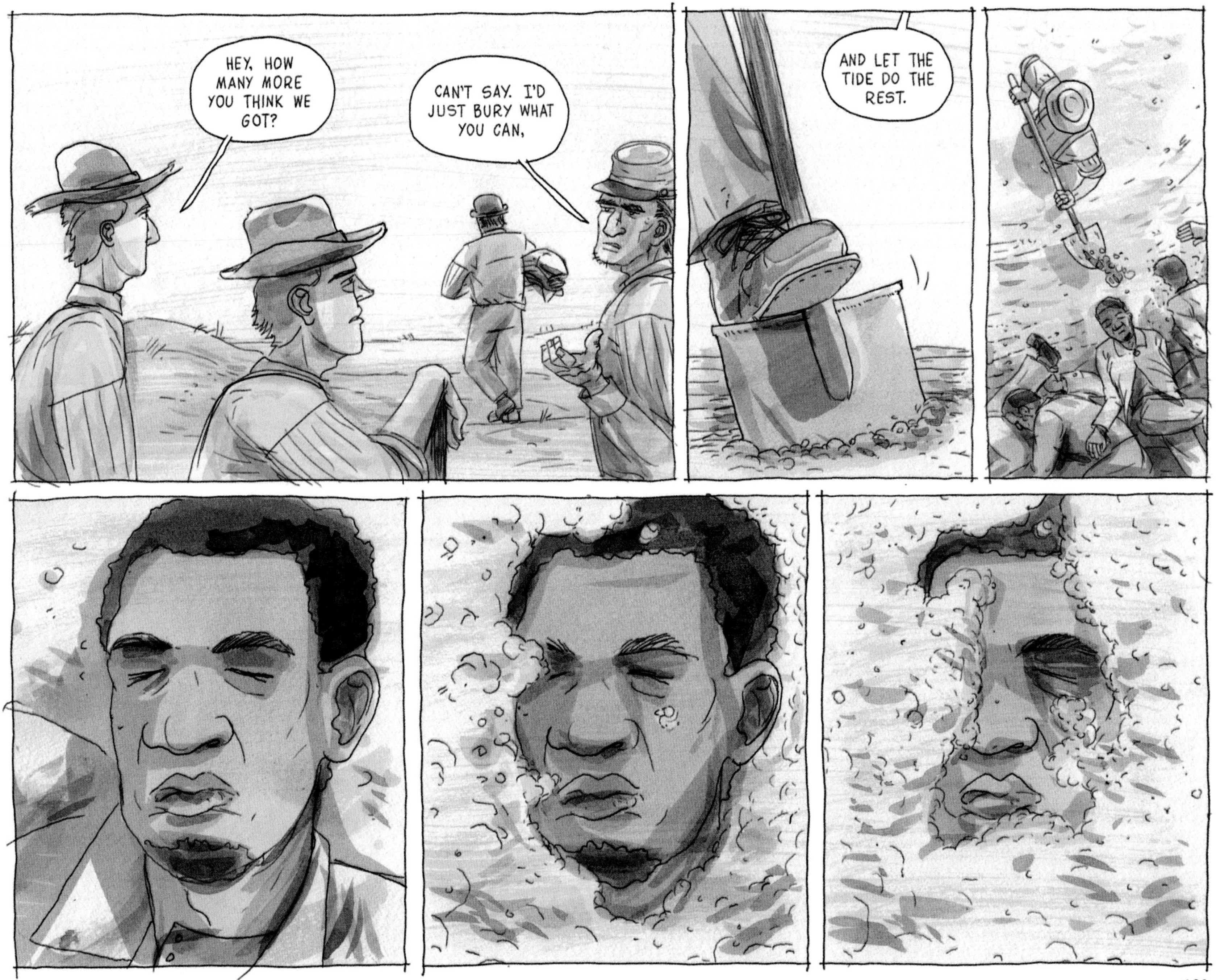
HEY, HOW MANY MORE YOU THINK WE GOT?
CAN'T SAY. I'D JUST BURY WHAT YOU CAN,
AND LET THE TIDE DO THE REST.

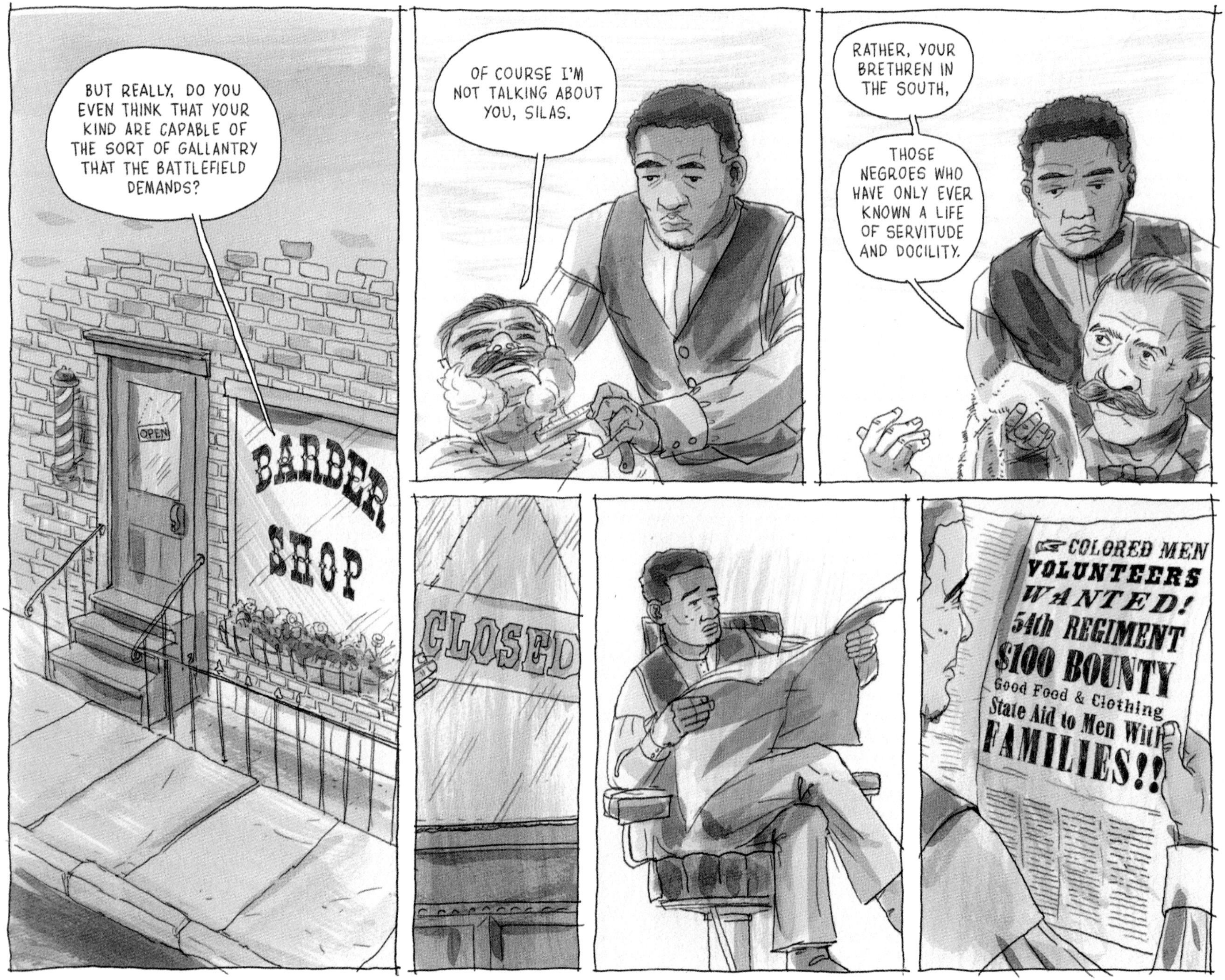
BUT REALLY, DO YOU EVEN THINK THAT YOUR KIND ARE CAPABLE OF THE SORT OF GALLANTRY THAT THE BATTLEFIELD DEMANDS?
OPEN
BARBER SHOP
OF COURSE I'M NOT TALKING ABOUT YOU, SILAS.
RATHER, YOUR BRETHREN IN THE SOUTH,
THOSE NEGROES WHO HAVE ONLY EVER KNOWN A LIFE OF SERVITUDE AND DOCILITY.
CLOSED
COLORED MEN
VOLUNTEERS
WANTED!
54th REGIMENT
$100 BOUNTY
Good Food & Clothing
State Aid to Men With
FAMILIES!!

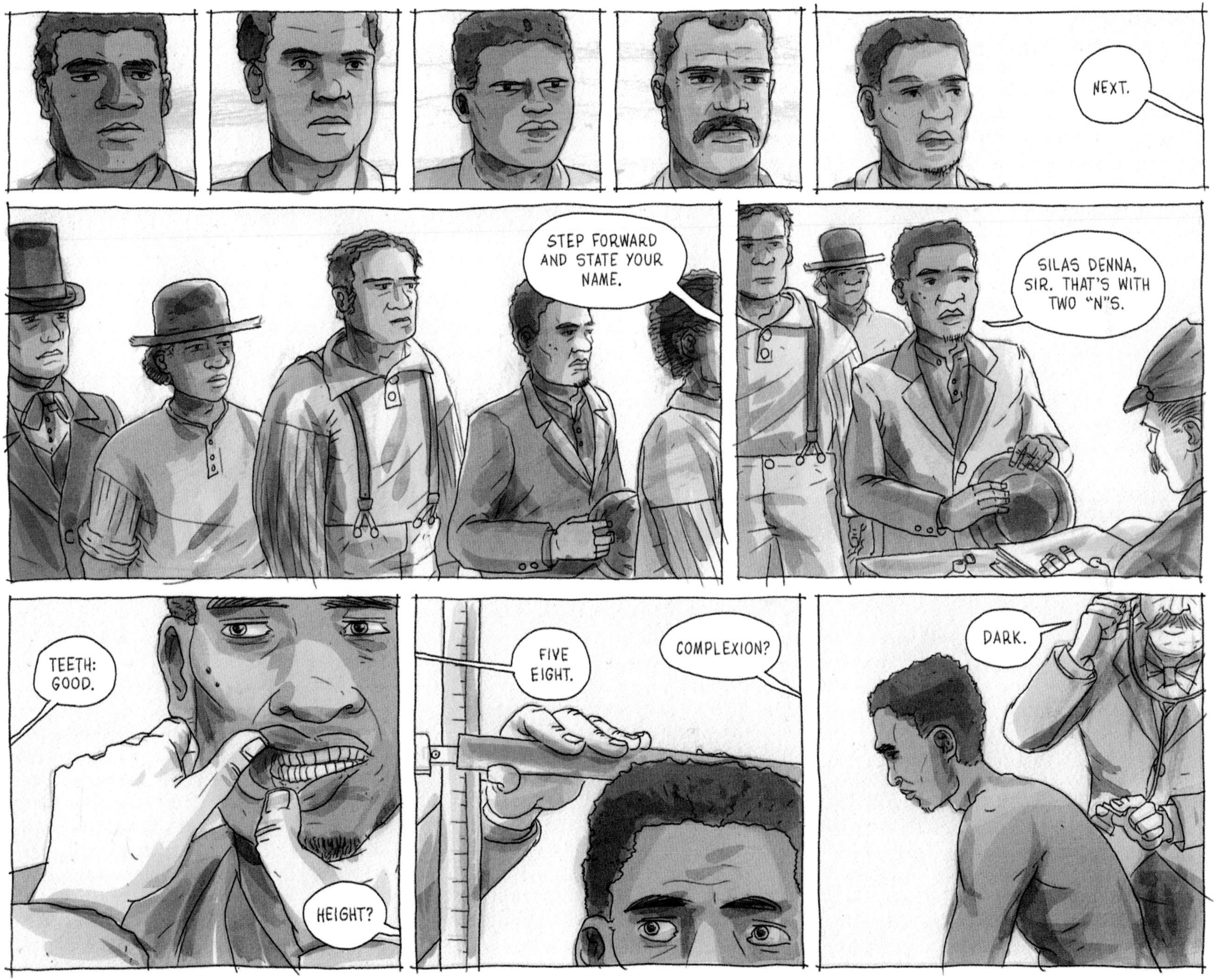
NEXT.
STEP FORWARD AND STATE YOUR NAME.
SILAS DENNA, SIR. THAT'S WITH TWO "N"S.
TEETH: GOOD.
HEIGHT?
FIVE EIGHT.
COMPLEXION?
DARK.

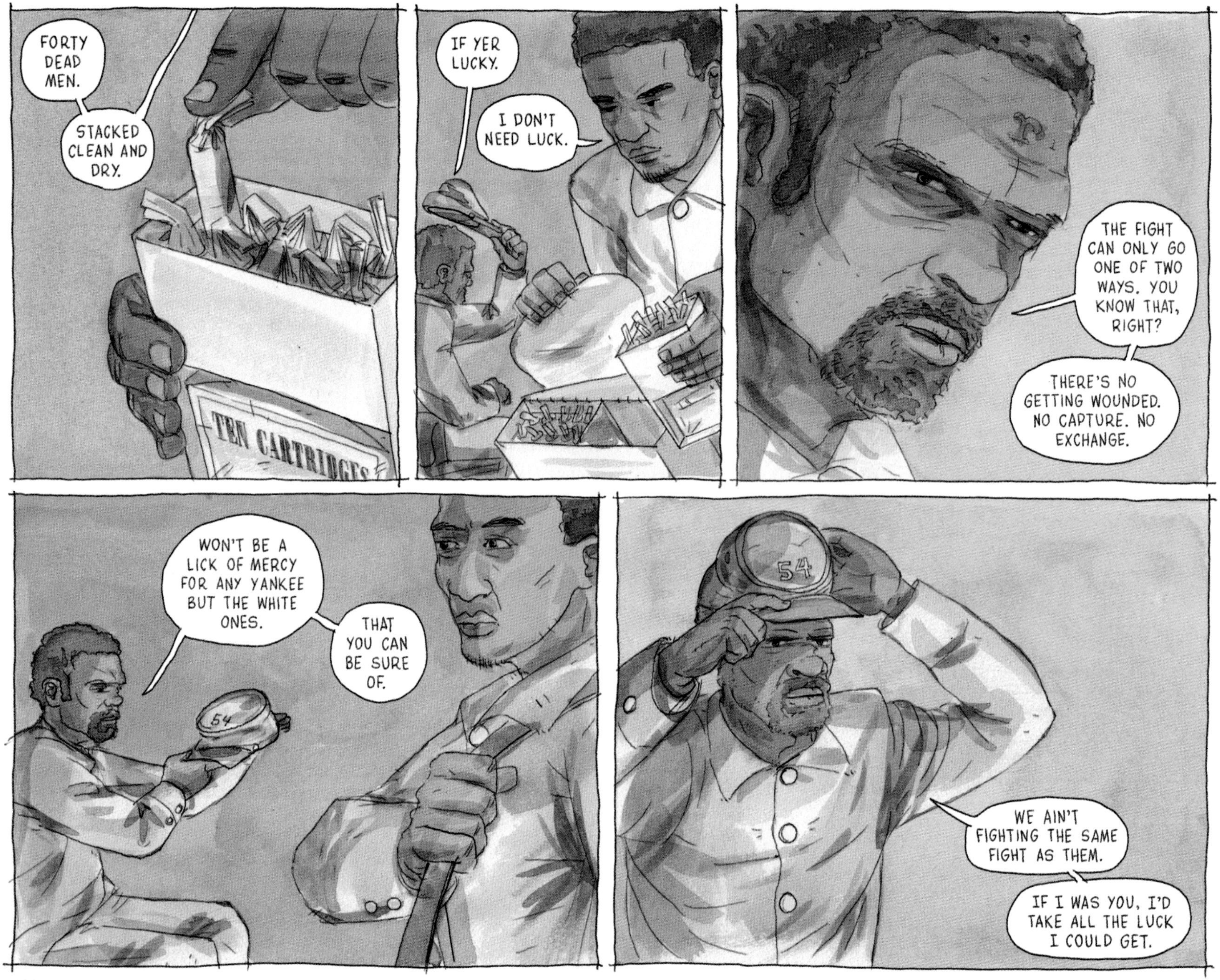
FORTY DEAD MEN.
STACKED CLEAN AND DRY.
TEN CARTRIDGES
IF YER LUCKY.
I DON'T NEED LUCK.
THE FIGHT CAN ONLY GO ONE OF TWO WAYS. YOU KNOW THAT, RIGHT?
THERE'S NO GETTING WOUNDED. NO CAPTURE. NO EXCHANGE.
WON'T BE A LICK OF MERCY FOR ANY YANKEE BUT THE WHITE ONES.
THAT YOU CAN BE SURE OF.
54
54
WE AIN'T FIGHTING THE SAME FIGHT AS THEM.
IF I WAS YOU, I'D TAKE ALL THE LUCK I COULD GET.

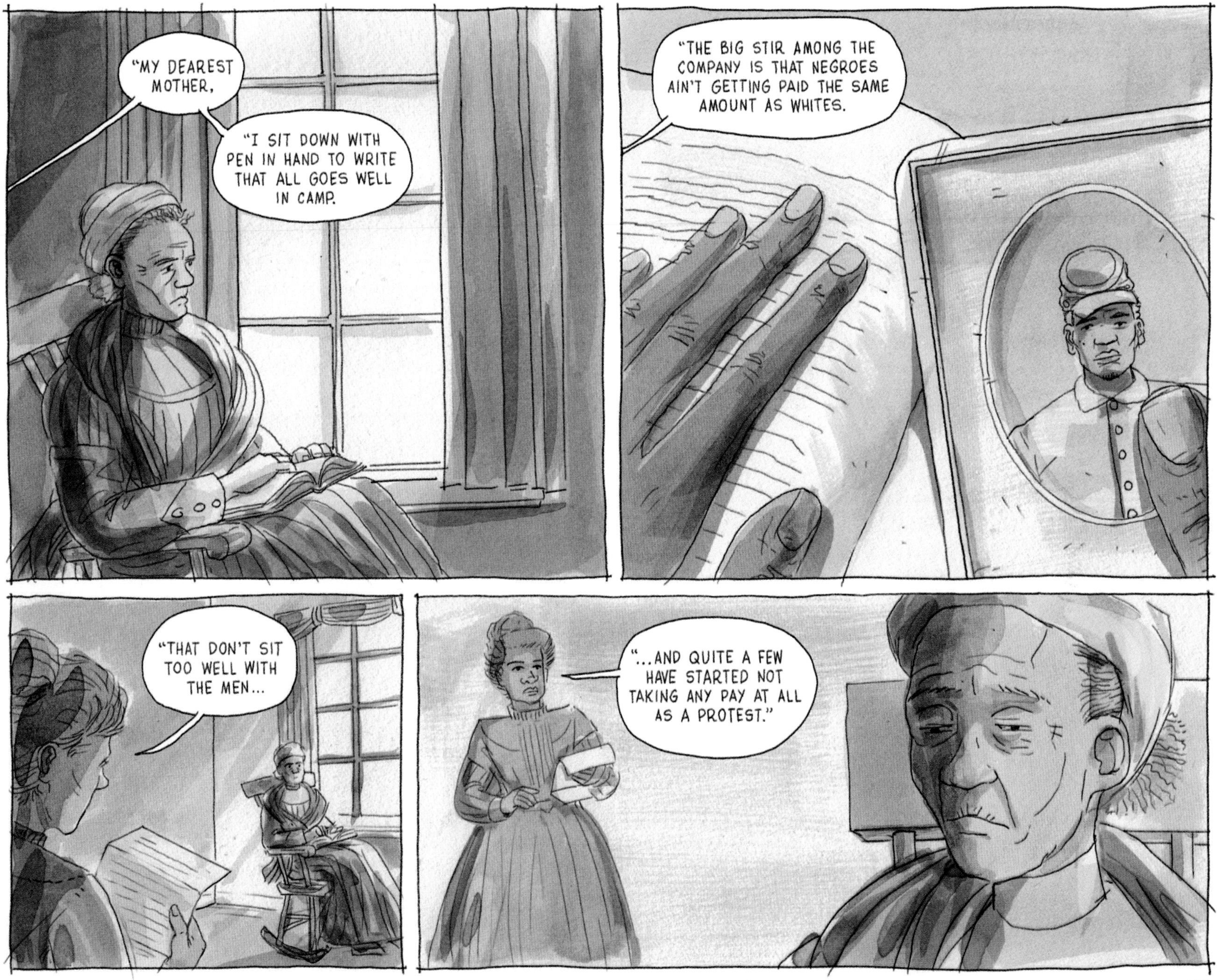
"MY DEAREST MOTHER,
"I SIT DOWN WITH PEN IN HAND TO WRITE THAT ALL GOES WELL IN CAMP.
"THE BIG STIR AMONG THE COMPANY IS THAT NEGROES AIN'T GETTING PAID THE SAME AMOUNT AS WHITES.
"THAT DON'T SIT TOO WELL WITH THE MEN...
"...AND QUITE A FEW HAVE STARTED NOT TAKING ANY PAY AT ALL AS A PROTEST."

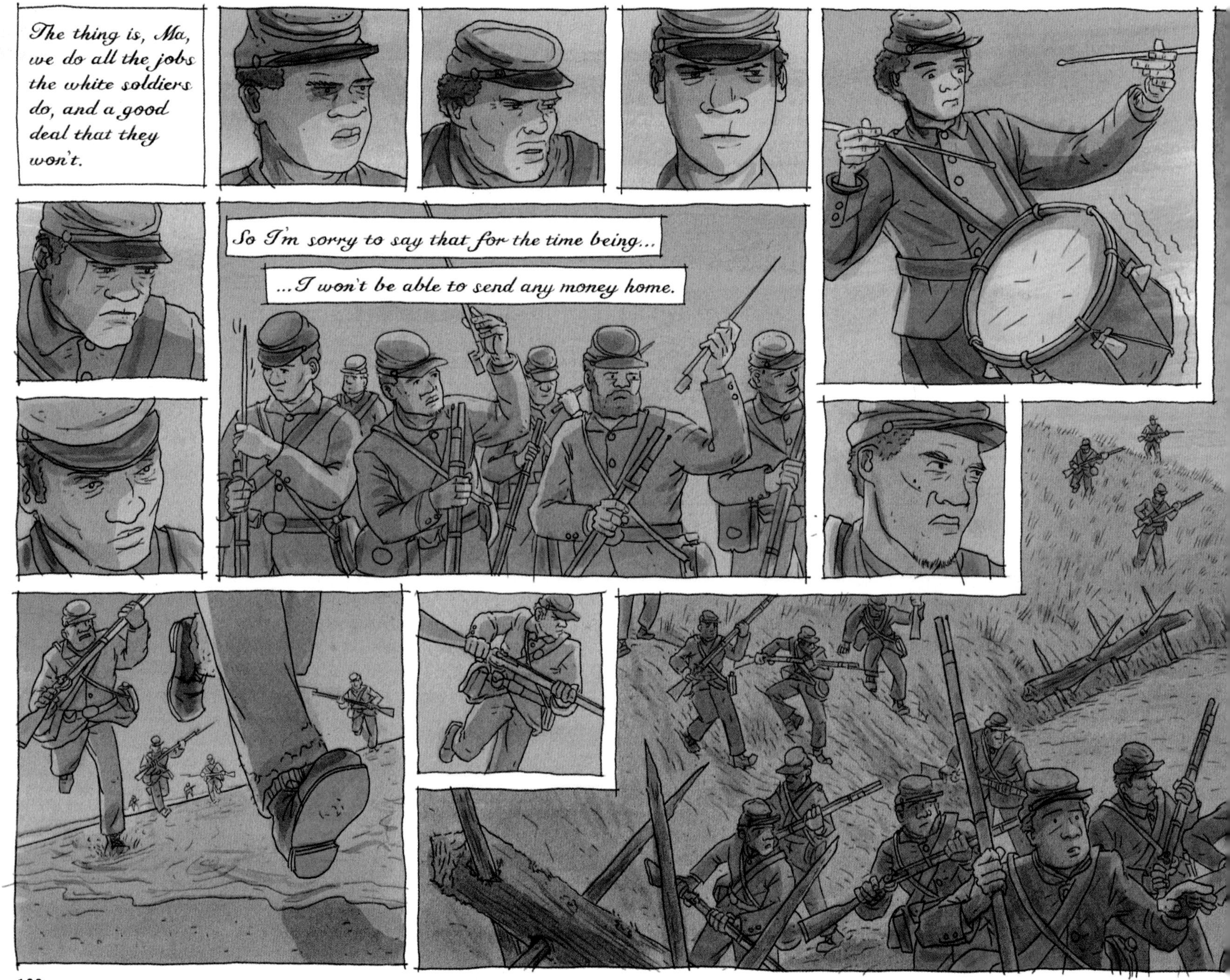

The thing is, Ma, we do all the jobs the white soldiers do, and a good deal that they won't.
So I'm sorry to say that for the time being...
...I won't be able to send any money home.

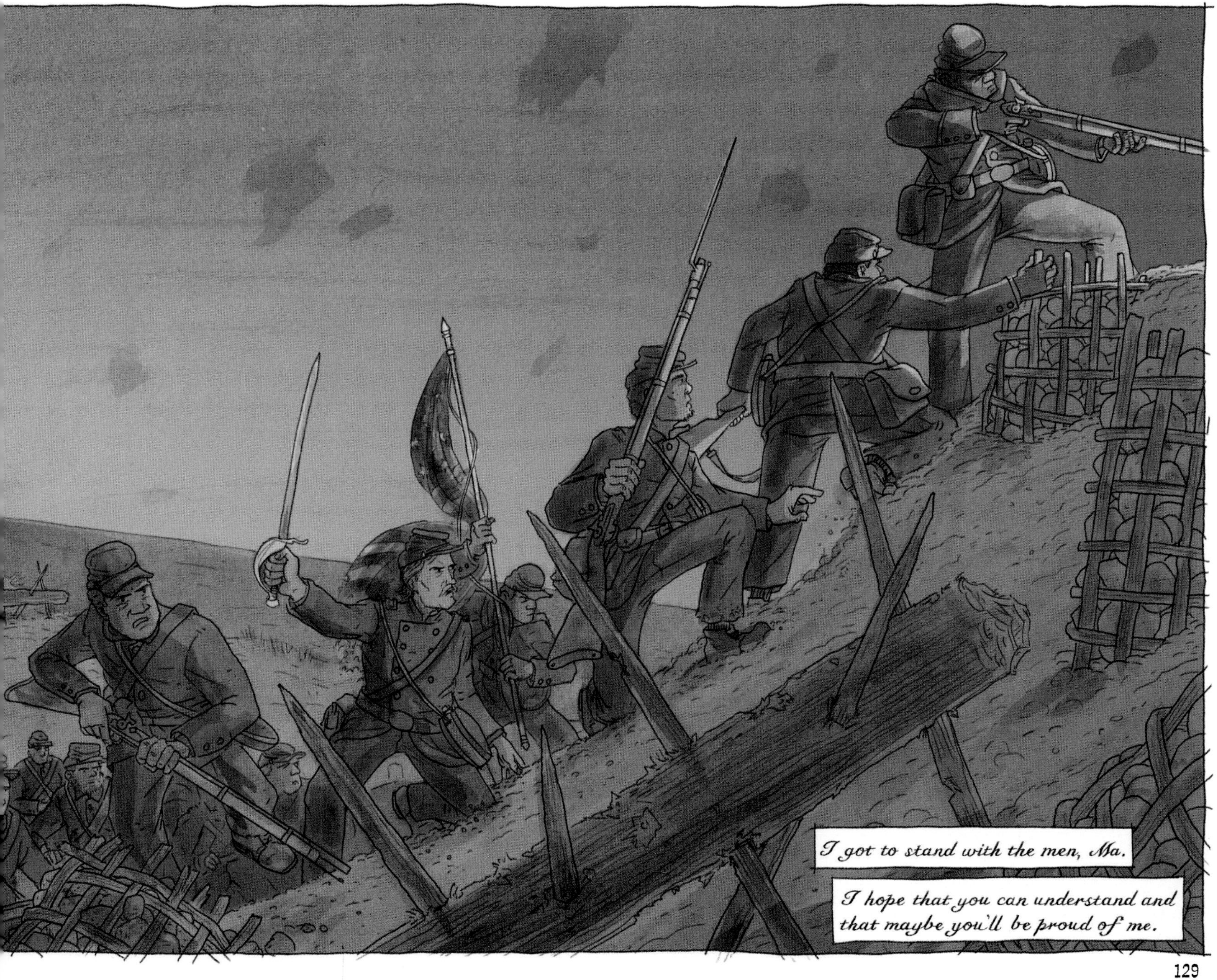
I got to stand with the men, Ma.
I hope that you can understand and that maybe you'll be proud of me.

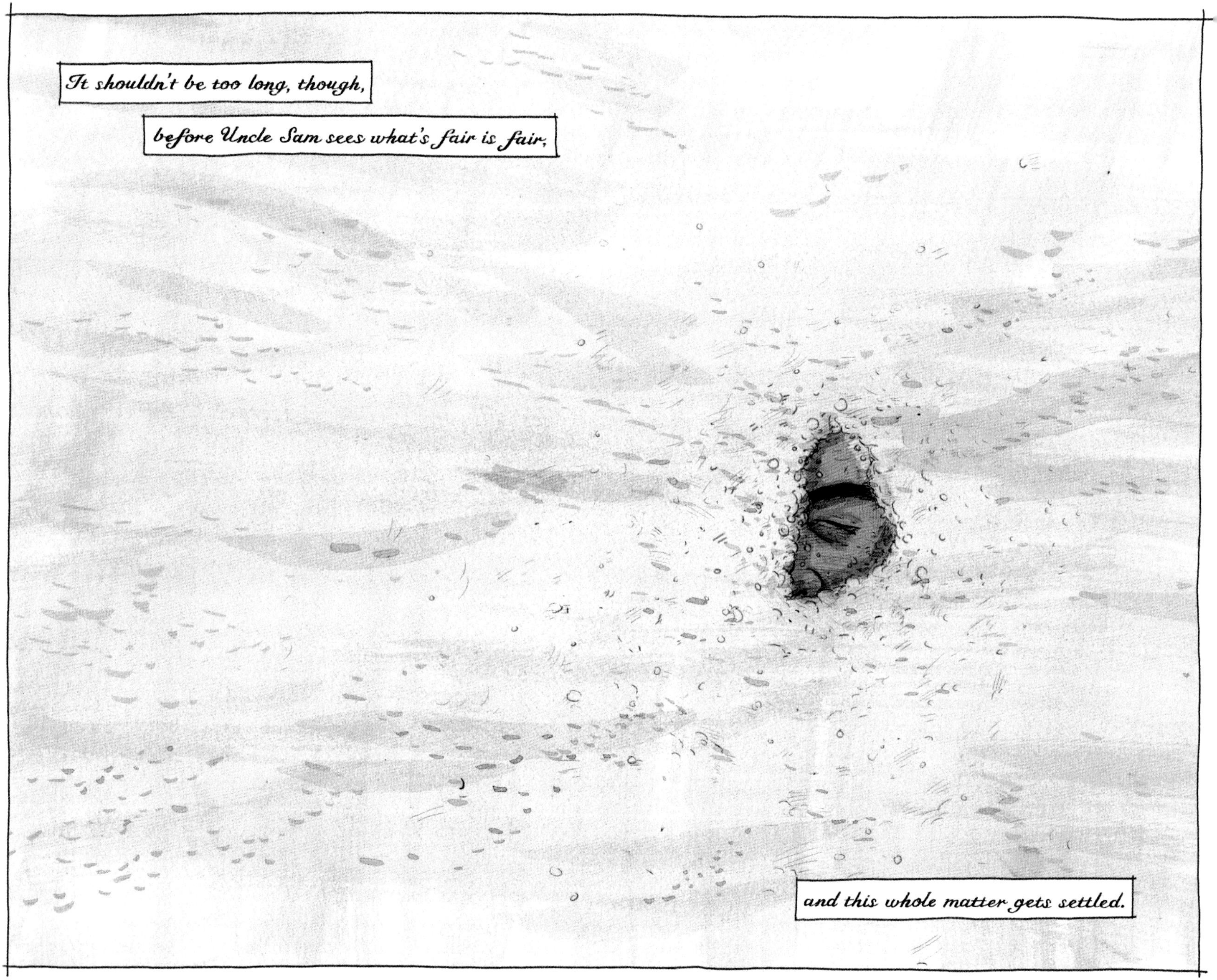
It shouldn't be too long, though,
before Uncle Sam sees what's fair is fair,
and this whole matter gets settled.

Chapter 11: Death Letter

FREDERICKSBURG SENTINEL

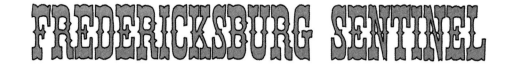

May 4, 1864

UNION RECONSIDERS WAR'S MEANING AFTER DRAFT RIOTS AND FORT WAGNER

Less than a week after Union regiments quelled rioting in Manhattan, Federal troops attacked Fort Wagner, outside Charleston, South Carolina. The Massachusetts 54th Regiment, composed of African American soldiers, led the charge across open marshland and rolling dunes. The assault on the Confederate fortifications was doomed from the start. Almost half the men in the 54th were killed or wounded. Their commander, Colonel Robert Gould Shaw, the son of prominent abolitionists in Boston, lay among the dead.

The heroism of the Massachusetts 54th gave the lie to pervasive stereotypes suggesting that African American men were too childlike or untrustworthy to be effective soldiers. When coupled with grim images of race hatred coming out of the riots in New York City, the tragic exploits of this regiment forced some Northerners to reconsider their prejudices.

Shaw's father drove the point home when he responded to a Confederate officer who refused to turn over his son's body so that it could receive a proper burial. The officer reportedly said of Colonel Shaw, "We have buried him with his niggers." Shaw's father ignored the officer's attempt at scorn, replying publicly, "We hold that a soldier's most appropriate burial place is on the field where he has fallen."

President Lincoln captured the shifting mood in the North with an open letter to Democrats, scolding: "You say you will not fight to free Negroes. Some of them seem willing to fight for you."

RATHER DIE FREEMAN THAN LIVE TO BE SLAVES
3RD UNITED STATES COLORED TROOPS

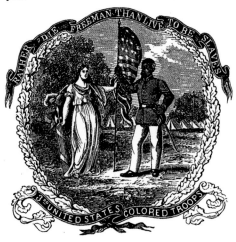

VETERANS' PENSIONS:
The Federal Apparatus Expands

The federal government exploded in size and scope during the Civil War, levying the United States' first income taxes, unifying the nation's currency, drafting citizens to serve in the armed forces, laying the groundwork for public institutions of higher learning across the country, and creating a new pension system.

Modest military pensions dated back to the Revolutionary War. But starting in July 1862, with the Union's fortunes suffering on the front lines and the cruelty of the fighting hitting home, enlistments diminished. Federal authorities passed a new law, increasing the size of payouts and expanding eligibility beyond surviving soldiers whose disability could be "directly traced to injuries received or diseases contracted while in military service" to include widows, orphans, and dependent orphaned sisters of men who died fighting for the Union.

The law prohibited the disbursement of funds to "any person who in any manner aided or abetted the rebellion," leaving it to the Southern states to mount their own pension systems in later years.

Federal pensions, meanwhile, grew in generosity and complexity, until, early in the twentieth century, they were meted out to any veteran who had served honorably. A military pension, born of war, had evolved into an old-age pension, a precursor to the nation's Social Security system.

RUMORS FROM THE FRONT

Union and Confederate Forces Locked in Combat Outside Spotsylvania Courthouse

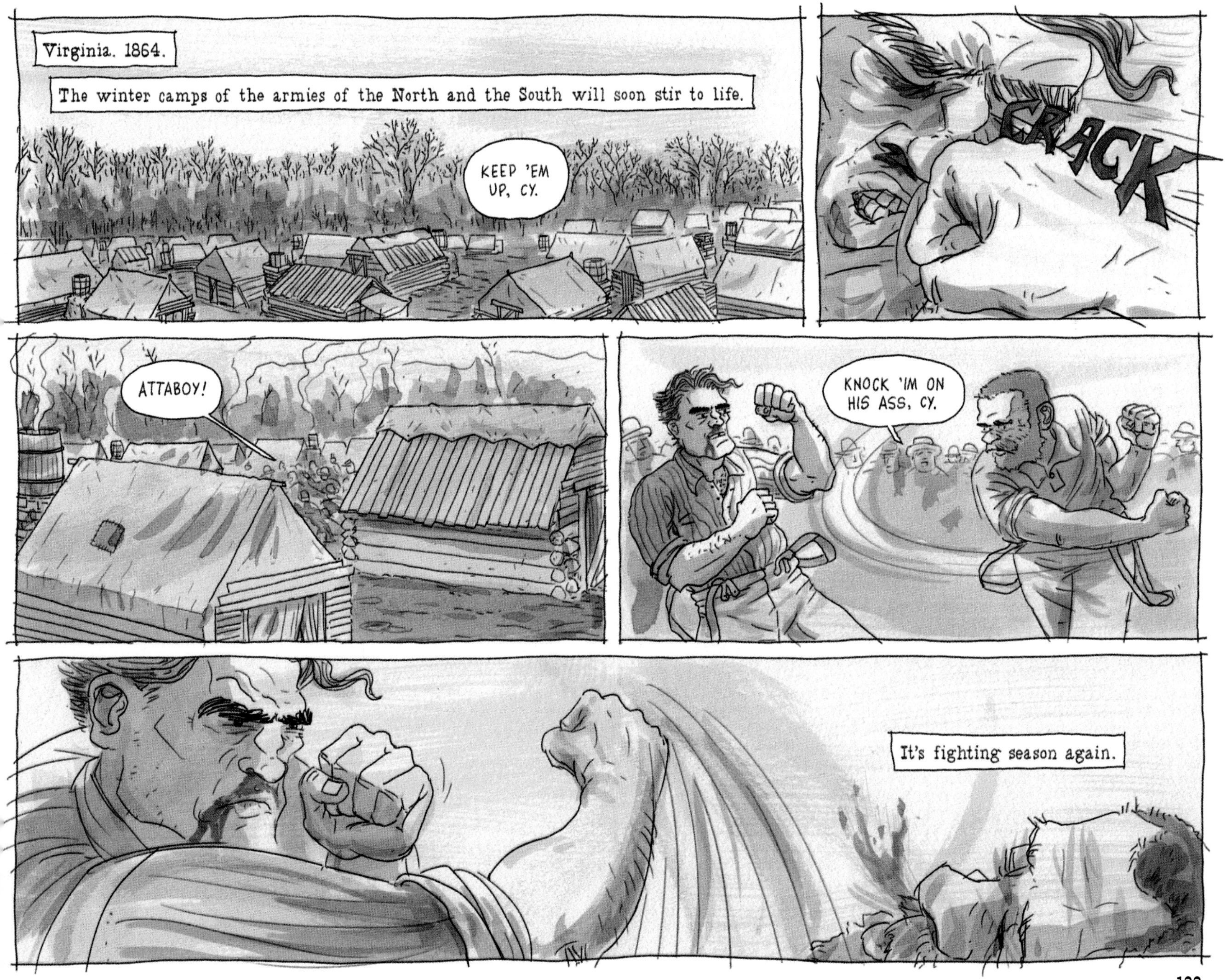
Virginia. 1864.
The winter camps of the armies of the North and the South will soon stir to life.
KEEP 'EM UP, CY.
CRACK
ATTABOY!
KNOCK 'IM ON HIS ASS, CY.
It's fighting season again.

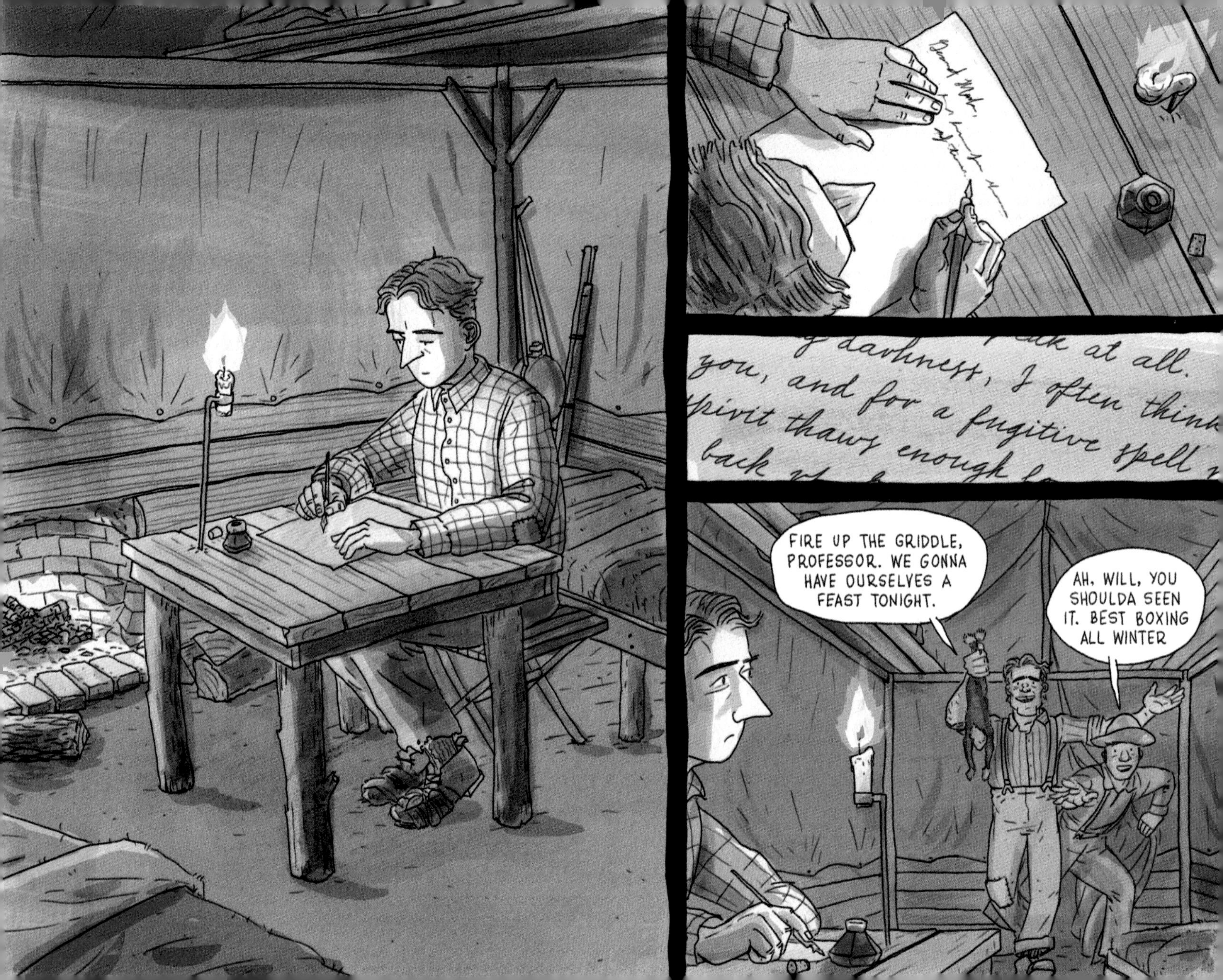
FIRE UP THE GRIDDLE, PROFESSOR. WE GONNA HAVE OURSELVES A FEAST TONIGHT.
AH, WILL, YOU SHOULDA SEEN IT. BEST BOXING ALL WINTER

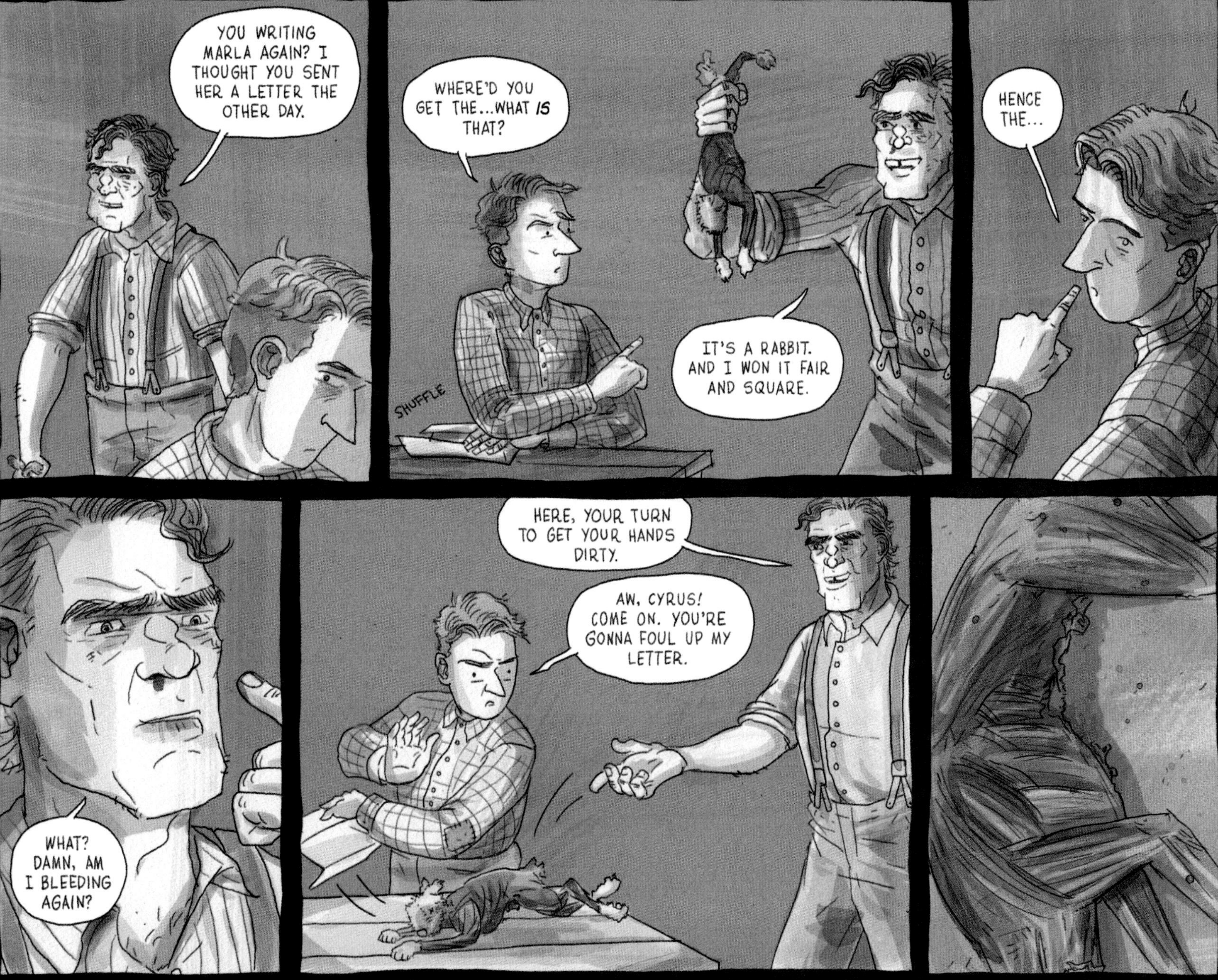
YOU WRITING MARLA AGAIN? I THOUGHT YOU SENT HER A LETTER THE OTHER DAY.
WHERE'D YOU GET THE...WHAT *IS* THAT?
SHUFFLE
IT'S A RABBIT. AND I WON IT FAIR AND SQUARE.
HENCE THE...
WHAT? DAMN, AM I BLEEDING AGAIN?
HERE, YOUR TURN TO GET YOUR HANDS DIRTY.
AW, CYRUS! COME ON. YOU'RE GONNA FOUL UP MY LETTER.

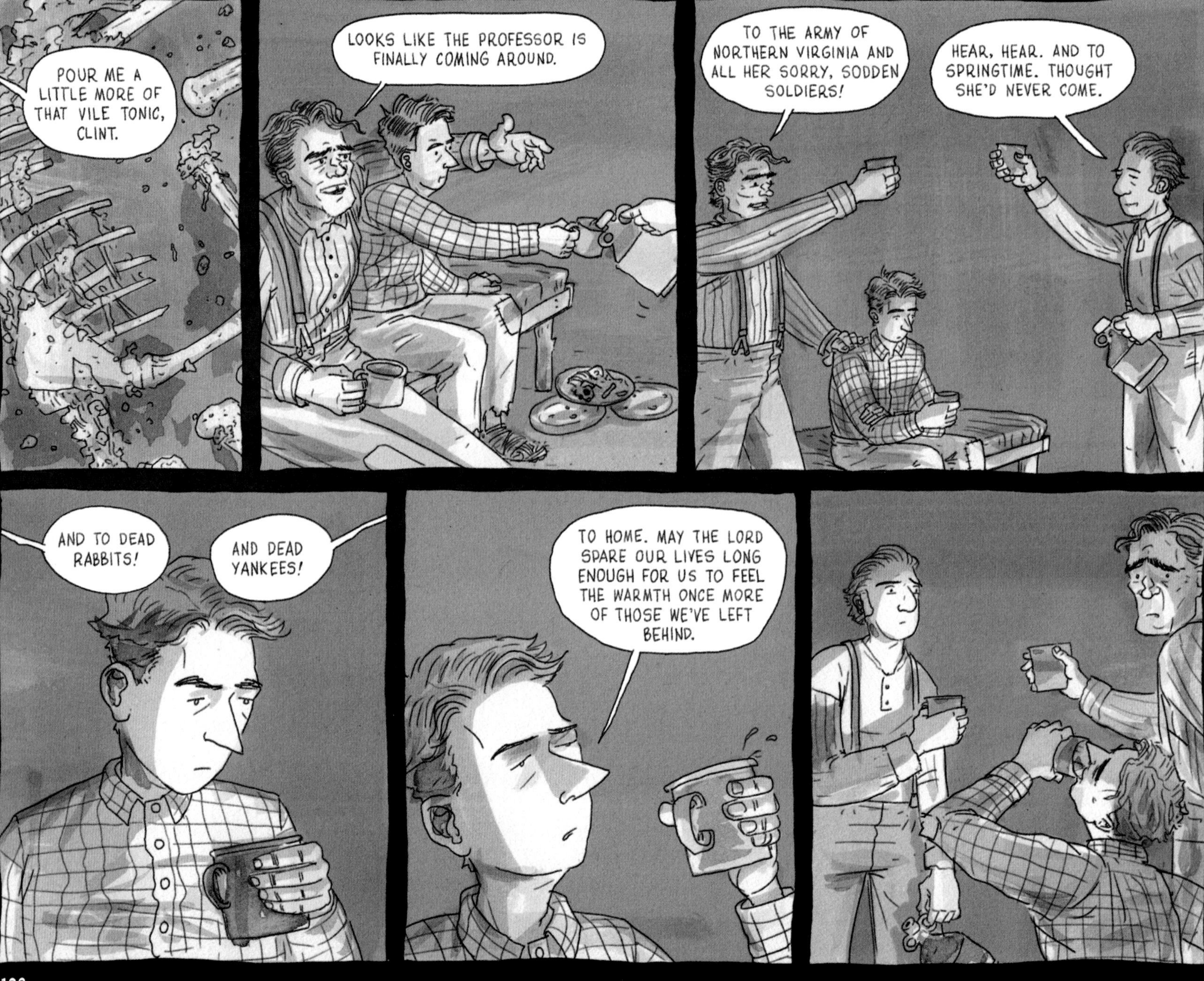
POUR ME A LITTLE MORE OF THAT VILE TONIC, CLINT.
LOOKS LIKE THE PROFESSOR IS FINALLY COMING AROUND.
TO THE ARMY OF NORTHERN VIRGINIA AND ALL HER SORRY, SODDEN SOLDIERS!
HEAR, HEAR. AND TO SPRINGTIME. THOUGHT SHE'D NEVER COME.
AND TO DEAD RABBITS!
AND DEAD YANKEES!
TO HOME. MAY THE LORD SPARE OUR LIVES LONG ENOUGH FOR US TO FEEL THE WARMTH ONCE MORE OF THOSE WE'VE LEFT BEHIND.

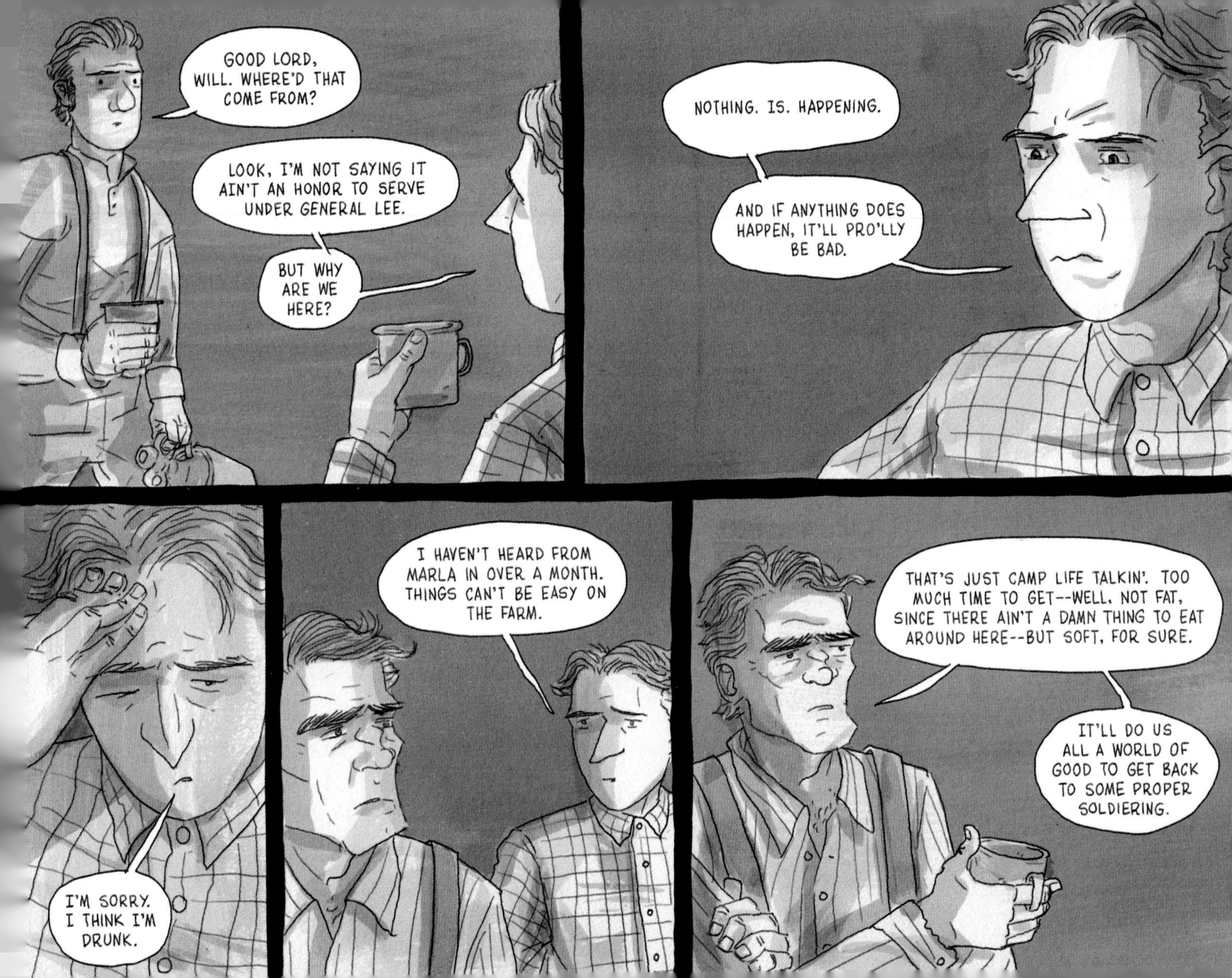
GOOD LORD, WILL. WHERE'D THAT COME FROM?
LOOK, I'M NOT SAYING IT AIN'T AN HONOR TO SERVE UNDER GENERAL LEE.
BUT WHY ARE WE HERE?
NOTHING. IS. HAPPENING.
AND IF ANYTHING DOES HAPPEN, IT'LL PRO'LLY BE BAD.
I'M SORRY. I THINK I'M DRUNK.
I HAVEN'T HEARD FROM MARLA IN OVER A MONTH. THINGS CAN'T BE EASY ON THE FARM.
THAT'S JUST CAMP LIFE TALKIN'. TOO MUCH TIME TO GET--WELL, NOT FAT, SINCE THERE AIN'T A DAMN THING TO EAT AROUND HERE--BUT SOFT, FOR SURE.
IT'LL DO US ALL A WORLD OF GOOD TO GET BACK TO SOME PROPER SOLDIERING.

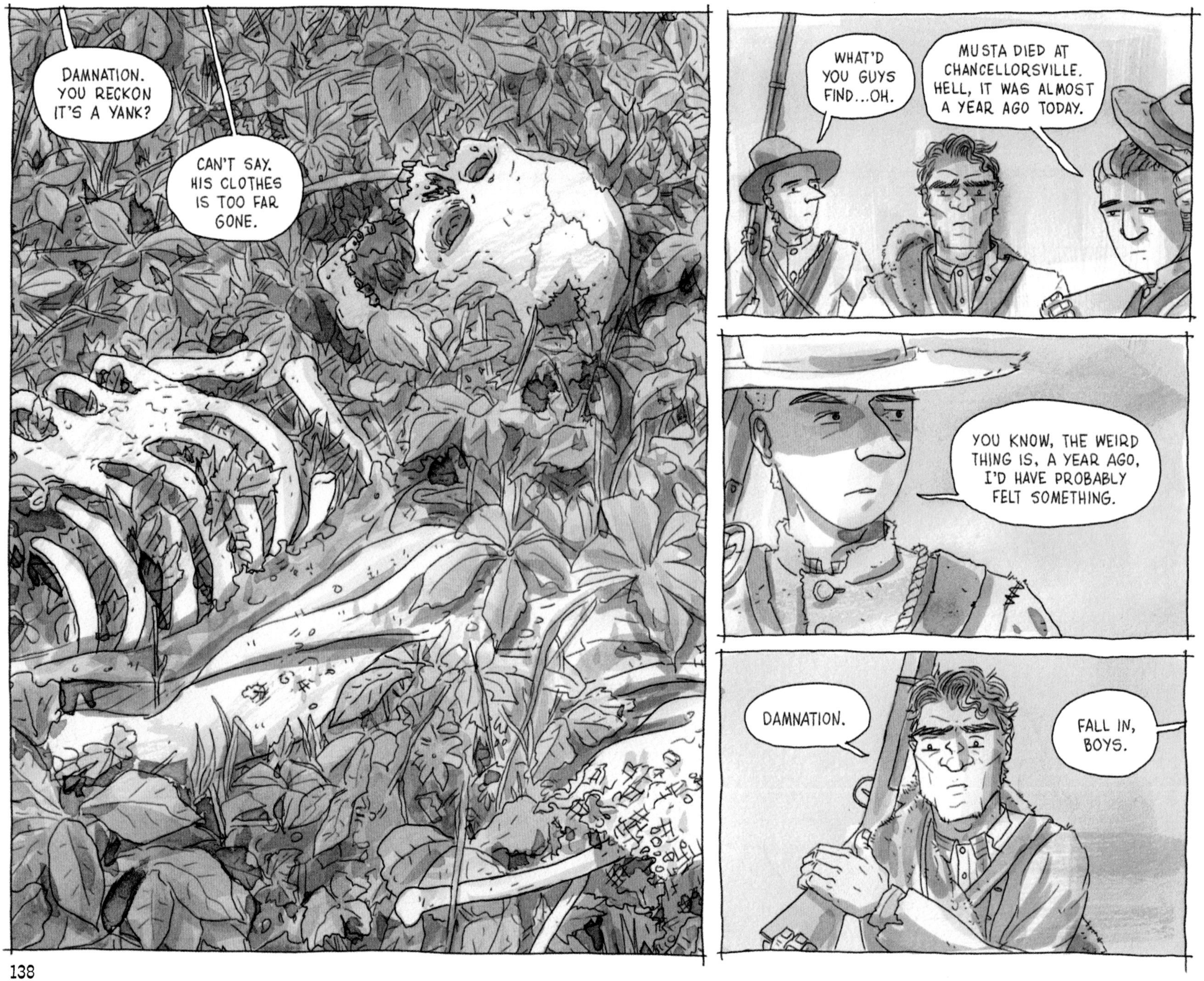
DAMNATION. YOU RECKON IT'S A YANK?
CAN'T SAY. HIS CLOTHES IS TOO FAR GONE.
WHAT'D YOU GUYS FIND...OH.
MUSTA DIED AT CHANCELLORSVILLE. HELL, IT WAS ALMOST A YEAR AGO TODAY.
YOU KNOW, THE WEIRD THING IS, A YEAR AGO, I'D HAVE PROBABLY FELT SOMETHING.
DAMNATION.
FALL IN, BOYS.

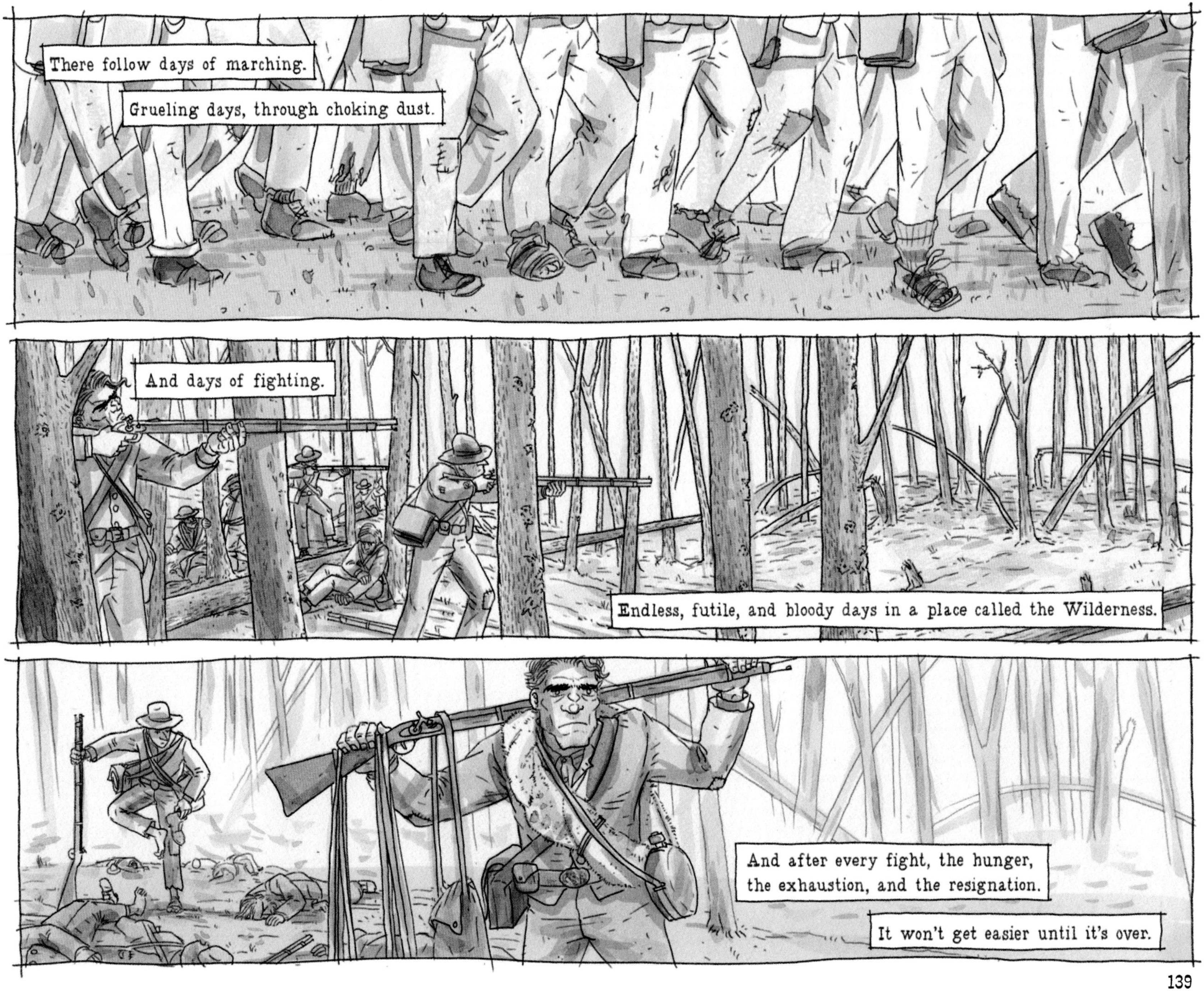
There follow days of marching.
Grueling days, through choking dust.
And days of fighting.
Endless, futile, and bloody days in a place called the Wilderness.
And after every fight, the hunger, the exhaustion, and the resignation.
It won't get easier until it's over.

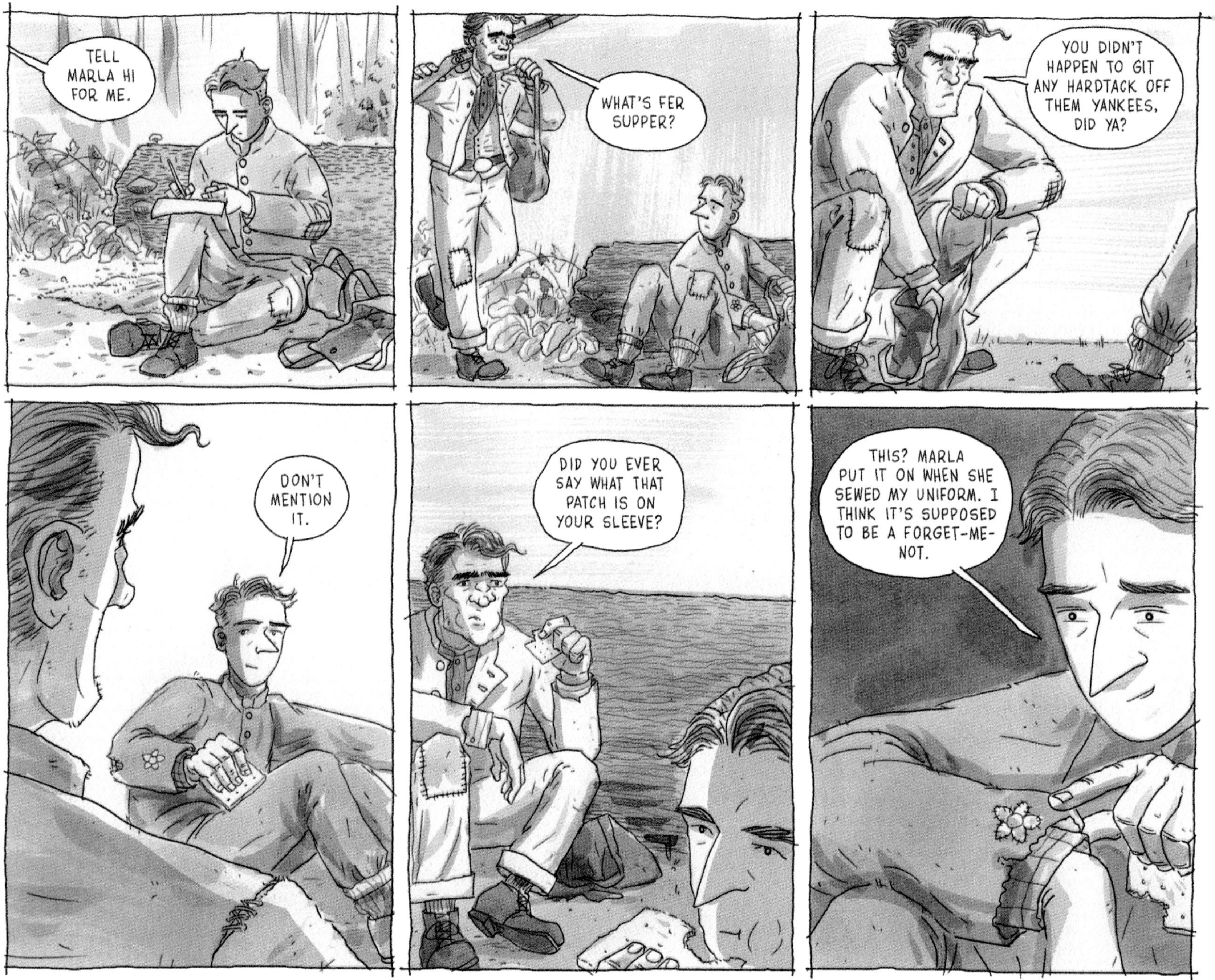
TELL MARLA HI FOR ME.
WHAT'S FER SUPPER?
YOU DIDN'T HAPPEN TO GIT ANY HARDTACK OFF THEM YANKEES, DID YA?
DON'T MENTION IT.
DID YOU EVER SAY WHAT THAT PATCH IS ON YOUR SLEEVE?
THIS? MARLA PUT IT ON WHEN SHE SEWED MY UNIFORM. I THINK IT'S SUPPOSED TO BE A FORGET-ME-NOT.

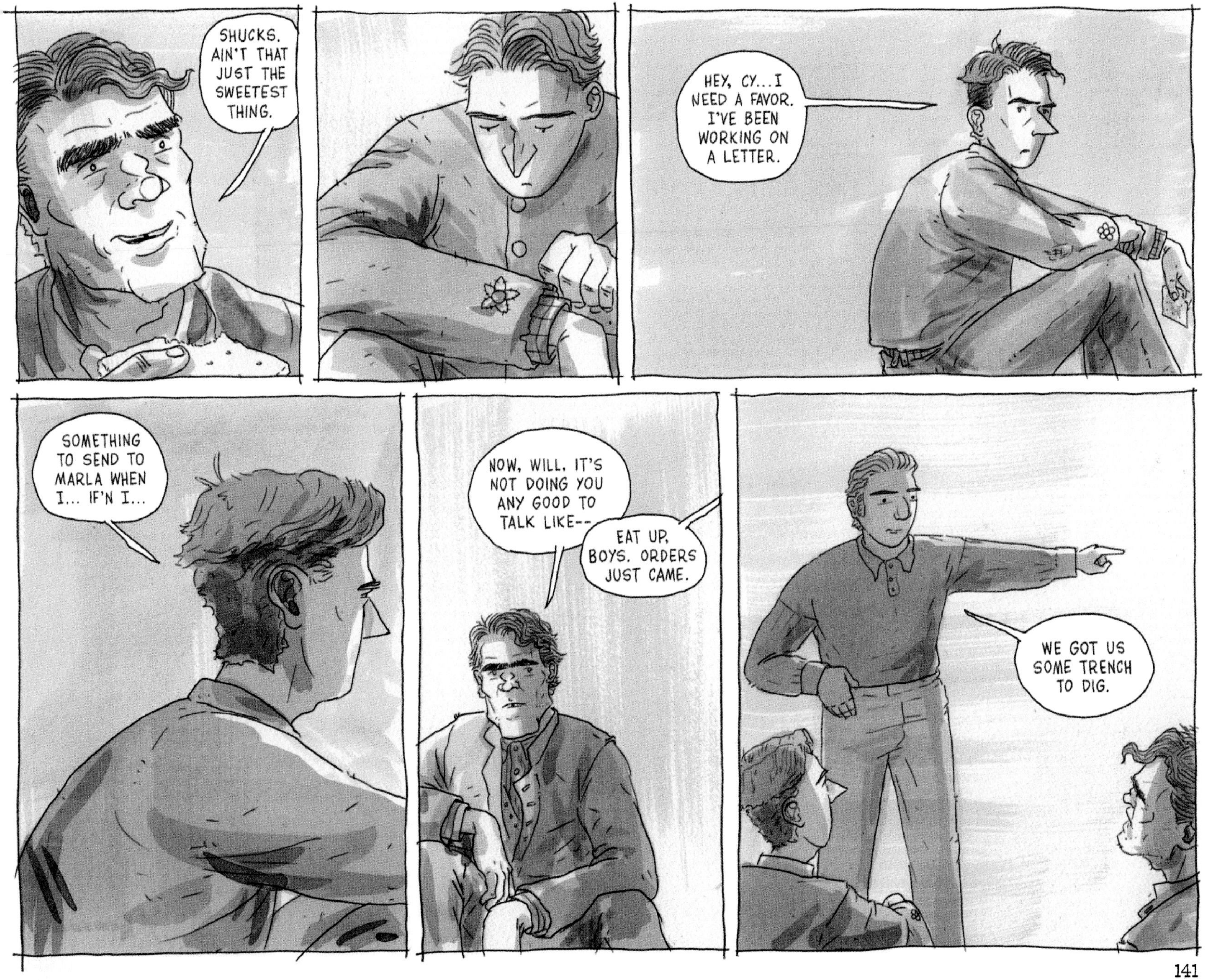
SHUCKS. AIN'T THAT JUST THE SWEETEST THING.
HEY, CY... I NEED A FAVOR. I'VE BEEN WORKING ON A LETTER.
SOMETHING TO SEND TO MARLA WHEN I... IF'N I...
NOW, WILL, IT'S NOT DOING YOU ANY GOOD TO TALK LIKE--
EAT UP, BOYS. ORDERS JUST CAME.
WE GOT US SOME TRENCH TO DIG.

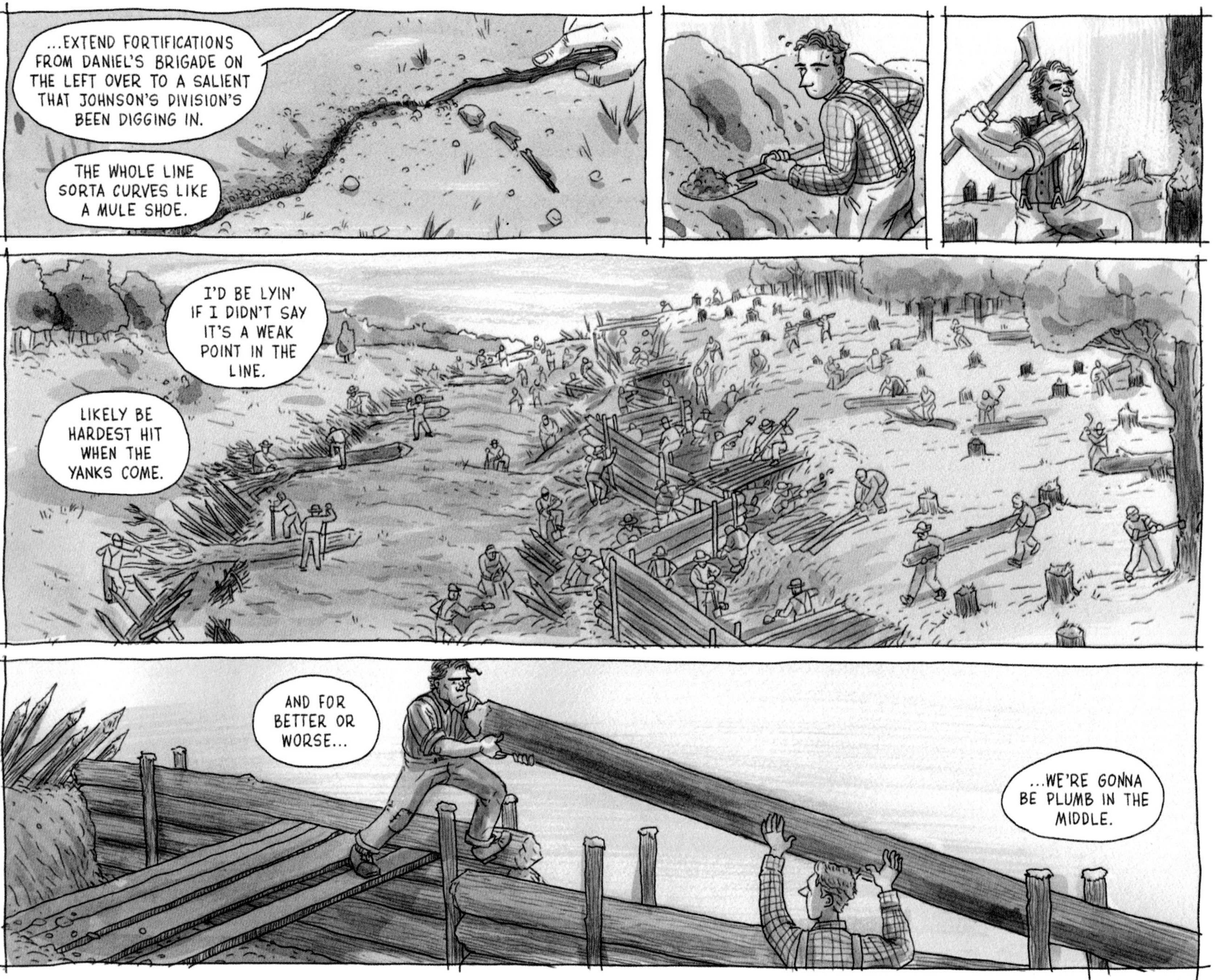
...EXTEND FORTIFICATIONS FROM DANIEL'S BRIGADE ON THE LEFT OVER TO A SALIENT THAT JOHNSON'S DIVISION'S BEEN DIGGING IN.
THE WHOLE LINE SORTA CURVES LIKE A MULE SHOE.
I'D BE LYIN' IF I DIDN'T SAY IT'S A WEAK POINT IN THE LINE.
LIKELY BE HARDEST HIT WHEN THE YANKS COME.
AND FOR BETTER OR WORSE...
...WE'RE GONNA BE PLUMB IN THE MIDDLE.

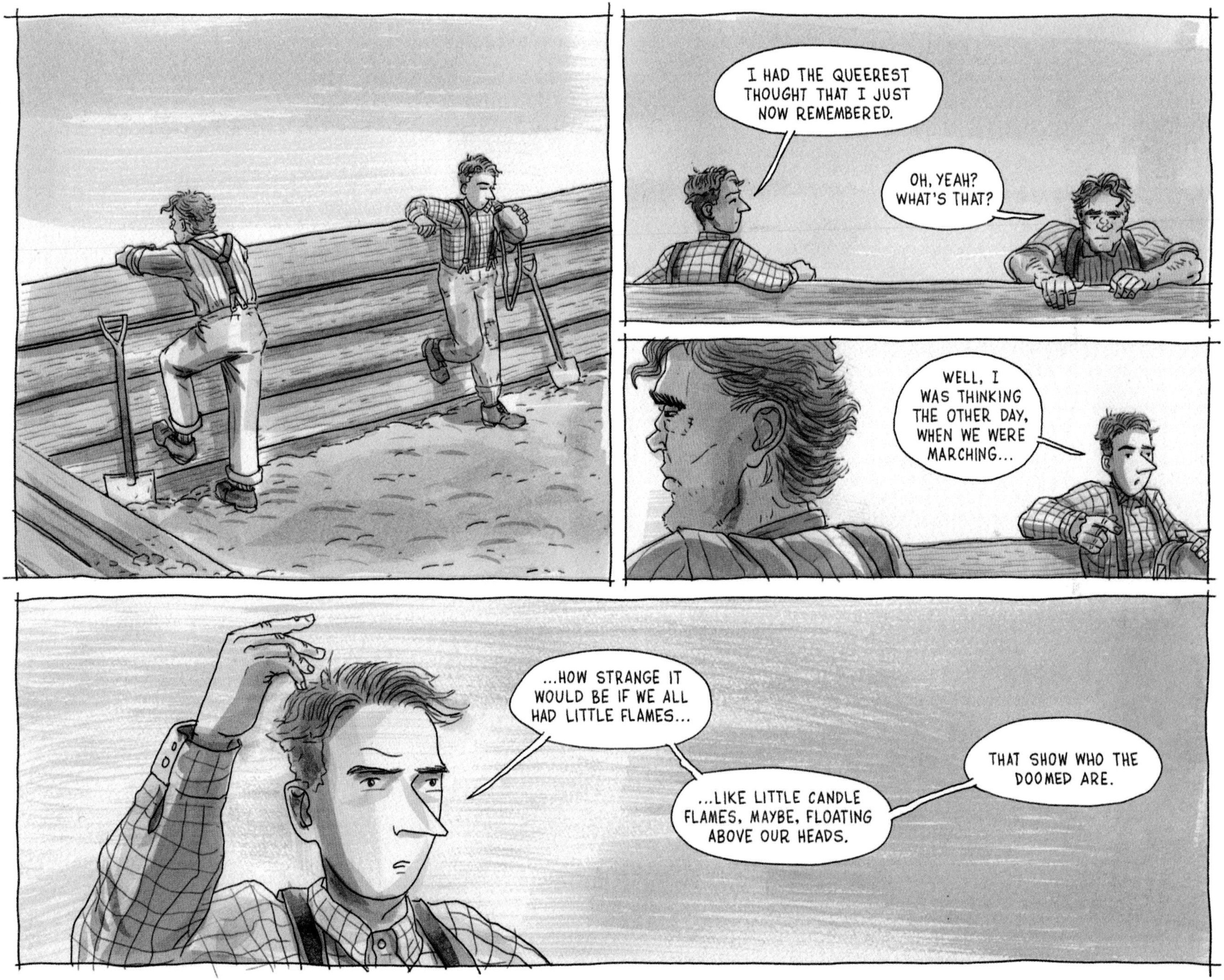
I HAD THE QUEEREST THOUGHT THAT I JUST NOW REMEMBERED.
OH, YEAH? WHAT'S THAT?
WELL, I WAS THINKING THE OTHER DAY, WHEN WE WERE MARCHING...
...HOW STRANGE IT WOULD BE IF WE ALL HAD LITTLE FLAMES...
...LIKE LITTLE CANDLE FLAMES, MAYBE, FLOATING ABOVE OUR HEADS.
THAT SHOW WHO THE DOOMED ARE.

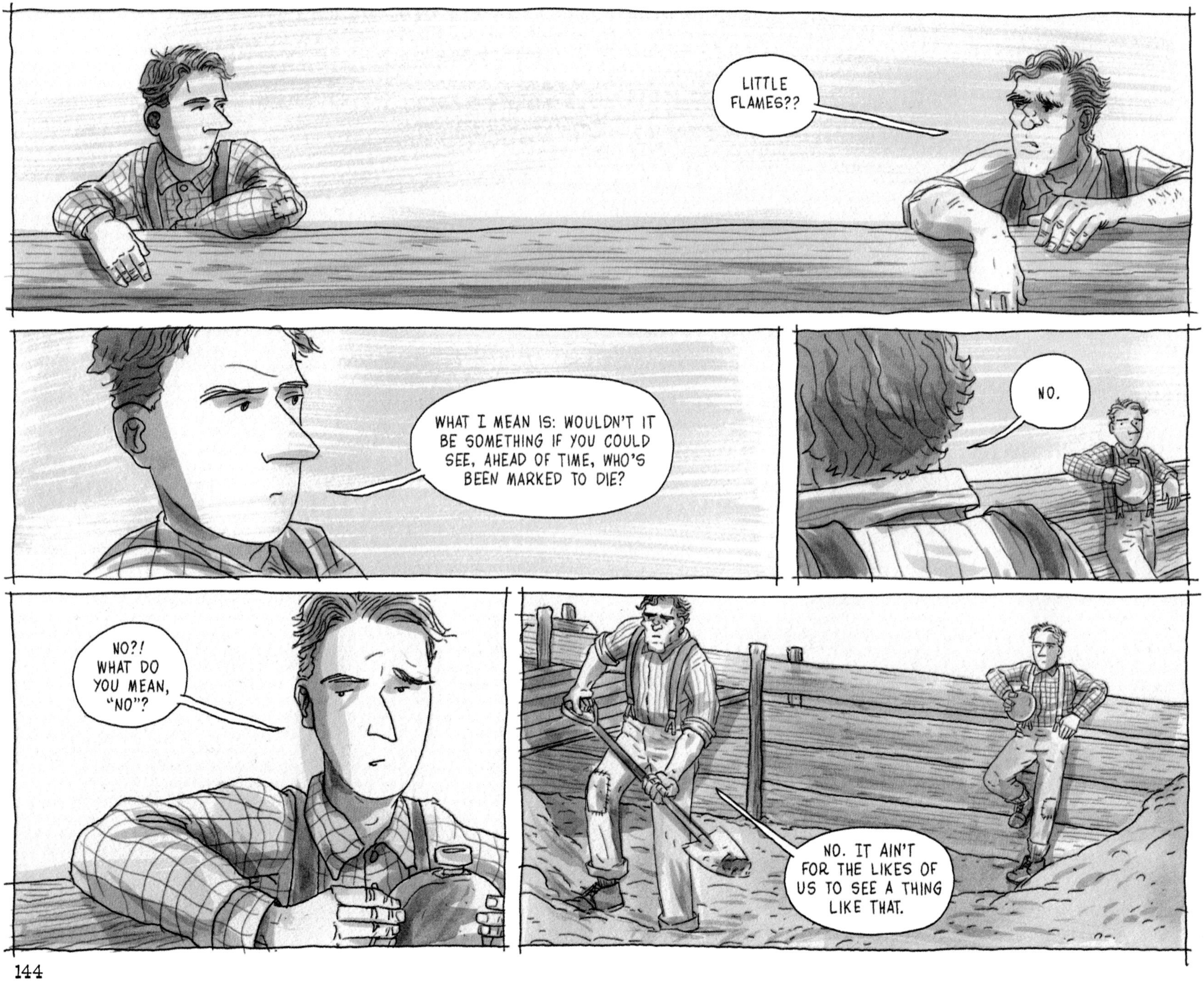
LITTLE FLAMES??
WHAT I MEAN IS: WOULDN'T IT BE SOMETHING IF YOU COULD SEE, AHEAD OF TIME, WHO'S BEEN MARKED TO DIE?
NO.
NO?! WHAT DO YOU MEAN, "NO"?
NO. IT AIN'T FOR THE LIKES OF US TO SEE A THING LIKE THAT.

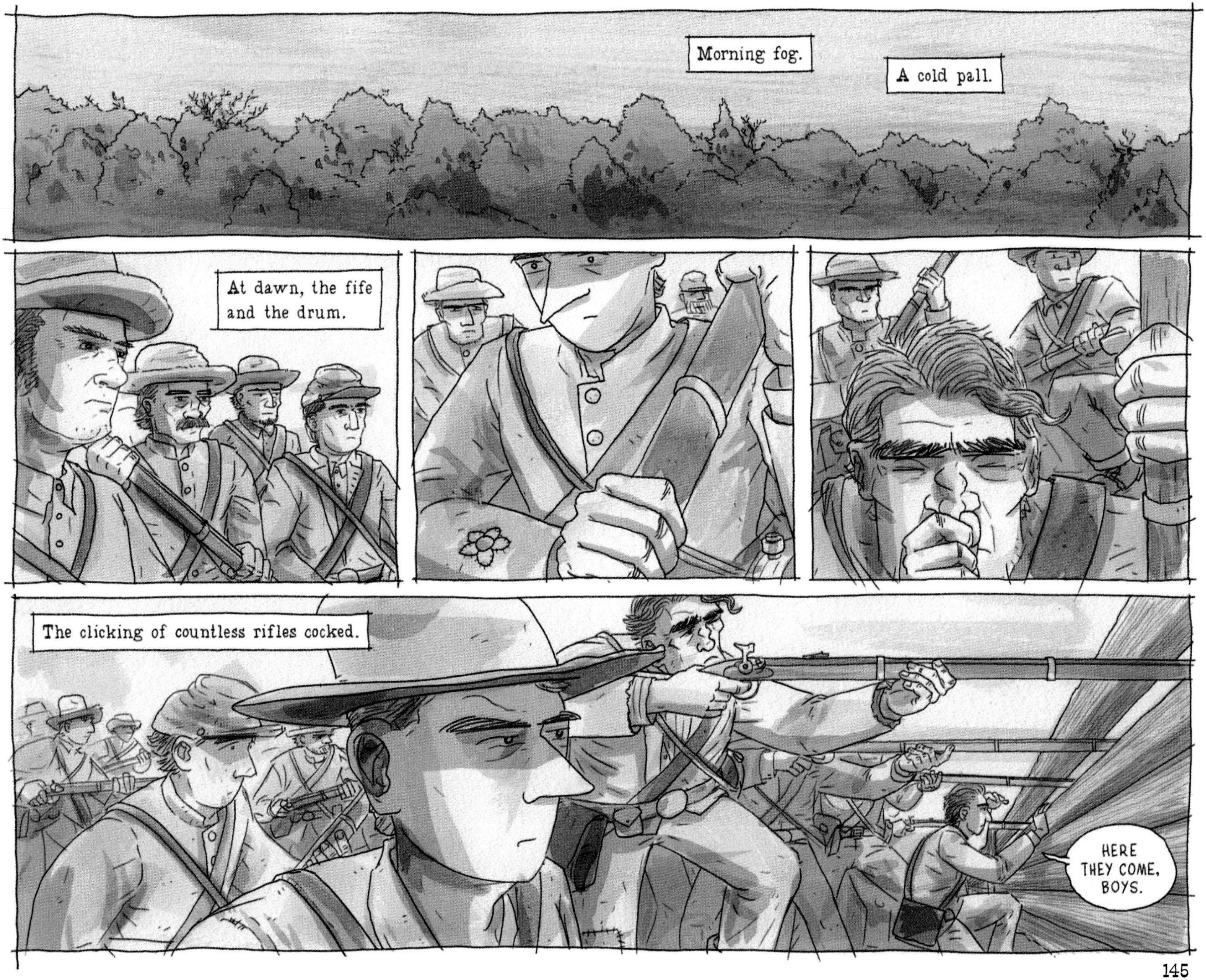
Morning fog.
A cold pall.
At dawn, the fife and the drum.
The clicking of countless rifles cocked.
HERE THEY COME, BOYS.

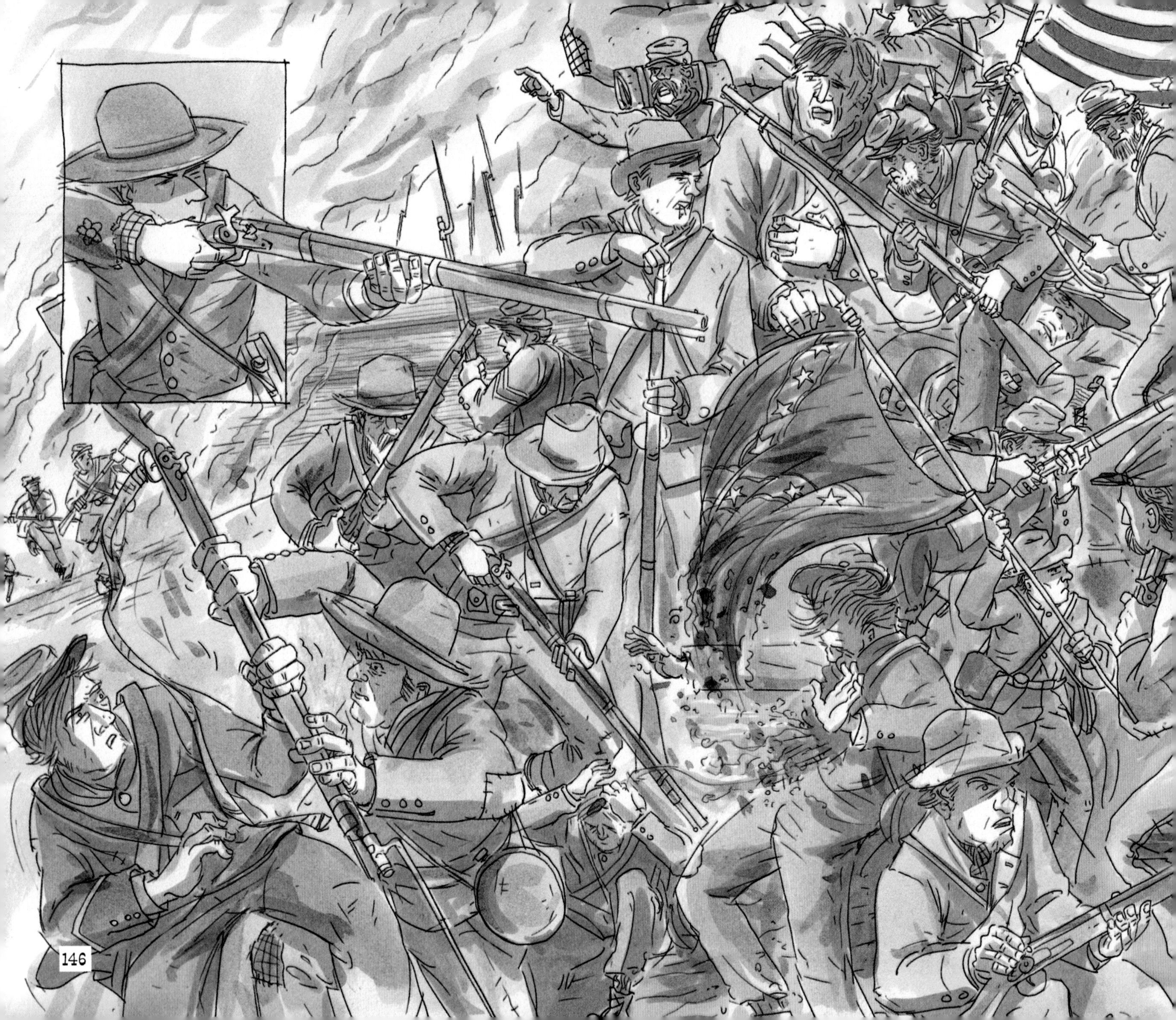

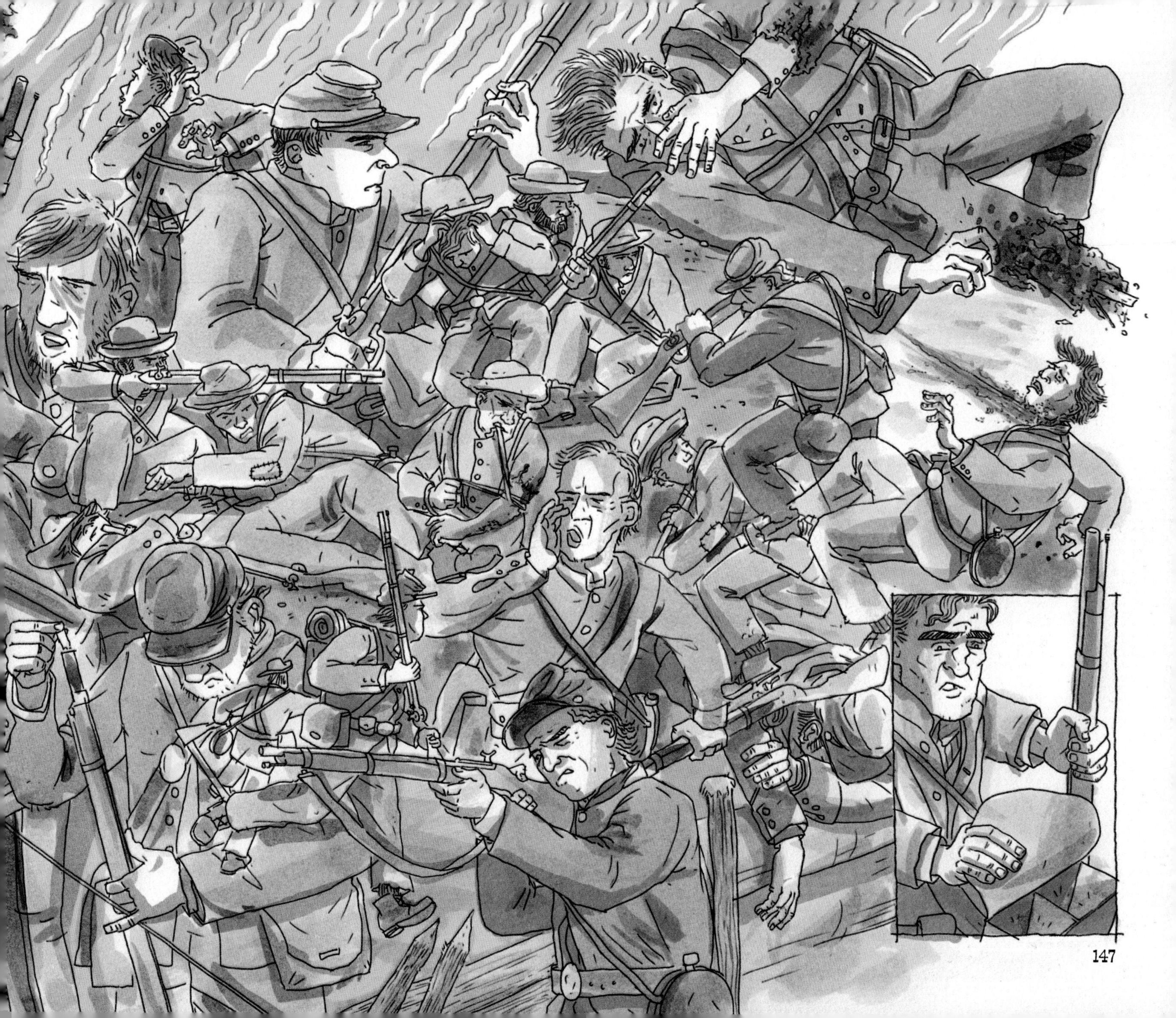

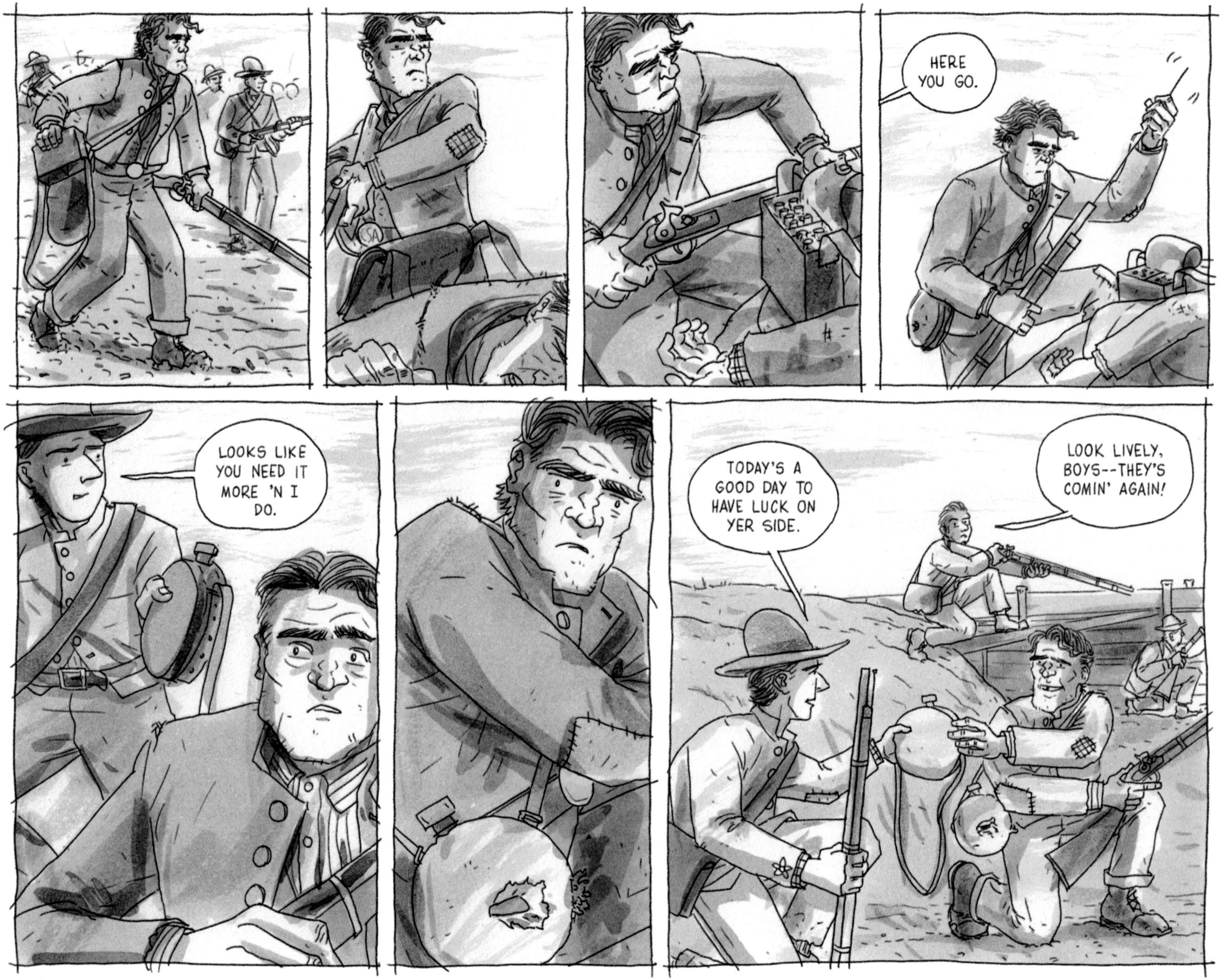
HERE YOU GO.
LOOKS LIKE YOU NEED IT MORE 'N I DO.
TODAY'S A GOOD DAY TO HAVE LUCK ON YER SIDE.
LOOK LIVELY, BOYS--THEY'S COMIN' AGAIN!

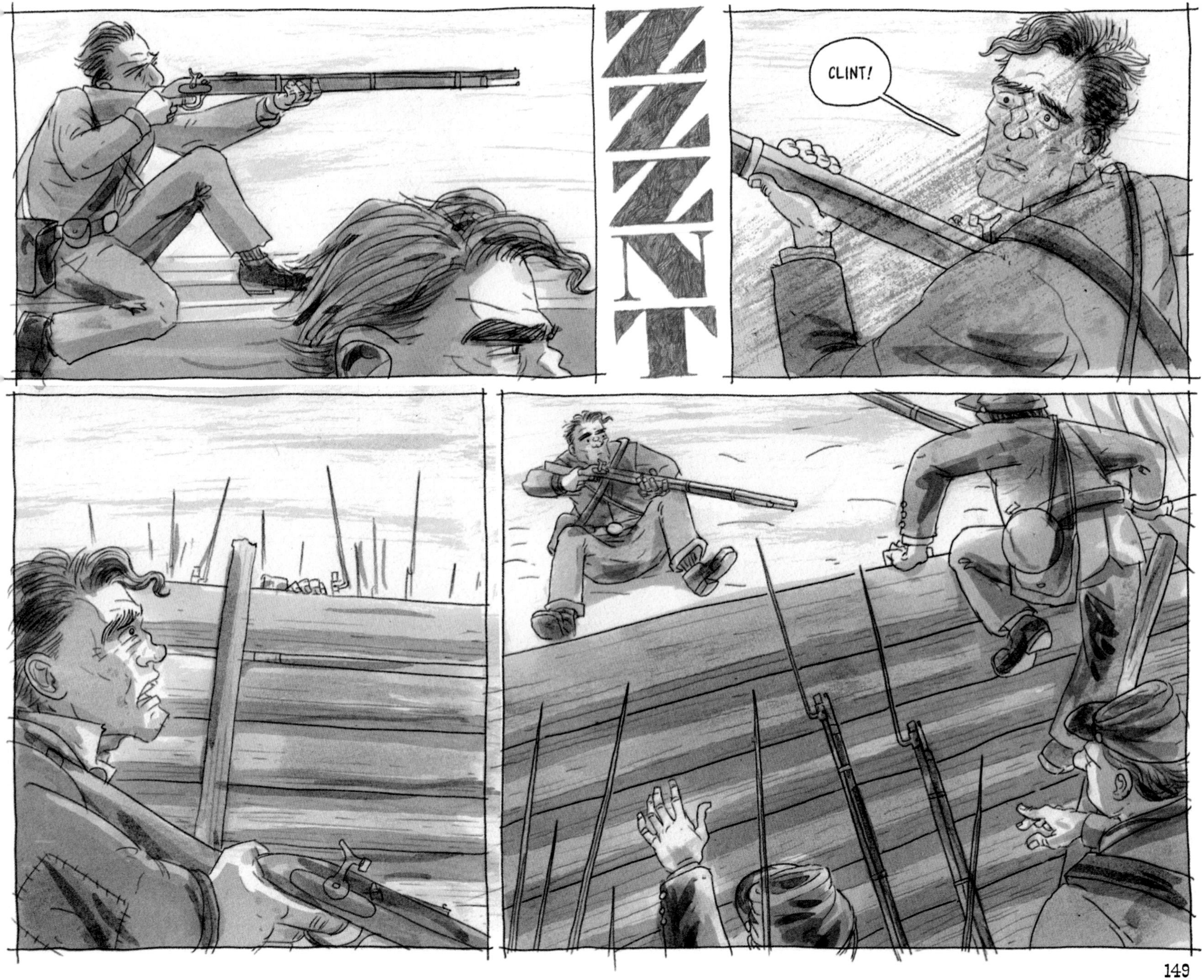
ZZZNT
CLINT!

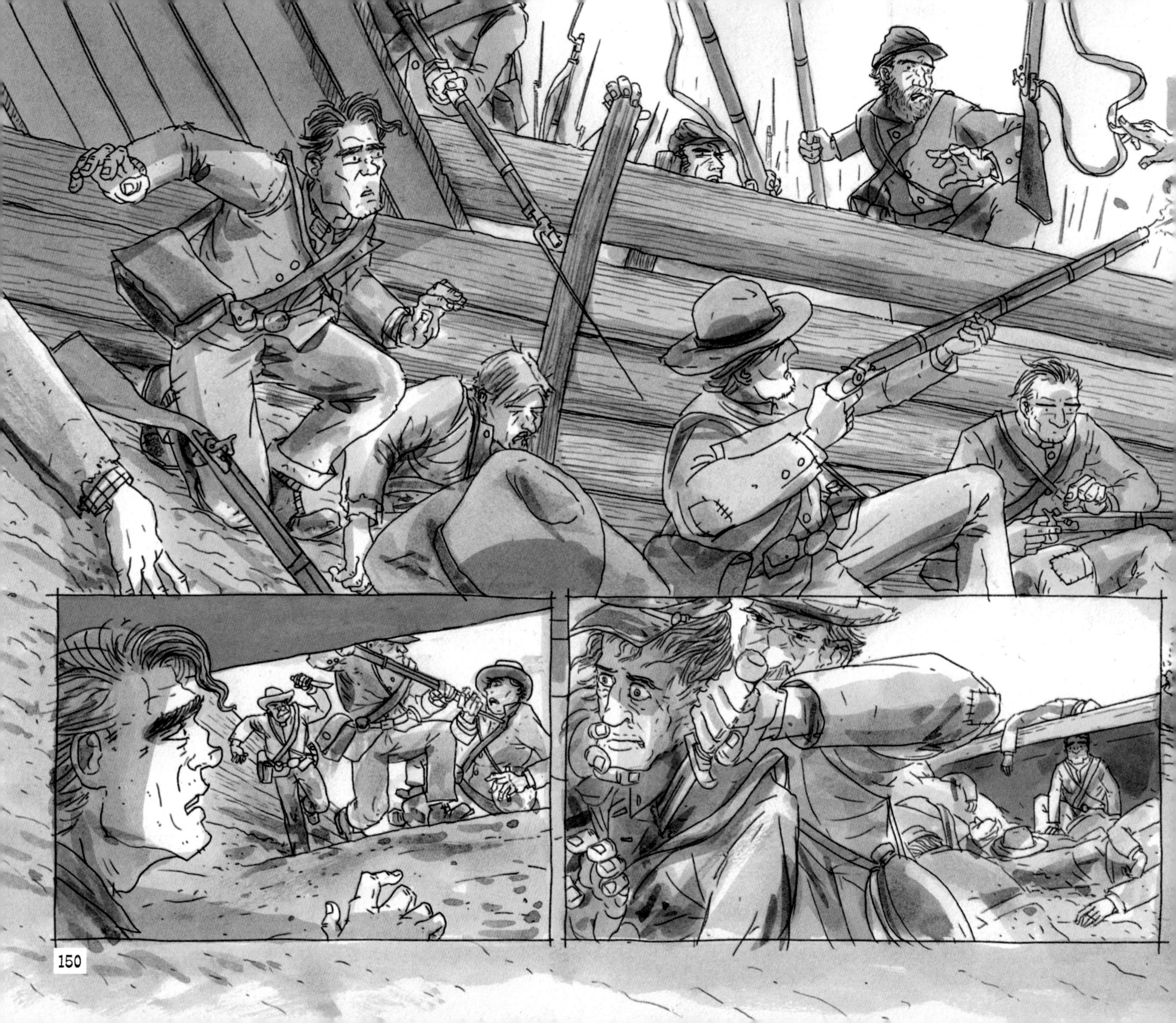

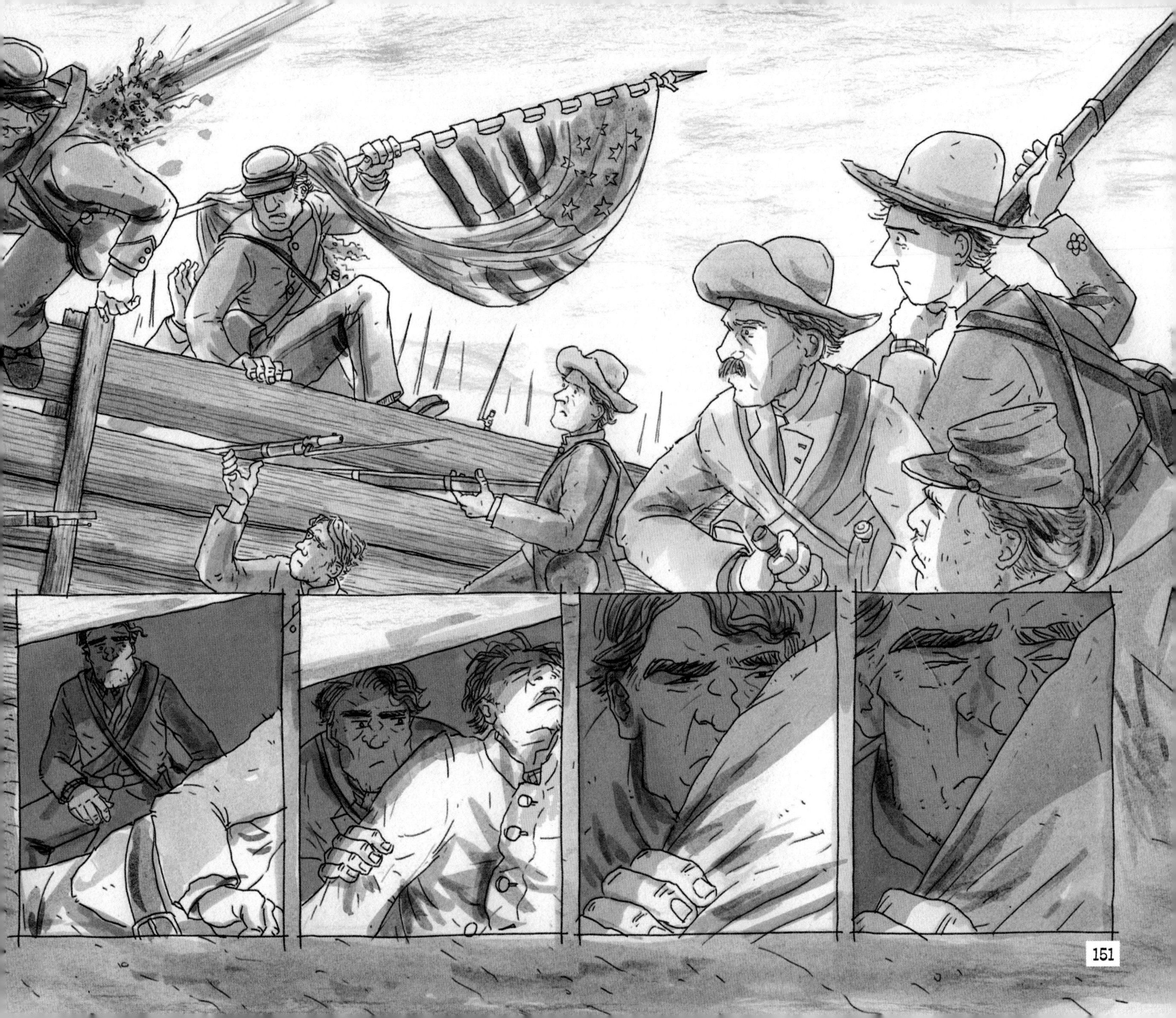

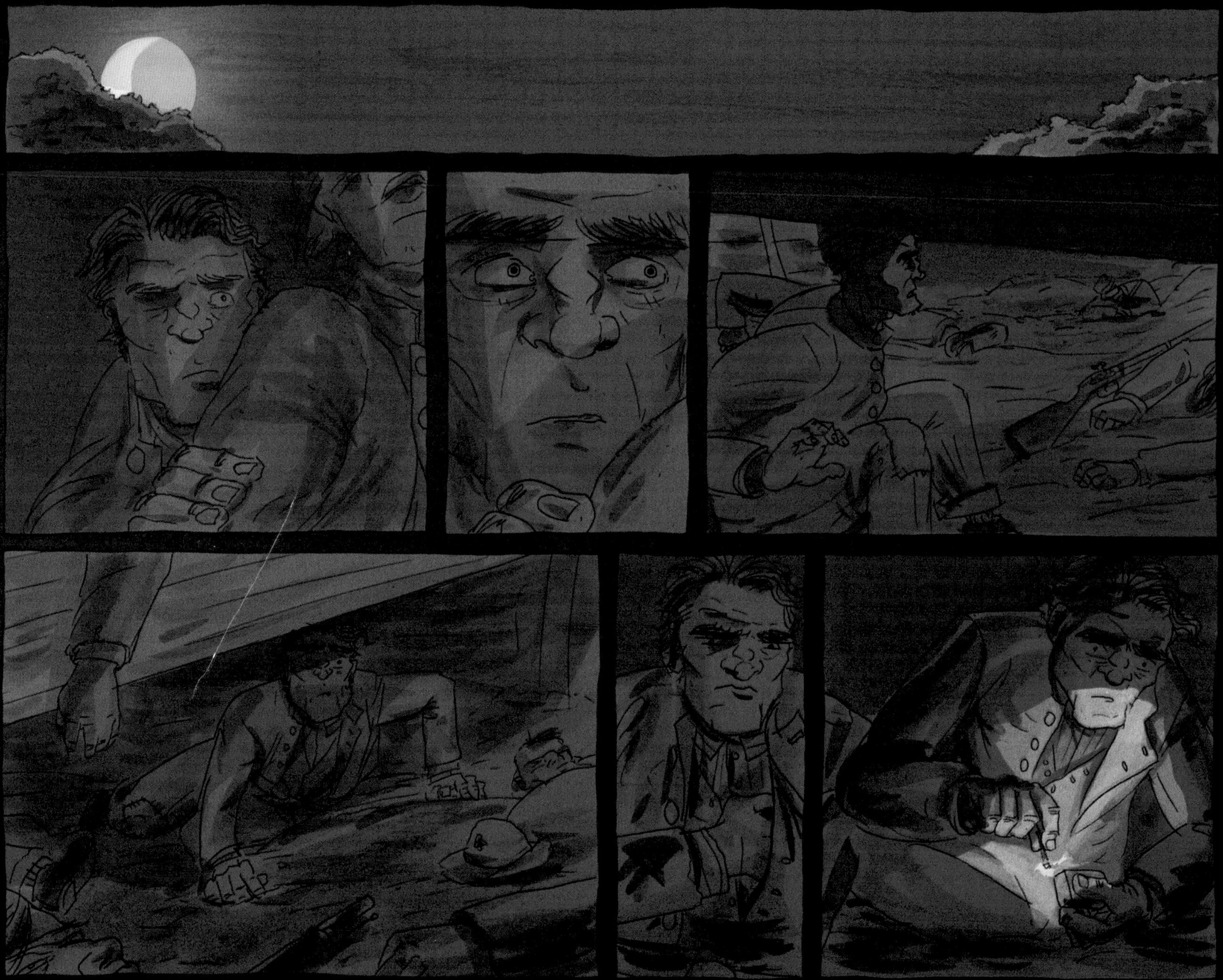

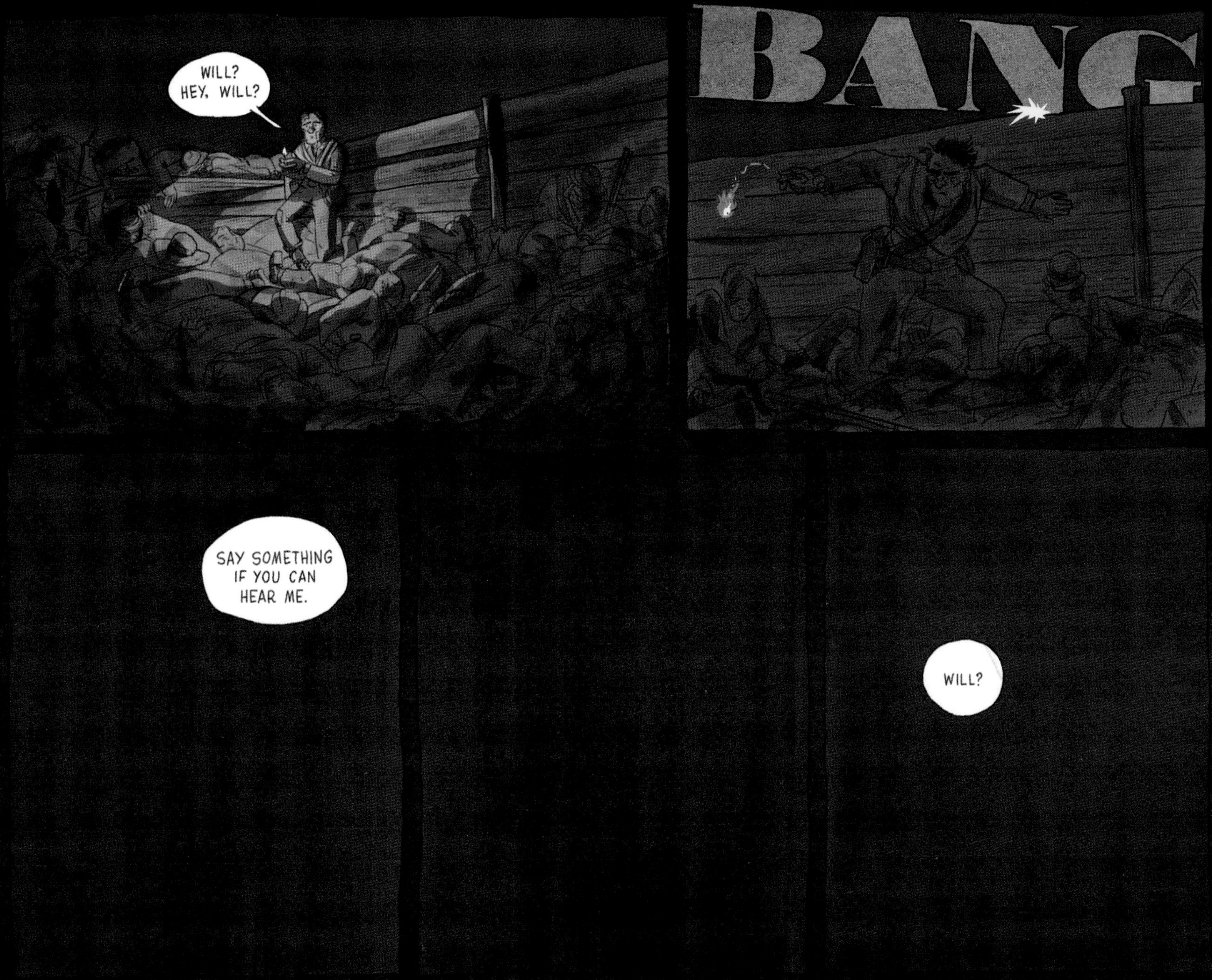
WILL?
HEY, WILL?
BANG
SAY SOMETHING IF YOU CAN HEAR ME.
WILL?

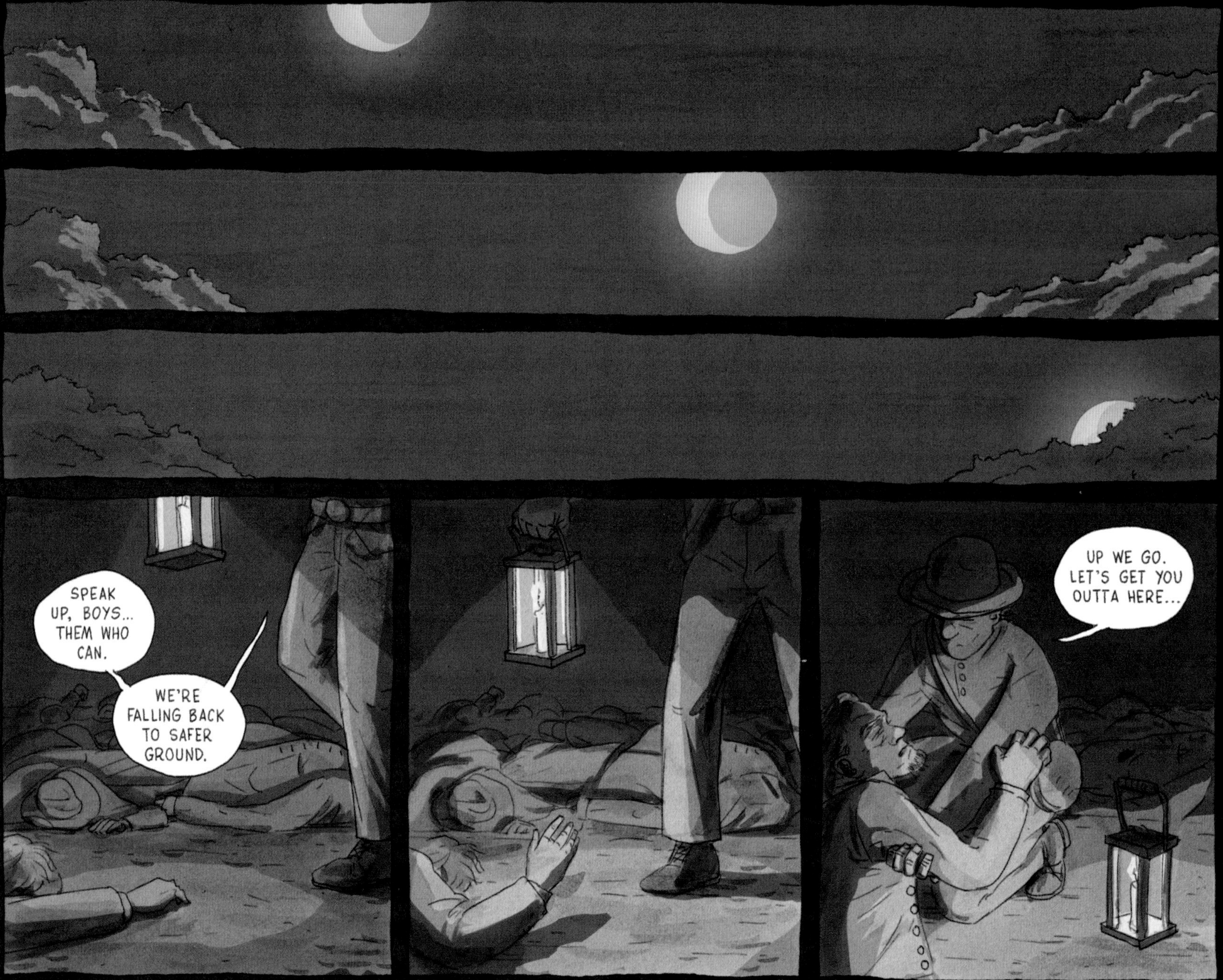
SPEAK UP, BOYS... THEM WHO CAN.
WE'RE FALLING BACK TO SAFER GROUND.
UP WE GO. LET'S GET YOU OUTTA HERE...

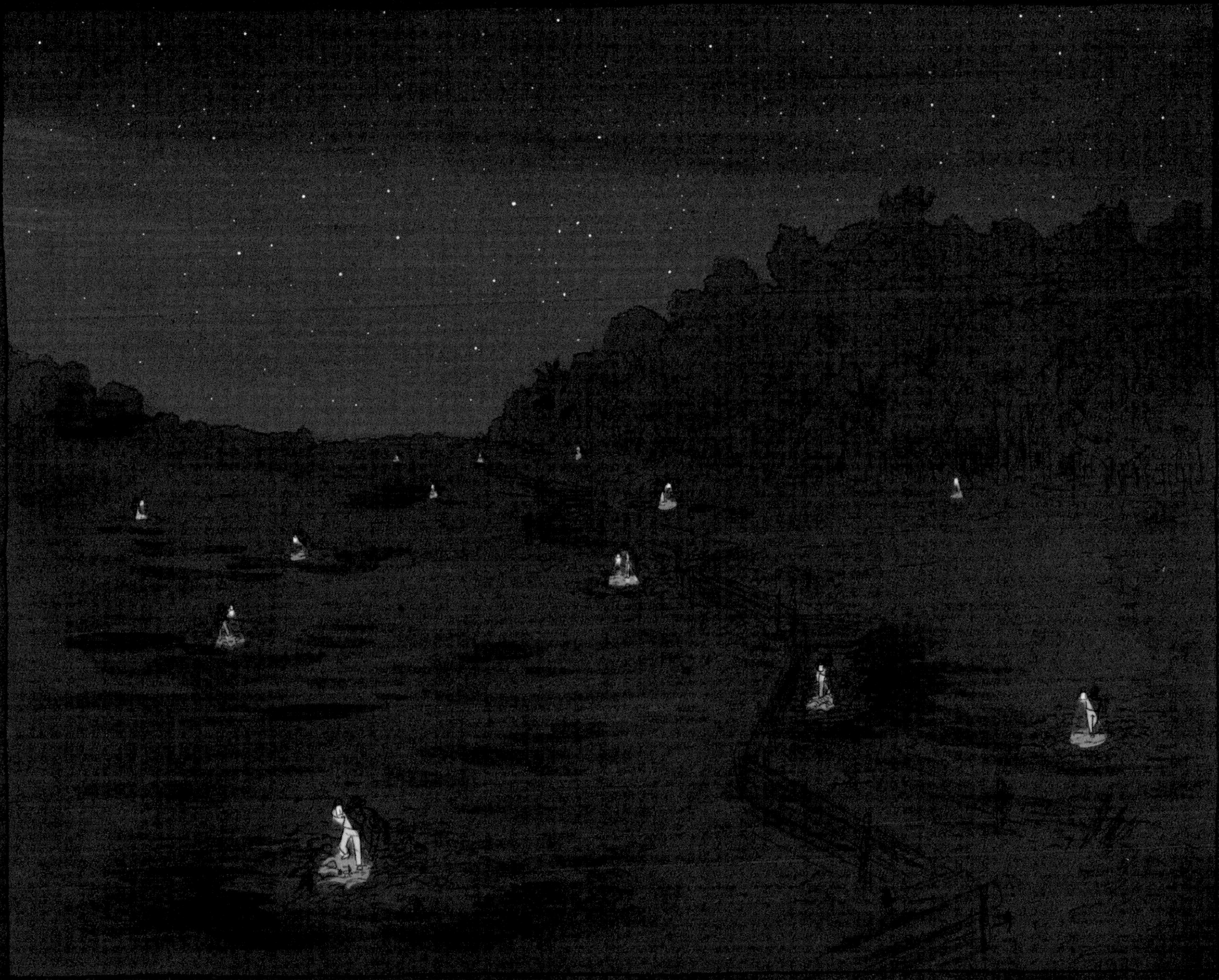

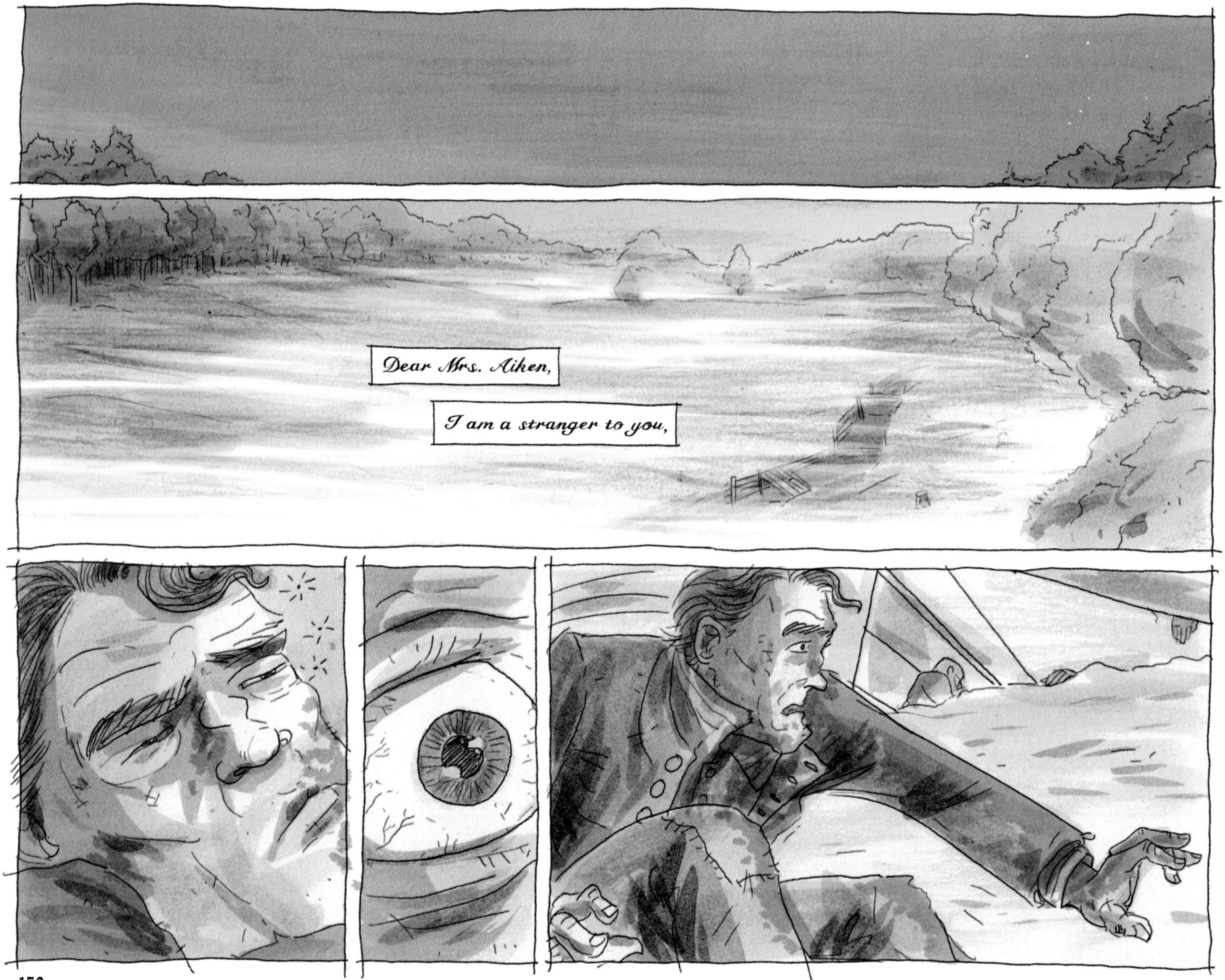

Dear Mrs. Aiken,
I am a stranger to you,

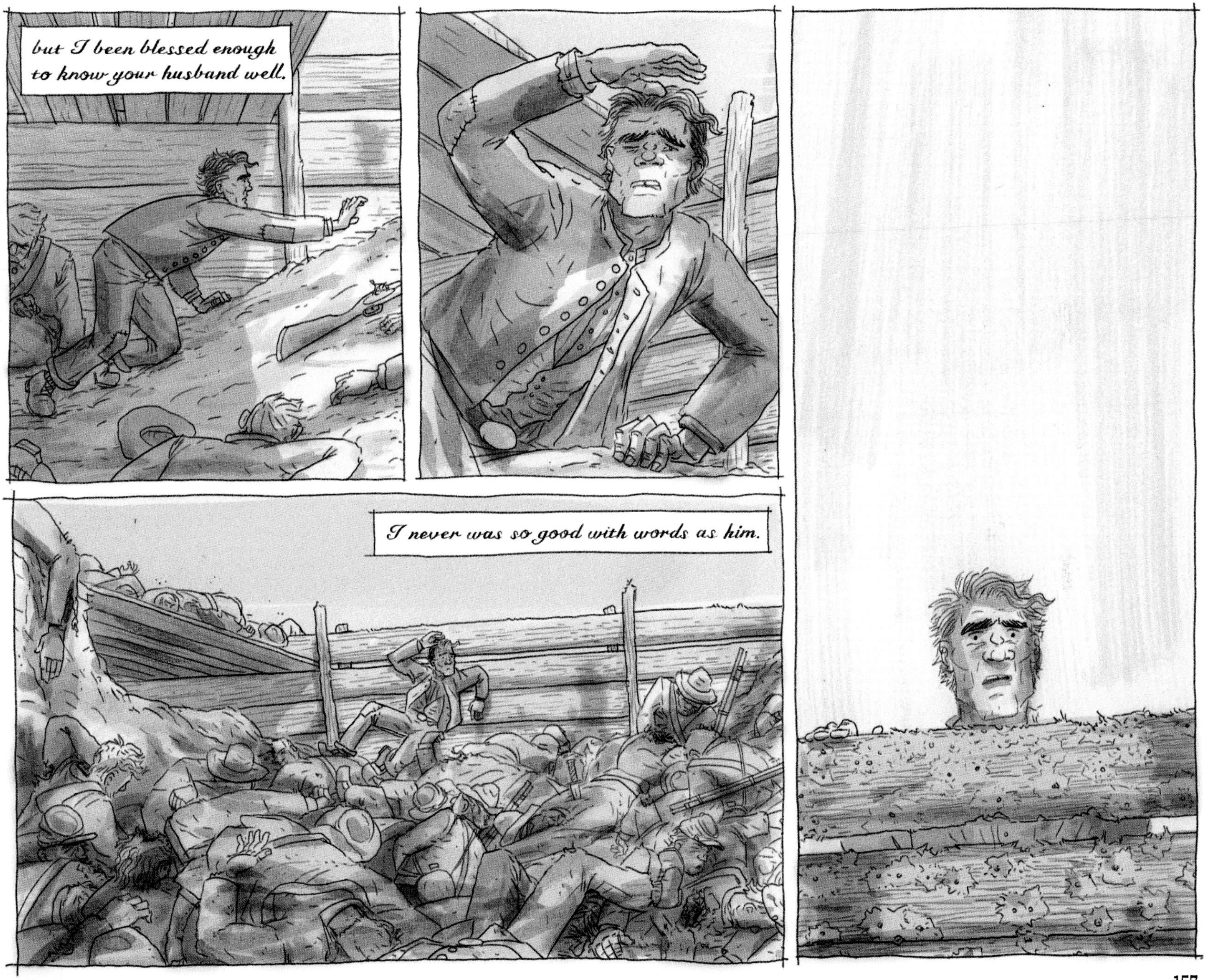
but I been blessed enough to know your husband well.
I never was so good with words as him.

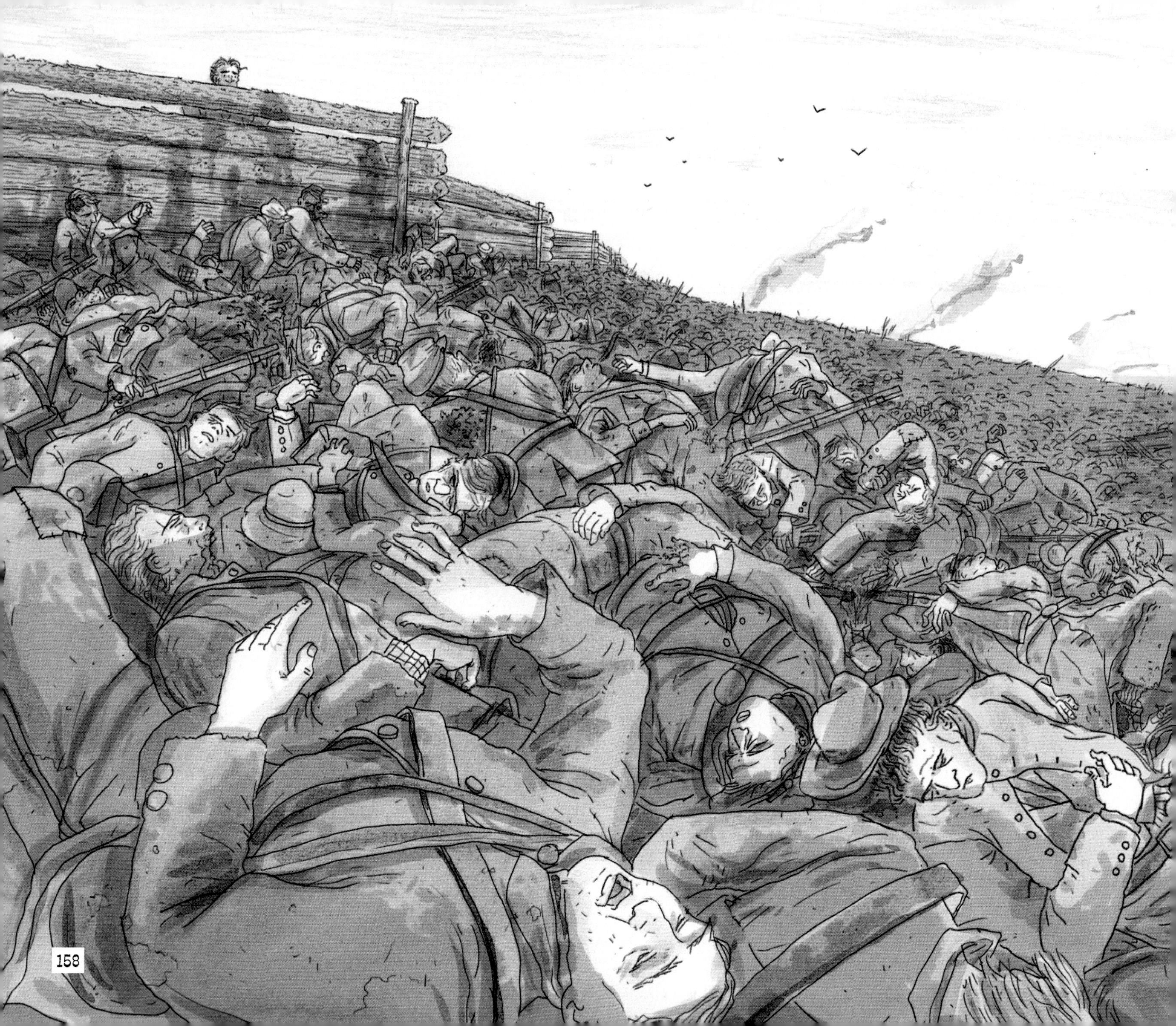

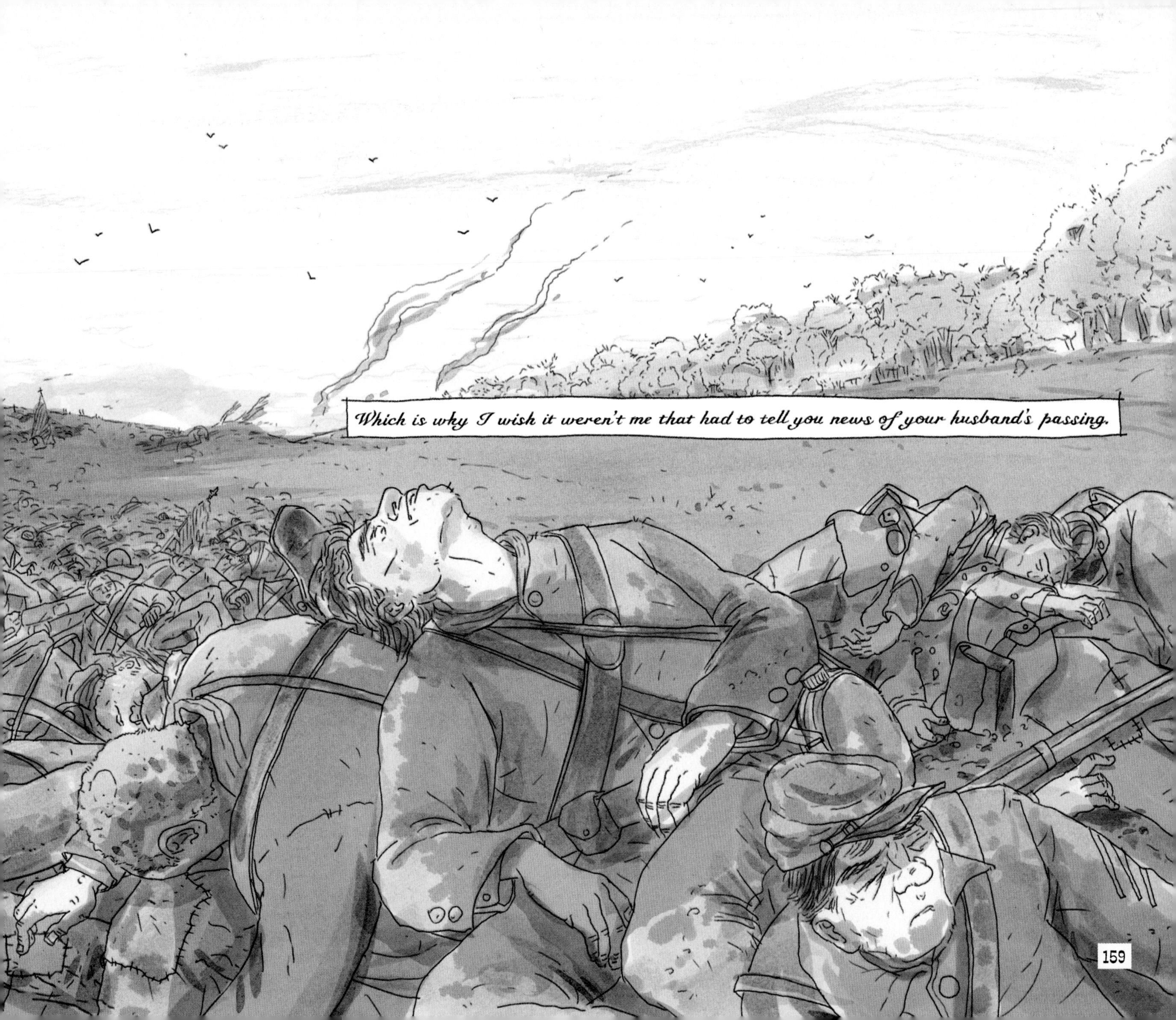
Which is why I wish it weren't me that had to tell you news of your husband's passing.

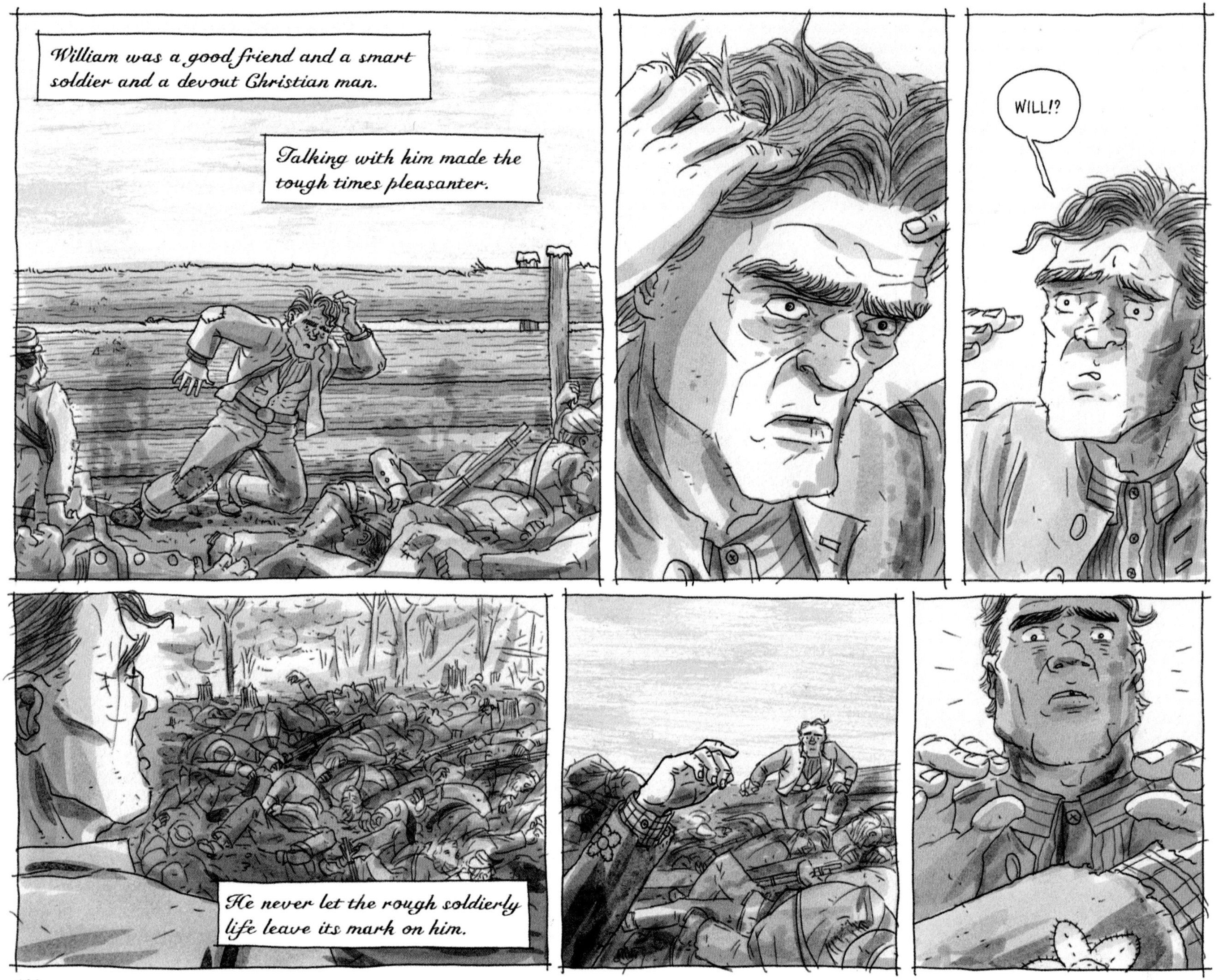
William was a good friend and a smart soldier and a devout Christian man.
Talking with him made the tough times pleasanter.
WILL!?
He never let the rough soldierly life leave its mark on him.

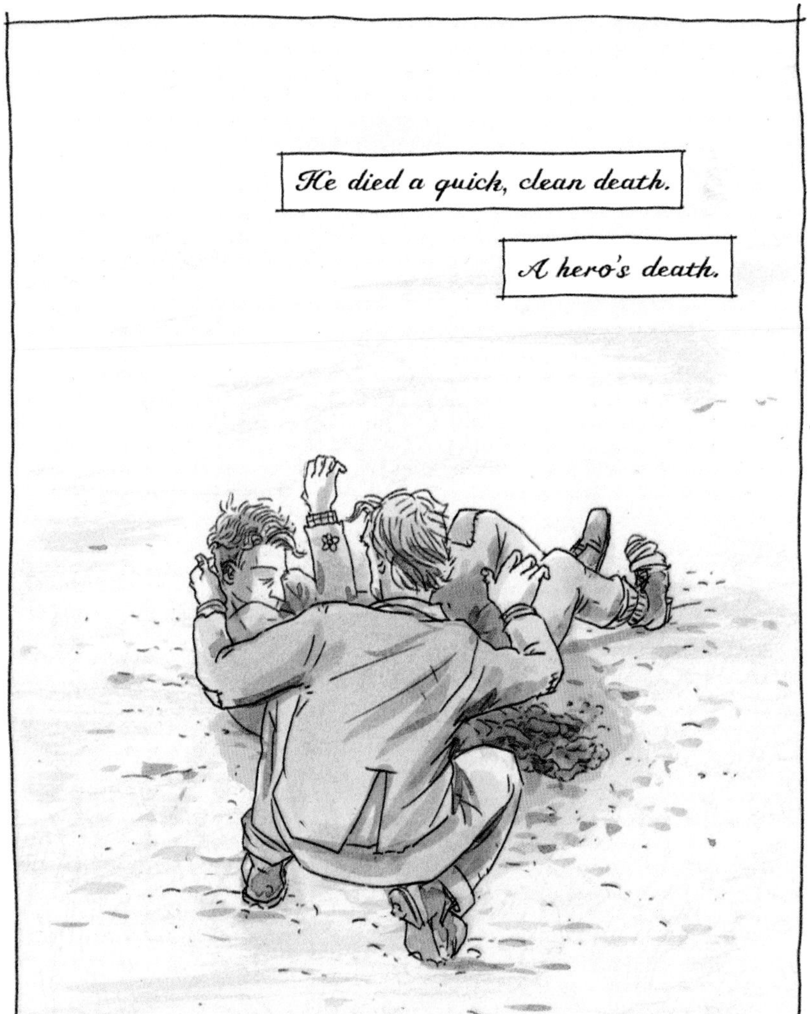
He died a quick, clean death.
A hero's death.

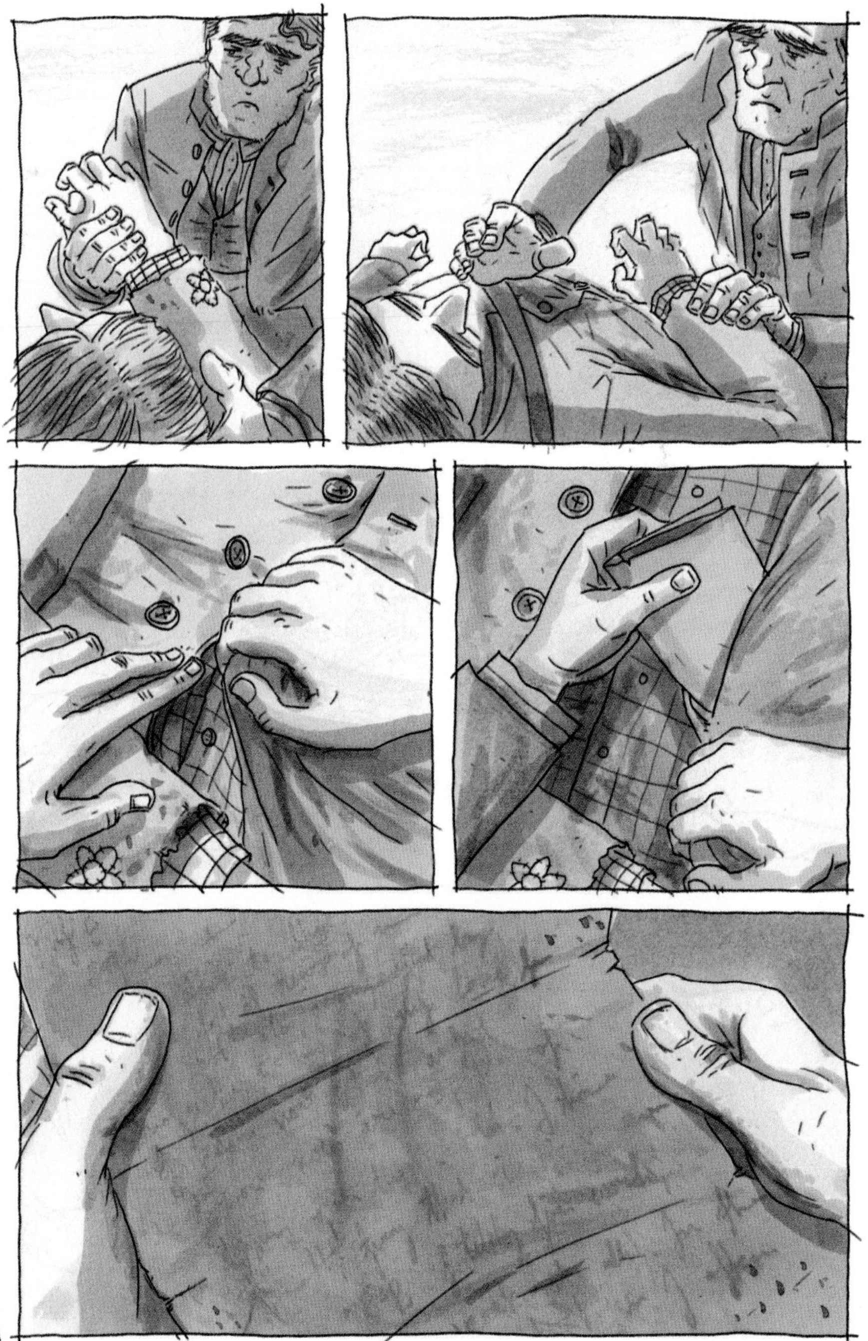

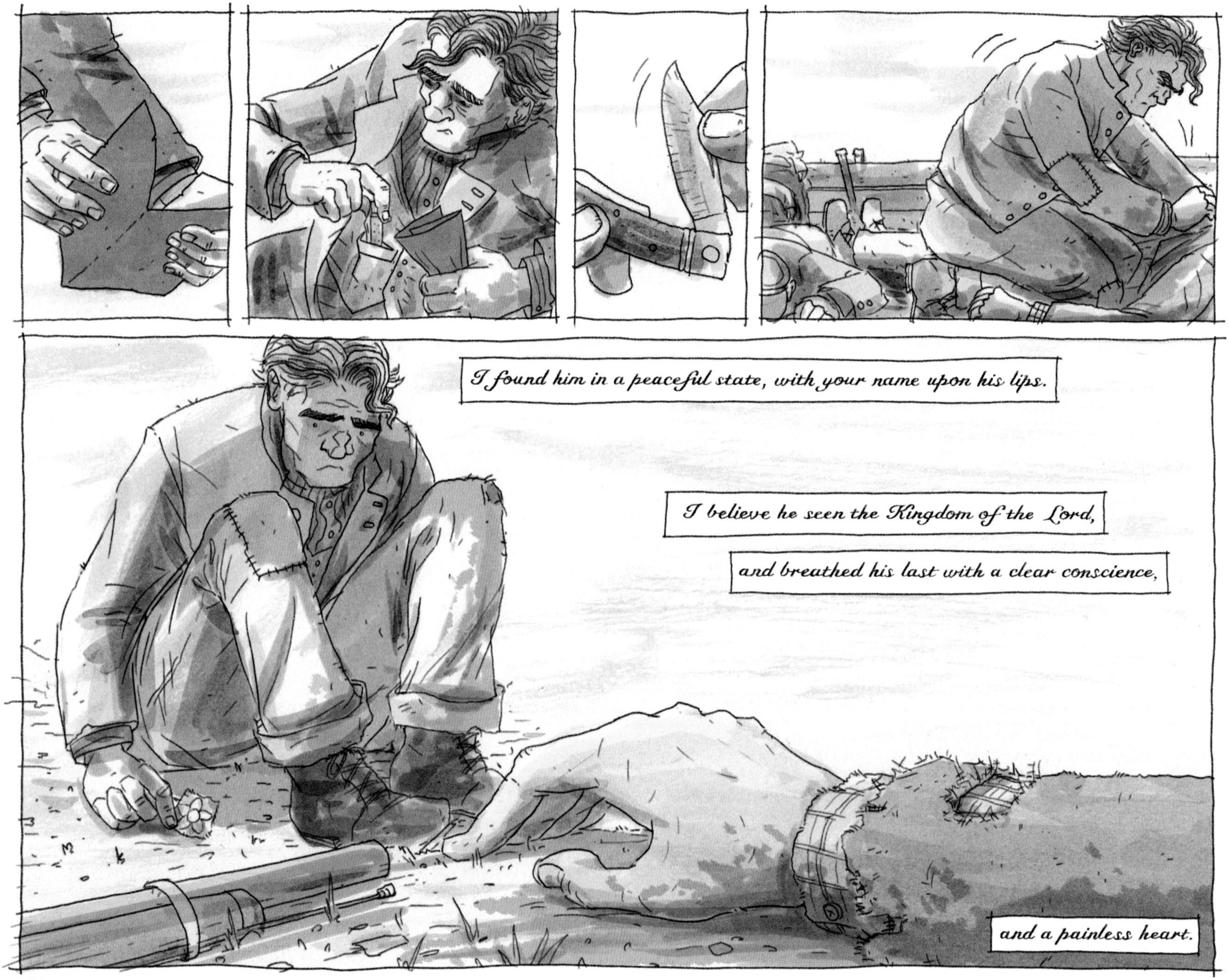
I found him in a peaceful state, with your name upon his lips.
I believe he seen the Kingdom of the Lord,
and breathed his last with a clear conscience,
and a painless heart.

Chapter 12: Ink

ATLANTA ENQUIRER

August 7, 1864

GENERAL GRANT TAKES CHARGE

In the spring of 1864, President Lincoln promoted Ulysses Grant to command of all the Union's armies. Grant moved east, tapping William Sherman to lead the Federal forces in the West.

Still the rebels fought on, pinning their hopes on the upcoming election in the North. If voters could be persuaded to boot Lincoln from office and replace him with a Democrat, a hasty peace might secure independence for the Confederacy.

To that end, General Lee planned to have his Army of Northern Virginia inflict as much damage as possible on Federal troops. From early May though mid-June, battle-hardened rebels killed or wounded some fifty thousand federals (the South lost half that number) at the Wilderness, Spotsylvania, and Cold Harbor.

But Grant, unlike his predecessors, remained undaunted by the carnage. He ordered his men to keep grinding toward Richmond. Lee countered by entrenching his army in Grant's path, outside Petersburg. So began a period of trench warfare--fighting marked by equal parts brutality and boredom.

Lincoln, for his part, wondered how he could win reelection against a backdrop of soaring casualties and tactical blunders.

AN IMPASSE OVER PRISONER EXCHANGE

Early in the war, the Union and the Confederacy, eager to avoid the expense and logistical nightmare of caring for prisoners of war, regularly exchanged captives. But after President Lincoln issued the Emancipation Proclamation and former slaves and free people of color began mustering into the Union army, Southerners insisted that the practice of arming African Americans was an abomination, evidence of Lincoln's disregard for the rule of law and the protocols of civilized warfare.

In July of 1863, the Confederate Congress adopted a policy of re-enslaving or executing captured African American soldiers. The Union War Department responded by imprisoning captured rebel troops.

By early 1864, both sides held thousands of POWs. The Confederacy dealt with the situation by building a prison camp at Andersonville, in southwest Georgia. It was designed to hold ten thousand captives, but by August 1864 more than thirty thousand Union troops languished there without shelter in the heat and humidity.

Democrats, looking toward the fall election, charged that the Lincoln administration valued the welfare of African American troops more highly than that of white soldiers. Lincoln himself--bolstered by General Grant's request that captured rebels remain in prison, where they could not aid the Confederate war effort--refused to budge in the run-up to the election.

RUMORS FROM THE FRONT ☞

Union POWs Suffer Unspeakable Horrors

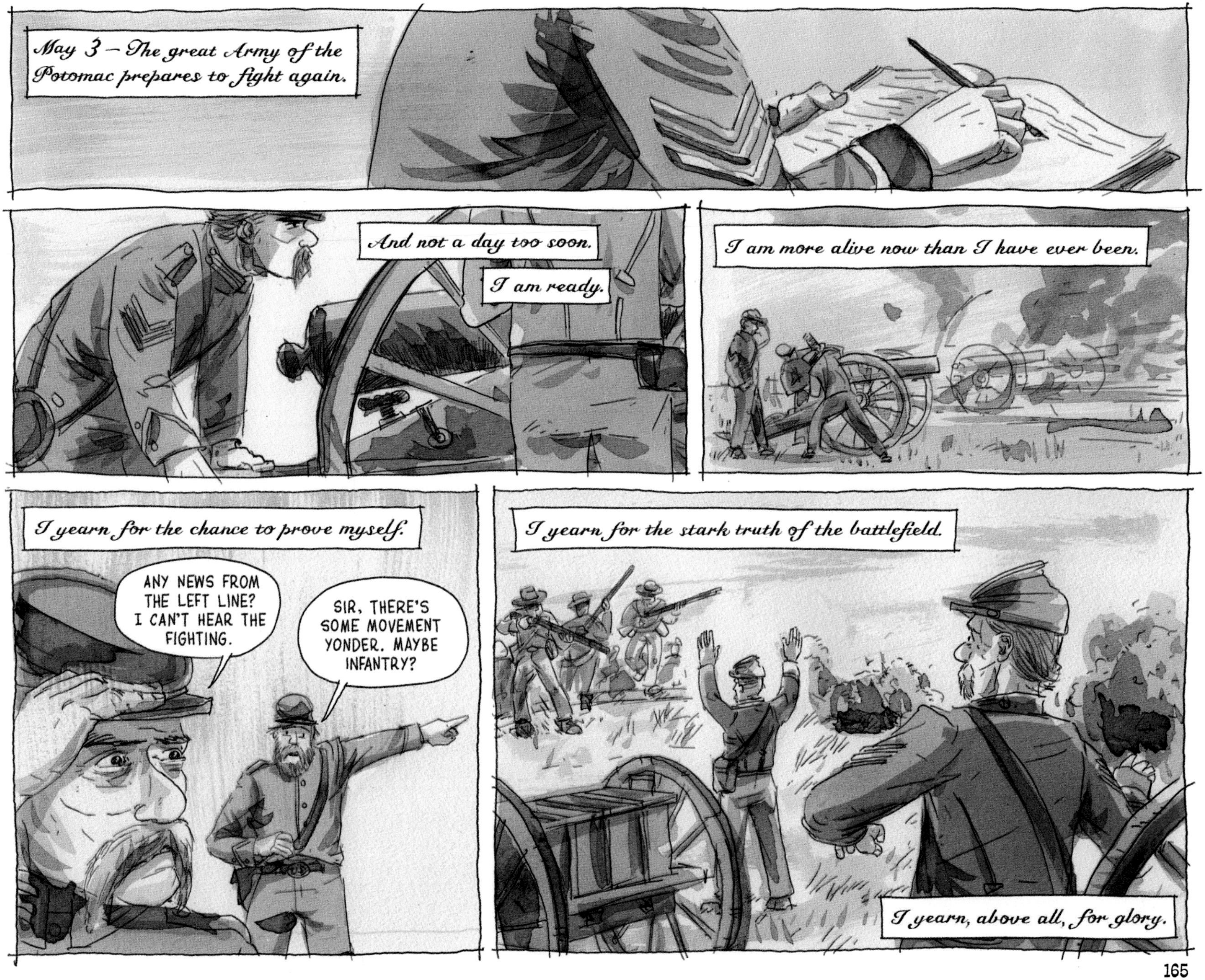
May 3 — The great Army of the Potomac prepares to fight again.
And not a day too soon.
I am ready.
I am more alive now than I have ever been.
I yearn for the chance to prove myself.
ANY NEWS FROM THE LEFT LINE? I CAN'T HEAR THE FIGHTING.
SIR, THERE'S SOME MOVEMENT YONDER. MAYBE INFANTRY?
I yearn for the stark truth of the battlefield.
I yearn, above all, for glory.

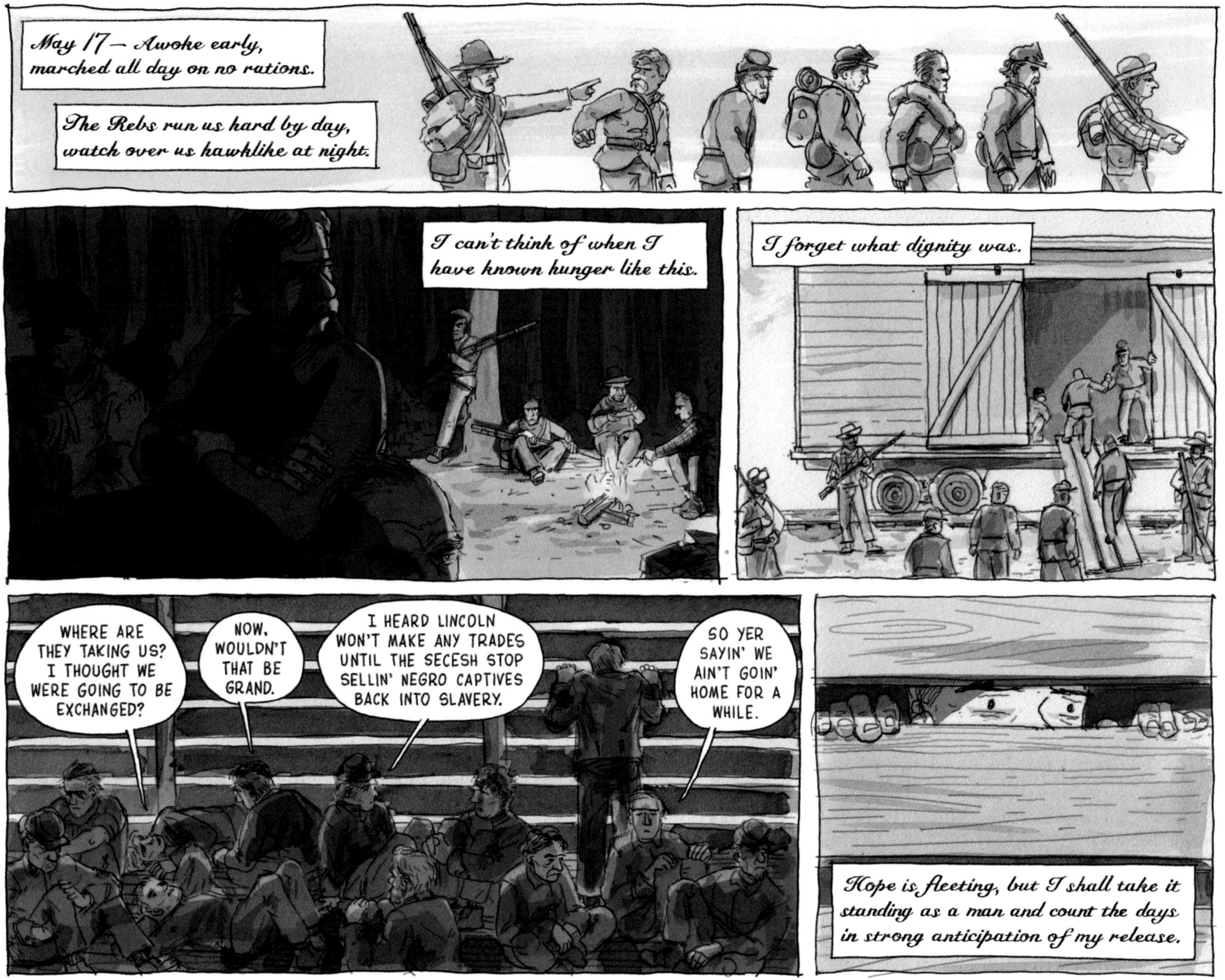
May 17— Awoke early, marched all day on no rations.
The Rebs run us hard by day, watch over us hawklike at night.
I can't think of when I have known hunger like this.
I forget what dignity was.
WHERE ARE THEY TAKING US? I THOUGHT WE WERE GOING TO BE EXCHANGED?
NOW, WOULDN'T THAT BE GRAND.
I HEARD LINCOLN WON'T MAKE ANY TRADES UNTIL THE SECESH STOP SELLIN' NEGRO CAPTIVES BACK INTO SLAVERY.
SO YER SAYIN' WE AIN'T GOIN' HOME FOR A WHILE.
Hope is fleeting, but I shall take it standing as a man and count the days in strong anticipation of my release.

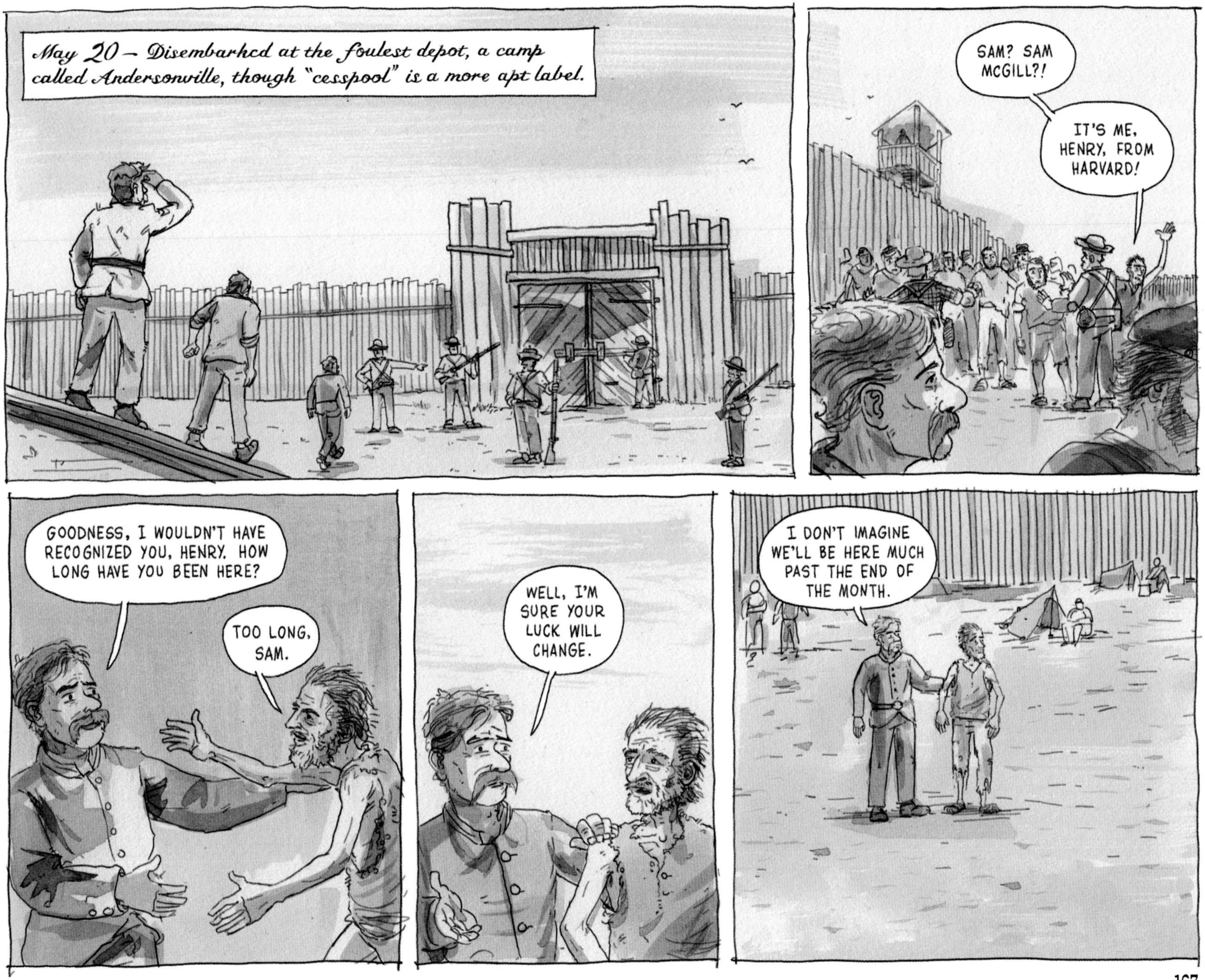
May 20 – Disembarked at the foulest depot, a camp called Andersonville, though "cesspool" is a more apt label.
SAM? SAM MCGILL?!
IT'S ME, HENRY, FROM HARVARD!
GOODNESS, I WOULDN'T HAVE RECOGNIZED YOU, HENRY. HOW LONG HAVE YOU BEEN HERE?
TOO LONG, SAM.
WELL, I'M SURE YOUR LUCK WILL CHANGE.
I DON'T IMAGINE WE'LL BE HERE MUCH PAST THE END OF THE MONTH.

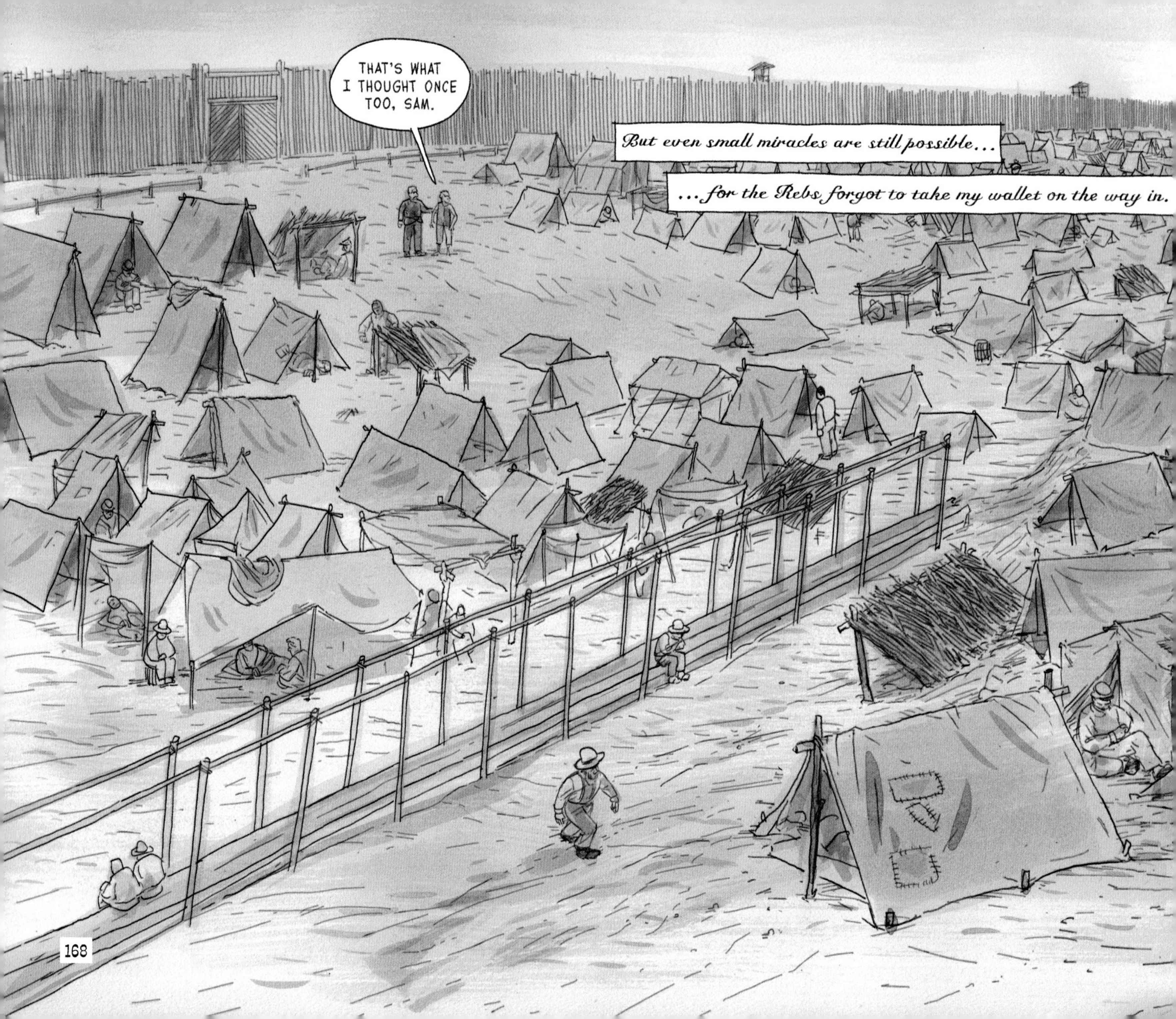
THAT'S WHAT I THOUGHT ONCE TOO, SAM.
But even small miracles are still possible...
...for the Rebs forgot to take my wallet on the way in.

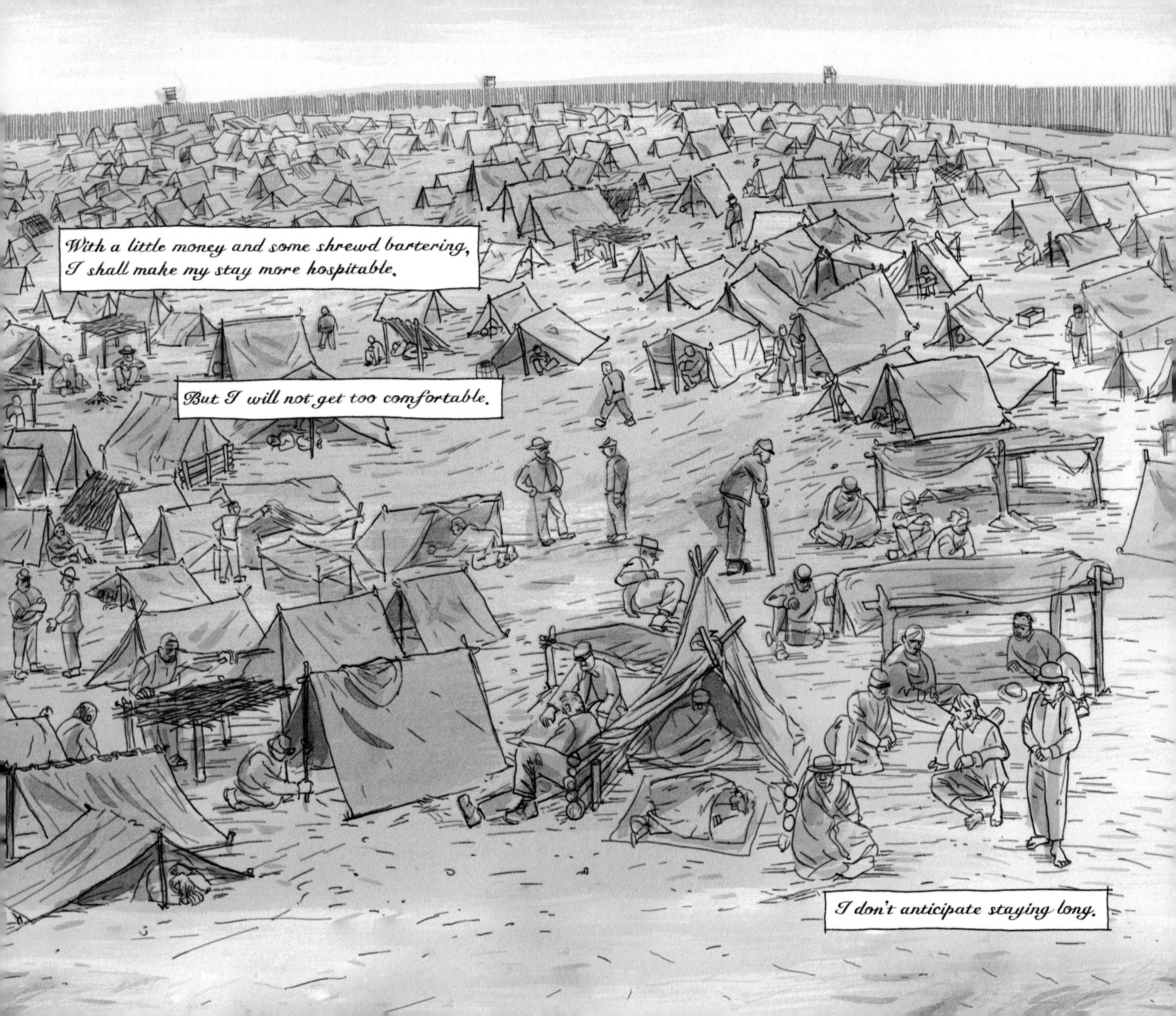
With a little money and some shrewd bartering, I shall make my stay more hospitable.
But I will not get too comfortable.
I don't anticipate staying long.

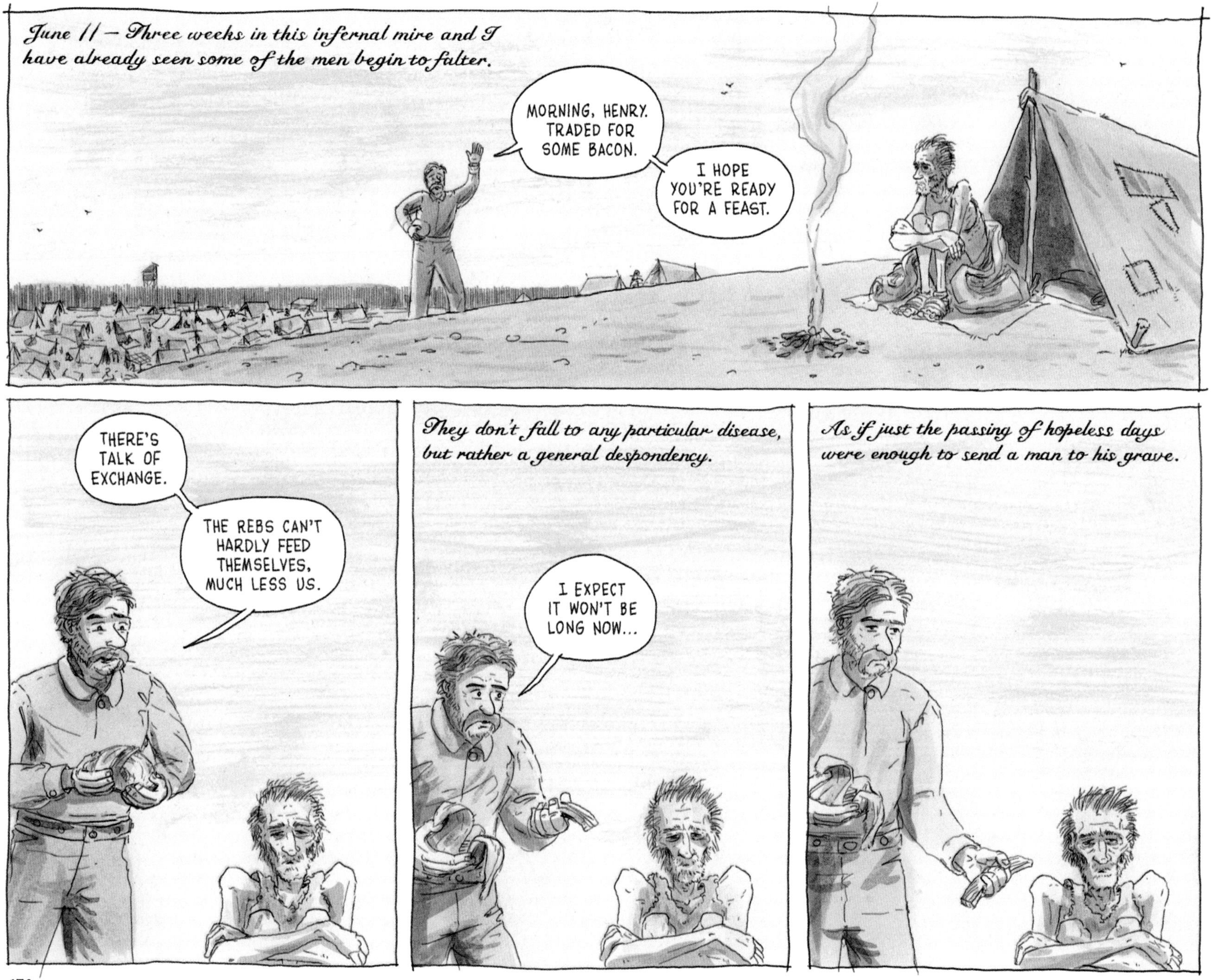
June 11 – Three weeks in this infernal mire and I have already seen some of the men begin to falter.
MORNING, HENRY. TRADED FOR SOME BACON.
I HOPE YOU'RE READY FOR A FEAST.
THERE'S TALK OF EXCHANGE.
THE REBS CAN'T HARDLY FEED THEMSELVES, MUCH LESS US.
They don't fall to any particular disease, but rather a general despondency.
I EXPECT IT WON'T BE LONG NOW...
As if just the passing of hopeless days were enough to send a man to his grave.

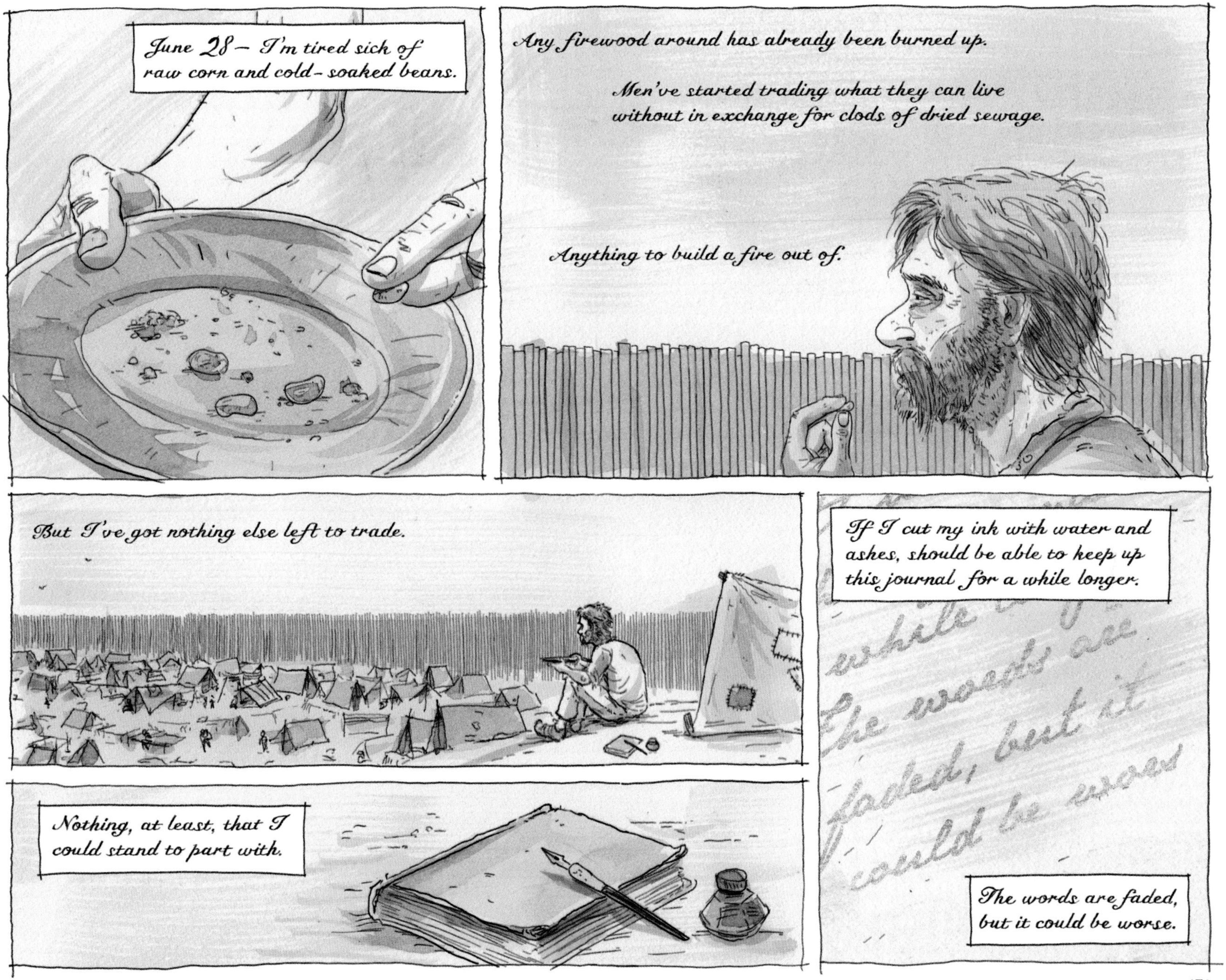
June 28 – I'm tired sick of raw corn and cold-soaked beans.
Any firewood around has already been burned up.
Men've started trading what they can live without in exchange for clods of dried sewage.
Anything to build a fire out of.
But I've got nothing else left to trade.
If I cut my ink with water and ashes, should be able to keep up this journal for a while longer.
Nothing, at least, that I could stand to part with.
The words are faded, but it could be worse.

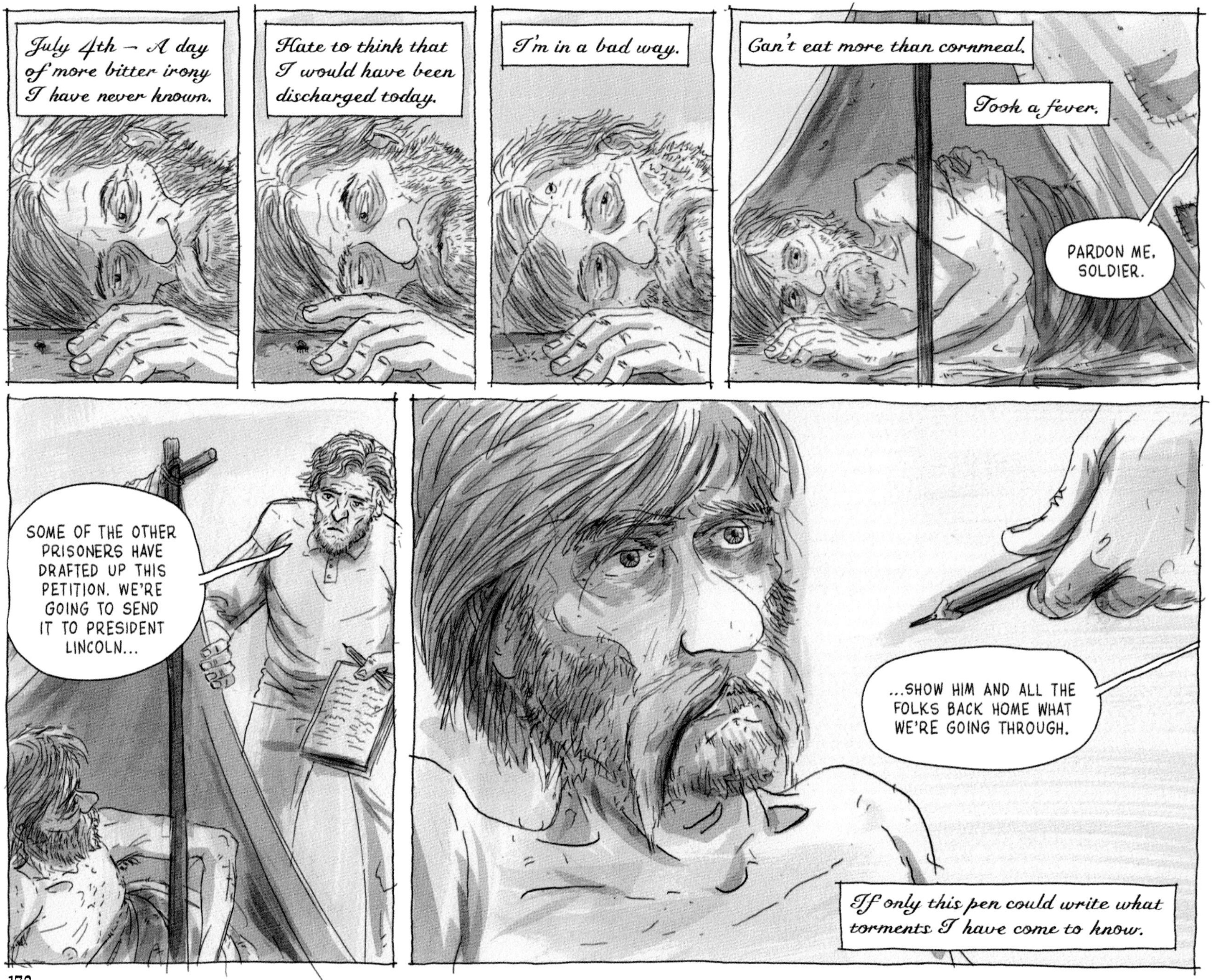
July 4th – A day of more bitter irony I have never known.
Hate to think that I would have been discharged today.
I'm in a bad way.
Can't eat more than cornmeal.
Took a fever.
PARDON ME, SOLDIER.
SOME OF THE OTHER PRISONERS HAVE DRAFTED UP THIS PETITION. WE'RE GOING TO SEND IT TO PRESIDENT LINCOLN...
...SHOW HIM AND ALL THE FOLKS BACK HOME WHAT WE'RE GOING THROUGH.
If only this pen could write what torments I have come to know.

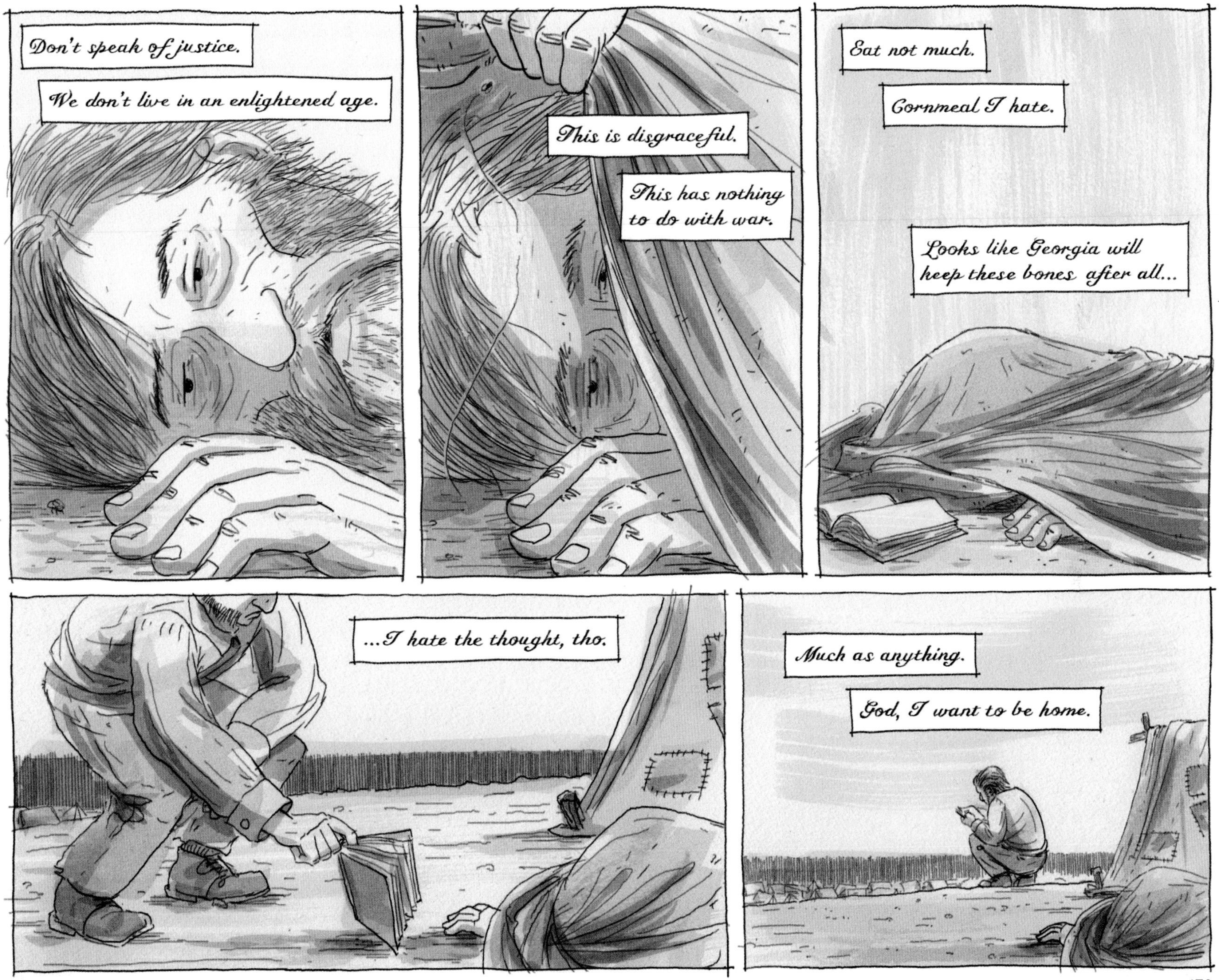
Don't speak of justice.
We don't live in an enlightened age.
This is disgraceful.
This has nothing to do with war.
Eat not much.
Cornmeal I hate.
Looks like Georgia will keep these bones after all...
...I hate the thought, tho.
Much as anything.
God, I want to be home.

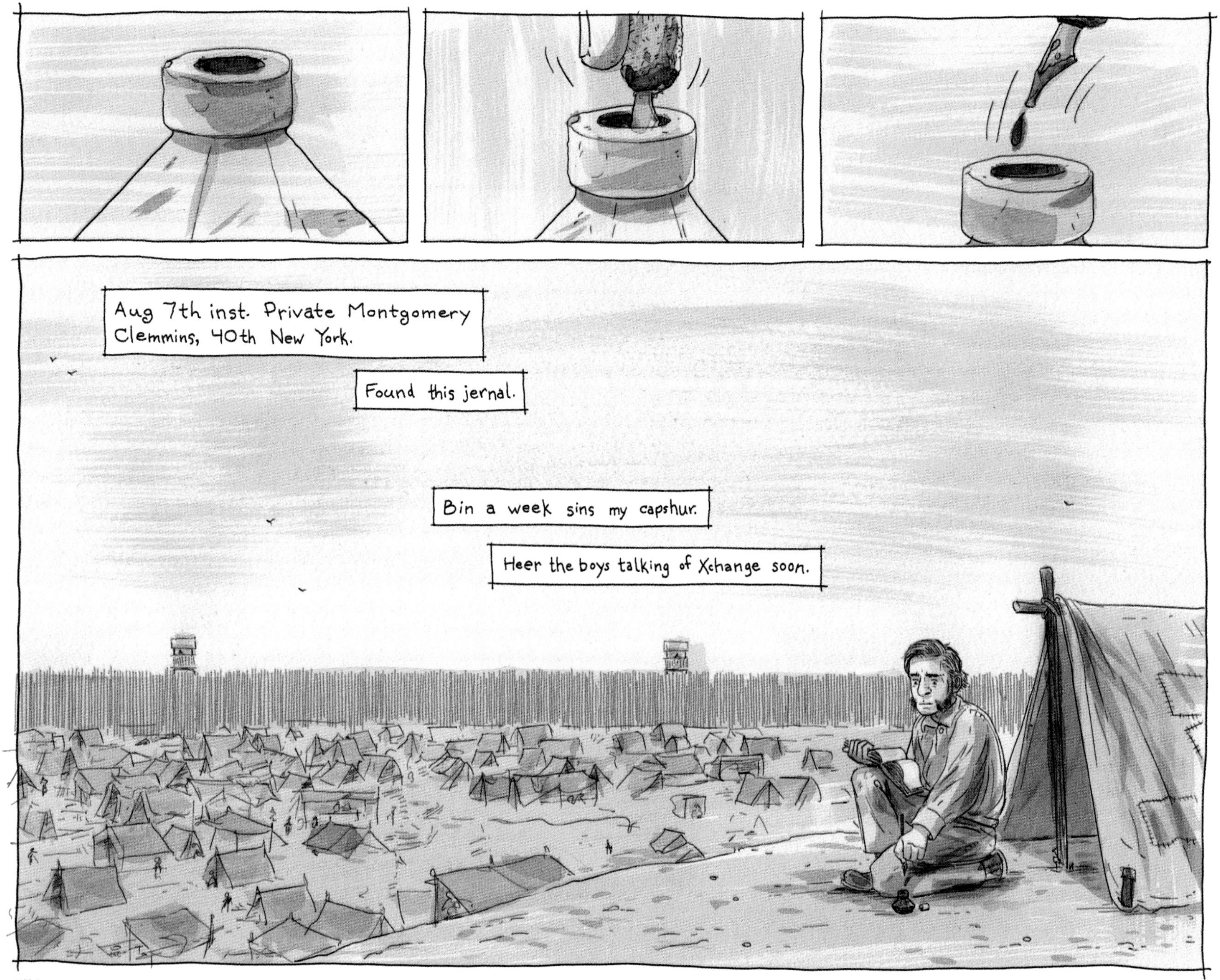
Aug 7th inst. Private Montgomery Clemmins, 40th New York.
Found this jernal.
Bin a week sins my capshur.
Heer the boys talking of Xchange soon.

Chapter 13: General Lee's Sword

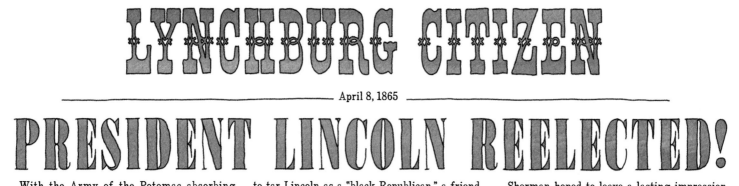

LYNCHBURG CITIZEN

April 8, 1865

PRESIDENT LINCOLN REELECTED!

With the Army of the Potomac absorbing massive casualties in the trenches outside Petersburg, and General Sherman's men making only incremental progress on the road to Atlanta, President Lincoln's electoral prospects looked bleak in the summer of 1864.

Democratic editorialists and politicians berated the President for choosing emancipation over a negotiated peace. Some Republicans, too, thought Lincoln should consider settlement overtures from Jefferson Davis. Lincoln listened but held fast: any agreement would have to reunite the Union and preserve emancipation.

By late August, Lincoln thought he would lose the upcoming contest to his former subordinate, George McClellan. McClellan, though, had problems of his own: the Democrats were divided between peace and war wings. Trying to split the baby, they nominated McClellan but inserted a peace plank into the party platform. Just days later, Atlanta fell. An infuriated McClellan repudiated the Copperheads, who considered running a candidate of their own.

By contrast, the Republicans were united, and President Lincoln looked stalwart and strong. During the campaign the Democrats continued to tar Lincoln as a "black Republican," a friend of African Americans rather than whites, but in November the President secured reelection in a landslide.

General Sherman

SHERMAN MARCHES
THROUGH GEORGIA & S. CAROLINA
Leaves Wake of Ruin

Having taken Atlanta, perhaps securing reelection for his Commander in Chief, William Tecumseh Sherman decided that he wanted to march his army through Georgia to the Atlantic Coast. He would, he said, "make Georgia howl!"

Sherman hoped to leave a lasting impression on Southerners, to "make them so sick of war that generations would pass away before they would again appeal to it." Exactly a week after the 1864 election, he got to work.

Sherman's men left Atlanta in flames as they began their march to the sea. Along the way, they fed themselves by pillaging and plundering the countryside. They arrived in Savannah just before Christmas, and Sherman telegrammed Lincoln to offer him the city as a gift.

A month into the new year, Sherman turned his army north, cutting through South Carolina, the cradle of secession, and meting out what he saw as fair recompense for the state's sins against the sanctity of the Union. Columbia burned. And though Sherman would always claim that rebels, hoping to keep valuable cotton away from the Union, had started the fires, few Southerners believed him.

Sherman marched on, his gaze fixed on Virginia, where he hoped to help General Grant end the war.

RUMORS FROM THE FRONT ☞
General Lee Contemplates Surrender

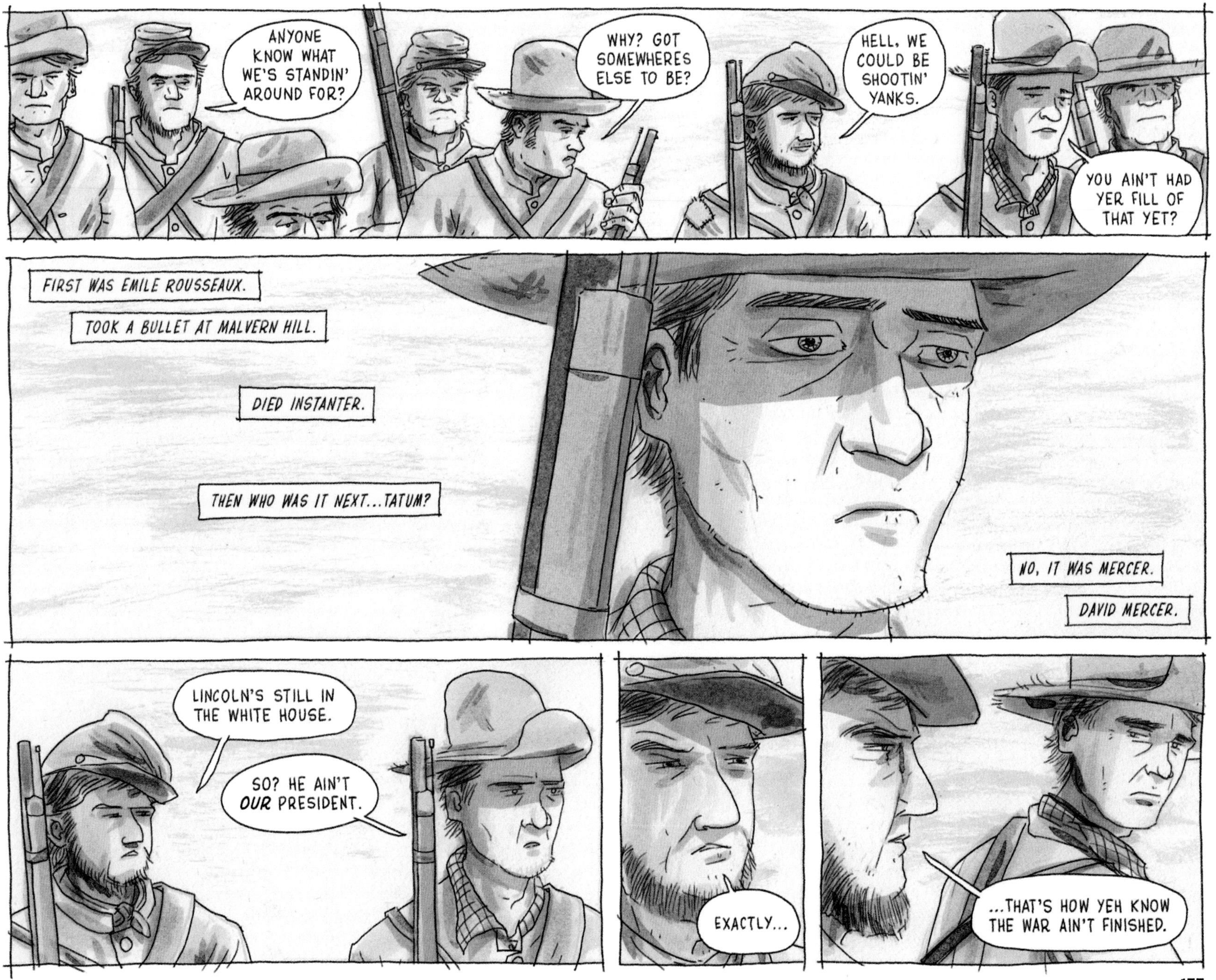
ANYONE KNOW WHAT WE'S STANDIN' AROUND FOR?
WHY? GOT SOMEWHERES ELSE TO BE?
HELL, WE COULD BE SHOOTIN' YANKS.
YOU AIN'T HAD YER FILL OF THAT YET?
FIRST WAS EMILE ROUSSEAUX.
TOOK A BULLET AT MALVERN HILL.
DIED INSTANTER.
THEN WHO WAS IT NEXT...TATUM?
NO, IT WAS MERCER.
DAVID MERCER.
LINCOLN'S STILL IN THE WHITE HOUSE.
SO? HE AIN'T OUR PRESIDENT.
EXACTLY...
...THAT'S HOW YEH KNOW THE WAR AIN'T FINISHED.

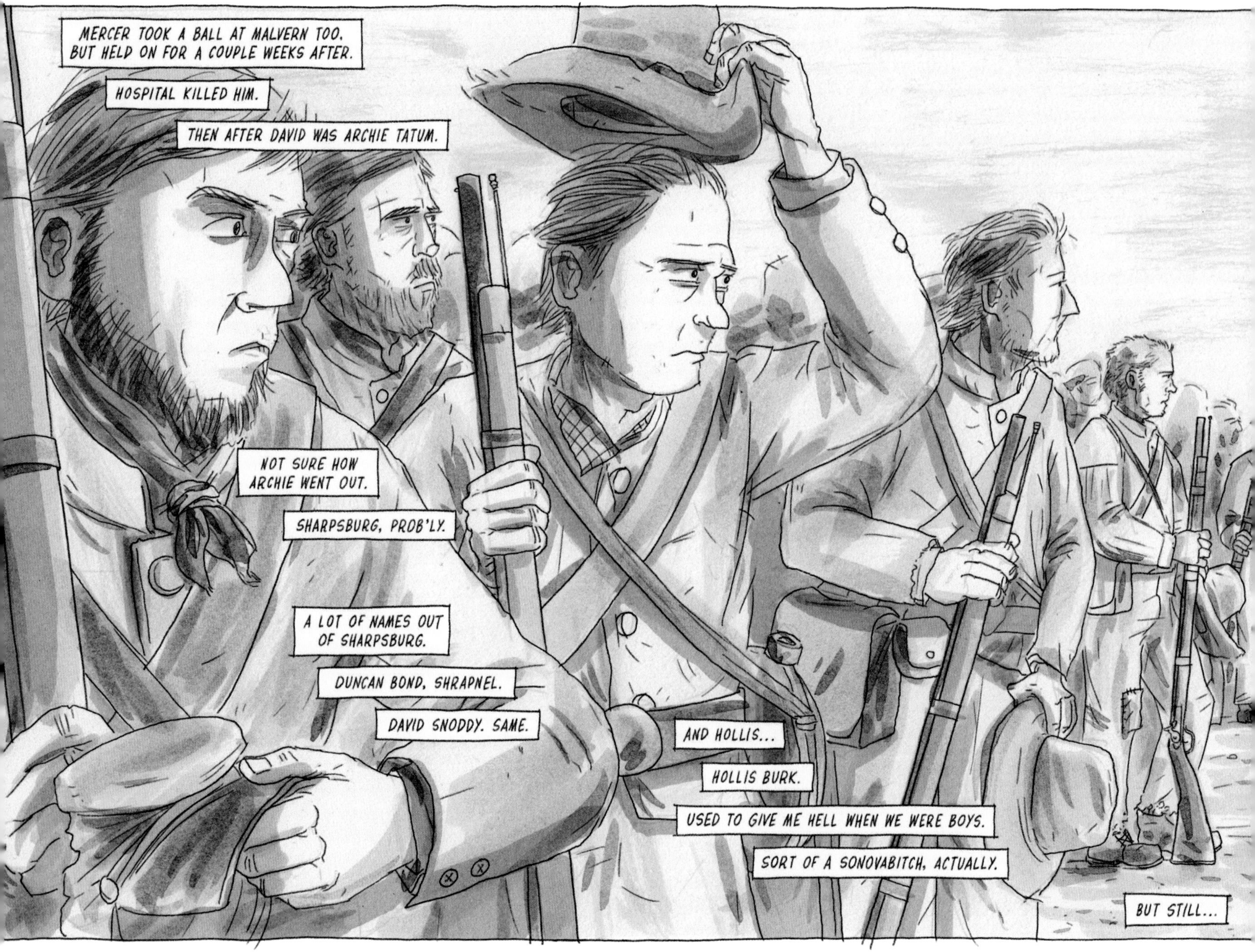

MERCER TOOK A BALL AT MALVERN TOO. BUT HELD ON FOR A COUPLE WEEKS AFTER.
HOSPITAL KILLED HIM.
THEN AFTER DAVID WAS ARCHIE TATUM.
NOT SURE HOW ARCHIE WENT OUT.
SHARPSBURG, PROB'LY.
A LOT OF NAMES OUT OF SHARPSBURG.
DUNCAN BOND, SHRAPNEL.
DAVID SNODDY. SAME.
AND HOLLIS...
HOLLIS BURK.
USED TO GIVE ME HELL WHEN WE WERE BOYS.
SORT OF A SONOVABITCH, ACTUALLY.
BUT STILL...

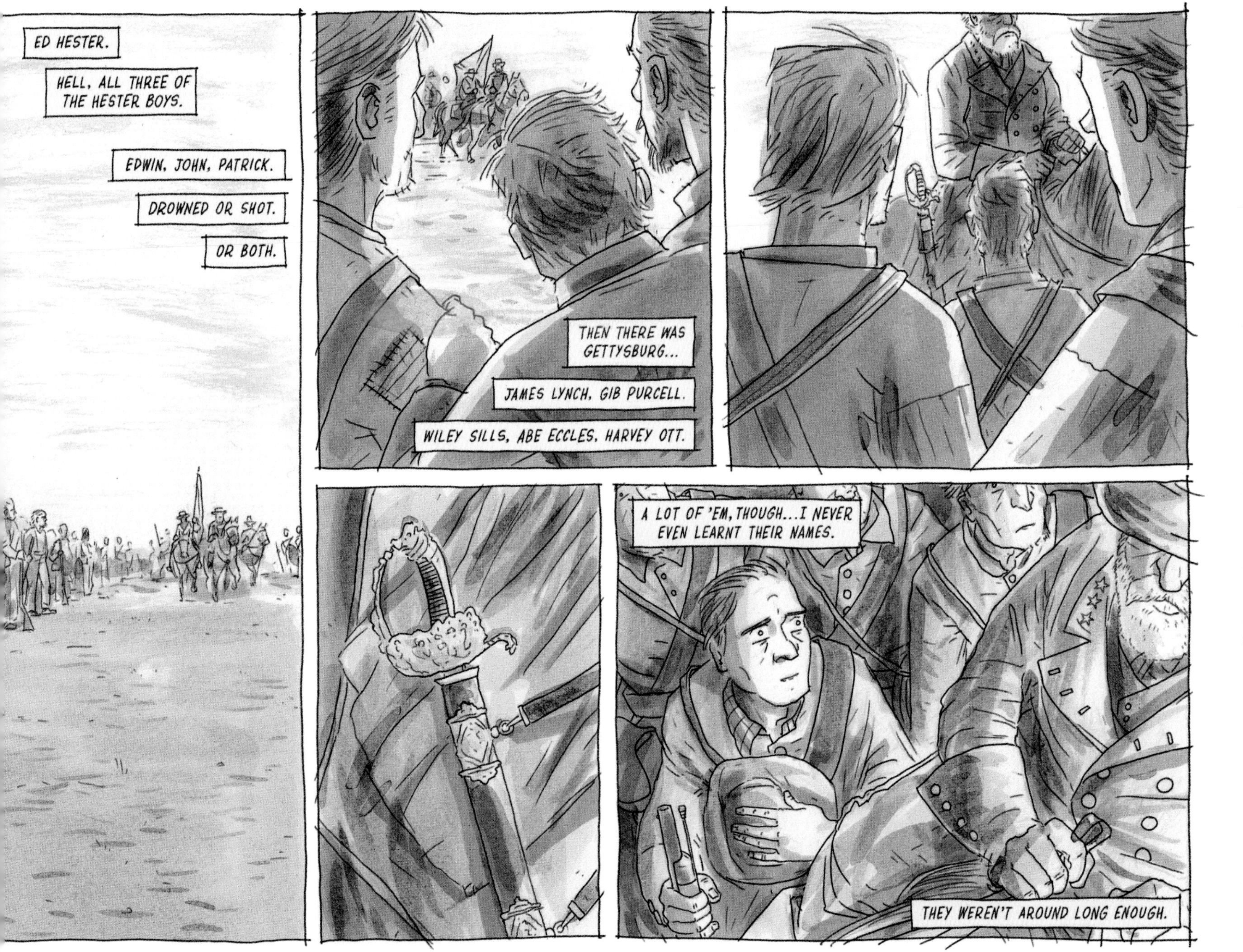
ED HESTER.
HELL, ALL THREE OF THE HESTER BOYS.
EDWIN, JOHN, PATRICK.
DROWNED OR SHOT.
OR BOTH.
THEN THERE WAS GETTYSBURG...
JAMES LYNCH, GIB PURCELL.
WILEY SILLS, ABE ECCLES, HARVEY OTT.
A LOT OF 'EM, THOUGH...I NEVER EVEN LEARNT THEIR NAMES.
THEY WEREN'T AROUND LONG ENOUGH.

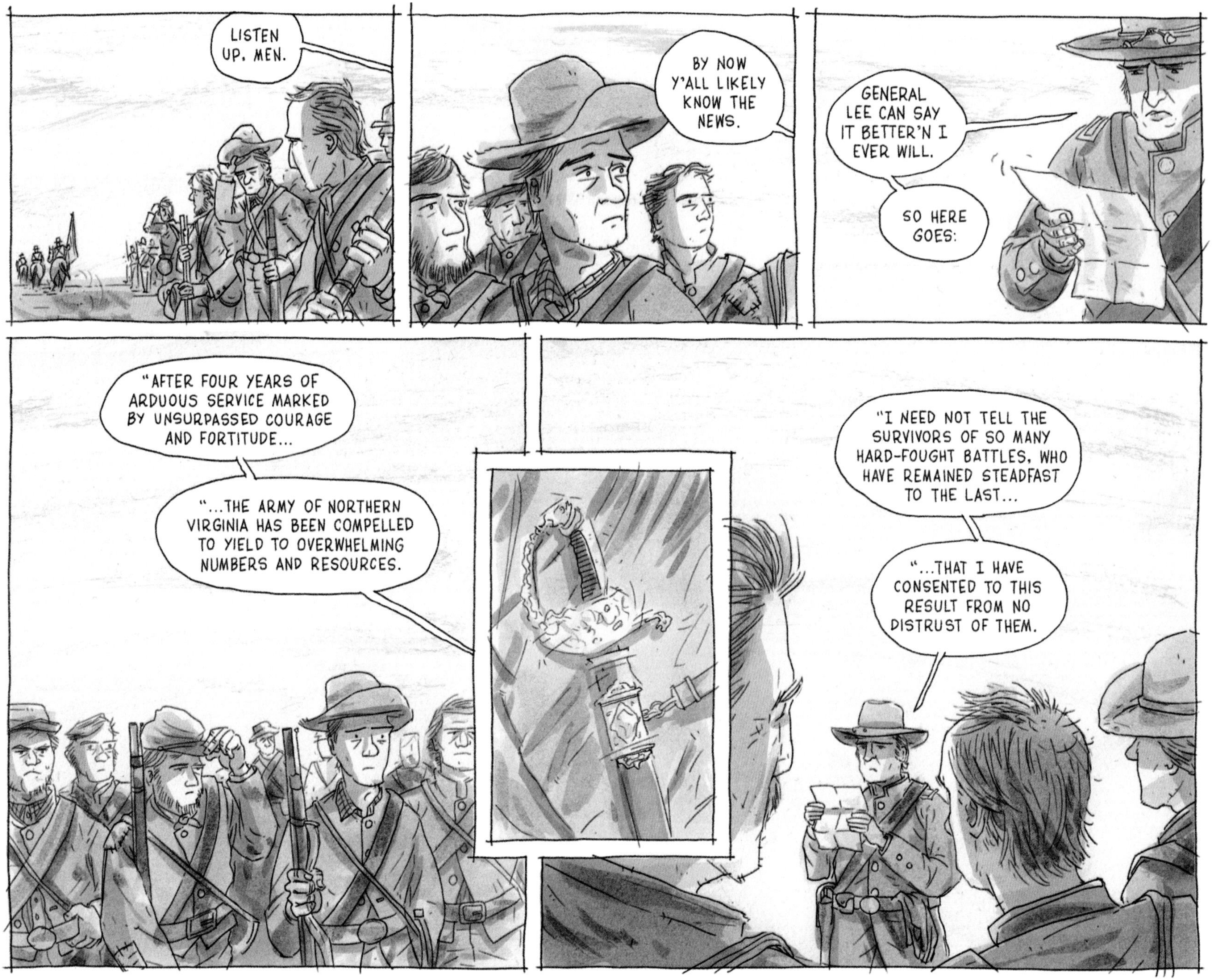
LISTEN UP, MEN.
BY NOW Y'ALL LIKELY KNOW THE NEWS.
GENERAL LEE CAN SAY IT BETTER'N I EVER WILL.
SO HERE GOES:
"AFTER FOUR YEARS OF ARDUOUS SERVICE MARKED BY UNSURPASSED COURAGE AND FORTITUDE...
"...THE ARMY OF NORTHERN VIRGINIA HAS BEEN COMPELLED TO YIELD TO OVERWHELMING NUMBERS AND RESOURCES.
"I NEED NOT TELL THE SURVIVORS OF SO MANY HARD-FOUGHT BATTLES, WHO HAVE REMAINED STEADFAST TO THE LAST...
"...THAT I HAVE CONSENTED TO THIS RESULT FROM NO DISTRUST OF THEM.

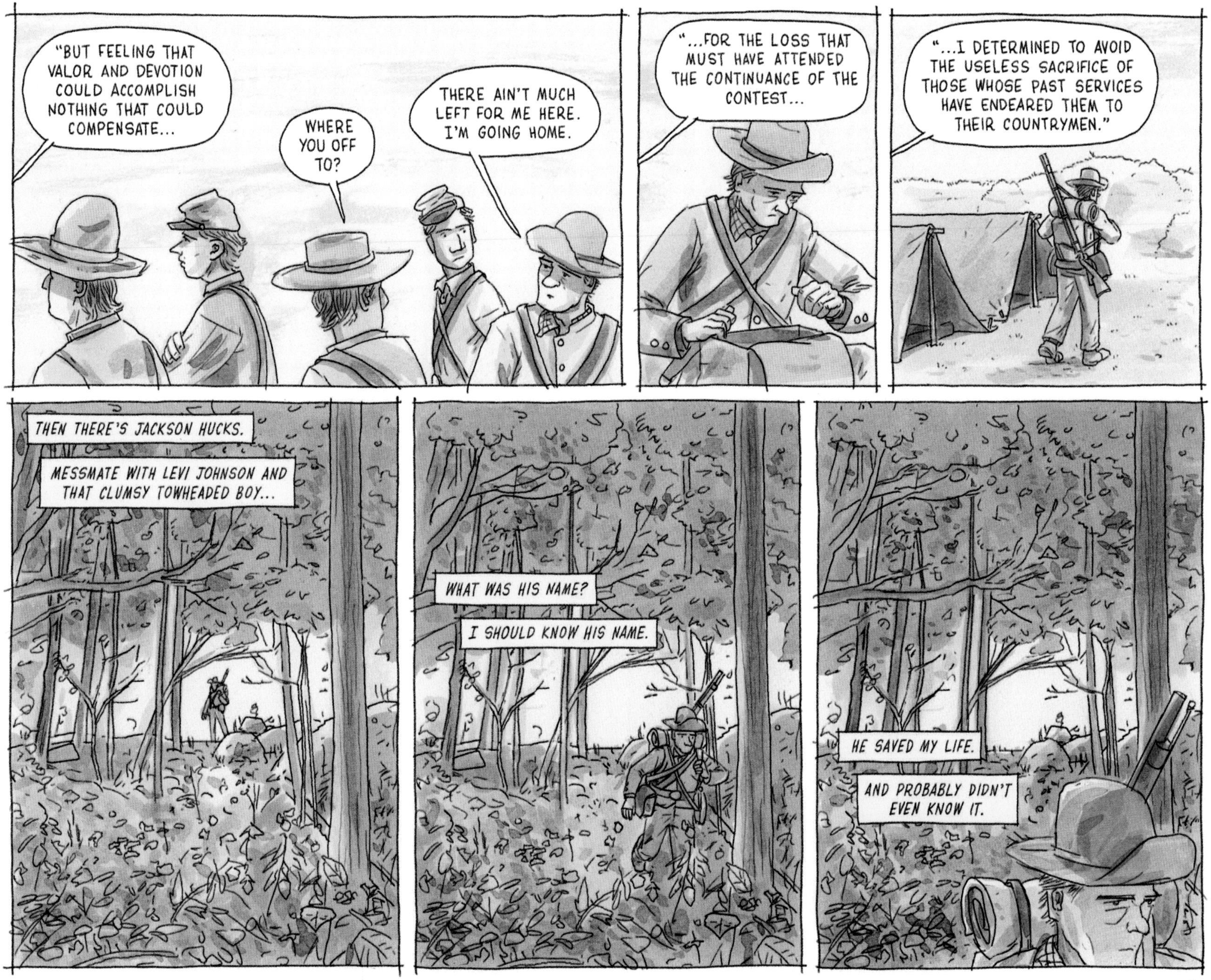
"BUT FEELING THAT VALOR AND DEVOTION COULD ACCOMPLISH NOTHING THAT COULD COMPENSATE...
WHERE YOU OFF TO?
THERE AIN'T MUCH LEFT FOR ME HERE. I'M GOING HOME.
"...FOR THE LOSS THAT MUST HAVE ATTENDED THE CONTINUANCE OF THE CONTEST...
"...I DETERMINED TO AVOID THE USELESS SACRIFICE OF THOSE WHOSE PAST SERVICES HAVE ENDEARED THEM TO THEIR COUNTRYMEN."
THEN THERE'S JACKSON HUCKS.
MESSMATE WITH LEVI JOHNSON AND THAT CLUMSY TOWHEADED BOY...
WHAT WAS HIS NAME?
I SHOULD KNOW HIS NAME.
HE SAVED MY LIFE.
AND PROBABLY DIDN'T EVEN KNOW IT.

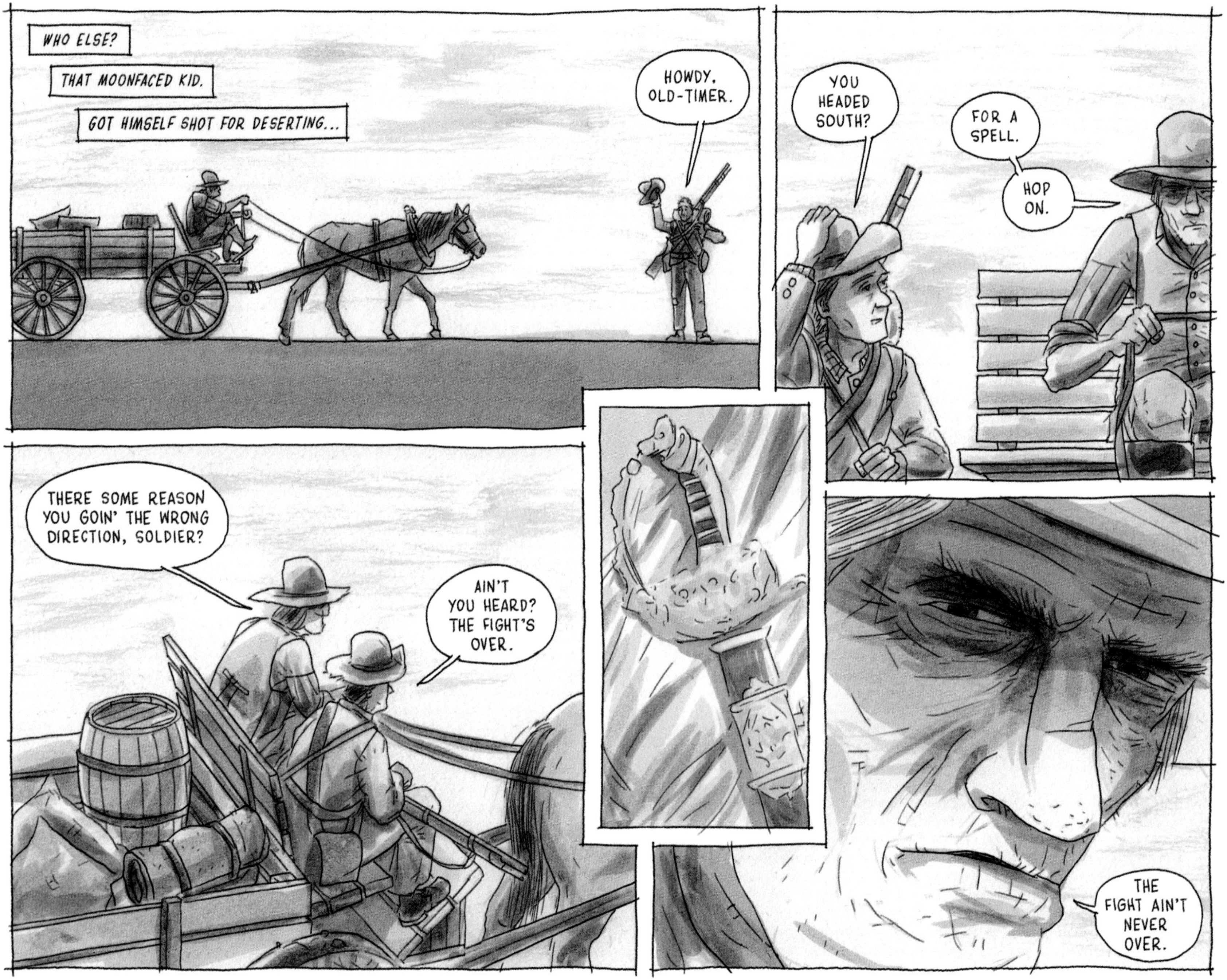
WHO ELSE?
THAT MOONFACED KID.
GOT HIMSELF SHOT FOR DESERTING...
HOWDY, OLD-TIMER.
YOU HEADED SOUTH?
FOR A SPELL.
HOP ON.
THERE SOME REASON YOU GOIN' THE WRONG DIRECTION, SOLDIER?
AIN'T YOU HEARD? THE FIGHT'S OVER.
THE FIGHT AIN'T NEVER OVER.

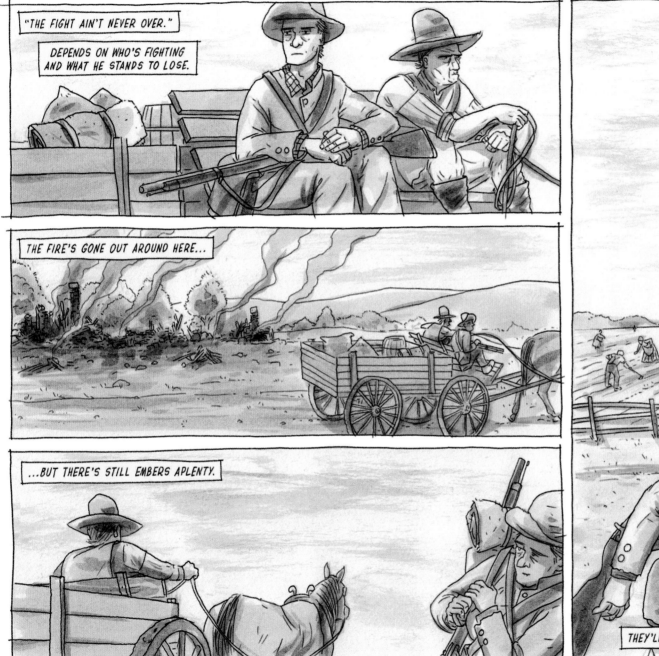

"THE FIGHT AIN'T NEVER OVER."

DEPENDS ON WHO'S FIGHTING AND WHAT HE STANDS TO LOSE.

THE FIRE'S GONE OUT AROUND HERE...

...BUT THERE'S STILL EMBERS APLENTY.

THEY'LL SMOLDER WHO KNOWS HOW LONG.

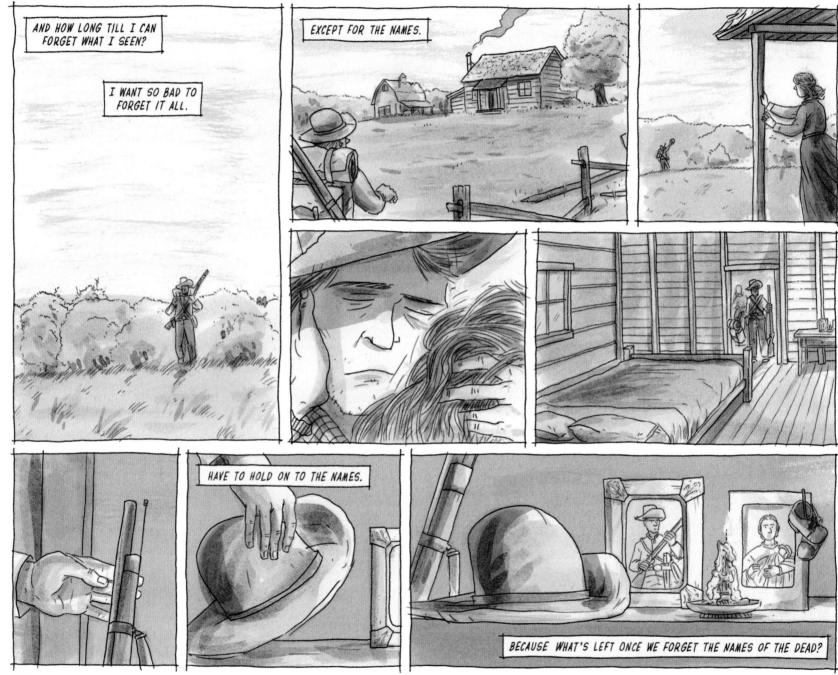

AND HOW LONG TILL I CAN FORGET WHAT I SEEN?

I WANT SO BAD TO FORGET IT ALL.

EXCEPT FOR THE NAMES.

HAVE TO HOLD ON TO THE NAMES.

BECAUSE WHAT'S LEFT ONCE WE FORGET THE NAMES OF THE DEAD?

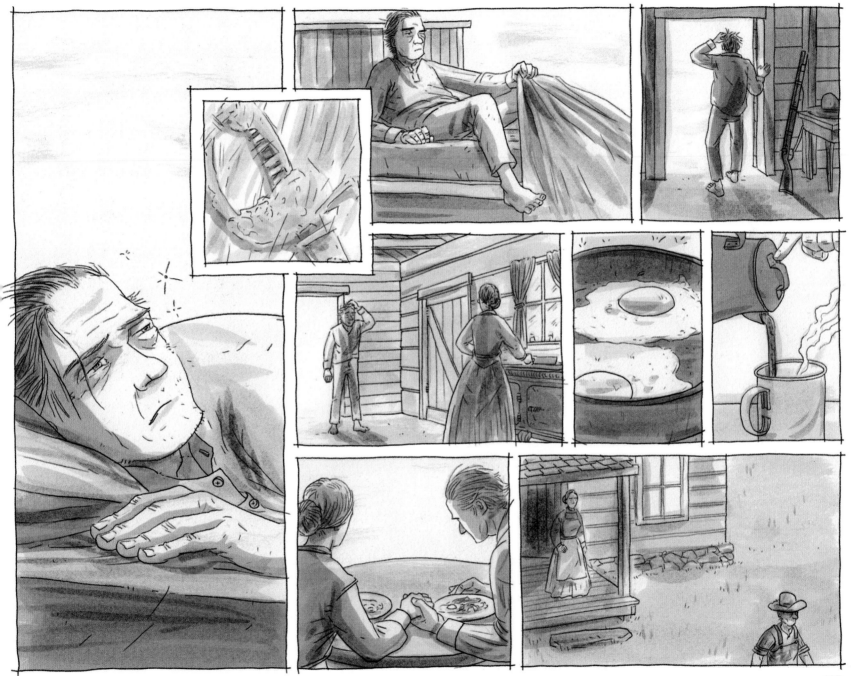

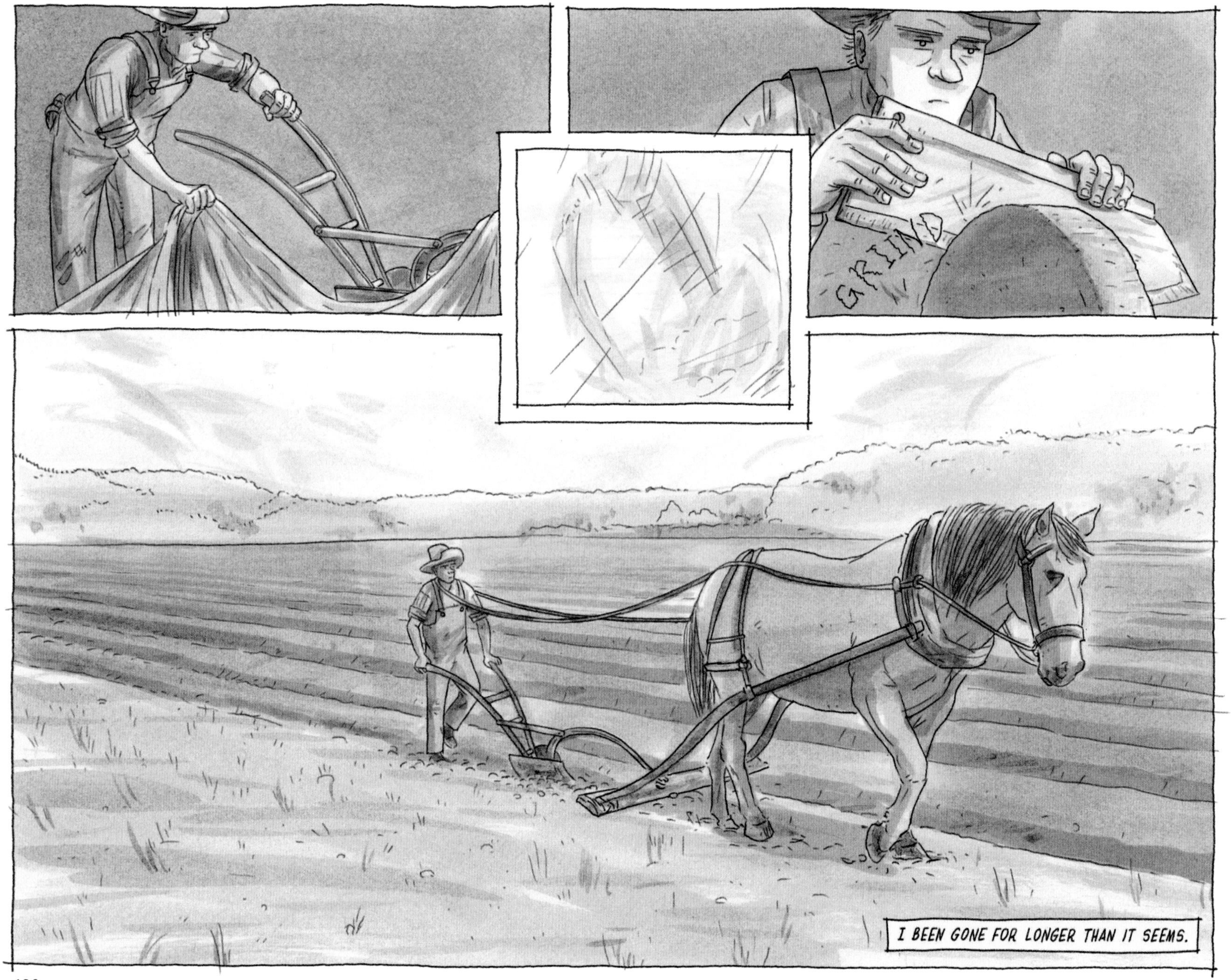
I BEEN GONE FOR LONGER THAN IT SEEMS.

Chapter 14: Nooses

SHREVEPORT MERCURY

April 14, 1865

THIRTEENTH AMENDMENT:
SLAVERY ABOLISHED

On January 31, 1865, the U.S. House of Representatives passed the Thirteenth Amendment by a vote of more than two to one. Sixteen Democrats joined the majority, a rare episode of bipartisanship during the war years. The victory thrilled President Lincoln, who had been prepared to call Congress into special session if the vote failed.

When the final tally was announced, Republicans on the House floor erupted into cheers, and observers in the gallery, including a number of African American onlookers, wept tears of joy. Outside, cannons roared, announcing to the nation's capital what the slaves who had freed themselves over the previous two years already knew: the South's "peculiar institution" was another casualty of the war.

"Neither slavery nor involuntary servitude," the text read, "except as a punishment for crime whereof the party shall have been duly convicted, shall exist within the United States, or any place subject to their jurisdiction."

It would be another year—during which the war would end and the President would be killed—before, on December 6, 1865, Georgia became the final state needed to ratify the Thirteenth Amendment.

SEEKING RECONCILIATION
Amid the Ruins

Grant handled Lee's surrender with an eye on reconciliation. Aware that many Southerners were going hungry, he allowed Lee's men to return home with their horses, hoping they would "put in a crop to carry themselves and their families through the next winter."

Lee remarked that such generosity would "do much toward conciliating our people." But kindness could not erase the fact that some 260,000 rebels had died in the war, that large swaths of the South lay in ruins, and that the dream of an independent Confederacy had been crushed.

And so, while some Southerners would in the coming years try to build a "New South," envisioning progressive racial attitudes and economic modernization, Confederate ideologues, having lost the war, struggled to win the peace. These men, including Jefferson Davis, would argue that the South had fought bravely and honorably but that the Confederate project had been doomed from the start. Union forces had so outnumbered the rebels; Union generals, including Sherman and Grant (Southern mythmakers cast Grant as a butcher opposite Lee's surgeon), had been so bloodthirsty; the North's industrial output had so overwhelmed the South's war-making capacities, that the noble Confederacy never stood a chance.

When linked, these after-the-fact justifications for losing the war became known as the Lost Cause.

RUMORS FROM THE FRONT ☞

President Slain by Assassin's Bullet

188

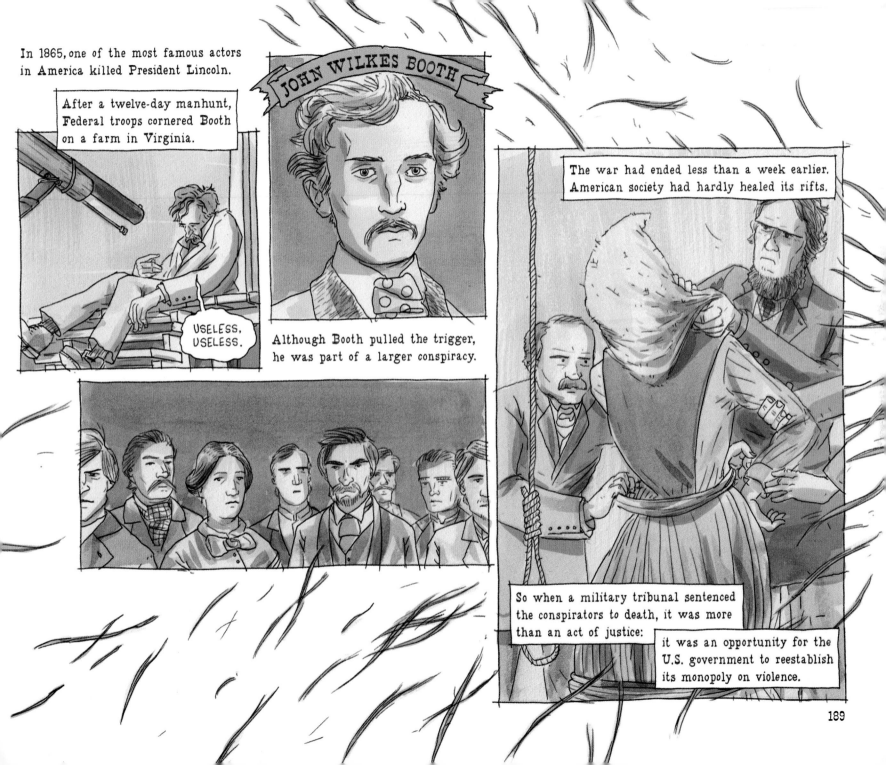

In 1865, one of the most famous actors in America killed President Lincoln.

After a twelve-day manhunt, Federal troops cornered Booth on a farm in Virginia.

USELESS, USELESS.

JOHN WILKES BOOTH

Although Booth pulled the trigger, he was part of a larger conspiracy.

The war had ended less than a week earlier. American society had hardly healed its rifts.

So when a military tribunal sentenced the conspirators to death, it was more than an act of justice: it was an opportunity for the U.S. government to reestablish its monopoly on violence.

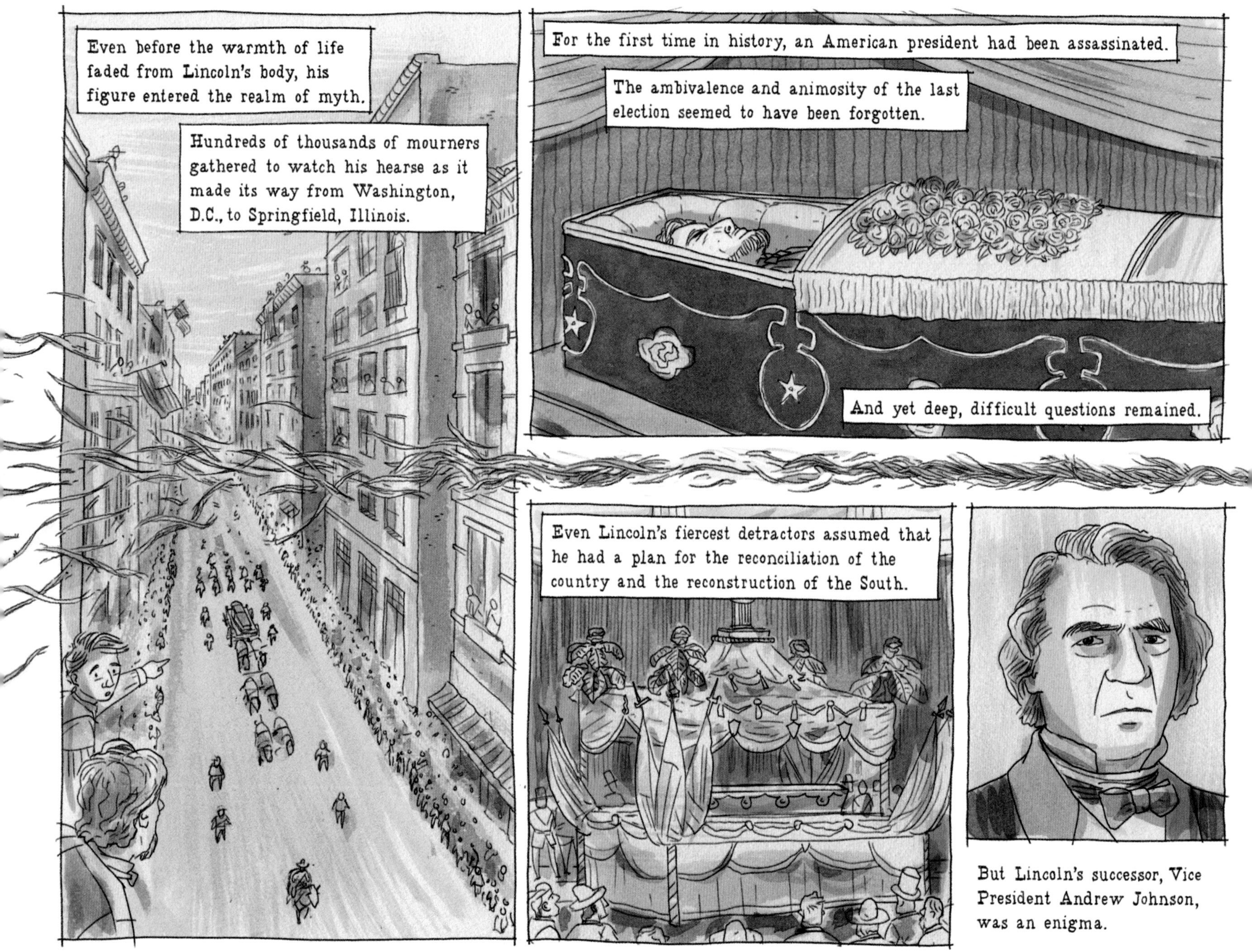
Even before the warmth of life faded from Lincoln's body, his figure entered the realm of myth.
Hundreds of thousands of mourners gathered to watch his hearse as it made its way from Washington, D.C., to Springfield, Illinois.
For the first time in history, an American president had been assassinated.
The ambivalence and animosity of the last election seemed to have been forgotten.
And yet deep, difficult questions remained.
Even Lincoln's fiercest detractors assumed that he had a plan for the reconciliation of the country and the reconstruction of the South.
But Lincoln's successor, Vice President Andrew Johnson, was an enigma.

In 1868, Congress announced the ratification of the Fourteenth Amendment to the Constitution:

"ALL PERSONS BORN OR NATURALIZED IN THE UNITED STATES, AND SUBJECT TO THE JURISDICTION THEREOF, ARE CITIZENS OF THE UNITED STATES..."

The amendment overruled the Supreme Court's decision in the Dred Scott case.

And it extended citizenship to African Americans.

Another feature of the amendment was to prohibit states from denying anyone the rights guaranteed under the Constitution. Due process would be afforded to all.

Except, that is, for Native Americans.

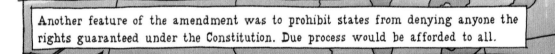

Arguably, the most significant clause of the Fourteenth Amendment was the guarantee that all citizens are entitled to "equal protection" under the law.

On questions of justice and inalienable rights, the federal government had decisively overruled the sovereignty of the individual states.

But it's one thing to write a law; it's another thing entirely to enforce it.

191

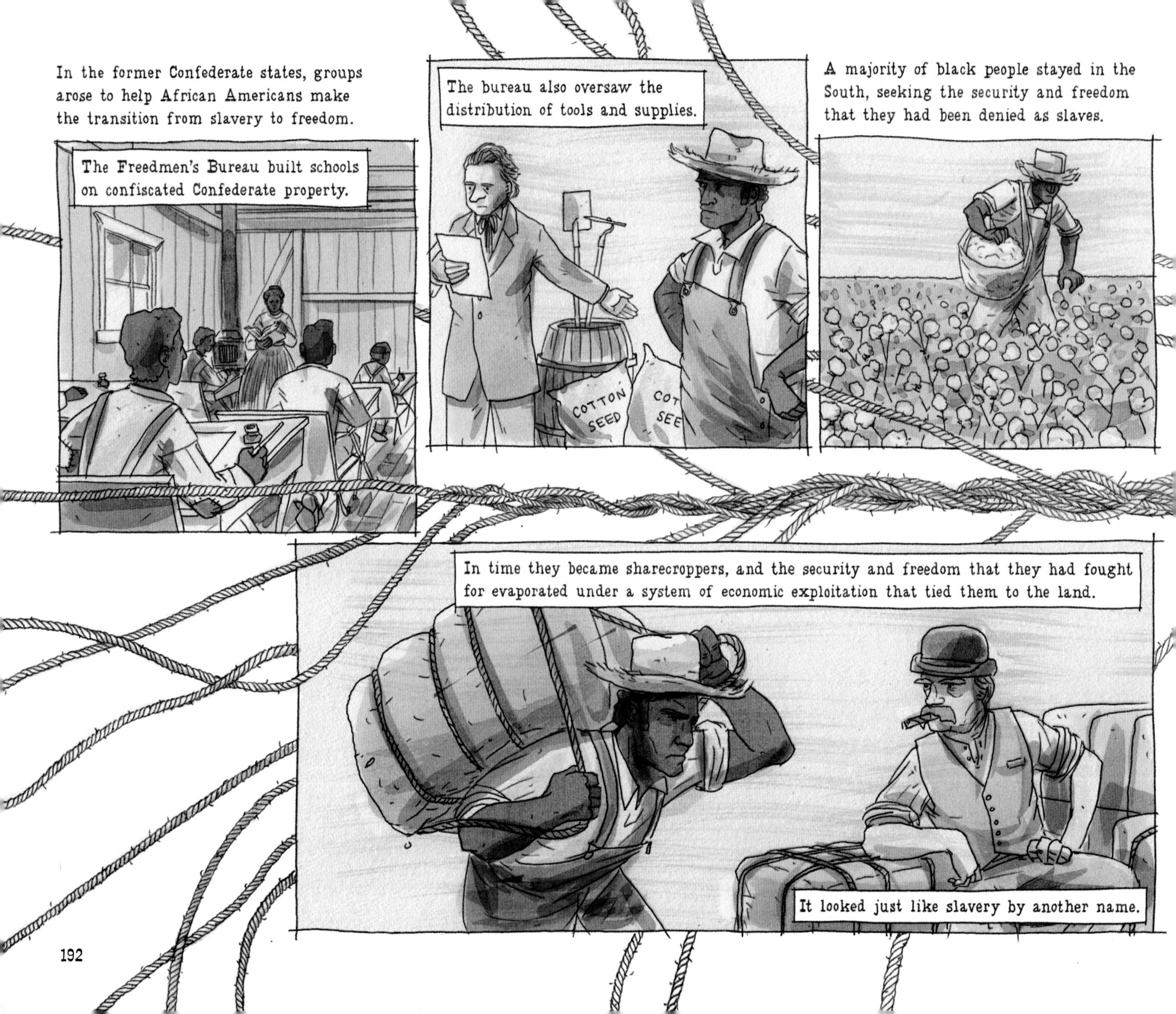
In the former Confederate states, groups arose to help African Americans make the transition from slavery to freedom.
The Freedmen's Bureau built schools on confiscated Confederate property.
The bureau also oversaw the distribution of tools and supplies.
COTTON SEED
COT SEE
A majority of black people stayed in the South, seeking the security and freedom that they had been denied as slaves.
In time they became sharecroppers, and the security and freedom that they had fought for evaporated under a system of economic exploitation that tied them to the land.
It looked just like slavery by another name.

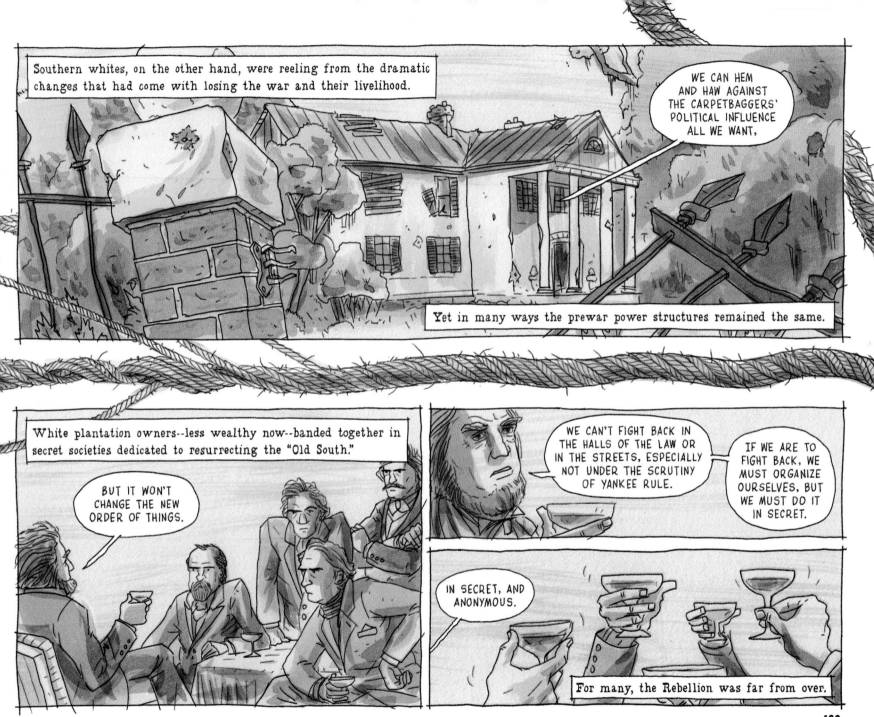

Southern whites, on the other hand, were reeling from the dramatic changes that had come with losing the war and their livelihood.

WE CAN HEM AND HAW AGAINST THE CARPETBAGGERS' POLITICAL INFLUENCE ALL WE WANT,

Yet in many ways the prewar power structures remained the same.

White plantation owners--less wealthy now--banded together in secret societies dedicated to resurrecting the "Old South."

BUT IT WON'T CHANGE THE NEW ORDER OF THINGS.

WE CAN'T FIGHT BACK IN THE HALLS OF THE LAW OR IN THE STREETS, ESPECIALLY NOT UNDER THE SCRUTINY OF YANKEE RULE.

IF WE ARE TO FIGHT BACK, WE MUST ORGANIZE OURSELVES, BUT WE MUST DO IT IN SECRET.

IN SECRET, AND ANONYMOUS.

For many, the Rebellion was far from over.

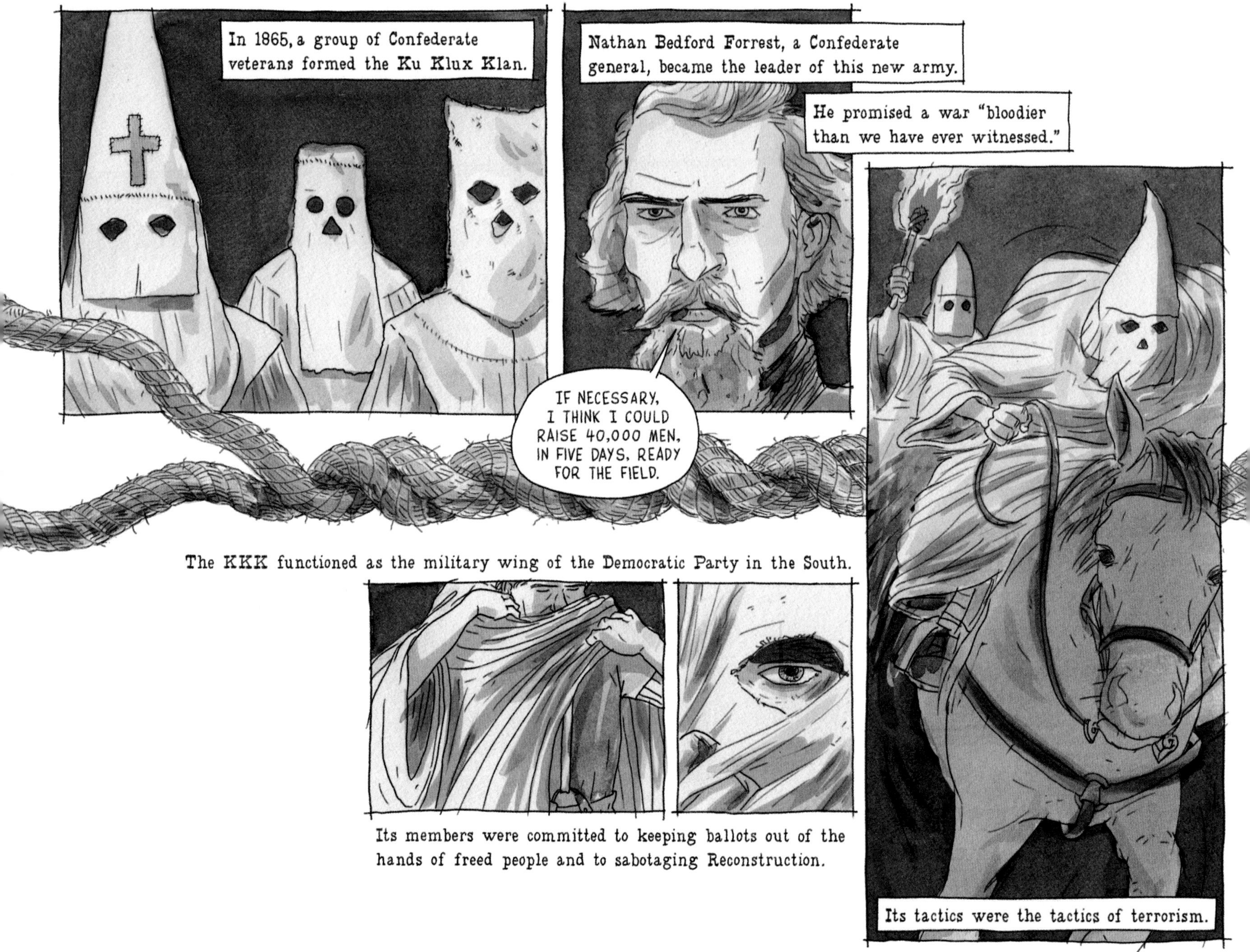
In 1865, a group of Confederate veterans formed the Ku Klux Klan.
Nathan Bedford Forrest, a Confederate general, became the leader of this new army.
He promised a war "bloodier than we have ever witnessed."
IF NECESSARY, I THINK I COULD RAISE 40,000 MEN, IN FIVE DAYS, READY FOR THE FIELD.
The KKK functioned as the military wing of the Democratic Party in the South.
Its members were committed to keeping ballots out of the hands of freed people and to sabotaging Reconstruction.
Its tactics were the tactics of terrorism.

The Fifteenth Amendment, which was ratified in 1870, secured for all black men the right to vote.

But once again, policies in Washington were no match for the intensity of white supremacists in the South.

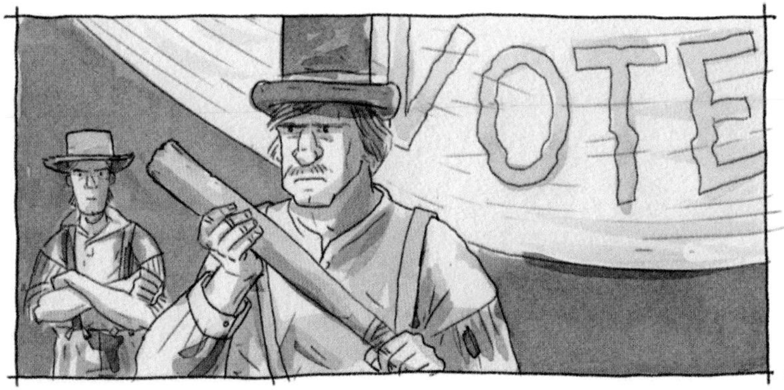
VOTE

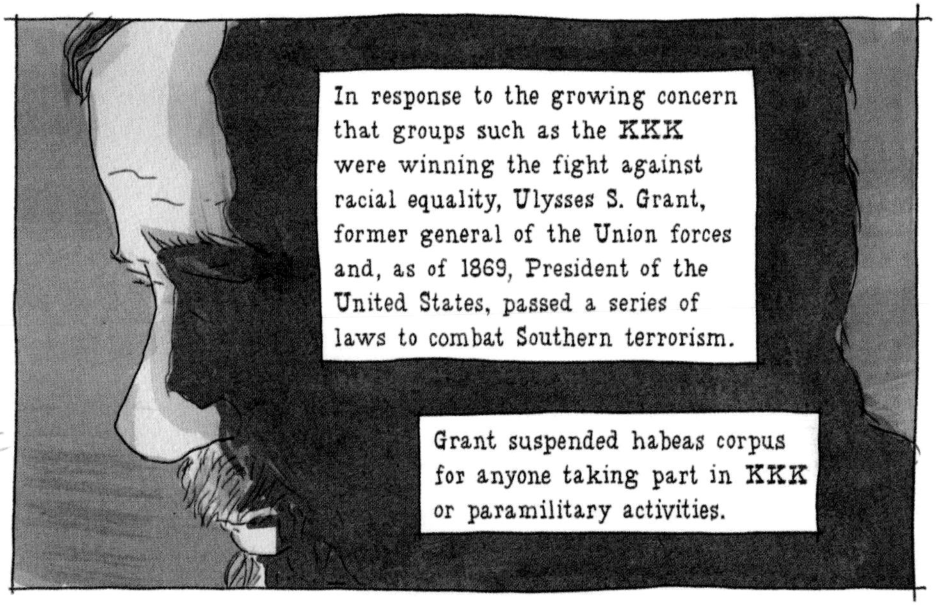
In response to the growing concern that groups such as the KKK were winning the fight against racial equality, Ulysses S. Grant, former general of the Union forces and, as of 1869, President of the United States, passed a series of laws to combat Southern terrorism.
Grant suspended habeas corpus for anyone taking part in KKK or paramilitary activities.

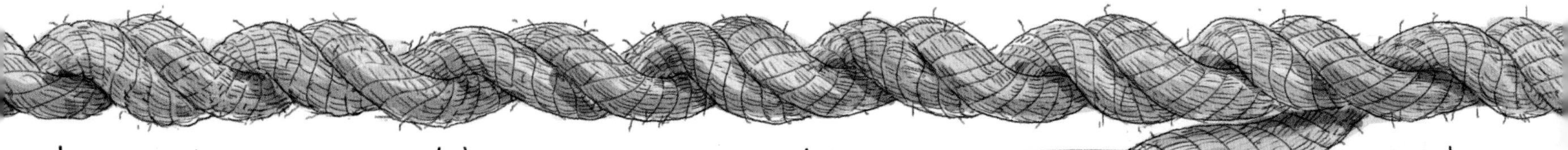

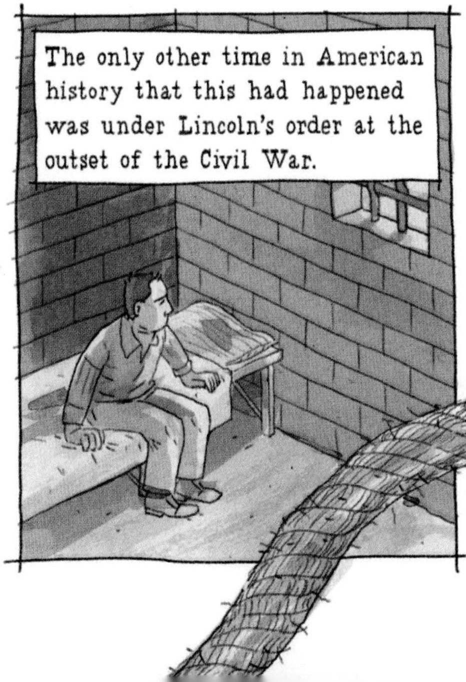
The only other time in American history that this had happened was under Lincoln's order at the outset of the Civil War.

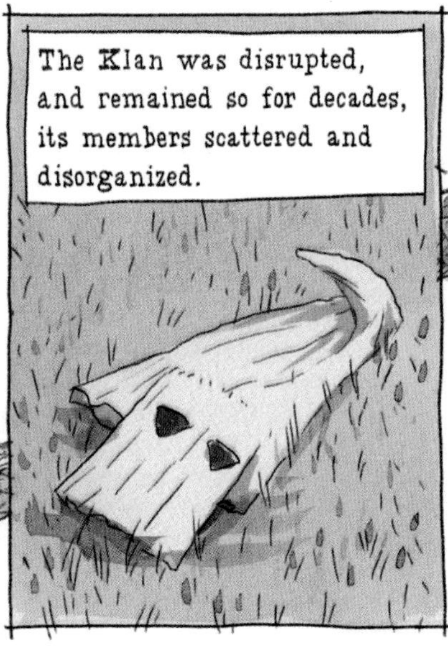
The Klan was disrupted, and remained so for decades, its members scattered and disorganized.

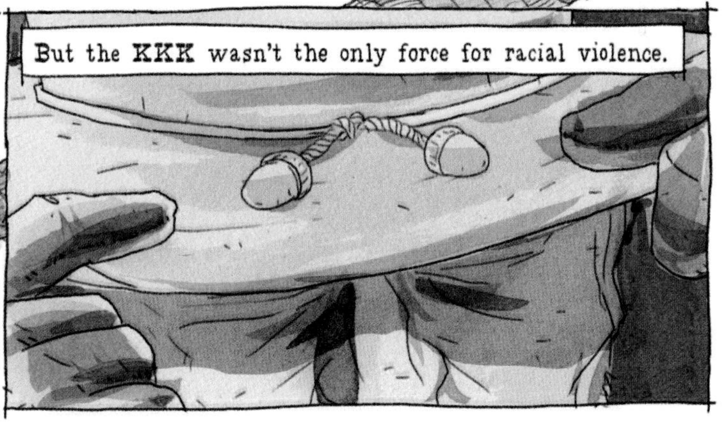
But the KKK wasn't the only force for racial violence.

In the Deep South, white supremacists could strike in broad daylight, even in Confederate uniform, without fear of reprisal.

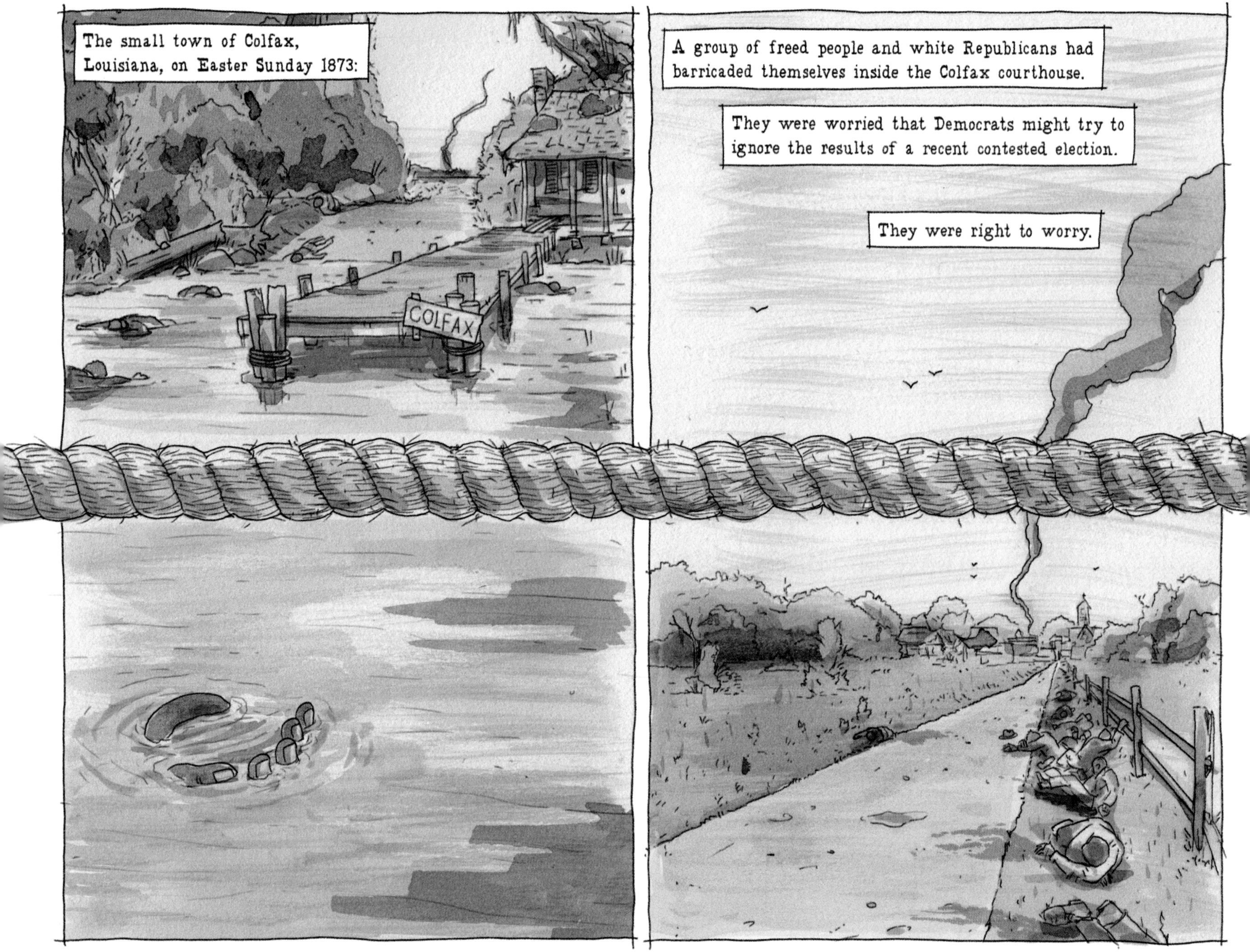
The small town of Colfax, Louisiana, on Easter Sunday 1873:
COLFAX
A group of freed people and white Republicans had barricaded themselves inside the Colfax courthouse.
They were worried that Democrats might try to ignore the results of a recent contested election.
They were right to worry.

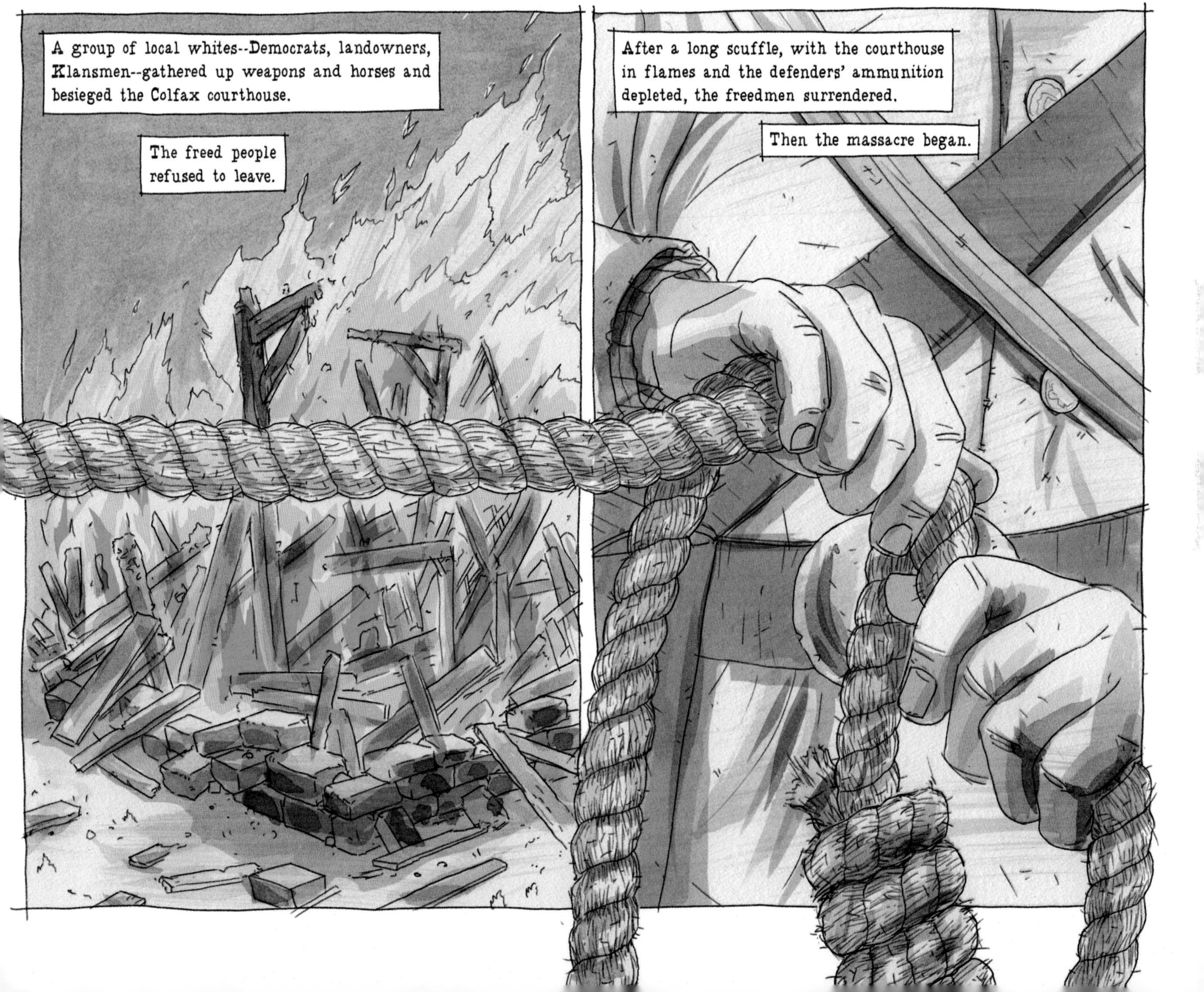
A group of local whites--Democrats, landowners, Klansmen--gathered up weapons and horses and besieged the Colfax courthouse.
The freed people refused to leave.
After a long scuffle, with the courthouse in flames and the defenders' ammunition depleted, the freedmen surrendered.
Then the massacre began.

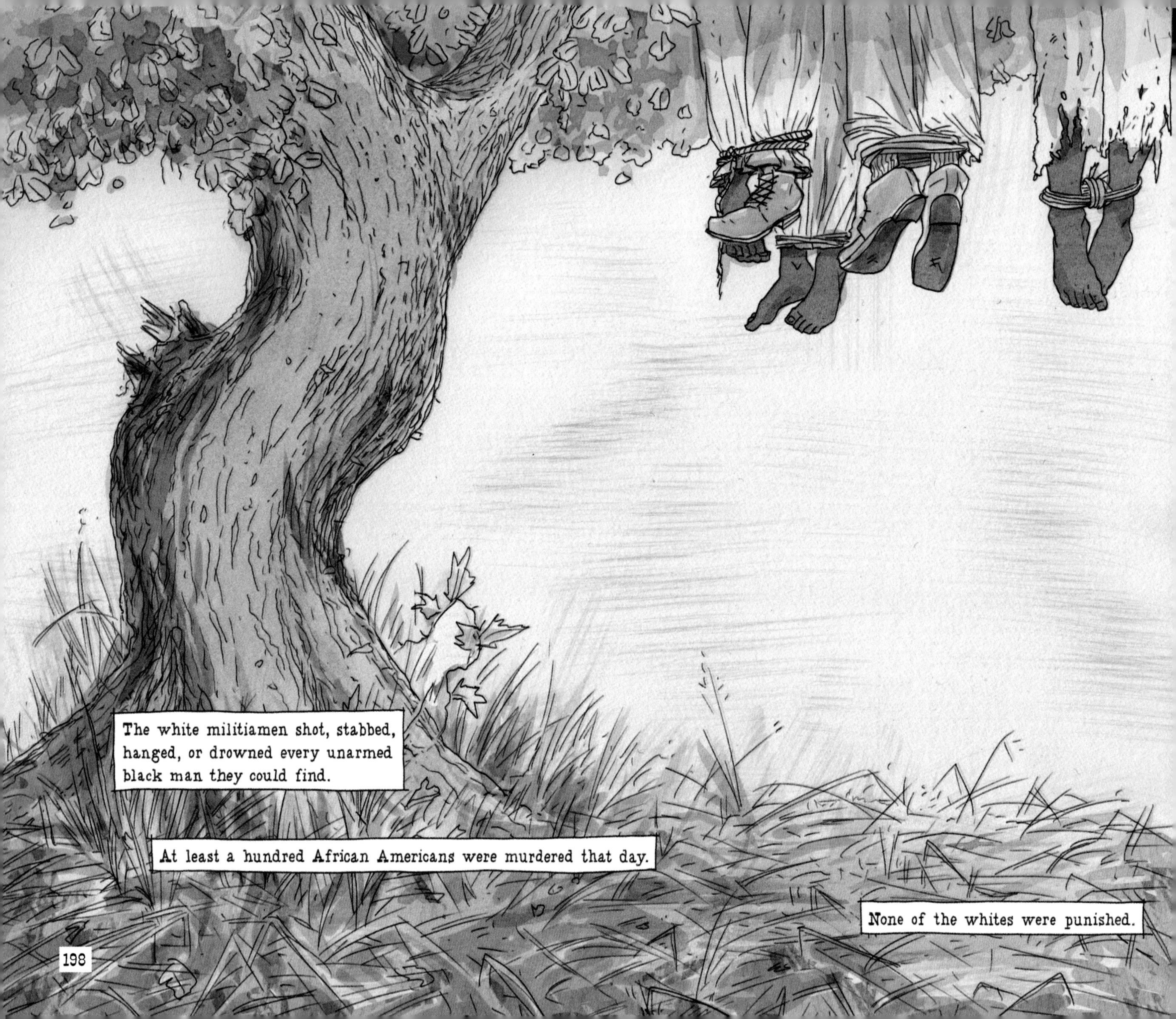
The white militiamen shot, stabbed, hanged, or drowned every unarmed black man they could find.
At least a hundred African Americans were murdered that day.
None of the whites were punished.

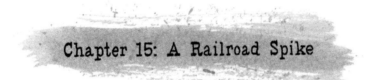

Chapter 15: A Railroad Spike

CHICAGO  PHOENIX

March 2, 1877

A WHITE MAN'S REPUBLIC IN THE WEST

The Civil War exploded out of disputes over whether the West would remain free soil or allow slavery to take root. Then, during the war itself, the Republican Party promised its loyalists that the West would soon be theirs, payment for patriotic sacrifices made during the conflict.

To that end, in 1862 a Republican–dominated Congress passed three pieces of landmark legislation, and the Lincoln administration created the United States Department of Agriculture. Together, those laws, and that new piece of the federal apparatus, broadened the sweep of government authority and catalyzed the conquest and colonization of the West after the war.

The Department of Agriculture offered farmers who struggled to make ends meet in an uncertain and sometimes hostile environment access to expert advice. The Morrill Land Grant Act underwrote an expansion of the nation's system of public education, which was particularly valuable to communities in the sparsely populated West. The Homestead Act granted 160 acres of public land to individuals who resided on and improved their parcels for a period of five years. The Pacific Railroad Act handed out millions of acres of federal property, along with substantial loans, to private corporations that linked Omaha, Nebraska, with San Francisco, California. On May 10, 1869, Leland Stanford drove the "Golden Spike" at Promontory Summit, Utah, connecting the Central Pacific and Union Pacific railroads.

With the Atlantic and Pacific coasts stitched together by rails, land available to pioneers for the taking, and U.S. troops working to remove Native peoples from the West, hundreds of thousands of settlers flooded into the region.

1876 ELECTION: NO CLEAR WINNER

The 1876 election was, until the year 2000, the closest in the nation's history. When the ballots were counted, Samuel Tilden, a Democrat, had outpolled Rutherford B. Hayes, a Republican, by more than 3 percent of the popular vote. But in a race to 185 in the Electoral College, Hayes had 184 to Tilden's 165. Twenty electoral votes––all of Louisiana's, Florida's, and South Carolina's tallies plus one of Oregon's––remained up for grabs, with each side claiming victory in the contested states.

In the run-up to the election, Democrats had accused Republicans of using memories of the war as a political cudgel, of "waving the bloody shirt." There was some truth to the charge, as Republicans had suggested that voters couldn't count on Democrats to be loyal to the Union. Meanwhile, on Election Day, armed gangs had roamed the Deep South, disfranchising African American voters who likely would have cast their ballots for Republican candidates.

In the end, Congress appointed a commission to adjudicate the results. Less than a week before Inauguration Day, that body awarded the disputed electoral votes to Hayes, handing him victory. Hayes, apparently making good on an arrangement struck with leading Democrats, then withdrew federal troops from the South, ending Reconstruction. Critics have since labeled this backroom deal one of the most "corrupt bargains" in American history.

RUMORS FROM THE FRONT ☞

Republicans Give Up On Reconstruction, Gain the White House

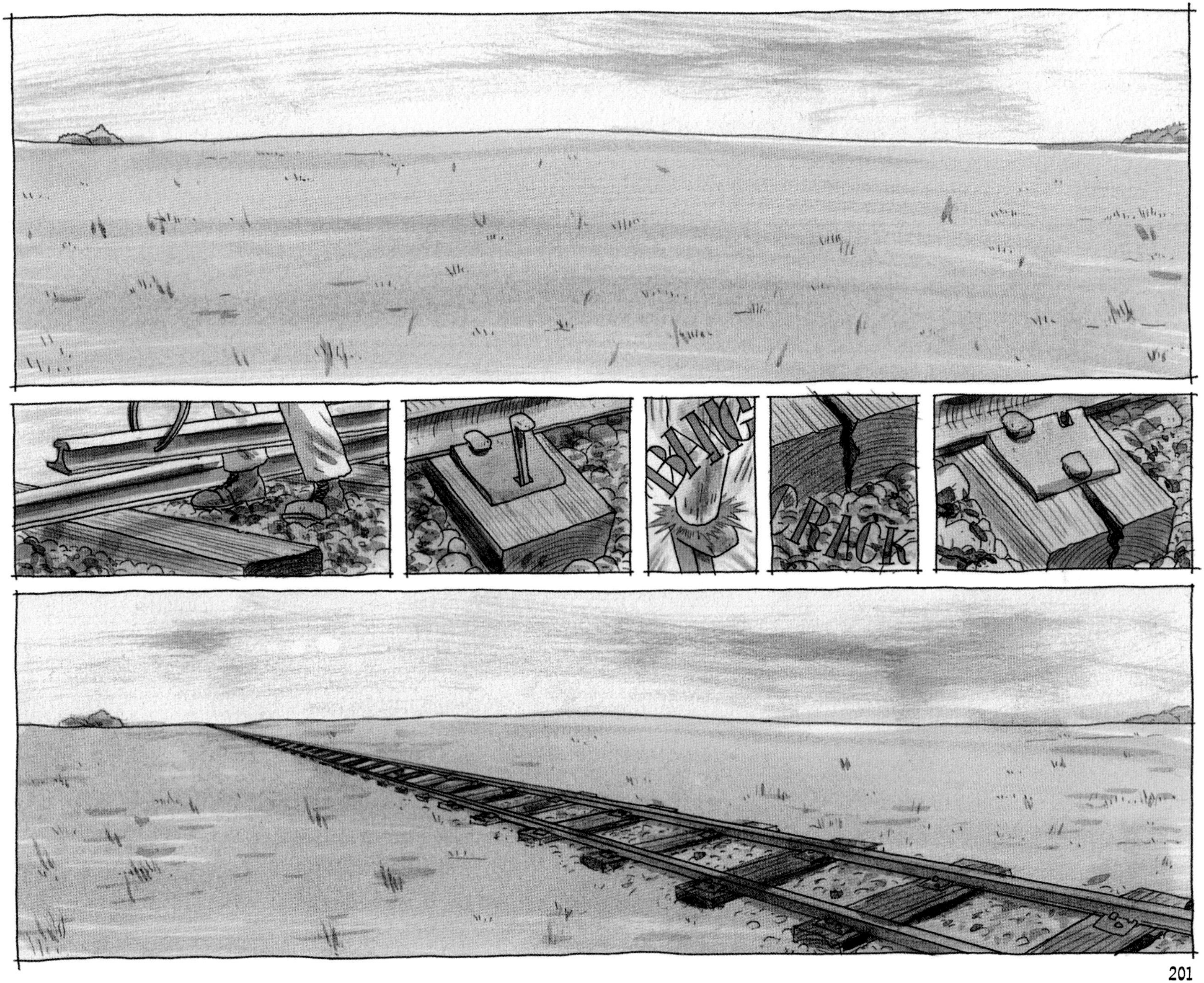
BANG
CRACK

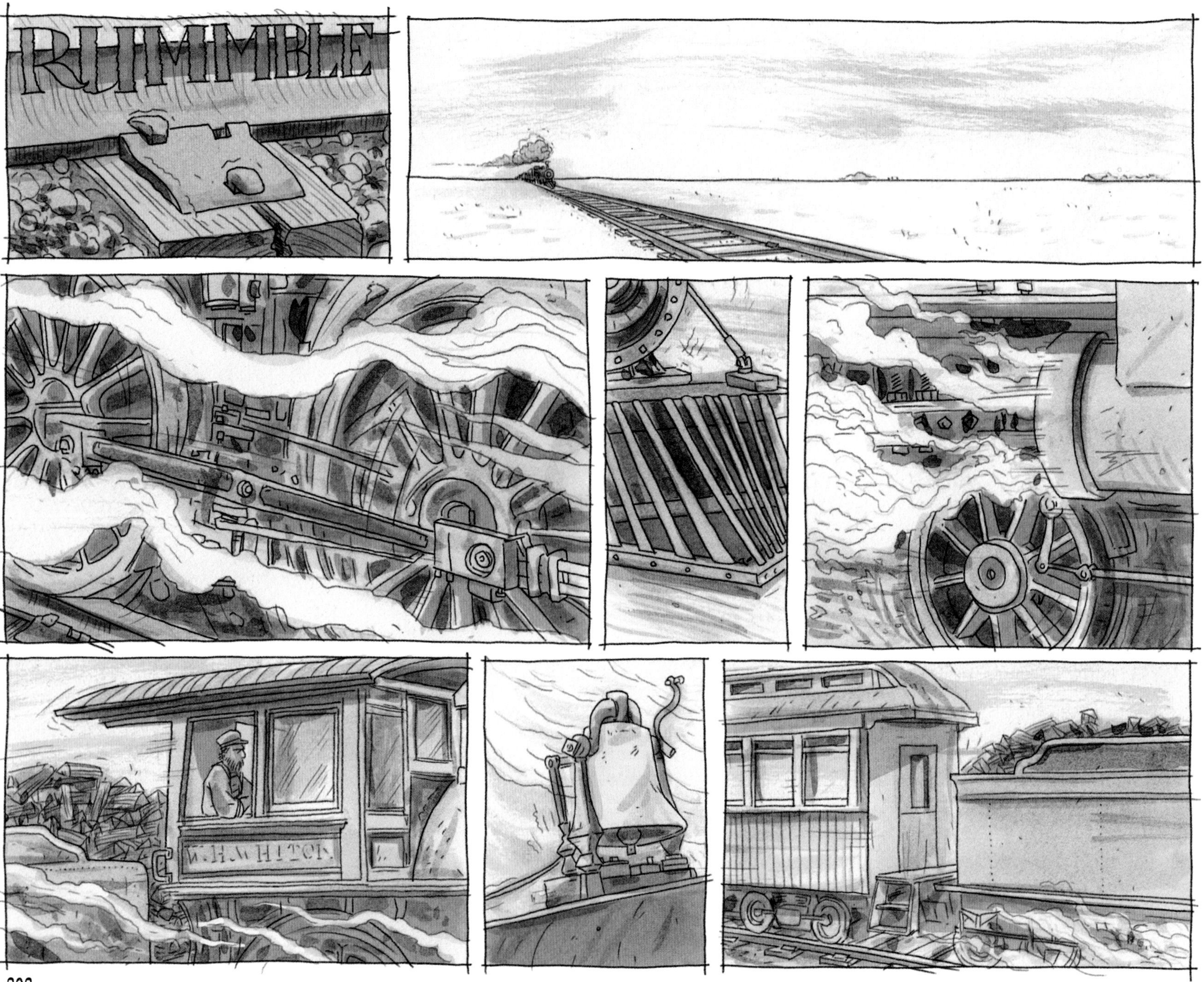
RUMMBLE
W. H. WHITON.

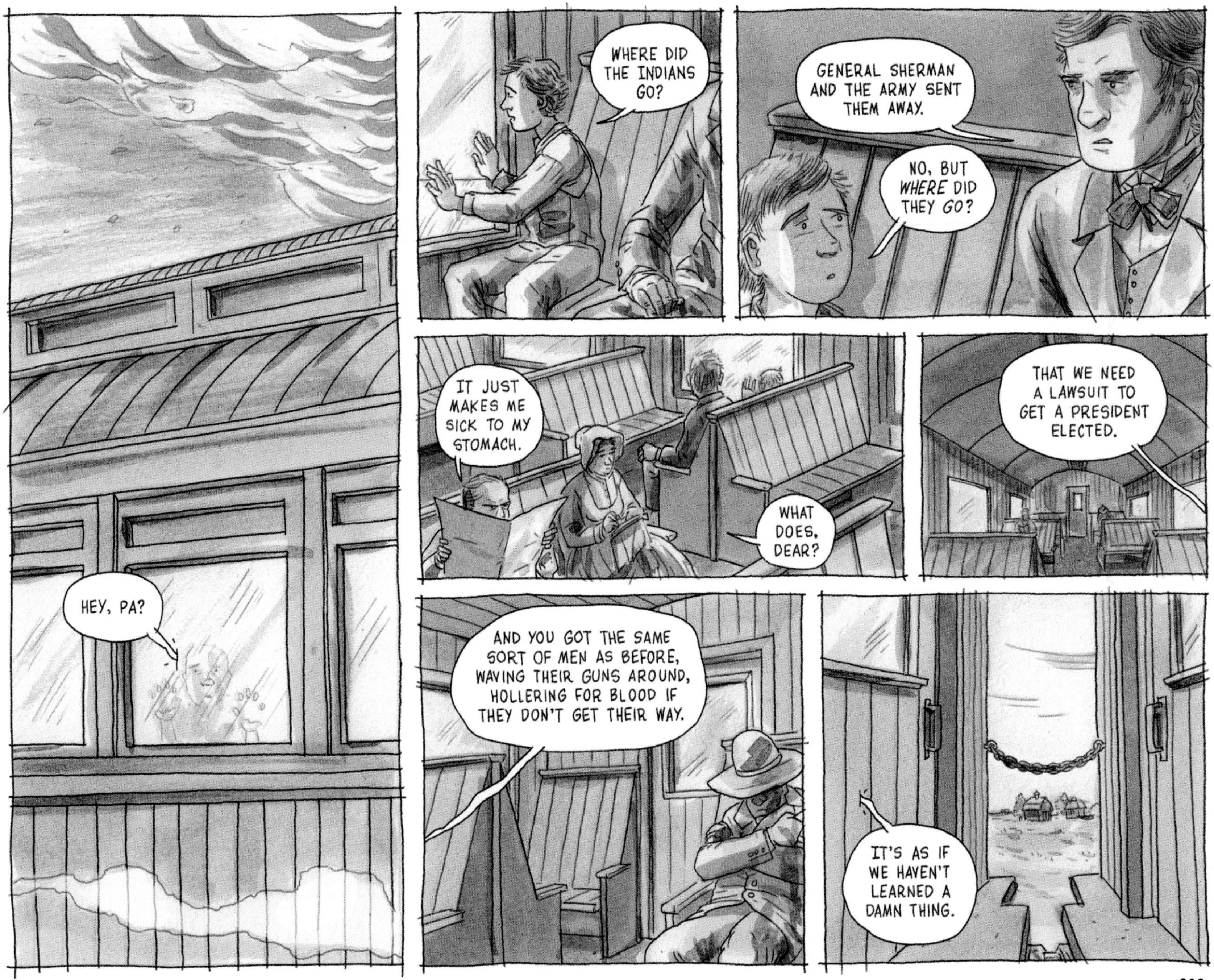
HEY, PA?
WHERE DID THE INDIANS GO?
GENERAL SHERMAN AND THE ARMY SENT THEM AWAY.
NO, BUT WHERE DID THEY GO?
IT JUST MAKES ME SICK TO MY STOMACH.
WHAT DOES, DEAR?
THAT WE NEED A LAWSUIT TO GET A PRESIDENT ELECTED.
AND YOU GOT THE SAME SORT OF MEN AS BEFORE, WAVING THEIR GUNS AROUND, HOLLERING FOR BLOOD IF THEY DON'T GET THEIR WAY.
IT'S AS IF WE HAVEN'T LEARNED A DAMN THING.

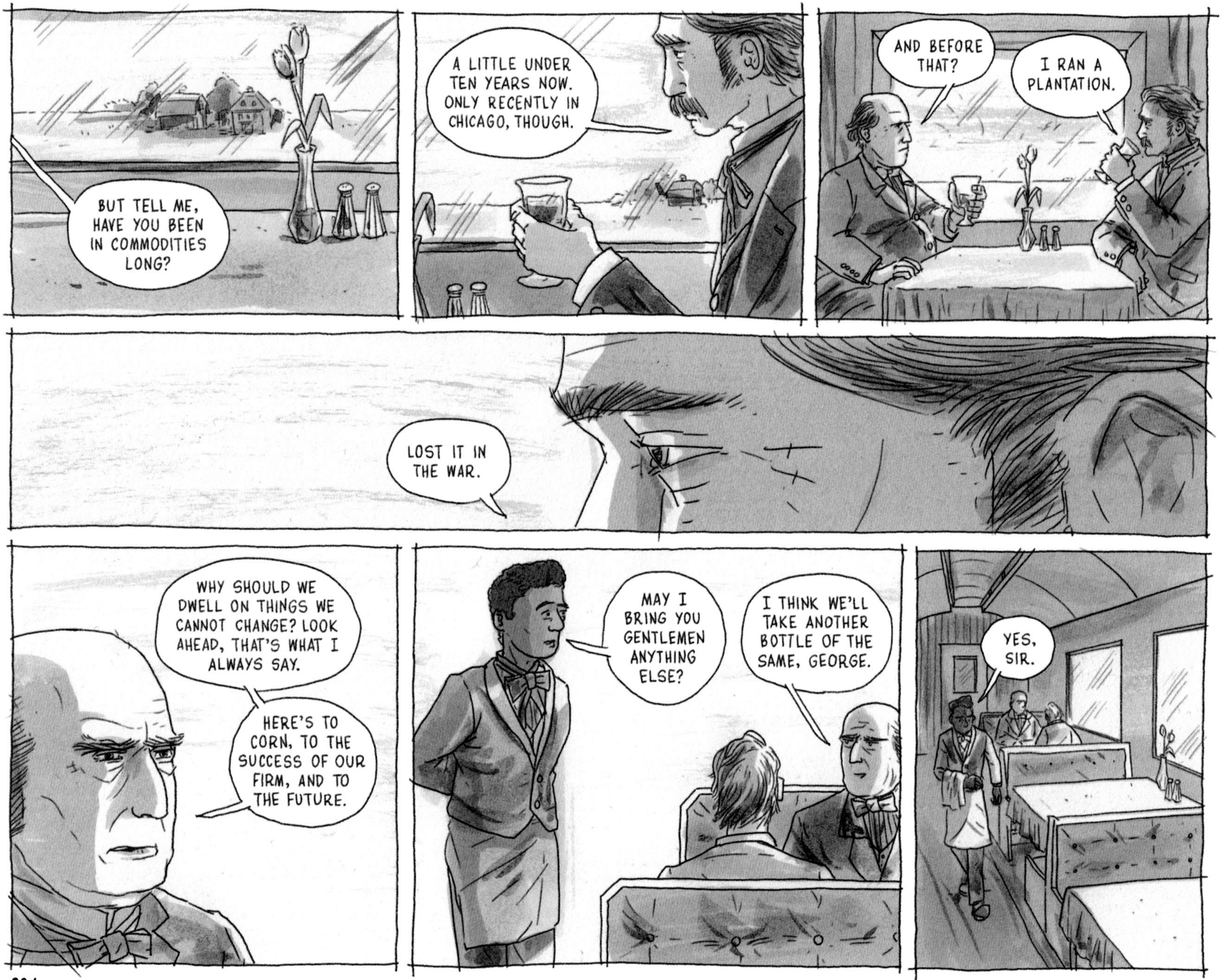
BUT TELL ME, HAVE YOU BEEN IN COMMODITIES LONG?
A LITTLE UNDER TEN YEARS NOW. ONLY RECENTLY IN CHICAGO, THOUGH.
AND BEFORE THAT?
I RAN A PLANTATION.
LOST IT IN THE WAR.
WHY SHOULD WE DWELL ON THINGS WE CANNOT CHANGE? LOOK AHEAD, THAT'S WHAT I ALWAYS SAY.
HERE'S TO CORN, TO THE SUCCESS OF OUR FIRM, AND TO THE FUTURE.
MAY I BRING YOU GENTLEMEN ANYTHING ELSE?
I THINK WE'LL TAKE ANOTHER BOTTLE OF THE SAME, GEORGE.
YES, SIR.

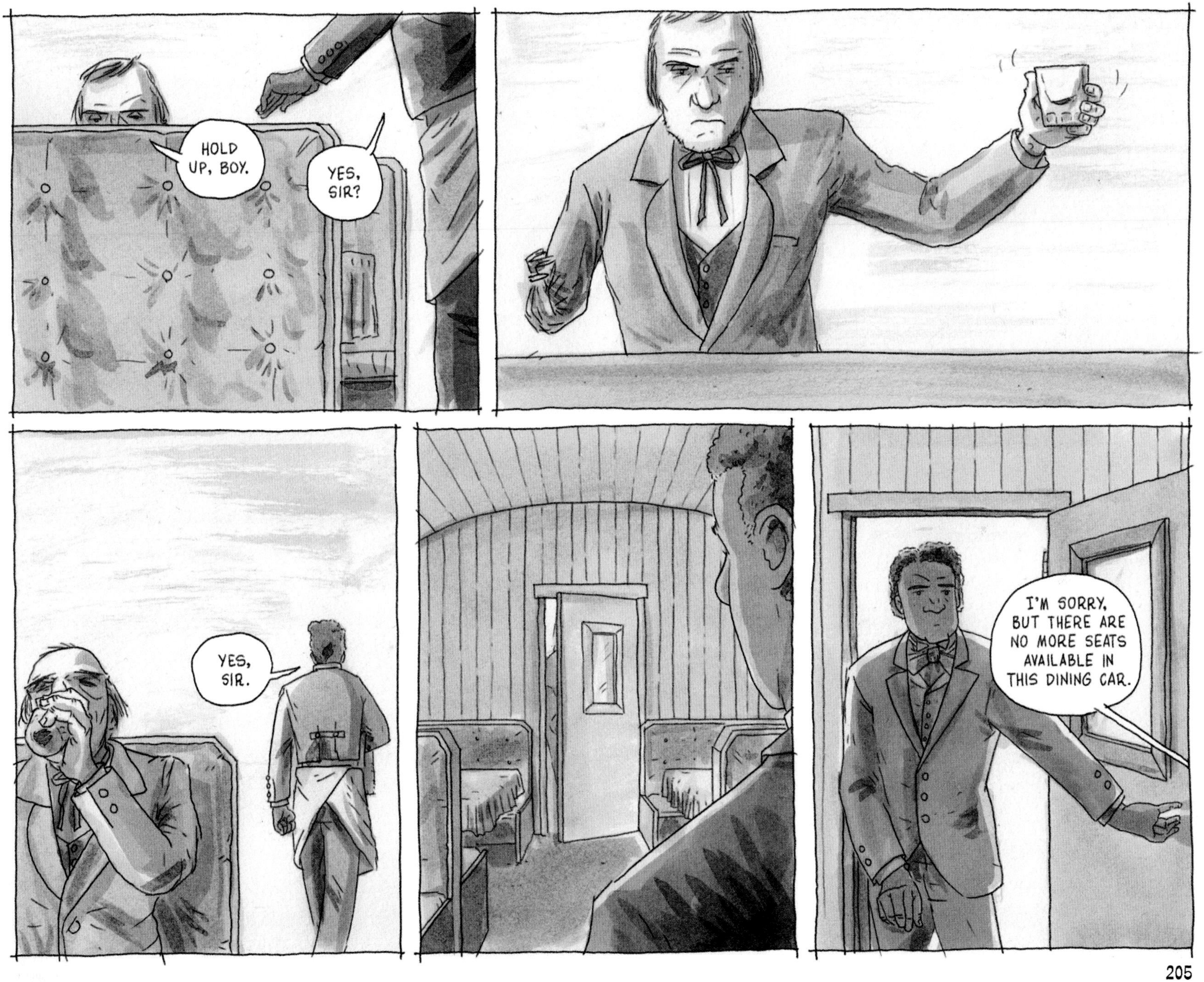
HOLD UP, BOY.
YES, SIR?
YES, SIR.
I'M SORRY, BUT THERE ARE NO MORE SEATS AVAILABLE IN THIS DINING CAR.

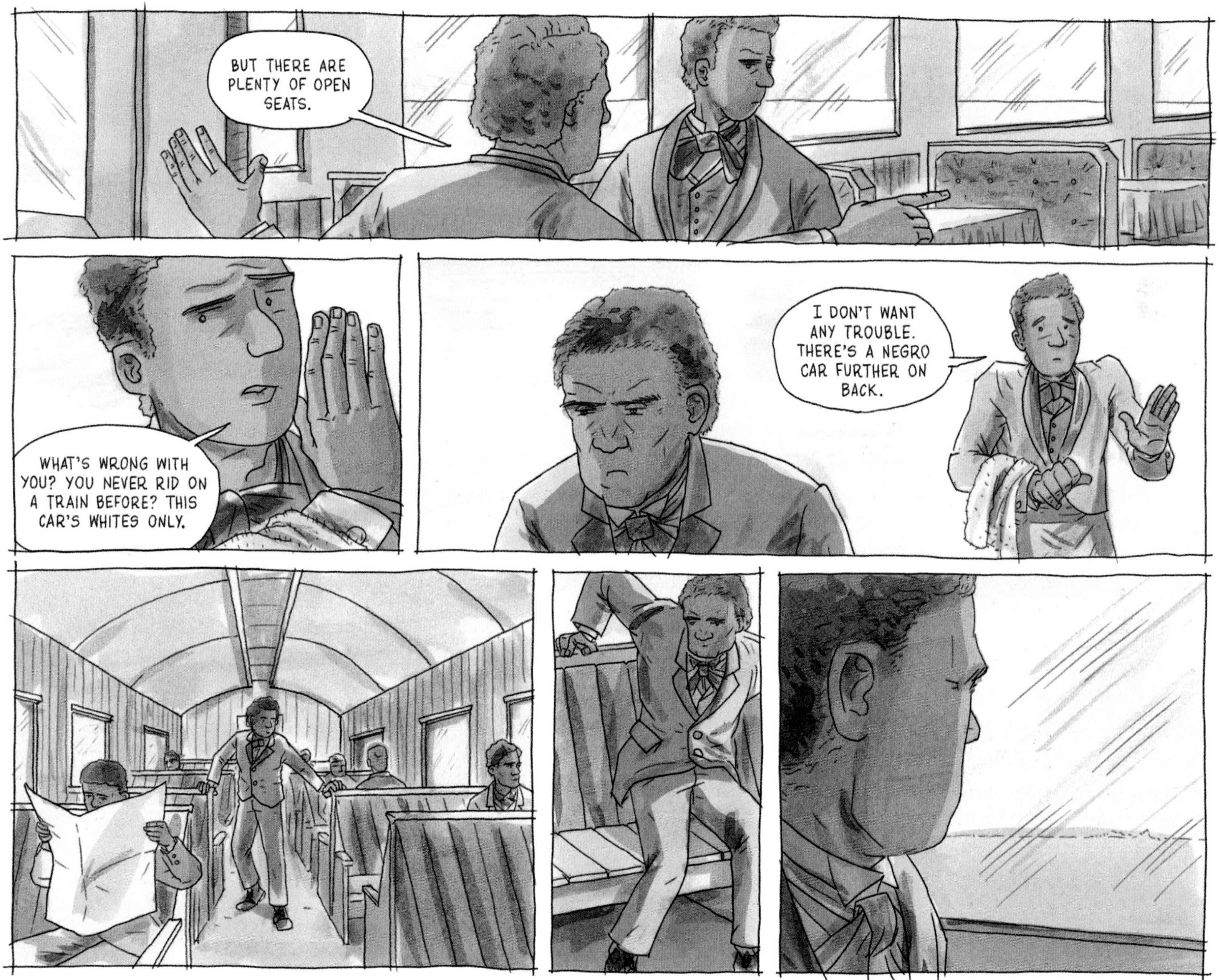
BUT THERE ARE PLENTY OF OPEN SEATS.
WHAT'S WRONG WITH YOU? YOU NEVER RID ON A TRAIN BEFORE? THIS CAR'S WHITES ONLY.
I DON'T WANT ANY TROUBLE. THERE'S A NEGRO CAR FURTHER ON BACK.

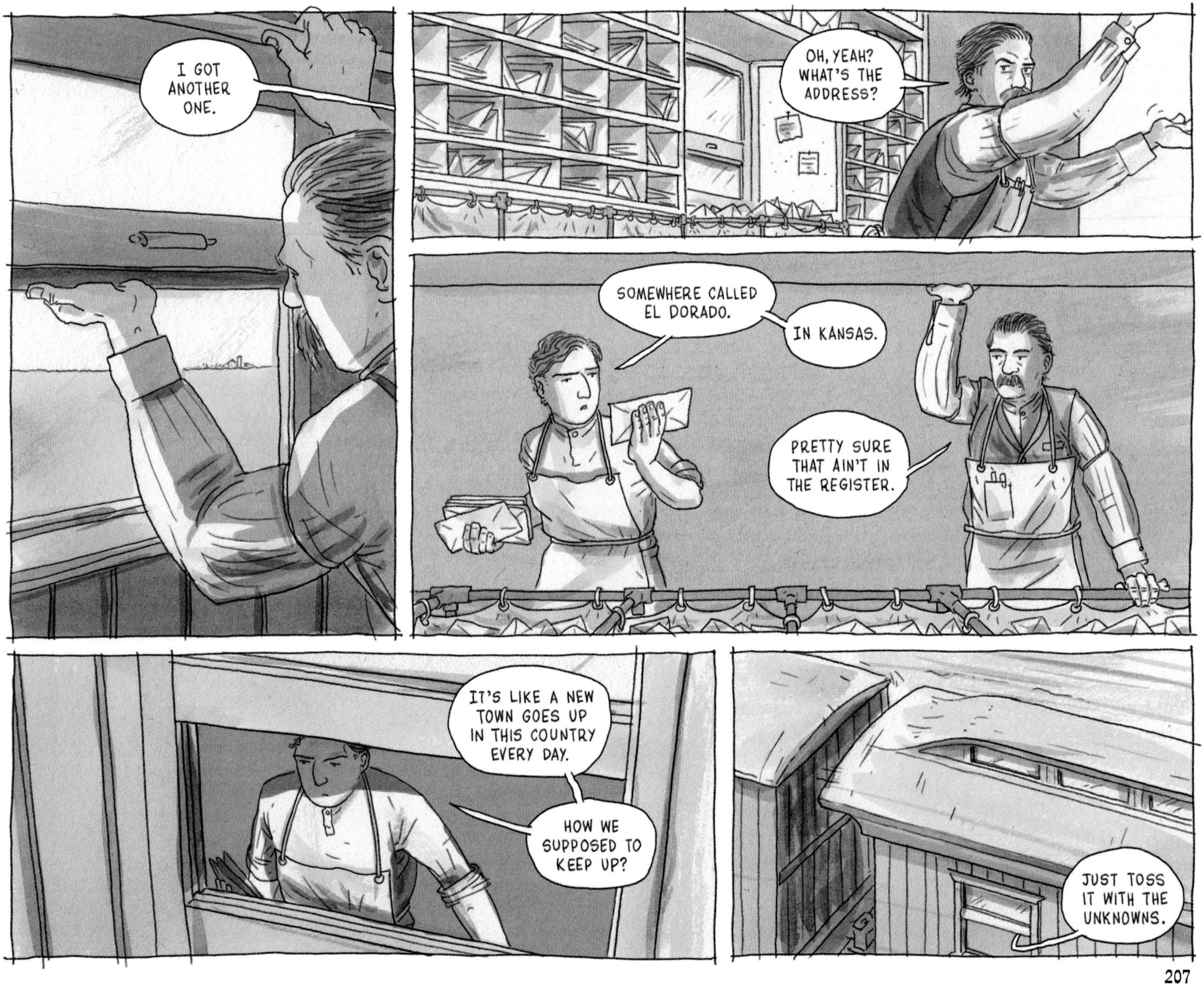
I GOT ANOTHER ONE.
OH, YEAH? WHAT'S THE ADDRESS?
SOMEWHERE CALLED EL DORADO.
IN KANSAS.
PRETTY SURE THAT AIN'T IN THE REGISTER.
IT'S LIKE A NEW TOWN GOES UP IN THIS COUNTRY EVERY DAY.
HOW WE SUPPOSED TO KEEP UP?
JUST TOSS IT WITH THE UNKNOWNS.

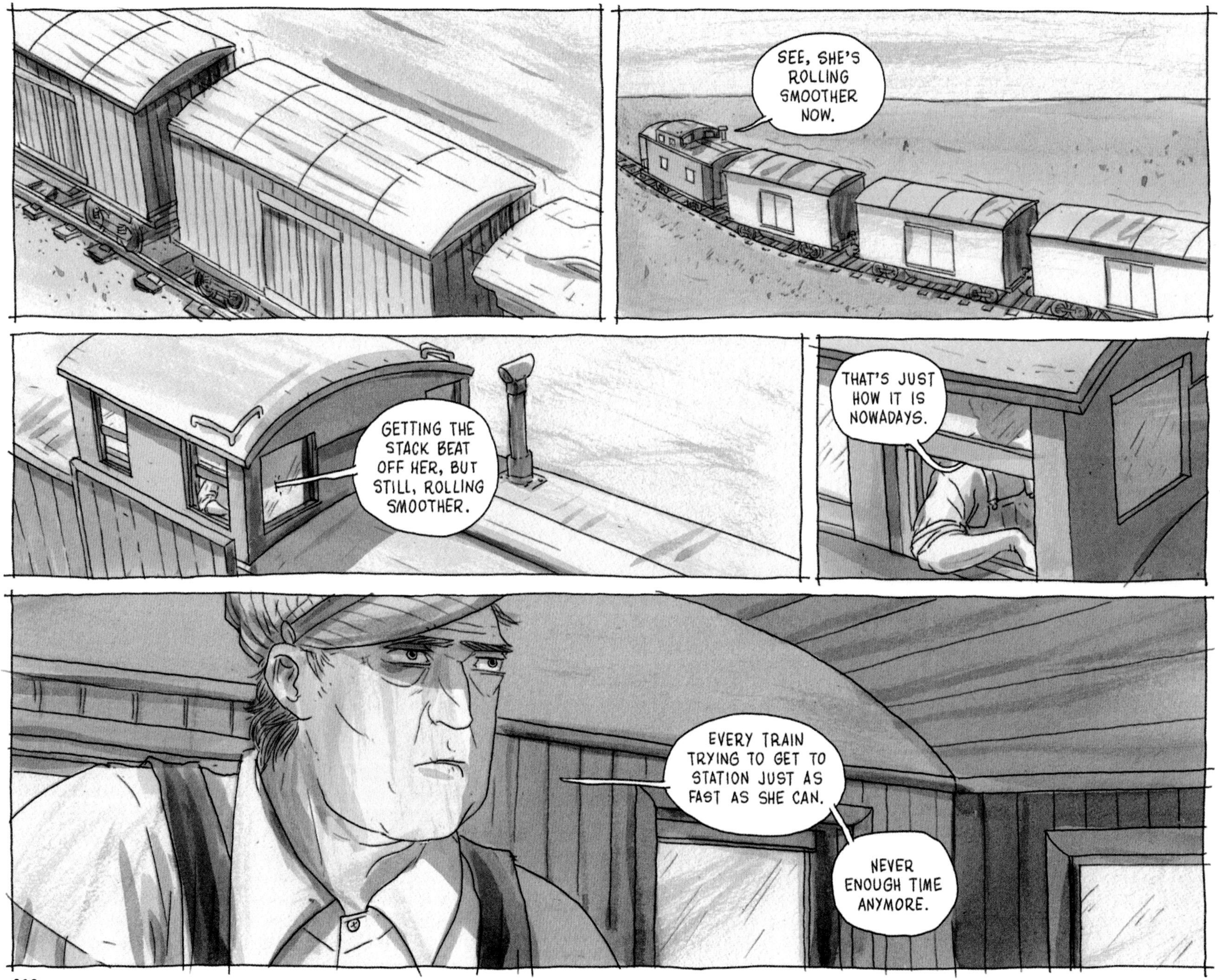
SEE, SHE'S ROLLING SMOOTHER NOW.
GETTING THE STACK BEAT OFF HER, BUT STILL, ROLLING SMOOTHER.
THAT'S JUST HOW IT IS NOWADAYS.
EVERY TRAIN TRYING TO GET TO STATION JUST AS FAST AS SHE CAN.
NEVER ENOUGH TIME ANYMORE.

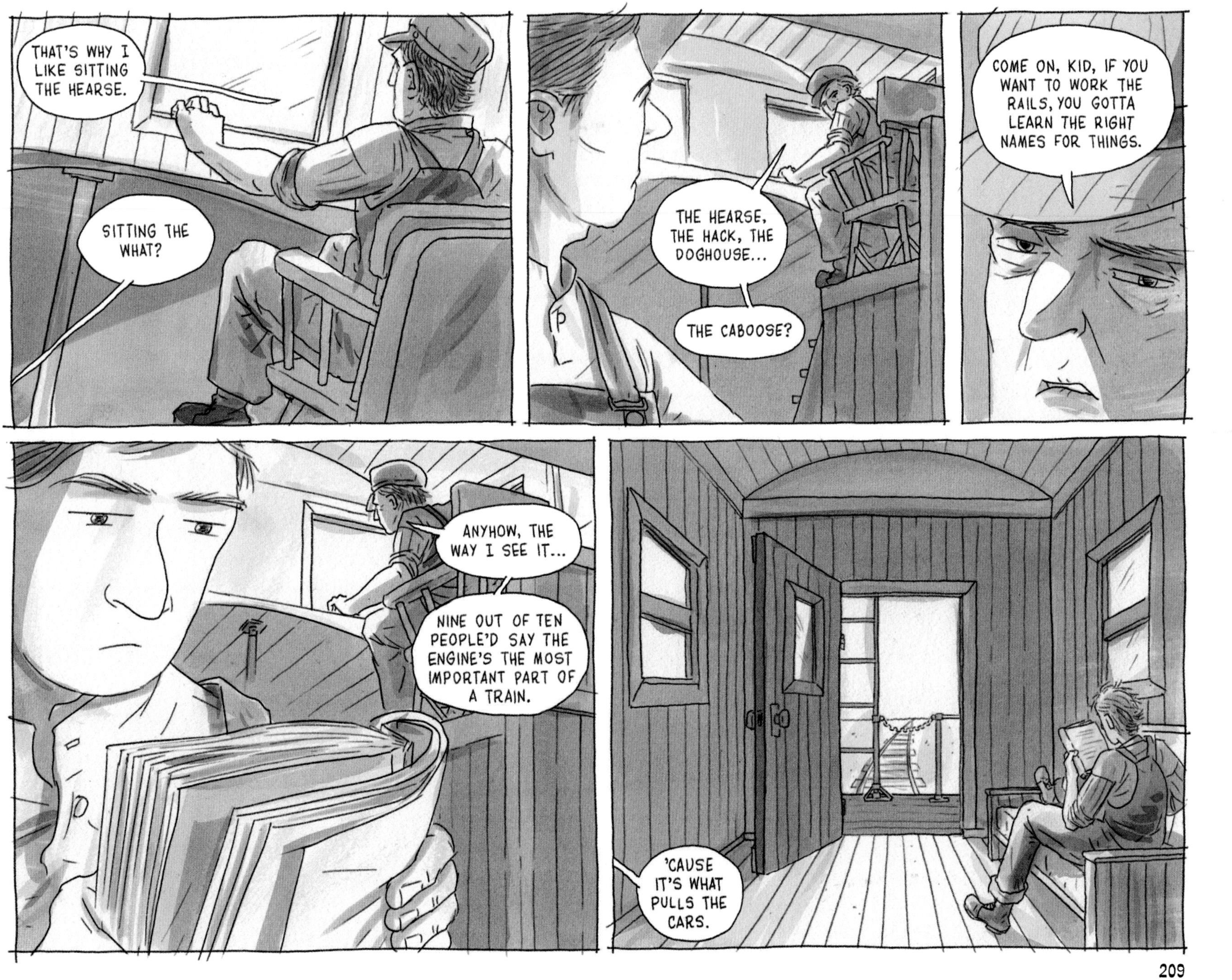
THAT'S WHY I LIKE SITTING THE HEARSE.
SITTING THE WHAT?
THE HEARSE, THE HACK, THE DOGHOUSE...
THE CABOOSE?
COME ON, KID, IF YOU WANT TO WORK THE RAILS, YOU GOTTA LEARN THE RIGHT NAMES FOR THINGS.
ANYHOW, THE WAY I SEE IT...
NINE OUT OF TEN PEOPLE'D SAY THE ENGINE'S THE MOST IMPORTANT PART OF A TRAIN.
'CAUSE IT'S WHAT PULLS THE CARS.

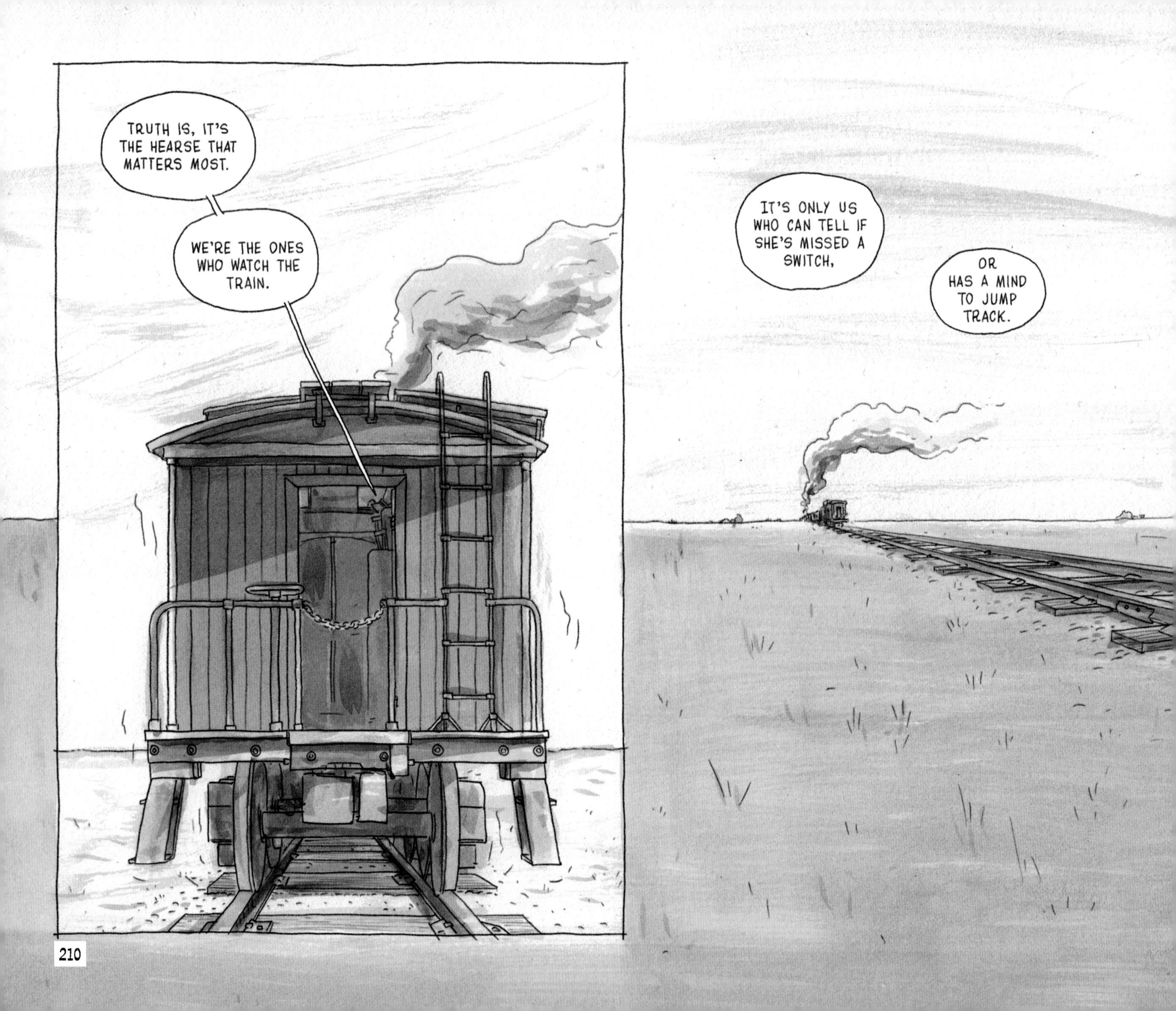
TRUTH IS, IT'S THE HEARSE THAT MATTERS MOST.
WE'RE THE ONES WHO WATCH THE TRAIN.
IT'S ONLY US WHO CAN TELL IF SHE'S MISSED A SWITCH,
OR HAS A MIND TO JUMP TRACK.

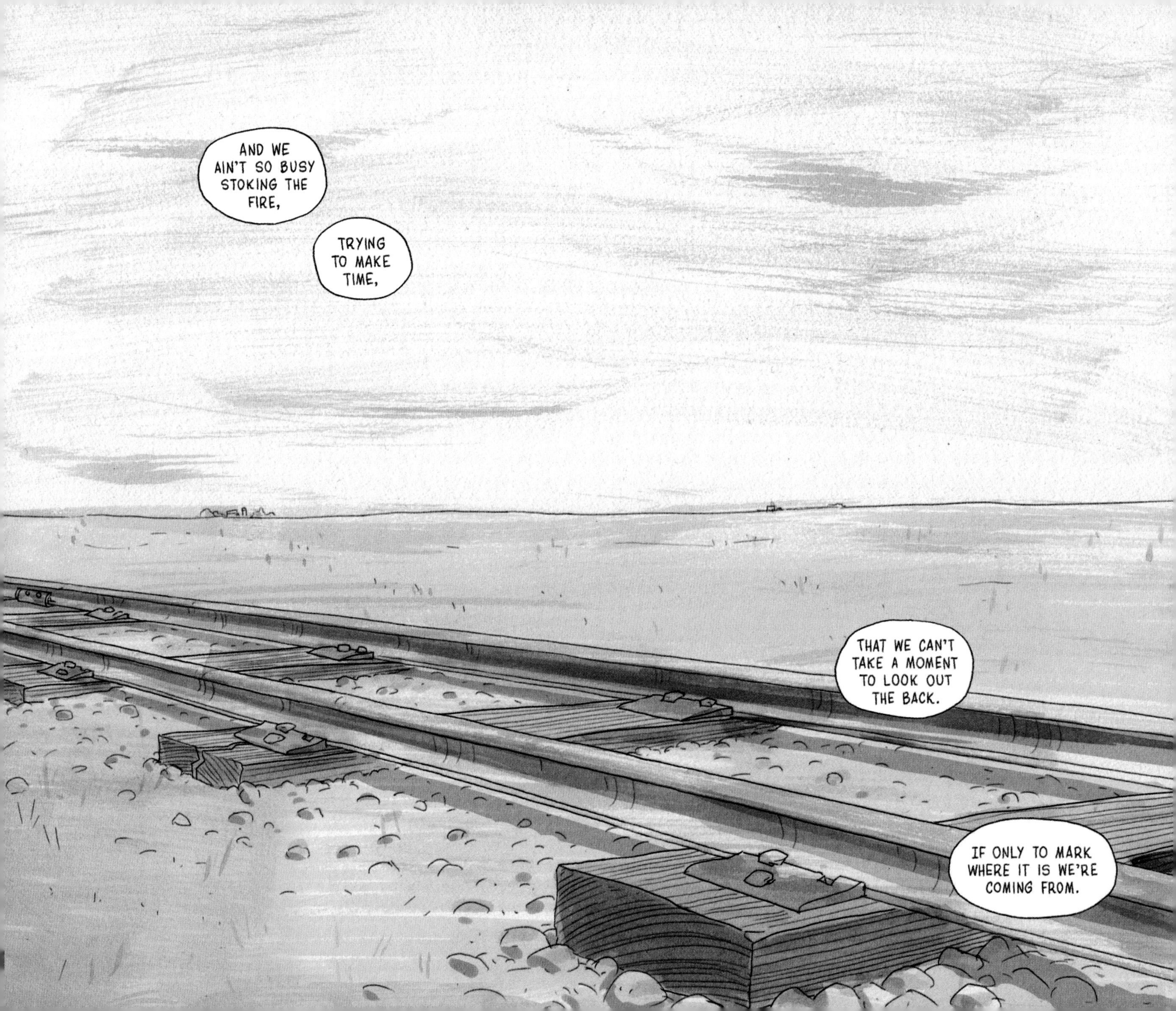
AND WE AIN'T SO BUSY STOKING THE FIRE,
TRYING TO MAKE TIME,
THAT WE CAN'T TAKE A MOMENT TO LOOK OUT THE BACK.
IF ONLY TO MARK WHERE IT IS WE'RE COMING FROM.

NOTES AND SUGGESTED READING

In several cases, we have relied on historical documents for source material. The book's epigraph, for instance, is drawn from Walt Whitman's *Prose Works*. In Chapter 2, the abolitionist Sarah T. Smith's words are taken from a speech titled "Loosening the Bonds of Prejudice." In that same chapter, we have used lines from Henry David Thoreau's "Civil Disobedience" and Chief Justice Roger Taney's opinion in *Dred Scott v. Sandford*, and "Charlie Suttle's slave" refers to the infamous Anthony Burns case (Burns was owned by a man named Charlie Suttle), which prompted widespread indignation over the impact of the Fugitive Slave Act of 1850.

The journalist in Chapter 3 is based on the reporter William Howard Russell, who traveled throughout the United States during the Civil War. His words are drawn from a *New York Times* article on Bull Run. He later expanded that piece into a book titled *My Diary: North and South*. Passages from Walt Whitman's *Leaves of Grass* and Frederick Douglass's "What to the Slave is the Fourth of July?" appear in Chapter 4. The photographer in Chapter 8 is Alexander Gardner, and his image "The Home of a Rebel Sharpshooter" first appeared in *Gardner's Photographic Sketch Book of the War*. Chapter 12 hews closely to the experience of Samuel Melvin, a Massachusetts soldier who kept a diary of the last days of his life at Andersonville prison camp.

The passages quoted in Chapter 13 are from Robert E. Lee's "Farewell Address to the Army of Northern Virginia" (also known as General Order No. 9). Finally, in Chapter 14, John Wilkes Booth's last words appear in Gene Smith's *American Gothic*, and Nathan Bedford Forrest's words are drawn from an interview Forrest sat for with the *Cincinnati Commercial* on August 28, 1868.

More broadly, we often took inspiration from a wide variety of primary sources, including Ambrose Bierce's essays (especially his extraordinary "What I Saw of Shiloh"), Mary Boykin Chesnut's *Mary Chesnut's Diary*, Mathew Brady's extensive portfolio of Civil War photographs, Frederick Douglass's *Narrative of the Life of Frederick Douglass*, George Fitzhugh's *Cannibals All!*, Ulysses Grant's *Personal Memoirs*, Thomas Wentworth Higginson's *Army Life in a Black Regiment*, Harriet Jacobs's *Incidents in the Life of a Slave Girl*, Abraham Lincoln's speeches, and the various declarations of causes of the seceding states.

Turning to secondary sources, we frequently looked to James McPherson's magisterial *Battle Cry of Freedom*, which we think is the best single-volume history of the war. Other useful texts include Bruce Catton's *The Centennial History of the Civil War*, which focuses on the Army of the Potomac; Michael Fellman, Lesley Gordon, and Daniel Sutherland's *This Terrible War*; David Potter's *The Impending Crisis*; and Richard Sewell's *A House Divided*.

A number of recent books have examined the pervasiveness of violence during the era of the Civil War. Drew Faust's *This Republic of Suffering* provided us with many eclectic and chilling facts about the horrors of war. We also relied on Mark Neely's *The Civil War and the Limits of Destruction*, Megan Kate Nelson's *Ruin Nation*, and Lisa Brady's environmental history, *War Upon the Land*.

Among books chronicling the experiences of slaves and free people of color on the road to, during, and after the war, we especially admire David Cecelski's *The Fire of Freedom*, Leslie Harris's *In the Shadow of Slavery*, Steve Kantrowitz's *More than Freedom*, James McPherson's *Marching Toward Freedom*, Edmund Morgan's *American Slavery, American Freedom*, Peter Kolchin's *American Slavery*, Walter

Johnson's *Soul by Soul*, Thavolia Glymph's *Out of the House of Bondage*, Leon Litwack's *Been in the Storm So Long*, and Alan Taylor's *The Internal Enemy*.

When it came to material on antislavery, abolitionism, and emancipation, we leaned heavily on Eric Foner's *Free Soil, Free Labor, Free Men* and *The Fiery Trial*, Christopher Hager's *Word by Word*, Tony Horwitz's *Midnight Rising*, Richard Huzzey's *Freedom Burning*, Bruce Levine's *Confederate Emancipation*, Chandra Manning's *What This Cruel War Was Over*, James Oakes's *The Radical and the Republican* and *Freedom National*, and Michael Vorenberg's *Final Freedom*.

We drew material on women's experiences during the era of the war from Drew Faust's *Mothers of Invention*, Stephanie McCurry's *Confederate Reckoning*, Hannah Rosen's *Terror in the Heart of Freedom*, Stephanie Camp's *Closer to Freedom*, Nina Silber's *Daughters of the Union* and *Gender and the Sectional Conflict*, Martha Hodes's *The Sea Captain's Wife*, Lyde Sizer's *The Political Work of Northern Women Writers and the Civil War*, and Jane Schultz's *Women at the Front*.

Eric Foner's *Reconstruction* served as our guide to the struggles in the postwar years. We also looked to Michael Perman's *Reunion Without Compromise* and *Struggle for Mastery*, Douglas Egerton's *The Wars of Reconstruction*, Nicholas Lemann's *Redemption*, C. Vann Woodward's *Origins of the New South*, W.E.B. Du Bois's *Black Reconstruction in America*, Edward Ayers's *The Promise of the New South*, and Charles Lane's *The Day Freedom Died*.

The literature on collective memory of the Civil War has exploded in recent years. We consulted David Blight's *Race and Reunion*, Michael Kammen's *Mystic Chords of Memory*, Gaines Foster's *Ghosts of the Confederacy*, Gary Gallagher's *The Union War* and *Lee and His Generals in War and Memory*, Elizabeth Varon's *Appomattox*, and two collections of essays: Alice Fahs and Joan Waugh's *The Memory of the Civil War in American Culture* and Alan Nolan and Gary Gallagher's *The Myth of the Lost Cause and Civil War History*.

ACKNOWLEDGMENTS

We wish to thank the following people for their help: Thomas Andrews, Adam Arenson, Phillip Barron, Tom Biby, Robert Borg, Otto Braided Hair, Kellan Cummings, Carolyn de la Peña, Brian DeLay, Jonathan Earle, Max Edelson, Chris Fluetsch, Gary Gallagher, Joan Hilty, Charlotte Housel, Ben Johnson, Anna Kelman, Sam Kelman, Brendan Leach, Jacob Lee, Thomas LeBien, Kevin Levin, Randolph Lewis, Chandra Manning, Kathryn Shively Meier, Mary Mendoza, Brian Craig Miller, Amanda Moon, Johann Neem, Megan Kate Nelson, Kathy Olmsted, Pablo Ortiz, Andrew O'Shaughnessy, Matthew Phelan, Eric Rauchway, Andres Resendez, Joshua Rothman, Simon Sadler, Margaret Sankey, Christina Snyder, Rachel St. John, Ellen Stroud, Julie Sze, Alan Taylor, Kim Todd, Cecilia Tsu, Susannah Ural, Elizabeth Varon, Charles Walker, Clarence Walker, and Louis Warren.